ANDREW KUYVENHOVEN

daylight

FAITH
ALIVE®
Christian Resources

Grand Rapids, Michigan

This book was originally published by Paideia Press in 1977.

Daylight: 366 Daily Devotional Readings. Revised edition © 2009 by Faith Alive Christian Resources, 2850 Kalamazoo Ave. SE, Grand Rapids, MI 49560. All rights reserved. With the exception of brief excerpts for review purposes, no part of this book may be reproduced in any manner whatsoever without written permission from the publisher.

Library of Congress Cataloging-in-Publication Data
Kuyvenhoven, Andrew.
    Daylight: daily readings with the Bible / Andrew Kuyvenhoven.
        p. cm.
    Originally published: Grand Rapids: Zondervan, 1978, © 1977.
    Includes index.
    ISBN 978-1-59255-518-5
    1. Devotional calendars. I. Title.
    BV4811.K88 2009
    242'.2—dc22

                                                                          2009042823

10 9 8 7 6 5 4 3 2 1

Contents

Preface

Although this book was well received and often reprinted between 1977 and 1990, I had not expected a new publisher to take enough interest in *Daylight* to update and reprint it in the year 2009. But here it is.

I express gratitude to God, whom I want to glorify by this book, and thankfulness to the publisher who is taking a risk. I miss my wife, Ena, who used to critique my writings and sermons. I had her for more than 56 years and God holds her forever.

Over the years I have received numerous thankful remarks of people who were enriched by the words in this book. But I know to whom such credit is due. May the Lord continue to use it.

Andrew Kuyvenhoven
October 2009

Publisher's Note

Faith Alive Christian Resources thanks Andrew Kuyvenhoven for consenting to this reprinting of his book. This new edition of *Daylight* includes Scriptures from Today's New International Version (TNIV) and additional updates as needed. We've also added a "Reflections" question at the end of each devotional for personal reflection or discussion.

Your Kingdom Come

The kingdom is coming, for the King has been anointed with heavenly power. He's on his way.

daylight

Run the Race

HEBREWS 11:29-12:2

> *. . . Since we are surrounded by such a great cloud of witnesses, let us throw off everything that hinders and the sin that so easily entangles. And let us run with perseverance the race marked out for us, fixing our eyes on Jesus. . . .* —*Hebrews 12:1-2*

We do not drift into another year like pieces of wood on the stream of time. The new year is before us like a race to be run. God calls us to the race and tells us how to run it.

"Let us throw off everything that hinders and the sin that so easily entangles." If you try running a race in your winter coat, you'll lose it before you start. The coat will hinder your movements. And if you are out of condition, sluggish and fat, your chances are slim at best.

God's athletes may not carry their sinful habits into the race. They must "throw off" the worldly cares that grow on Christians like extra pounds on obese North Americans. When you are called to the kingdom, you cannot run for the prize with your arms full of treasures and your heart divided by desires. You must have a single purpose, and you must train to stay in shape.

The race is very difficult. Some must "run" while they are sick in bed, others are in the race as business people bracing themselves for the after-Christmas slump. A few are persecuted for their faith by public authorities, and many are students who have just begun a new term. But all of us are in the race. And all of us must run "by faith."

The stadium of our lives is surrounded by bleachers filled with spectators. They aren't ordinary spectators. They are all veteran athletes who have run the race. This whole cloud of witnesses tells us to run "by faith." That's the secret of the runner. The whole gallery of Hebrews 11 urges us to keep running and to take all the hurdles "by faith."

The focus of our faith is Jesus. Keep looking at Jesus. As long as the eye of our faith is fixed on Jesus, we will overcome all obstacles and receive the crown at the finish.

Take courage and run.

REFLECTIONS

Think about what drags you down in the race, and then ask God to help you throw it off.

Land of Hope and Glory

ISAIAH 35

*". . . your God will come, he will come with vengeance; with divine
retribution he will come to save you."* —Isaiah 35:4

Every person has hope. A hope-less person is dead. Our expectations
have just been rekindled by the start of a new year. But now we must ask
ourselves what we are hoping for and on whom our hope relies.

Christians have set their hopes on Christ, and they await the coming
of the kingdom of God.

As a matter of fact, all humanity, yes, the whole creation, is looking
for this land of hope and glory which Bible believers call the kingdom
of God.

Isaiah 35 pictures the land of hope and glory for us. The wilderness
has turned into a garden, and the desert teems with life. The lame man
is leaping. The mute person is singing. Sin and terror, the dragon and the
lion, have disappeared. The place is secure. Sorrow and sighing are not
at home in this country. They "will flee away." This is the country of our
hopes. It's the land of everyone's dreams; it's the kingdom of God in the
world of humans.

And here is the secret. Here is how it will come about: "Your God will
come." Therefore we must set our hopes on God and direct our prayers to
him. Industry and labor, philosophy and medicine, business and banking
cannot bring the land of hope and glory. "Your God will come. . . ."

God comes with vengeance and salvation. Vengeance is for the oppressors, salvation for the oppressed. Punishment is for those who hate God,
and deliverance for those who long for God. With this double-edged
sword of vengeance and salvation, God will open the promised land.

Nothing is more human than to hope. But we set our hopes on different things. Blessed are those who have set their hopes on God. They are
the only people who will not be disappointed.

REFLECTIONS
How would you express the hope you have as a Christian?

Prepare the Way

MATTHEW 3:1-12

"Repent, for the kingdom of heaven has come near."

—Matthew 3:2

"Now it is coming," said John the Baptist. Finally God is coming to the earth, coming with vengeance and salvation. All that is wicked God will burn away, but whatever is clean and good he will gather and preserve forever.

John thought that the final judgment was coming. That's because he was the last of the Old Testament prophets. The Old Testament sees Jesus' first and second comings as one event, one double act of salvation and judgment. We know more than John the Baptist, for we live after the death and resurrection of Jesus. We know that Jesus was judged for our sins when he came the first time. Later he will come back as Judge.

This does not mean, however, that John made a mistake. The kingdom was really coming, and the King really came. John performed the task for which God had appointed him. John told the Jews and, ultimately, all of us that nobody can enter the kingdom without repentance and cleansing.

What is repentance? It's not just feeling sorry for what we have done; it's a break with the old pattern. We give up our former love and our former ways. We turn to God and his ways.

Wherever the kingdom is proclaimed, the message of the forerunner must be heard: We cannot reach for the treasures of God's kingdom as long as our hands are dirty. We cannot enter God's kingdom as long as we are building our own.

We tend to postpone repentance. We tend to postpone *all* cleanup work: in our rooms, around the house, and in our lives. One of Satan's demons must be called Procrastinator. He keeps people out of the kingdom by telling them that they can repent tomorrow.

Do it now. For the kingdom of heaven is at hand.

REFLECTIONS

Daily confession of sin is part of repentance. Take time now to ask God, once again, for forgiveness.

The King Revealed

MATTHEW 3:13-17

Then Jesus came from Galilee to the Jordan to be baptized by John.
—*Matthew 3:13*

The greatest surprise came on the day when Jesus made his way through the crowd and approached John the Baptist, "to be baptized by John." He wanted to be cleansed!

Here was the one who is worthy of all praise. Everyone should bow the knee before him. The greatest prophet is not worthy to kiss his feet or carry his sandals. And he said, "Let me be baptized."

In consternation John refused.

But with the serenity of a man who knows the goal and the way to the goal, Jesus said, "You have to do it, John, for this is how we fulfill all righteousness; this is what God requires."

The will of God is the end of all reluctance for John. Jesus steps into the Jordan. Now he takes the place of the sinner—as if he himself were a sinner. And while he stands where the polluted people should be standing, the voice is heard from heaven: "This is my Son." The Spirit descends. The power comes down. And the Anointed One goes out to fulfill his mission.

What a mission!

Now the kingdom is coming because the King has been anointed with heavenly power. Baptized with the Spirit, he is going to dethrone the devil. But what a surprise! What a divine turn of events! The Lord of all takes the place of all, where the sins of the world are washed away. And when John the Baptist—or you or I—would be inclined to say, "He is the wrong man for this place," God and Jesus say that this is how it is going to happen and must happen. "This is my Son." This is the right man in the right place.

The Son comes to save God's people. Therefore he steps onto the spot where sinners deserve to stand.

REFLECTIONS

Picture Jesus being baptized, standing in your place, as a sinner. Give thanks.

Rejoice, You Fools of God

MATTHEW 5:1-12

> *"Blessed are the poor in spirit . . . those who mourn . . . the meek . . .*
> *those who hunger and thirst for righteousness . . . the merciful . . .*
> *the pure in heart . . . the peacemakers . . . those who are persecuted*
> *because of righteousness, for theirs is the kingdom of heaven."*
> —Matthew 5:3-10

There are about 6.8 billion people in the world. And one billion is one thousand times a million people. It's an unimaginable number. All these people have their hopes, their desires, their ambitions.

Among them is a group of people unknown to most and unsung by our poets yet served by the angels. They are all over the globe, and God knows their names.

What distinguishes all these undistinguished people? They have set their hopes on God. They take God's Word with utter seriousness, and they expect his kingly rule to be established in this world. Therefore they are always somewhat out of step with the people of this world, even if they look very much like all the others.

They are poor in spirit, while the others glory in their possessions and think they know it all.

They mourn, while the others seem to be having a ball.

They are meek, while the others are pushy.

Their hearts burn with desire for God. Everybody else is grabbing while the grabbing is good, but they refuse to give up and give in. They remain hungry and thirsty for God's righteousness.

In the midst of rugged individualism, they are merciful.

Although lust and adultery have become celebrated entertainment, they remain pure in heart. When quarrels erupt, they do not become defensive but establish peace. Jesus stretches out his hand over them. "Blessed are you. Yours is the kingdom of heaven."

Take heart, people of God. Resist the pressures of the world. Hope steadfastly in God. Jesus your Lord will give you the kingdom as your inheritance.

REFLECTIONS

Is your life marked by the qualities Jesus described? How have you experienced his blessing?

The Hope of the World

MATTHEW 5:13-16

"You are the salt of the earth. . . . You are the light of the world. . . ."
—*Matthew 5:13-14*

God's fools are the salt of the earth. The earth will never believe it and God's people can hardly be convinced of it, but the Creator of the earth has revealed it: all the preserving power on earth is stored in the little flock of God.

The salt metaphor spoke even louder to ancient people than it does to us. Long before freezers and refrigerators were invented, there was only one thing that could keep food from spoiling. And that one thing was salt. Only salt had the power to prevent spoiling and make the perishable imperishable. Therefore ancient people praised their God or gods for the gift of salt.

Now, when Christ says that his people are the salt of the earth, he means that God has appointed his people to hold back the decay and save what is being spoiled.

The Lord also spoke of the frightful possibility of the salt losing its taste. If that happens, it will not be because of the world's persecution. Only an inner deterioration of God's people could bring it about. When God's fools start tasting like "the world," when they think and act just like all their neighbors, they have lost the power to save. Why? Because anything can be flavored with salt except salt itself. When salt is not salt anymore, that is, when Christians no longer bear the imprint of God's kingdom, they are worthless themselves and the whole world is robbed of its hope. The saving power of the world is in the Church—as long as it remains the Church.

Christians are also the light of the world. If they were taken out of the world, it would be utter darkness. The knowledge of God would be gone.

We can hardly believe we are that important. All the saving power is in the little flock of God. That's why God keeps us in the world—to serve as a saving power. But if we aren't salt and light anymore, God has no use for us.

REFLECTIONS

What does it mean for you to be the salt of the earth and the light of the world?

Hallowed Be Your Name

ISAIAH 11:1-9

> . . . *the earth will be filled with the knowledge of the* LORD *as the waters cover the sea.*   —*Isaiah 11:9*

Here, in Isaiah 11, is another picture of the land of hope and glory. First we read about the excellent King who rules over this country. This "branch," who grew out of the fallen tree of the house of David, is Jesus Christ. Under his rule, says the prophet, the country has justice, peace, and rest. The King has removed wickedness, he has been fair to the poor and the meek, and now the peace of the country extends to man and beast. All is harmony. All is shalom.

What makes this world so good is the rule of the Messiah. You might also say this country is the promised land because "the earth will be filled with the knowledge of the Lord." These two things always go together. When God's name is hallowed, the kingdom has come, and when the kingdom has come, the earth is full of the knowledge of the Lord.

A taxi driver was trying to park in a crowded street when he scraped the fender of another car. The angry owner got out of his house of chrome and tin and loudly profaned the name of Jesus Christ. Then the taxi driver said: "Sir, why don't you use the name of somebody you know?"

Swearing is not only a vulgar habit, it is also a sure sign of ignorance. As soon as someone knows Jesus, she will stop swearing and start praying. Therefore we aren't sure what hurts us more—the careless swear word or the ignorance that it reveals.

You could say that Christ came into the world to establish the kingdom, but you could also say that he came to teach all of us about God. That's the same thing. And Christ sent the Holy Spirit to make us obey Christ as our King—*or* to teach us about God as our Father.

When the kingdom has come, the earth will be full of the knowledge of the Lord.

REFLECTIONS

In what ways did you attempt to "hallow God's name" today?

Total Renewal

MATTHEW 9:1-8

> *"Take heart, son; your sins are forgiven. . . . Get up, take your mat*
> *and go home."*   *—Matthew 9:2, 6*

The Old Testament prophecies speak of the coming kingdom as a land flowing with milk and honey. Some say that we must take these words literally, while others maintain that we must understand them figuratively. When the Old Testament says that the desert shall be full of roses, some believe that we are really waiting for flower gardens, but others say that it means happiness and spiritual joy.

Jesus is God's appointed King in the kingdom that is and is coming. When he did his mighty works on earth, he showed what he meant by the kingdom he preached.

A helpless man was brought to Jesus. The Lord said: "Take heart, son; your sins are forgiven." And then, to prove that he had the power to forgive sins, he made the lame man leap.

In the kingdom, all misery must disappear. Christ came to renew the whole world. He has the power to do so, for he has the power to forgive sins. Our reform movements and renewal projects can do no more than patch up some battered places on the face of the earth. We may (must!) clear up some slums and we may (must!) defeat certain diseases. Sometimes we can even repair a broken home. But we cannot heal a broken heart.

Christ attacks our problems at their root. The root of all the problems, the cause of every curse, is the evil in the human heart. He has given us a new heart and new hope. But he does not stop there. He finishes by giving us a new heaven and a new earth. If our sins are forgiven today, tomorrow we will see the lame man leap. And the desert will be full of flowers.

REFLECTIONS

Reflect on the scope of God's "renewal projects," beginning with yourself and ending with the new creation. Bow in silence before our awesome God.

What's Really Necessary

LUKE 10:38-42

*"Martha, Martha . . . you are worried and upset about many things,
but few things are needed—or indeed only one."*   —*Luke 10:41*

We must not infer from the story of Martha and Mary that it is better
to sit still than to work. We know of one church where the people were
inclined to sit still and merely talk about the return of Christ. Then they
were told to get to work (1 Thess. 4:11). God hates laziness.

Yet work can kill a person. That happens when a person is too busy to
listen to Jesus. Nothing is more important than to know Jesus. Our lives
depend on it. And we learn to know Christ by listening to him.

Some say our society is so corrupt that when you apply for a job, it's
more important to know someone on the inside than to have all the possible qualifications. It doesn't help if you know the right thing; everything depends on knowing the right person.

In one respect, at least, that statement is true. Everything depends on
the question *Do you know Jesus?* Not what you know but who you know is
going to be decisive. Therefore listening to his voice, his Word, his Spirit
is more important than anything you could possibly mention.

Our Master knows our needs. He also knows that we need to eat, that
we have to pay our bills, that there is work we simply have to get done.
However, there may be good reason for Christ to look at us now and say,
with the same concern he once showed to Martha, "My dear child, you
are worried and upset about many things, but few things are needed—or
indeed only one." Only one thing is really necessary.

Not everything we consider necessary is really necessary. To a large
extent, the art of living is getting our priorities straight. If we believe
Christ when he says that we really need only one thing, life is already a
lot simpler, isn't it?

REFLECTIONS

Are you taking enough time in your busy life to listen to Jesus? How do
you do that?

Our Needs Are Known

MATTHEW 6:5-15

". . . your Father knows what you need before you ask him."
—Matthew 6:8

We must tell our needs to God. However, we cannot tell God anything he does not know already. God knows our needs before we ask. It takes much grace and years of experience before we know our own needs.

We're not very good at finding out what our needs are. For one thing, we always get our "wants" and our "needs" confused. Besides, we often deceive ourselves. Some husband may think that he needs another wife, whereas he really needs to learn how to be a husband. Psychiatrists can be helpful because they can show some people what their real needs are. Our emotional lives are often so murky that we need help straightening out the tangle of wishes and disappointments and guilt feelings.

There is great comfort in the thought that God knows our needs. Once a lame man was taken to Jesus. When that pitiful, paralyzed person looked at Jesus, you would think that the Master, along with everybody else, knew the lame man's greatest need. The need was crying out: the man needed to be healed! Yet Jesus said to him: "Your sins are forgiven." Christ knew of a need that was more basic than any need we could discern.

Often our God must be wearied when we tell him our needs. He must say to himself that these are not our real needs. That's why Jesus, when he instructed us in prayer, told us to ask that the Father's name be hallowed and that his kingdom come. Those are our needs as he knows them.

The question is still whether we know that these are our needs. We must not simply say these first lines of the prayer out of politeness, so that we can proceed to our own daily needs. If that's our (unconscious) reasoning, we still have a long way to go, for our real need is God.

REFLECTIONS

Try praying the first two petitions of the Lord's Prayer in your own words.

And Thus the Kingdom Comes

MATTHEW 13:3-14

"A farmer went out to sow his seed." —*Mathew 13:3*

When Jesus told this story, there were many people who did not catch the meaning. In fact, only those understood it who had "ears to hear," and to whom "the knowledge of the secrets of the kingdom of heaven" had been given. What made this story so hard to understand?

The people were all waiting to see the coming of the kingdom. John the Baptist had said that it was now very close. He had said that the Reaper was coming: "He will gather the wheat into his barn, but he will burn up the chaff with unquenchable fire."

Jesus speaks of the same kingdom. But Jesus does not talk of the Reaper; he speaks of the sower or farmer. There is nothing spectacular about the work of the farmer. He sows the seed. He waits patiently. He knows that much seed will go to waste—at least in the type of field sown by the ancient Palestinian farmer. There are stones and rocks, there are thorns and thistles, and some of the seed is simply carried off by the birds. Yet there is going to be a crop. At harvest time there is going to be a good yield.

That's how the kingdom comes. That's how God gains back his world. Not by sending fire from heaven, not yet by sending the Reaper, but by sending the sower. If you have ears, you will hear. If it is given to you to know the goals of God, you will sense that the indestructible kingdom comes through the humble work of the sower.

As yet nothing spectacular has happened. The King has come—but in the form of a servant. Everything seems to remain as it has always been. But those who know the mystery of the kingdom are tense with expectation and multiply their prayers. Because a farmer went out to sow. . . .

REFLECTIONS

What does this parable tell you about how the kingdom comes into the world?

Wisdom of God

1 CORINTHIANS 2:1-9

> *. . . we declare God's wisdom, a mystery that has been hidden.*
> *. . . None of the rulers of this age understood it. . . .*
> *—1 Corinthians 2:7-8*

Paul is not speaking about the kind of secret knowledge that some cults and secret societies claim. The hidden wisdom is the gospel, the good news about Christ. This wisdom of God is Christ crucified, the Son of God who died for our salvation. This wisdom was hidden; nobody could know it until it was revealed. And nobody could think it up, because it was the wisdom of God. God had prepared salvation in a way that shows his wisdom and makes a mockery of the salvation schemes of all religions. No eye had seen it and no ear had heard it—the death and resurrection of Christ.

At the cross, all the powers of sin were pitched against Christ. He was not a mere individual who died a horrible death; he was the head of a new humanity. He acted as the representative of his people. Then he arose. Again, he was not a mere individual who returned from the grave; he was the beginning of a new harvest.

In the death of Christ, then, the last power of Satan was spent; in the resurrection of Christ, the first power of God was manifested. The gates of a new age opened at that moment. Heavenly power descended. The Holy Spirit brings new and everlasting life to all who believe in Christ.

This is the gospel. The way of salvation in Christ has now been revealed. It is being proclaimed in simple words, and it is sown all over the world as seed over a field. It is by this Word that humanity must be saved and the world restored.

We must take time and effort to appropriate that gospel, to make it our own. And since it is only by the Spirit of God that we learn the wisdom of God (vv. 10-13), we must beg for the Spirit while we study God's Word.

REFLECTIONS

Are you taking "time and effort" to make the gospel your own? Have you asked the Spirit to help you as you study God's Word?

The Law of the Seed

JOHN 12:23-33

". . . unless a kernel of wheat falls to the ground and dies, it remains only a single seed, But if it dies, it produces many seeds."
—*John 12:24*

The tension in Jerusalem was mounting. People whispered that this Jesus might be the promised deliverer. The whisper became a roar when Jesus rode into the city on the donkey. "Hosanna!" they cried. "Long live the King!"

Then he said it himself: "The hour has come for the Son of man to be glorified." And how will this happen? "Unless a kernel of wheat falls to the ground and dies . . ."

Jesus knows that there will be no crown without a cross. His Father will have no harvest unless Jesus is the seed. So he gave himself. He gave his life for us. Therefore we thank and praise him forever.

But Jesus was not the only one who had to fulfill this law of the seed. He said that this law applied to his followers as well. We are inclined to forget that. We must learn and believe that the only crop this earth will ever bear will sprout out of the sacrifice of Jesus. But we must also understand that the sacrifice of Jesus gives us the power to obey the law of the seed.

A kernel of wheat that is kept in the granary remains alone. It is unfruitful. That it may serve as flour and finally as bread is not the point now. It can yield fruit only if it falls into the ground and "dies."

Jesus clarifies this law of the seed in the next sentence: If you love your life, if your only concern is self-preservation, you are unfit for the kingdom. Life in the kingdom follows the law of the seed. It is by giving that we receive, it is by blessing that we are blessed, and it is by dying that we live.

If I call Jesus my Lord, my life is subject to the law of the seed.

REFLECTION

What does it mean to you that your life as a follower of Christ is subject to the law of the seed?

The Sword of the Lamb

REVELATION 1:9-18

. . . coming out of his mouth was a sharp, double-edged sword.
—Revelation 1:16

All that the Old Testament prophesied about the Messiah has been fulfilled in Jesus. Yet everything turned out to be so divinely different from what anyone would have expected.

For instance, Israel was made to expect a deliverer who would be a warrior. The Messiah (that is, the Anointed One, the King) would scatter all his enemies. He would lead his people into a holy war. He would establish lasting peace and bring back the golden age to Israel and to the world.

What happened to the prophecies of the warrior king?

At this very moment, Jesus is the King. At least one man has seen him in his royal splendor. That man was John, on the island of Patmos. But what about the sword of the King? Yes, he does have a sword. However, he does not wear it where every other warrior keeps his sword, at his left side, ready to be drawn. The sword comes out of his mouth!

It's all part of the great surprise, the news of the gospel of the kingdom. The lion came as a lamb. The judge came with mercy. The reaper came as the sower. And the sword of the King comes out of his mouth. It is the Word that battles for him.

Nevertheless, the Word of the Lord is the sword of the Lord. Christ used to warn the cities where his Word had been heard that if they did not listen and obey, there would be no hope for them on the day of judgment. Christ says the same thing to our continent, once filled with churches and Bibles.

We must not be deceived by the seemingly harmless character of the gospel, or by the free-and-easy way in which people handle that Word. (They like it or dislike it; they take it or leave it.) In reality the gospel has the power to open and close the entrance to the kingdom. The sword is a word, but the Word is a sword!

REFLECTIONS

What does this passage and reading say to you about the Word of God in your own life?

The Sword Does Kill

ISAIAH 66:18-24

"And they will go out and look on the dead bodies of those who rebelled against me. . . ."   —*Isaiah 66:24*

God establishes his kingdom with vengeance and salvation. These two sides of God's mighty work always go together. It is the business of the church to preach the good news, the gospel of salvation. But it is unfair not to warn of judgment. Even if we have little understanding of the nature of God's final punishment, we know that it's coming. Many of us are slow to speak of salvation in Christ because we aren't quite convinced of damnation outside of Christ.

There is no book in the Old Testament that speaks in more jubilant tones about God's salvation than the book of Isaiah. In this book are immortal words of comfort. Isaiah contains descriptions of the love of God that sound as if they were written after God's love was revealed in Jesus. Yet this book ends with a sob. It ends with a picture of the damned.

Of course, anyone who relishes these pictures should be rebuked. We have all heard of "fire and brimstone" preachers who have abused the power of these pictures to pummel the public. But we should not have to excuse ourselves for bringing up the subject of eternal punishment. In heaven there is sorrow over unbelief and joy when a sinner repents. God's people on earth should reflect both the joy and the sorrow. If our sorrow is not very profound, the joy cannot be very deep either.

At least thirty times, Isaiah calls God "the Holy One of Israel." Even though we, by the blood and Spirit of Jesus, might know the same God in more tender and personal ways, he remains God—the Holy One. God cannot tolerate sin, and he must come with vengeance and salvation. Either our sins are punished in Jesus Christ, or we have to bear the punishment ourselves.

O God, be merciful to us and to our neighbors.

REFLECTIONS

Thoughtfully pray aloud the prayer found in the last line of the reading for a minute or so.

Suicide

ACTS 13:44-49

Since you reject [the Word of God] and do not consider yourselves
worthy of eternal life, we now turn to the Gentiles. —Acts 13:46

A person commits suicide when he or she rejects the Christ.

The church does not always give the impression that its work is so serious. Parsons and politicians seem to be forever smiling and shaking hands. The world is getting used to friendly young people handing out tracts. If someone wants attention, he or she can have people of the church come to the door nearly every week with the same polite invitation. In the local newspaper, the church on the corner claims to be "The Friendly Church," and the church downtown assures you that "A Big Welcome Awaits You." They all seem to be interested in You. If You would only show a mild interest in them, chances are that You would be courted for years.

I hope we all agree that friendliness and genuine personal interest ought to mark our congregations. In the cold, concrete jungles of our cities, lonely people should be able to find true fellowship among Christians. But it is not impossible that in the midst of the courtesy and advertising, people outside the church are missing the point: anyone who rejects Christ commits spiritual suicide. Anyone who places herself above the Word of God judges herself unworthy of eternal life. Not intentionally, of course. But this is how Paul and Barnabas interpret what people are really doing when they turn down the gospel.

The Word of God is and remains the Word of God. Even ordinary human beings of reasonable integrity will honor their word and their signature. But it is totally unthinkable that God would say one thing and do another. God's Word and his signature are in Christ Jesus. When you honor him, you receive all that God has promised. God will back up both his promises and his threats without fail.

REFLECTIONS

Reflect on your own approach to the Word of God. Do you sense both its promise and its threat?

Please, Come Down

ISAIAH 63:15-64:2

"Oh, that you would rend the heavens and come down. . . ."

—*Isaiah 64:1*

Some situations appear to be so hopeless that we say: "Unless a miracle happens, unless God himself does something . . ." We have heard people make such comments when someone was critically ill. For a long time it was going up and down; one day a little better, the next day a relapse. Finally it was going downhill altogether. "Unless a miracle happens . . . Unless God himself does something . . ."

A father has talked to his boy for a long time, and the boy's mother has spoken to him often. Yet he does not want to listen. He goes from bad to worse. Then the parents get on their knees and say: "Please, God, do something. Oh, that you would rend the heavens and come down. . . ."

Here, in this Bible verse, a man of God is on his knees. He points at the hopeless situation of God's people in the world. They lost the truth and lost the way. They lost their freedom and lost their temple. "Please, God, do something about it. Oh, that you would rend the heavens and come down. . . ."

God always answers prayer. This particular Old Testament prayer was answered in a way Isaiah could not have imagined. In the fullness of time, the Lord himself came to our planet as a baby in Bethlehem. The heavens were rent, and the angels assembled to give glory to God.

Since the heavens were rent and the Son came down, God has been doing something about our seemingly hopeless situation. God invaded our world, and the beginnings of the new world are already here in the lives and works of God's people. But the fullness of the kingdom has not yet appeared. We must cry again and pray without ceasing: "Come, Lord Jesus. Oh, that you would rend the heavens and come down."

REFLECTIONS

Do you long for God's kingdom to be complete? Do you pray for the return of Jesus?

God Has Done It

PSALM 130

He himself will redeem Israel from all their sins. —*Psalm 130:8*

". . . you are to give him the name Jesus, because he will save his people from their sins." —*Matthew 1:21*

The night watch of the ancient watchman must have seemed even longer than the night shift of the modern worker. The watchman in Israel did not have a clock. He did not know how many hours he had left to go. All he could do was look to the east and wait for the first sign of the new day. The writer of Psalm 130 compares this anxious waiting of the night watchman to his own longing: "I wait for the Lord more than watchmen wait for the morning."

The first watchmen we meet in the New Testament are shepherds "keeping watch over their flock by night." It became the most memorable night in history, for light came before the night was over. Those watchmen were the first to hear that Jesus was born.

Jesus was the one for whom the poet of Psalm 130 was waiting. Why? Because Jesus can do what only God can do: save from sin.

Let's be sure that we don't overlook this truth. The Old Testament waits for the Lord God to bring the Day and "redeem Israel from all their sins." The New Testament announces that the time of waiting is over: "Give him the name Jesus, because he will save his people from their sins."

If Jesus is not God, we are still in darkness. But since Jesus is God, he has the power to forgive and renew. Our night has ended. The day has begun. "Wake up, sleeper, rise from the dead, and Christ will shine on you" (Eph. 5:14).

The darkness is over. There is no reason to wait for the light anymore, for Jesus has come. There is no reason to be burdened by sin any longer, for Jesus has come. The work of salvation is perfect, for God has done it.

REFLECTIONS

Reflect on how God has brought you from darkness into light, and then give God the glory.

False Prophets

JEREMIAH 28:1-11

> *Then the prophet Hananiah . . . said before all the people: "This is what the LORD says. . . ."* —*Jeremiah 28:10-11*

A prophet is someone who speaks for God. When he opens his mouth, he does not speak for himself. Instead he proclaims: "This is what the LORD says," or, as some Bible versions forcefully put it, "Thus says the LORD." This man Hananiah also said that he spoke for God. But he was lying. Hananiah was a false prophet.

There are countless false prophets in the world today. Every one of them has a following. Often they proclaim their message with more zeal than the true prophets. Yet they are lying.

How are you going to tell whether a prophet is true or false?

If you want to know if a certain painting is an "old master" or an imitation, you have it judged by an expert. It's not that simple when it comes to the truth or falsehood of the Christian faith. Yet there is a similarity. The Christian faith rests on historical facts. The report of those facts is contained in historical documents. Those documents, the books of the Bible, are open to scientific examination, such as is applied to any historical document.

You would think that in a matter as important as the question of right or wrong, the truth or the lie, people would spend a bit more time in investigation. If cancer is worth millions of research dollars, shouldn't some research be done into the lives and writings of the founders of certain "churches"? If Joseph Smith, the founder of Mormonism, was a false prophet, his teachings have deluded more than twelve million people around the world.

Too many Christians are apathetic when it comes to the deceivers against whom God himself has warned us. We must consistently oppose false teachings and continually pray that God will destroy the works of the lying prophets. We should also give more generous and enthusiastic support to schools and seminaries that are faithful to the truth.

Above all, we must live close to Christ and have his Word in our hearts.

REFLECTIONS

What "false prophets" are deceiving people today? How?

The Apostolic Teaching

1 TIMOTHY 1:12-17

> *Here is a trustworthy saying that deserves full acceptance: Christ*
> *Jesus came into the world to save sinners. . . .* —1 Timothy 1:15

When Paul wrote his first letter to Timothy, he was most concerned that the sound teaching be preserved: "Timothy, guard what has been entrusted to your care" (6:20).

This apostolic teaching which Timothy must expound and preserve concerns Jesus Christ. On this witness to Jesus the church is built, and by this teaching the people of God continue to live. No wonder the aging apostle is so passionate both in recommending the sound gospel truth and in warning against deceivers.

In the Bible verse quoted above, Paul gives a brief statement of the purpose for which Jesus came into the world—"to save sinners." Moreover, he says that this word is "trustworthy," and that it deserves full acceptance.

It is wonderful that the heart of the gospel can be stated in such simple and reliable terms: "Christ Jesus came into the world to save sinners." All the talk about Jesus can become very confusing. More books have been written about Christ than any one of us can ever read. But whenever we become confused, we must remember to return to the basic truth. We must find our resting point on the reliable rock bottom of the Christian faith: "Here is a trustworthy saying that deserves full acceptance: Christ Jesus came into the world to save sinners."

This saying is not comforting only because it is so brief and clear. What comforts us especially is that Jesus came to save sinners. Perhaps we all go through moods when we feel quite acceptable to God, while there are other times when we know that we are "not good enough." But it is exactly when we realize that we are unworthy of his love that we may believe he came for us. Christ Jesus came to save sinners. Those are the people who are "not good enough."

REFLECTION

Sing the first verse of "Amazing Grace," John Newton's expression of the truth that Jesus came to save sinners.

The Hope of Salvation

ROMANS 8:18-25

For in this hope we were saved. But hope that is seen is no hope at all. Who hopes for what they already have? —Romans 8:24

Salvation is present and salvation is future. We have been saved and we hope for salvation. If we mean by salvation that our sins have been forgiven, salvation is present. "Are you saved?" "Yes, I am." But we are still subject to pain and death, and we are still liable to fall into sin. "Are you saved?" "I expect to be saved." Salvation is also future. Remember: hope that is seen is no hope.

We understand this situation better if we think of forgiveness as one of the first fruits of the kingdom. Since Jesus came into the world, the powers of the kingdom are present. But God's kingdom is not yet fully established. For that we will have to wait until Jesus comes again. That will be our full and final salvation.

We should not expect too little of the effect of Christ's Spirit in the present life. If we belong to Christ, our sins have been forgiven and we can do good works. Sin does not rule us anymore. Christ rules us through his Spirit. Our hearts are changed.

At the same time, we may not expect too much of the Christian life in the present world. Our lives are not going to prove to us that we are saved. That certainty is always outside of us—in Christ Jesus. We hold on to salvation only by faith. In other words, we live "in this hope." And hope refers to the future.

This is the tension that is necessarily present in every Christian's experience: we have it already and we don't have it yet. Why? Because the kingdom has come and yet has not fully come. Therefore we pray even more earnestly: "Your kingdom come!" Or: "Lord, fulfill my hope. Haste the day when my faith shall be sight."

As a matter of fact, when you can pray this with your whole soul, you are a Christian.

REFLECTIONS

How do you experience the tension described in this reading?

Volunteers

PSALM 110

Your troops will be willing on your day of battle. . . .

—*Psalm 110:3*

This psalm is quoted in the New Testament more often than any other psalm. The psalm speaks of Jesus Christ. There are two things in the psalm that made it hard for the Jews in Jesus' days. First of all, the Son of David is called the Lord of David. How can a son be more than his father? (This is precisely the riddle Jesus put to the Pharisees in Matthew 22:45.)

Secondly, this Messiah-King of Psalm 110 is at the same time a priest: "You are a priest for ever, in the order of Melchizedek."

The riddle is solved when you know Jesus. Jesus was indeed the Son of David, but he was also the Lord of David because he was the Son of God. And Jesus was not only king but also a "priest forever," because he offered himself as a sacrifice. Thus he became king and remained priest.

Now is the day that Jesus is in power. Today King Jesus has an army. The army consists of volunteers who offer themselves willingly. Jesus invites everybody, but he forces nobody. It is true that everyone who enlists in his army has been conquered by his love, and it is beyond doubt that everyone who puts on God's gospel armor has first been captured by the insistence of the Spirit. Nevertheless, a person always assumes a place in Christ's army freely and willingly. Christ wants only cheerful givers and volunteer soldiers.

The soldiers are also priests, which is not surprising when we know that the general is the Priest-King. And the victory of this army—which is a sure thing with such a general—comes "not with swords' loud clashing, or stir of rolling drums." No, "with deeds of love and mercy, the heavenly kingdom comes."

The priestly soldiers in God's army win the victory by prayer and sacrifice.

REFLECTIONS

Think back on an act of "love and mercy" that you performed for the Lord. Did you do so "freely and willingly"? Give thanks for the opportunities God gives you to serve.

Transferred to the Kingdom

COLOSSIANS 1:9-14

For he has rescued us from the dominion of darkness and brought us into the kingdom of the Son he loves. . . . —*Colossians 1:13*

The Bible says that we are either living under the dominion of the devil or have been transferred to the rule of Jesus. It's either black or white. Perhaps we would like to assign each other and ourselves to a gray area between the devil and the kingdom. But the fact of the matter is that you are either in or out; you belong to the devil or to Christ.

Christians may freely praise God for delivering them from the dominion of darkness and transferring them to the kingdom of the beloved Son. From now on they may and must and can live by the rules of their new Lord.

Notice that there are two separate operations in this saving work of God. The first is that he rescued or delivered us from the darkness, and the second is that he brought or transferred us to the kingdom of Christ. The first was the rescue operation. He got us out of the cage. The second operation is the resettlement of those who were rescued: He transferred us to the kingdom of his beloved Son.

Christians acknowledge this double work of Christ when they call him their Savior and their Lord. When we say "Savior," we mean that he rescued us. When we say "Lord," we mean that he transferred us to his domain, kingship, or authority. He is our Savior because he got us out of the old house. He is our Lord because we are now under his blessed rule.

It is obvious, then, that we cannot have Christ as our Savior unless he is now our Lord. Christ does not leave us in the old house, nor does he leave us halfway between the old and the new. Only when he has transferred us to his own domain are we saved.

In other words, our obedience to the Lord is evidence of our salvation.

REFLECTIONS

Praise God for rescuing you from darkness and transferring you to the light of Christ's kingdom. Ask that your life may show your gratitude for what Christ has done for you.

Time Goes On

GALATIANS 4:1-7

But when the set time had fully come [literally, when the fullness of time came], God sent his Son . . . —Galatians 4:4

It seems natural to think of time and history in terms of circles, for that's the way life appears to our unenlightened eyes. A person's life runs through the cycle of birth, growth, maturity, and death. A nation seems to run the same gamut: it rises, becomes vigorous, grows prosperous, becomes decadent, and disappears. And the seasons of the year seem to be four spokes in the wheel of nature.

Once we have admitted that everything runs in cycles, we are at a loss to make any sense of life or to attach meaning to history. What is up will come down, and what is down will come up again. We are running in circles, and we ourselves are part of a bigger circle. We are not only turning, we are being turned. Perhaps there is somebody or something at the wheel. Who knows?

The Bible teaches us a different view of life and time. It speaks of the "fullness" of time, when God sent his Son, and of the "last day," when the Son will come again. The word *fullness* makes us think of water flowing into a barrel. Every drop adds to the total volume. And finally the barrel is full.

Life and time and history are not what they appear to be. We are not enmeshed in a circle. And today, the 24th of January, is not just another spoke in the big wheel that turns and turns. It's not another round on the merry-go-round, and it's not another race through the vicious circle. But it is another drop in God's barrel. The days and weeks are flowing by, and we are getting older. But all these days flow to a goal, with God watching and regulating the stream. Soon we will hear the archangel's voice. The trumpet will blast because the Day has come. "Stop!" "Full!"

Time goes on. We should learn how to use it. Don't be afraid or reckless. The kingdom is coming.

REFLECTIONS

Reflect on the fact that your life—and all of time—is moving not in a circle but toward a goal. What difference does this make for the way you live?

Faithfulness

MATTHEW 24:45-51

*It will be good for that servant whose master finds him doing so
when he returns.* —Matthew 24:46

Stewardship is very important in the Bible, but modern life offers little that helps explain what a steward is and does.

In Bible times, when a man went on a journey, he might well stay away for more than a year. Then he would entrust his belongings or his business to a steward for the duration of his absence. That person, the steward, had full authority to transact business or rule the household until the master returned. The return of the master was also the day of reckoning. And since the master's trip was not scheduled by a travel agency, the date of his return was uncertain.

You can see what an excellent example this institution of stewardship provided when the Lord wanted to warn his followers to wait and work in expectation of his return. That's why a number of parables are about stewards who work in their master's business and who must constantly keep in mind that their master will return unexpectedly. The point of the parables is not that the master will stay away for a long time but that he will return unexpectedly.

Now, if you had to choose a person to whom you were to entrust your business or your farm, what would be the most desirable traits to look for? They would be reliability, loyalty, faithfulness. The most important thing in a steward is not brilliance but faithfulness.

In every decision the faithful steward thinks first of the master. Every night the books and the master's business are organized so that if the master should come home during the night, the steward would be ready to give an account.

"So you also must be ready, because the Son of Man will come at an hour when you do not expect him" (Matt. 24:44).

REFLECTION

If the Lord were to return tonight, would he find you ready? Faithful?

We Must Wait

MATTHEW 25:1-13

"Therefore keep watch, because you do not know the day or the hour."
—Matthew 25:13

These ten girls were to take part in a bridal procession. We should imagine that they were waiting in a house halfway between the homes of the bride and the groom. There they sat, all dressed up, holding their little lamps, ready to go out as soon as the bridegroom came. Then they would join the friends of the groom. Singing happy songs, they would lead the couple to the hall where the wedding was to take place.

But it took much longer than they had expected. Their excited chatter died down, they became drowsy, and they fell asleep. Then, suddenly, they were startled by a shout that the bridegroom was coming. Quickly they trimmed their lamps, which had burned up all the oil. Five of the girls had had enough foresight to bring some extra oil, and they went out to meet the bridegroom with brightly burning lamps. But the others had not taken any precautions and now found themselves without the lights they were supposed to carry. Since there was not enough oil to share, they ran off to buy some. But when the five foolish girls came running to the wedding hall, the door was closed. They were shut out. They were too late.

The point of the story is that since we do not know the day or the hour of Christ's return, we must be prepared to meet him anytime. When Christ comes, it is too late to get ready. We must *be* ready!

Throughout the New Testament, we are told what terror the sudden coming of the Lord will bring to those who aren't expecting him. The parable of the ten girls is about the friendliest, most innocent setting to choose in making this point. As a matter of fact, we feel just a bit sorry for these five girls.

Don't you feel sorry for the majority of the people you meet, who don't give a thought to the coming of the Lord?

REFLECTIONS

How can you live in such a way that you are prepared to meet Christ? What does "being ready" mean for your day-to-day living?

Impatient Waiting

LUKE 18:1-8

"However, when the Son of Man comes, will he find faith on the earth?"   *—Luke 18:8*

If the kingdom is our hope and treasure, we must persist in prayer and knock on the door of heaven until we receive what we are asking.

In driving home this point about persistence and endurance, the Lord told a story about a woman who had been done an injustice. In spite of the fact that the judge was callous, a fellow who "neither feared God nor cared what people thought," the woman received justice at last because she was insistent. The point Christ was making was that we, who have a righteous Judge in heaven, must not stop asking for what we have coming according to his own promise.

The question is not whether the Judge in heaven will listen; the question is whether the church will continue to cry out. "When the Son of Man comes, will he find faith on earth?" Faith, in this connection, means insistent prayer that keeps knocking on the gates of heaven.

By asking that disturbing question ("Will he find faith?"), the Lord implied that we are inclined to give up on the promise and to give in to "ordinary life." We take sin for granted, and we accept injustice as part of our existence. We shrug our shoulders when people walk all over each other, and we don't expect the cause of the righteous to be victorious. We admit that there is much wrong in the world, in the church, in our own lives, but we figure we can't do anything about it anyway.

The greatest danger that threatens Christendom is not atheism or immorality but apathy. It is a state in which the vision of the kingdom is no longer before the minds of Christians. They no longer pound on the door of heaven. They don't really believe that the Judge is listening and the Lord is coming.

Will the Lord find faith? Will there be men and women who live not by the standards of the world but by the strange music of the kingdom of God?

REFLECTIONS

About what kinds of things does the Lord want us to be "insistent in prayer"?

The Kingdom Is Here

MATTHEW 12:22-29

"But if it is by the Spirit of God that I drive out demons, then the kingdom of God has come upon you." —*Matthew 12:28*

The opposite of the kingdom of God is not the kingdom of man but the kingdom of Satan. People are either the victims of the devil's rule or they are set free in the kingdom of God.

There was a man who was completely in the devil's grip; he was "demon-possessed." He could not speak or hear as a result of the devil's work. Of course this does not mean that wherever there is deafness or inability to speak, we may conclude that a devil is responsible. But it does mean that both sickness and demon possession disappear when the kingdom has fully come.

This particular man was fully healed by Jesus. Then a discussion developed concerning the power with which Jesus operated. The idea that Jesus did this work by another devilish power had to be ruled out. Satan is not destroying Satan. "But if it is by the Spirit of God that I drive out demons, then the kingdom of God has come upon you."

This saying of Jesus is tremendously important for our understanding of the kingdom. The kingdom of God is not only a future reality for which we wait; it is already present wherever the stranglehold of Satan is broken. And the power that breaks the devil's hold is the Spirit of God. This Spirit first rested on Jesus and is now given to all those who believe in him.

Today Jesus Christ operates by his Spirit through his followers. The kingdom of Satan cannot stand against this power. To the extent that the Holy Spirit controls our present lives, to that extent the kingdom of God has come.

Vast areas of the present world seem to belong to the kingdom of Satan. But he who is with us and works through us is stronger than Satan. And he will win the battle.

REFLECTION

In what ways do you struggle against evil in your own life? What difference does Jesus' power make in these situations?

Already But Not Yet

MATTHEW 8:28-34

"What do you want with us, Son of God?" they shouted. "Have you come here to torture us before the appointed time?"
—*Matthew 8:29*

When you read the gospels, you notice that nobody recognizes Jesus for who he really is. Flesh and blood cannot recognize him. But the demons knew who Jesus was. They had a supernatural knowledge of Jesus and the significance of his coming.

When the devils saw the King, they heard the clock strike and they shuddered. They knew that the kingdom of God was going to be established because Jesus had come. Now the kingdom of Satan tottered.

The real battle is between the kingdom of God and the kingdom of Satan. Of course, people are not in the middle as innocent parties. We are either willing victims of the devil or saved by the grace of God. But the fact remains that our lot is decided in the spiritual realm—without us and about us—even if that truth hurts our pride. By God's Spirit we may become consciously engaged in the great battle, but this battle is never won by flesh and blood and is not fought against flesh and blood.

"Have you come here to torture us before the appointed time?" Apparently the devils know that their doom is sure, but they also know that the final hour has not yet come. They must leave their victims in the blessing, healing hands of Jesus. But the demons are allowed to go into the herd of swine. Jesus does not allow them to do so because he is moved with pity for the demons. Christ reserves his pity for people. He allows the demons to go because the "appointed time" has not yet come. Later he will consign them to the abyss.

This event is very instructive for the believer: It shows Jesus' power over the demons. They must surrender their victims to him. At the same time this happening shows that the victory is tentative—not yet complete. Christ permits them to carry on their destructive activity. The final hour of reckoning has not yet come.

REFLECTIONS

What does this story tell you about the kingdom of God?

Task and Shield

MATTHEW 28:16-20

> *"All authority in heaven and on earth has been given to me. Therefore go and make disciples of all nations. . . . . And surely I am with you always. . . ."*
> —*Matthew 28:18-20*

The work that Christ has accomplished by his death and resurrection is complete. Therefore he speaks in absolute terms when he meets with his disciples as their risen Lord. Notice how he uses the word *all*. *All* authority has been given to him in heaven and on earth. *All* nations must become his disciples. *All* the remaining days Jesus will be present with his people. Actually, he uses the word a fourth time, when he says that we must be taught to observe *all* that he has commanded. "All" leaves nothing that is not included.

Christ assigned his disciples an unlimited task: Make disciples of all nations. Disciples must go and make disciples. When someone believes, he must be baptized in the Name, and then he must learn to live as a disciple of Jesus. There may not be disciples of Peter, churches of John, or followers of Andrew. The task of every apostle and of every missionary is to make disciples of the one Master, Jesus Christ.

We must never forget that the task is assigned in the context of Christ's power. It would be impossible for the church of Christ to fulfill the commission of Christ, because we have no power of our own. But Christ lifted the shield of his power over his followers: I have all authority; therefore go and make disciples of all nations. And if this is not yet enough to make us lose our feeling of inferiority in view of the unlimited (and unfinished!) task, the King himself assures us of his presence. Not only does he lift the shield of his power over his missionaries, he himself goes with them.

To be disciples and to make disciples—that is our task. To believe in his power—that is our strength. To trust in his presence—that is our comfort.

REFLECTIONS

How do you feel about the task Jesus outlines in the Great Commission? What hope and strength do you find in this passage as you seek to follow Jesus?

The New Country

REVELATION 21:1-8

> *He who was seated on the throne said, "I am making everything new."*
> *—Revelation 21:5*

The great renovation is under way. To us it seems to take forever. But we must not forget that the reasons why it takes so long lie in God's wisdom and grace.

The beginnings of God's renewal of the world are despised by most, but they are greeted as the first signs of spring by all who have ears to hear and eyes to see. Just as God created by his Word, so God makes a new world by the gospel of his Son. The sower has gone forth to sow.

To us it seems impossible that the world could be entirely changed, for we are unable to change people. We cannot even change ourselves. But what is impossible with us is possible with God. In the beginning he gave us one father, Adam, whose blood flows in all of us. Now he has given us a second Adam, the Lord Jesus, whose Spirit flows in all who believe in him. Already we have received a new heart, a new hope, and a new power. We trust God to finish his work and make everything new.

We must never be discouraged. Nothing is so bad that God cannot make it good. Nothing is so old that God cannot make it new.

God did reveal to us that he has to use fire. The kingdom comes with judgment and salvation. Already the judgment came into the world. Good Friday was judgment day. On Golgotha the wrath of God was poured out on our sins. Therefore there is now no condemnation for those who are in Christ Jesus. For them the old things have passed away. Those who are in Christ Jesus have had their sins punished. God will not punish us twice.

We have now been brought into the kingdom of God's beloved Son. Under his rule we live a new life. Soon it will be revealed that God has given us a new name and a new country—the land of hope and glory.

REFLECTIONS

Imagine, if you will, what our world will look like when God restores creation and makes everything new. Then give thanks.

Living with God

Basic to true religion is our daily walk with God. This month's readings focus on Abraham, who knew what it meant to live by God's promises.

daylight

Father Abraham

ACTS 7:2-8

He is the father of us all. —*Romans 4:16*

Three world religions claim Abraham as their father. Rightly or wrongly, all Jews, Christians, and Muslims consider themselves the offspring of Abraham.

Undoubtedly people in each of these three groups believe they have good reasons for their claim on father Abraham. However, if any among these millions should think that this link with Abraham entitles them to preferential treatment with God, they are mistaken. God does not honor such credit cards.

God's people are counted by the faith of Abraham. Only those who believe as Abraham believed receive the promises of God. Abraham lived with God. This is a kind of life most people do not know.

Perhaps some reader of this page recently got married. He or she is now finding out what it means to live with a wife or a husband. At first you have to get used to it. Time and again you are amazed by the all-pervasive influence of your partnership. Later you find that you cannot even think of your own life apart from your spouse.

But a life lived with God is even stranger to an outsider than married life is to a single person. It's an amazing partnership that affects every thought, word, and deed.

Models for this kind of life are hard to find. Perhaps you are fortunate enough to have a friend or relative who is your picture of a person who lives with God. Let's hope so. But for an authentic model of this kind of life, you still have to go to the Bible. The life of Abraham, in particular, shows what it means to live with God. Abraham is the father of all whose lives are governed by the presence and promise of God.

REFLECTIONS

Who do you look to as a person who truly "lives with God"? What influence has this person had on your life?

With God on His Way

GENESIS 12:1-4

So Abram went, as the LORD had told him. . . . —*Genesis 12:4*

The obedience of faith is stated very simply: "So Abram went, as the LORD had told him." God spoke, and Abram did what God said.

At this point we must be very careful not to get all wrapped up in describing the sacrifices of our hero Abram. Usually we start talking about the pain of parting, the severance of ties, the burning of ships, and the courage of faith. We are inclined to talk this way because everybody understands such language. It is the language of ordinary human experience.

But this is not the line of reasoning followed by a man who lives with God.

Abram did not sacrifice anything. What he left behind was nothing in comparison with what lay ahead. He said goodbye to a burnt-out existence—especially if you remember how Joshua said that Abram's fathers served "other gods" (Josh. 24:2). Abram began to move onto a road that was bright with the promises of God. From the point of view of the man who has been gripped by the Word of God, Abram was the receiver and God was the giver.

The journey began with a word, a word from God addressed to a man. This is how a life with God begins. That's how those fishermen experienced it at the Sea of Galilee when the voice of Jesus said, "Follow me." A word comes to us from the other side, from God. It is the call of the gospel.

This Word of God cuts us loose from many old things. If we are wise and obedient, we are quick to break the ties rather than linger with regret. Those who are fascinated by the one who calls them do not pay attention to the pain of parting. Their lives have received a whole new dimension. They are now living in the magnetic field of the presence and promises of God.

REFLECTIONS

To what might God be calling you today? New ways of service? New places to serve? New people to contact?

From Altar to Altar

GENESIS 12:4-9

*So he built an altar [at Shechem] to the Lord, who had appeared
to him. . . . [At Bethel] he built an altar to the Lord and called on
the name of the Lord.*   —*Genesis 12:7-8*

The journey from the plains of the Euphrates to the hills of Judea is told
in five verses. Accompanied by Sarai, his childless wife, and his nephew
Lot, Abram left a prosperous country. Abram and his household moved
into Canaan from the north and went as far south as Bethel, in the
region of the Judean desert. This was the great trek, the historic journey
by which the center of attention and the focus of revelation was shifted
to Canaan for the next two thousand years. Yet the account is as sober as
it is brief. Hundreds of miles and numerous events are compressed into
a few sentences. But twice the writer mentions that Abram built an altar
to the Lord.

The altar marks the point where God has spoken and where Abram
has responded in faith. Altars are the sites where Abram has met his
God. All the dangers and delights of the long trip may be omitted from
the record. But the building of the altars is important.

Here is an outstanding feature of a life that is lived with God. Progress
is not measured by miles or ordinary events. All of that may be overlooked
when the account is written. But the points that must be mentioned are
the occasions for altar building.

Therefore the life that is lived with God remains a mystery to an outsider. Every other life is lived from diploma to promotion to paycheck.
People measure their journeys by the houses they lived in and the travels
they made. But the life of the man or woman who lives with God is measured from altar to altar.

Such a life reaches its goal when God's presence is uninterrupted and
when his last promise has been fulfilled. "Then I will go to the altar
of God, to God, my joy and delight. I will praise you . . . O my God"
(Ps. 43:4).

REFLECTIONS
What are the "altars" in your life?

Famine and Fright

GENESIS 12:10-16

Now there was a famine in the land. . . .   *—Genesis 12:10*

Abram's journey with God had hardly begun when he ran into troubles. Canaan was hit by a severe famine. Threatened by this disaster, Abram decided to go to Egypt. There he ran into more snags. He knew that the Pharaoh sometimes abducted the pretty wives of strangers. He feared that he might be killed. So Abram suggested to Sarai that she pose as his sister. And then the problems really started.

Why do these things happen? Why must a man who lives with God in faith and obedience be exposed to the threat of starvation on one hand and the advances of Pharaoh on the other?

We can never refrain from asking these questions. But such questions are useless; they lead to unfruitful discussions.

The only really important question is how a person behaves in the face of such threats. At such a time a person may not sit down and sigh, "Why does this happen to me?" These are occasions to say, "Who is the Lord in whom I trust?"

Of course the threats were real. But God is real too. Through Jesus Christ, you and I can face God. Therefore we can also face life and all circumstances. Faith is the refusal to panic.

Abram did very poorly in this test. He lied because he was afraid. He was afraid because he stopped trusting in God as his partner. And then he got entangled in his own scheming.

While we look at Abram, we had better listen to the word of wisdom: "Trust in the LORD with all your heart and lean not on your own understanding; in all your ways submit to him, and he will make your paths straight" (Prov. 3:5-6).

REFLECTION

What tests or troubles are you facing today or will you soon face? Ask God to help you trust him and bring you through whatever you're facing.

Back to God

GENESIS 12:17-13:4

> *"What have you done to me? . . . Why didn't you tell me she was your wife?"* —*Genesis 12:18*

Abram was rebuked by Pharaoh. Maybe the Pharaoh was not as noble as he sounded. But he was right. It is always hard for us to be rebuked by those who do not know the Lord. It makes us blush.

Notice that Abram did not say anything. He was ashamed.

God did not say anything either. At least the Bible does not record anything he said. God did something. God disentangled Abram from the predicament he had made for himself. The Lord remained faithful to his partner. Even the Pharaoh discovered how God was on the side of his undeserving friend Abram.

The caravan wound its way from Egypt to the desert of Judea. Abram's company was silent and ashamed. But there is grace in such a mood. When we are ashamed of ourselves, we can at least find God again, even if we hardly dare lift our eyes to heaven. When we are proud of ourselves, we do not need God and he hides his face.

Abram is learning that God does not give a promise and then leave us to find our own way. That is unthinkable. God never leaves us, day or night. When we are foolish enough to go our self-willed ways, God still haunts us and even disentangles us from the results of our own folly.

And now notice where the journey ends. If you or I were writing the story, we would close it with a tearful reunion of Abram and Sarai. Maybe they had such a reunion. But such a climax only fits novels; it cannot be the point of the Bible. At Bethel is a kneeling figure before an altar. A man has found his God again. Abram kneels at the altar.

Abram has returned to God. Now he lives again. It's like a New Testament Christian finding the cross, where God and people were reconciled. There we find life because there we know God.

REFLECTIONS

What kinds of experiences in your life drive you to God?

Comparing People (1)

GENESIS 13:5-13

> *Lot looked around and saw that the whole plain of the Jordan
> was well watered, like the garden of the LORD. . . . So Lot chose
> for himself the whole plain of the Jordan . . . and pitched his tents
> near Sodom.* —Genesis 13:10-12

The influence of those who have taught us in our youth is very deep. I can
still hear the voice of one of my teachers: "Abram was old and Lot was
young. Lot should have asked Abram to choose first. But Lot was greedy
and Abram was modest." Thus she taught us not to be the first to take a
cookie from the tray.

It was sweet of her and good for us, perhaps. But her story did not get
to the level of the Bible.

We always compare people with people. It's the only level we know.
That's how we decide whether a person is good or evil, selfish or generous, rich or poor. But this game can be played by any moralist.

The Bible always places us in our primary relationship—to God. The
weight of our deeds and decisions is measured against that awe-inspiring
backdrop—God! Once we have learned something of the biblical mea-
suring lines, we become increasingly hesitant to use our own.

Actually, Lot does not have a bad name in the Bible. He is called
"that righteous man" who was "tormented in his righteous soul" when he
saw the sins of Sodom (2 Pet. 2:8). But in this, his crucial hour, Lot did
not live with God. His desire for the Jordan Valley overruled all other
considerations.

Compared with other people, Lot did all right. He had what is called
the chance of a lifetime. Some people even have a philosophy about this
kind of thing. They say that opportunity knocks only once, and if you grab
your chance at that moment, everyone will agree that you did the right
thing. That's how so many people have landed just where they are. Their
eyes were blinded by the Jordan Valley or some other piece of real estate.
Now we can only pray that God will keep them awake at night, tossing
and turning, so that they pull up stakes before Sodom starts burning.

REFLECTIONS

Confess to God whatever may tempt you to think first about your own
needs and forget your relationship with God.

Comparing People (2)

LUKE 18:9-14

"God, I thank you that I am not like other people. . . ."

—*Luke 18:11*

Worldly people live on the person-to-person level because that's the only level they know. But religious people also find it easier to live with people than to live with God.

The Pharisee was a religious man: "God, I thank you . . ." He addressed God, but his thoughts were on the level of I-and-the-others: "I thank you that I am not like other people." Constantly he compared his religious behavior with the behavior of others. Many of us tend to do the same thing, in order to see how we are doing. As for the Pharisee, the comparison with others was in his favor. He was better in giving and in fasting. Compared with the tax collector, he was a pillar in church and society.

Jesus certainly did not say that the tax collector was "better." But the tax collector saw his life for the first time in terms of the staggering reality of God. And then he prayed. His prayer went to God. The prayer of the Pharisee remained on the level where it belonged. It would not get beyond the person-to-person level. The tax collector beat his breast and cried that he was a sinner.

The tax collector did not discover that he was a sinner because he found his behavior so wicked, comparatively speaking. Rather he confessed his sinfulness because he saw God. And once he—or anyone—has seen God, there is only one thing to say: "God, have mercy on me, a sinner."

Living with God is a strange life—strange to a natural man or woman. It's a life with an extra dimension. You don't know what this life is like until you know God.

If you don't know God, you might still be a nice person, comparatively speaking. But you could not possibly know the truth about yourself.

REFLECTIONS

What does it mean to you to see your life "in terms of the staggering reality of God"?

Comparatively Good

LUKE 18:18-23

"Why do you call me good? . . . Nobody is good but God alone."
—Luke 18:19

We are surprised by Jesus' question: "Why do you call me good?" If we may not call Jesus Christ a "good teacher," there aren't any good teachers.

"Nobody is good but God alone." But isn't Jesus the eternal Son of God? And doesn't the Bible itself say of a certain Joseph (Luke 23:50) and of a certain Barnabas (Acts 11:24) that they were "good men"?

Jesus is not denying his goodness, but he is correcting the one-level vision of the young man who came to him. This young ruler must learn to be very careful in his use of the word *good*. The young man is typical of a kind of religious moralism that continues to plague us. Our ideas of goodness are based on comparison with other people. And on that basis we get and give our grades, just as the marks in school are usually based on comparison with the performance of other students.

But Jesus always places a person before God. "Nobody is good but God alone." He teaches us to ask for the will of God for our lives. And when Christ revealed the will of God to the young man ("Sell everything you have. . . . Then come, follow me"), the ruler thought the demand was too high. When he compared himself to fellow believers, he was not doing badly ("All these I have kept since I was a boy"). But the new demand was incomparably high.

Every person lives in the presence of God. Our fellow believers do not set the standards. And we may not label others as "good" and "better" Christians. Our reward is from the Lord.

Those who know their Judge will not be swept off their feet by the compliments of people. And, by the same token, the condemnation of people is not final either.

REFLECTIONS
In what situations or settings might you be tempted to let other believers, rather than God, set the standard?

God's Generosity

LUKE 18:24-30

"Truly I tell you," Jesus said to them, "nobody who has left home or wife or brothers or sisters or parents or children for the sake of the kingdom of God will fail to receive many times as much in this age, and in the age to come eternal life." —Luke 18:29-30

When the rich young ruler refused to follow Jesus because the price was too high, the disciples asked what they would get. After all, they had given up everything to follow Jesus.

Once again Jesus gave a surprising answer. On more than one occasion we read in the gospels that Jesus rebuked his disciples for asking the wrong question. And in this case they certainly seem to have gone too far. We would expect Jesus to say: "Just follow me; never mind the reward." However, instead of chiding them, Jesus painted a picture of life with God in the most exciting colors.

Christ throws the doors of the castle wide open and exhibits the generosity of God. "You cannot be a loser if you follow me," he said. "You'll be the receiver in this life, and in the next age you'll have eternal life." For everything you give up, you will receive "many times as much." Any investor would be happy to get that kind of return.

We must often remind each other of Jesus' warning that those who would gain the whole world yet lose their soul have no profit whatsoever from their life's investment. But we should also remember his promise that those who give up on the worldly life will find a tremendous profit in the kingdom.

You and I are sinfully inclined to give little and expect little. Now let God teach us by the Spirit to give our all and expect all that Jesus has promised.

Jesus has spoken this cheerful word without reservation. We know that we have a generous God. And since we know this, it is much easier to burn our bridges and go on the pilgrimage with father Abraham and all who believe as he did.

REFLECTIONS

What tells you today that you have a generous God?

Was He Jealous?

GENESIS 13:14-18

> *The LORD said to Abram after Lot had parted from him, "Look around from where you are. . . ." There he built an altar to the LORD.* —Genesis 13:14, 18

How did Abram feel when Lot took the best part of the country, which belonged to Abram according to the promise of God?

God's people are hard to understand, especially in circumstances where they are being hurt by their neighbors. Jesus advised: "If anyone wants to sue you and take your shirt, hand over your coat as well" (Matt. 5:40). If they are after a dollar, give them two. Do we understand that attitude? Or do we despise it?

Other ancient teachers have advised their disciples to do the same thing. But then the reasoning was: "You should be far above that mundane attitude of grab while the grabbing's good. Let them have the stuff." They recommended an attitude of arrogance.

Jesus' teaching has a different frame of reference. He requires the style of someone who gathers treasures in heaven (Matt. 6:20) and who is therefore *free* with respect to his earthly possessions. It's what Paul called "having as not having."

God comes to Abram after Lot had left him. And God repeats the Word of promise: "Look around . . ." God always comforts us by repeating his Word. He wants us to set our sights on the promised future and live in the present by the power of faith. And when God's presence and promises constitute our wealth, our hearts do not cling to other treasures.

In the last lines of Genesis 13, we see a bit of this secret. Abram is picking stones from the meager soil to build an altar. For the way of one who lives with God does not go from rags to riches. Not even from good to better to best. It goes from altar, to altar, to God.

REFLECTIONS

Think about your own attitude toward earthly possessions. Ask God to give you an attitude of being "free" from the lure of things because your real treasures are God's presence and promise.

Abram and Melchizedek

GENESIS 14:13-24

Then Melchizedek king of Salem brought out bread and wine. He was priest of God Most High, and he blessed Abram. . . . Then Abram gave him a tenth of everything. —*Genesis 14:18-20*

After the battle a very significant event took place: Abram received a blessing from Melchizedek. This king, who was also a "priest of God Most High," is a mysterious figure in the history of the covenant. He does not really belong to the clan of God's own people.

(He is further mentioned in Psalm 110. And there is a long piece about him as a "type" of our Lord Jesus in Hebrews 5 and 7.)

This happening is strange indeed. After all, there was nobody in the whole world more important than Abram and his tribe. But here the head of the blessed nation, on whom all of God's promises rested, knelt before this stranger who had the power to bless. (Heb. 7:7 comments: "And without doubt the lesser is blessed by the greater.") Moreover, Abram acknowledged the religious authority of Melchizedek by paying a tax to him: "Abram gave him a tenth of everything."

This meeting with Melchizedek shows that Abram expected more than many children and a good country. This story is an indication that the hope and joy of Abram and his seed centered on a figure who would be more than a natural son of Abram. We know that, of course, because we have learned to read the Old Testament through the glasses of the New. We know that the ultimate hope of Abram was Jesus. "Your father Abraham rejoiced at the thought of seeing my day," said Jesus (John 8:56).

Jesus was the greatest son of Abram. But he is also the Son of God. Without the history of the natural children of Abram, we would not have Jesus. But the history of Abram's children is not enough to explain the coming of Jesus. He also came "from the outside," "from elsewhere"—a little like Melchizedek. And even Abram must kneel before this Priest-King to receive his blessing.

REFLECTIONS

How would you express your "ultimate hope"?

Faith

GENESIS 15:1-6

Abram believed the L<small>ORD</small>*; and he credited it to him as righteousness.* —*Genesis 15:6*

The coming of Christ divided the Jewish nation into two groups. A part of the children of Abraham accepted Jesus as the promised Messiah. But another part rejected him. An argument raged between these two groups. The issue was: Who were the real children of Abraham?

Paul, who was originally one of the Christ-rejecters but later became one of the Christ-confessors, was fond of quoting Genesis 15:6 as proof that those who accepted Christ were the real children of Abraham. You see, Paul used to say, the good news of Christ requires all people to believe—only believe. The gospel is not a reward for what you have done; it's a report of what God has done. You must believe this message. Then you will be right with God. God accepts you not because you are so good but because he is so good. You aren't right with God because you have accomplished something; you are righteous because Christ has accomplished everything. Only believe!

And as for Abraham, Paul pointed to Genesis 15:6: Righteousness is "credited" to Abraham in the same way it is credited to us, namely, by faith. "Understand, then, that those who have faith are children of Abraham" (Gal. 3:7; see also Rom. 4).

Now the children of Abraham have become as numerous as the stars in the sky. Thus Abraham's hope has been fulfilled. Through Christ we share in Abraham's blessing.

Belief in the gospel is the only gate through which one is admitted to God's people. That people is made up of all who walk by faith in God until the last promise has been fulfilled.

REFLECTIONS

What would you tell someone who asks you why you believe?

The Covenant

GENESIS 15:7-18

On that day the Lord made a covenant with Abram. . . .
—Genesis 15:18

In these verses we witness the making of a covenant between the Creator of the world and the ancestor of a nation that was to be God's instrument for bringing salvation to the world.

The elements for covenant making (the cut animals) were the same as those used in hundreds of binding contracts between ancient rulers.

A covenant means that *A* makes a promise to *B*. *B* may demand what *A* has promised, but *B* must provide what *A* requires in the terms of the contract. The cut animals are a solemn warning against unfaithfulness in the covenant.

Covenant making was not unusual as such. The unusual thing about this particular covenant was that God himself pledged fidelity to this man and his children. God stooped to use this human form of contract in order to assure Abram that God's promises are reliable.

Abram made the preparations, but his partner let him wait. Trusting that God would come, Abram kept the "elements" clean. Then Abram fell into a deep sleep, and the darkness descended. The "thick and dreadful darkness" not only fell around Abram but also "came over him." Under the spell of a deep religious fear, Abram met with his partner—God.

Smoke and fire signify the appearance of God. And it is God alone (instead of the two partners) who walks between the cut animals.

A covenant with God is, necessarily, more of a one-sided promise than a two-sided agreement. Therefore we call our relationship to God a covenant of grace. God has freely promised; we may ask with boldness.

God does require of his partners that they walk with him in faith and obedience: "And what does the LORD require of you? To act justly and to love mercy and to walk humbly with your God" (Mic. 6:8).

REFLECTIONS

Reflect on—and give thanks for—God's promises to you.

Off the Highway

GENESIS 16:1-3

"The LORD has kept me from having children."   —*Genesis 16:2*

What Sarai and Abram did was perfectly proper. According to the prevailing moral code, the childless woman could offer her slave woman to her husband. Note that Sarai says: "Perhaps I can have children *through her.*" It was an ancient form of adopting a child. Later this practice was taken up in the laws of Moses.

According to human insight and according to the rules of the existing order, this was the logical thing to do. Abram and Sarai had suffered long enough. The woman took the initiative, which was also quite proper. Everyone would have agreed that Abram and Sarai chose the right procedure.

But God had drawn this couple away from the sphere of human calculation and planning. Abram and Sarai had been placed on the highway of God's promise, and there they were to carry their cross by faith. God wanted them to stay on that highway and keep hoping in the promise. But with their adoption plan, they went onto the side road of their own solutions.

We do not judge them.

More than ten years of struggle lay behind this decision. Weren't those people entitled to some happiness?

In some Bible versions Sarai says, "*Behold* now, the Lord has prevented me from having children." Behold! Look and see for yourself. Faith is being certain of what we do not see (Heb. 11:1). But how can one always live by things we do not see? Look! Ten years and no children. We understand why Sarai faltered.

And Abram too lays down his burden. He leaves the highway of faith. Together they depart.

Of course this will lead to all kinds of trouble.

Why? Because living with God means that we carry our cross along the highway of faith toward the horizon of God's promise.

REFLECTIONS

In what areas of your life might you be tempted to "leave the highway of faith" and second-guess God?

On the Side Road

GENESIS 16:4-9

"May the LORD judge between you and me."   —*Genesis 16:5*

Once they had decided to take matters into their own hands, Abram and Sarai got themselves entangled in all kinds of difficulties. There was Sarai's jealousy. And Hagar's pride. Wasn't she, Hagar, the one who saved the household of Abram? The looks she gave Sarai and her bearing around the tents of Abram—she flaunted her pride before everyone!

The rest is so easy to understand because it is so utterly human. Also the final showdown: Sarai's pent-up grief and irritation burst out. Her words, invoking God's judgment ("May the Lord judge between you and me"), slapped Abram in the face. Abram was weary: "Your servant is in your hands." The Bible hides what happened under the veiled words "Then Sarai mistreated Hagar."

It makes no sense to ask who was wrong and who was right in the conflict between Abram and Sarai and Hagar. Why do people always want to know who is right and who is wrong after a series of conflicts have erupted? Who can give sensible judgment about right and wrong after people have become enmeshed in troubles, when lives have become twisted by corruption, infidelity, and greed? The fault lies way back. It began when Abram and Sarai left the highway. No use quarreling about who is right or wrong on the side roads. Back to life with God!

May God have mercy on the thousands of our neighbors and on many of us who use religion to do minor repairs to self-styled ways of living. These side road quarrels about right or wrong make no sense as long as the whole direction of life is wrong. Instead of quarreling, we should pray that the God of compassion will drive us back to the highway of faith.

As for Abram, Sarai, and Hagar, God picked up the pieces, just as he had done earlier back in Egypt. Again there is no rebuke. Only silent shame.

REFLECTION

What can you learn for your faith journey from this "side road" experience of Abram and Sarai?

God Almighty

GENESIS 17:1-7

> *When Abram was ninety-nine years old the* LORD *appeared to him and said, "I am God Almighty; walk before me faithfully and be blameless."*
> —*Genesis 17:1*

This is what Abram needed to hear: "I am God Almighty." The Bible does not say that Abram raised any questions, but it does tell us that he was ninety-nine years old. Human experience testifies that at such an age a man cannot expect much.

But living with God means one is drawn out of the sphere of human possibilities to God, with whom all things are possible. Therefore Abram must constantly ask himself: "Who is my God?" God said: "I am God Almighty; walk before me faithfully and be blameless." In other words: walk in such a way and live in such a manner that your life shows your faith in me as God Almighty.

Sometimes we would like to go to God with a long list of questions, for we are often unsure and perplexed. But God takes the list of questions out of our hands and says: "I am God Almighty." And God calls us to faith: "Walk before me faithfully and be blameless."

Abram must be called Abraham from now on. Even though the multitude was nowhere in sight, he is to be called "father of many nations." The promise is as good as the one who makes the promise. Therefore the name of this good and childless man will henceforth be a confession of faith in God Almighty. "Father of many nations"—Abraham.

The two covenant partners are having a meeting. God is speaking. And Abraham lies in the dust. Faith is adoration of God Almighty.

We belong to the multitude of those who by faith and endurance inherit the promises. That's why we must resolve to trust God with our whole heart. Silence now the questions that keep rising to our lips. Close the mouth that always wants to talk. We must think of God in greater terms. Therefore we ourselves must be more humble. He is God. Almighty is his name.

REFLECTIONS

Take a moment now to be silent and humble yourself before "Almighty God."

Sign and Seal

GENESIS 17:9-14

"This is my covenant with you and your descendants after you, the covenant you are to keep: Every male among you shall be circumcised."   —*Genesis 17:10*

God comes to people first with his Word of promise. This is what happened when God called Abram (Gen. 12). Next the Word of promise was ratified by a covenant (Gen. 15). And finally the covenant was sealed with the rite of circumcision (Gen. 17).

Married life is the best example of a contemporary covenant because it follows a similar pattern. First a young man calls on a girl. He makes promises, and they declare their love. Then the two of them make a covenant when they utter their wedding vows. Finally they exchange rings as signs of their fidelity to each other and as seals that their vows are unbreakable.

It was great goodness on the part of God to give people a sign of their bond with him. In the New Testament, God also gives signs of his bond with his people—baptism in God's name and holy communion. It is obvious, however, that a person does not get married by buying a wedding band in a jewelry store. If you have the money, you can buy a cupboard full of engagement rings and wedding bands. A ring without the partner and the promise is meaningless.

Just as the sign of God's promise became a mere sign and rite to many people of the Old Testament, so the two signs of the church are often accepted without faith in the promises. In such cases there is not really a marriage or a covenant. People are "christened" but they don't know the Christ; they partake of communion but they don't serve their Lord. God is very displeased when people make light of the signs and seals he has chosen.

But if the relationship is right, these signs are deeply meaningful: God, our partner, has sworn to be faithful. And God has pledged with his ring to never forsake us.

REFLECTIONS

When you see a baptism or share in the Lord's Supper, what do these signs tell you?

God Visits with Abraham

GENESIS 18:1-8

> *He then brought some curds and milk and the calf that had been*
> *prepared, and set these before them. While they ate, he stood near*
> *them under a tree.* —*Genesis 18:8*

What a picture! God is having lunch at Abraham's place.

It's almost embarrassing. God is almighty, and before him we must lie in the dust. So we are tempted to say that this is only a picture of God, that God is actually the Holy One, the Creator of the universe, the One who keeps all the planets in their courses.

But we may not spoil this revelation by such an explanation.

A person does not learn to live with God by trying to climb to God's level. That's the devil's road. The God of the Bible has come to our level. Human religion always thinks that we come closer to God when we become less human and more "spiritual." But the God of the Bible bridges the gap by becoming human. "The Word became flesh" (John 1:14). That's the center of the whole story.

The God of heaven and earth walked to the tent of Abraham in the company of two travelers. At Abraham's urgent request, the three men had lunch in the shade of a tree. God was sitting with his back to the door of the tent. Abraham was standing near the table, passing the milk and the meat. Sarah was peeking through the tent flap.

Later God came to us in Jesus Christ. He attended our weddings to make them more joyful, and he changed some funerals into song festivals. And that was not just a picture of God, as some people keep saying. He really came to our side.

We must get rid of the notion that we can speak to God only when we are on the mountaintop or in the cathedral; we must stop thinking that conversation with God is better from such perches. God is in the dining room, at school, at work. And if we have learned to love God's company, every ordinary day is bright.

REFLECTIONS

Where did you see God today?

Laughter of Unbelief

GENESIS 18:9-15

Then the LORD said to Abraham: "Why did Sarah laugh and say, 'Will I really have a child, now that I am old?' Is anything too hard for the LORD?" —Genesis 18:13-14

For twenty-five years Abraham and Sarah had been on their way with God. During all this time they had carried their burden of grief: they had no children.

Eight times the Bible says God comforted them by repeating his promise. This promise concerning the child was at first very general and became more and more specific as time went on. At first God spoke in broad terms, when he said that Abraham would have many descendants (12:3, 7; 13:6). Then Abraham began to think that God might want to count Abraham's descendants through his servant Eliezer. At that time the promise became more pointed: "This man will not be your heir, but a son coming from your own body will be your heir" (15:4).

Abraham and Sarah must have discussed the promise nearly every night. They saw that God's Word left room for a son of which Abraham would be the father without Sarah being the mother. Ishmael? But then the promise became even more specific: "Yes, but your wife will bear you a son" (17:19).

And God Almighty, who would later send an angel to Mary to announce the birth of Jesus, came himself to Sarah to say that "this time next year" the promised son would be born (18:10).

Then Sarah laughed.

Don't be too quick to condemn Sarah for her unbelieving, desperate laughter. Every person who takes God seriously and yet has to bear a burden day after day, year after year, will fall down sometime. She or he will cry and laugh in bitter unbelief. May God forgive us for those moments when we become cynical because his Word seems too good to believe, in a life that is too hard to bear. Only those who do not really believe don't have a struggle and never fall down.

Is anything too hard for the Lord? Anything?

REFLECTIONS

Where in your life do you need to hear God say, "Is anything too hard for the Lord?"

God Confides in Abraham

GENESIS 18:16-21

> *Then the* LORD *said, "Shall I hide from Abraham what I am about to do?"* —Genesis 18:17

Sometimes a member of the clergy or a police officer has to visit a certain house to bring the news that one of the members of that family has died in an accident. He or she arrives at the house with a heavy heart. The people don't know the shattering message. But then the look in their eyes turns from ignorance to suspicion to fright to terror.

God tells his secrets to his people. He confides in his earthly friends. What God has told us has cheered us more than anything else, for the message is happy, hopeful news. But God has also entrusted us with an awesome burden.

Here we are, living every day among people who are absorbed in the ordinary realities of human business. And we go our way among them as the ones-who-know. We know that one of these days God will walk into this ordinary routine of living. Suddenly all these people will be placed before a reality of which they have no inkling at present. They think it's a bad joke or a silly idea.

It's not easy to speak of this burden. Yes, of course there are people who can spout hell and damnation whenever they are turned on. But they don't give us the impression that they are carrying confidential information from their Lord.

No, it's not easy. But you can't keep quiet forever when you have a burden on your heart. After all, we know that it's going to happen. We believe that God's threats are as real as God's promises. We must first learn to speak freely and naturally of the promises. Then God will show us how to deliver the burden of his threats, wherever and whenever we have to speak out. God will give us the grace and courage.

REFLECTIONS

What difference might this Scripture passage and reading make in your day-to-day life?

Abraham as Intercessor

GENESIS 18:22-33

Then he said, "May the Lord not be angry, but let me speak just once more. What if only ten can be found there?" He answered, "For the sake of ten, I will not destroy it." —Genesis 18:32

Not only are God's people allowed to know God's plans for the world, their actions play a part in the way God deals with other people. Those who live with God are assigned to pray for the world.

When the covenant people struggle with God for the sake of the world, they must use boldness and humility. The boldness of their prayers rests on the knowledge of their God. Notice these expressions: "Will you sweep away the righteous with the wicked?" (v. 23 and again in v. 25). "Far be it from you!" (also repeated in v. 25). "Will not the Judge of all the earth do right?" (v. 25). The believers can pray so boldly because they know God's character.

Boldness is coupled with humility. We are deeply aware that we ourselves are but people and that God is God. "I am nothing but dust and ashes" (v. 27), says Abraham. "Now that I have been so bold as to speak to the Lord" (v. 27), "may the Lord not be angry" (vv. 30, 32). It is this combination of boldness and humility, freedom and fear, that makes Abraham a man of prayer.

Abraham and his children were called out of the world not because God wanted to forget about the rest of humanity but because he intended to bless all people through them. The first and most essential means by which believers become a blessing to the world is through their prayers on behalf of the world.

Especially since Christ has come, it is God's clear design that we should plead his cause with people and also that we should struggle with God for the salvation of the world. We must pray for those who do not pray. We plead with God to turn away his wrath. It is not our job to give up our cities to the fires from heaven. We pray and work so that the music of the name of Jesus may be heard in every town.

REFLECTIONS

Pray for someone you know who does not pray, who needs to be blessed with salvation.

"Isaac," That Is, "Laughter"

GENESIS 21:1-7

Sarah was afraid, so she lied and said, "I did not laugh."
Sarah said, "God has brought me laughter. . . ."

—Genesis 18:15; 21:6

We cannot suppress the question why this child of the promise had to come in such an impossible, almost ridiculous way. Why this burden for all those years? Why not a child in the normal, joyful way?

Very seldom does God answer this type of question. In John 9 we find the story of the man who was born blind. There Jesus answers the "Why?" of the disciples by saying that the work of God must be revealed. Even when God gives an explanation, he makes it clear that it is not the explanation that counts; it is God himself who makes the difference.

In other words, it is not God's purpose that we should know the answer to the riddles of our lives. In these perplexing matters, we will not receive an answer to our "Why?" But we will find God.

God does not want to be understood so that we will find out his reasons. God wants to be believed, so that he remains God. God gave no explanation to Abraham and Sarah. God wanted to give them more than an explanation: he wanted to give himself.

When spring came, Sarah bowed herself over the child of the promise. Then she spoke words that reflected her most intimate joy in the Lord. When she pressed her son to her breast, she herself found rest in the heart of God. Isaac! Laughter! All her bitterness and doubt melted in the laughter that God has prepared for all who hope steadfastly in his promise.

Take courage. We may have to sow with tears, but we shall reap with joy. The God of wisdom and of might gave a son to Sarah and a child to the virgin. God is faithful. Therefore the end will be laughter.

REFLECTIONS

Where has God recently brought "laughter" into your life?

The Last Test

GENESIS 22:1-3

Then God said, "Take your son, your only son, whom you love—
Isaac—and go to the region of Moriah. Sacrifice him there as a
burnt offering on a mountain I will show you." —*Genesis 22:2*

A man who lives with God must always surrender something. Abraham had to give up his native land and his father's house, he had to flee from Canaan to Egypt, and he had to part with his nephew Lot. Abraham and Sarah had to give up every normal possibility for a child. They had to abandon all human hope for a baby before God worked out his own possibilities. Only after they had suffered and after both had laughed in unbelief did God make them laugh the laughter of those who taste God's faithfulness.

And now Abraham had to prepare for the last test. The life of a person who lives with God is a course of study; it is a lesson plan designed to make him give up more and more, so that he will finally hope in God alone.

Here is Isaac, Abraham and Sarah's child, playing near the tent. Faith is proof of things not seen. But this child is proof of God's faithfulness. God and his promises are real in the boy who walks in the sunlight. Every time Isaac laughs, Abraham and Sarah laugh too, for God has remembered his mercy. The promise has been fulfilled, and the proof is tangible and beautiful—Isaac.

And now Abraham must give Isaac up.

Maybe we really meant it when we sang, "Jesus, I my cross have taken, all to leave and follow thee." But perhaps we did not know what we were singing. Don't resent it, then, when God takes more and more of ours, as long as we receive more and more of his.

This was the last test for the father of all believers. He was a man who walked with God. Or perhaps we should say that God walked with this man. And God's way with men and women is to make them give up more, so that they may get more.

REFLECTIONS

What have you had to surrender because you "live with God"?

By Faith He Passed the Test

GENESIS 22:3-14

> *When they first reached the place God had told them about, Abraham built an altar there and arranged the wood on it. He bound his son Isaac and laid him on the altar . . . and took the knife to slay his son.* —*Genesis 22:9–10*

During the night Abraham made his decision to obey. He rose early in the morning. That's strange, for we would expect him to dread the new day. But apparently the only thing Abraham dreaded was second thoughts. "Early the next morning, Abraham got up" (v. 3).

Then follows a detailed description of what Abraham did after he had gotten up. (Again, this seems strange for a writer who usually overlooks the details.) We get a description of Abraham's saddling the donkey, getting the servants, cutting the wood, calling Isaac. It's almost like a film. The camera gives us a close-up of all these little events. And when Abraham comes to the end of a three-day journey (what opportunities to have second thoughts!), we have a similar careful listing in verses 9 and 10, which are quoted on this page—building the altar, arranging the wood, binding Isaac, laying him down, reaching for the knife.

These little details are suddenly important, and every one of them must be noted. In these step-by-step preparations, Abraham is showing his decision to go, to obey, to set his feet on the highway of obedience. A decision that is not translated into obedient action is worthless. Big decisions must be followed through in bigger and smaller acts of obedience. Some people think faith is big talk without the details of work. When James, the servant of God, got to know some people like that, he wrote: "Was not our father Abraham considered righteous for what he did when he offered his son Isaac on the altar?" (James 2:21).

The two of them climbed the mountain. The boy was burdened with the wood for his own sacrifice. The father had the flint and the cleaver. "The two of them went on together." Theirs was the most eloquent silence ever reported.

REFLECTION

Reflect on how God may be testing you. What can you learn from Abraham's test that applies to your situation?

The Purpose of the Test

GENESIS 22:15-19

*"I swear by myself, says the LORD, that because you have done this
and have not withheld your son, your only son, I will surely bless
you. . . ."* —*Genesis 22:16–17*

The purpose of a test at school is to find out if the student knows the
material he or she has studied. The purpose of the test God gave Abraham was to find out if Abraham had learned to love God above all.

We can hardly believe that God would give such a test to all who walk
with him. It seems an extremely difficult test, reserved only for God's
honor students. And it was a final examination: it came during the last
miles of the road Abraham traveled with God.

Yet, if you believe your Bible, you will have to admit that Abraham's
test, though critical and ultimate, was by no means exceptional. The
decision Abraham had to make was no different from the crisis through
which the writer of Psalm 73 had to go. The psalmist came through with
the glorious confession "Whom have I in heaven but you? And earth has
nothing I desire besides you" (v. 25). Abraham had to arrive at the same
confession: There is nothing on earth to hold onto besides God.

You will also remember that the calling of Abraham, by which God
began to form the people of the old covenant, has much in common with
Jesus' calling of the disciples, by which he began to form the people of
the new covenant. Jesus said: "Follow me." And they left their nets and
followed him.

If you aren't convinced yet that Abraham's test is no exception,
read Matthew 10:37-39, where God says, not just to veteran saints but
in general terms, "Anyone who loves their father or mother . . . son or
daughter . . . more than me is not worthy of me." God takes his covenant
as seriously as any good husband or wife takes the covenant of marriage.
The Lord will not share us with another. And all of us must learn to confess: "There is nothing on earth that I desire besides you."

REFLECTIONS

Read all of Psalm 73. Then make verse 25 your own prayer to God.

He Really Sacrificed Him

HEBREWS 11:17-19

*Abraham reasoned that God could even raise the dead, and so in
a manner of speaking he did receive Isaac back from death.*
—*Hebrews 11:19*

When Abraham was making that three-day journey to Moriah, he "reasoned that God could even raise the dead." He did not indulge in self-pity, nor did he look at Isaac only. Instead he asked, "Who is my God?" He lived with God, and he had nothing left but God. During the whole test we see an unnatural calm in Abraham. It is the peace and assurance of a man whose heart rests in God.

We must not rationalize Abraham's behavior. He did not say, "God won't let it go to the end; he'll stop me at the last moment." Neither did he reason, "God is opposed to human sacrifices; he doesn't really mean it." On the contrary, as the letter to the Hebrews says, Abraham really sacrificed Isaac—and did so "by faith." It was *after* he had given up Isaac that Isaac was raised from the dead, figuratively speaking, and given back to Abraham.

Our efforts to explain Abraham's behavior in rational terms show our ignorance of life with God. Something in us refuses to believe that God would demand so much—just as we are never quite ready to believe that God can give so much. Even if we know that this is the plain teaching of the Bible, we don't quite grasp it. It appears that the pictures of people whom we know and love as Christians speak louder than a thousand Bible words. Countless people—in fact, all Christians—say that they want to live according to God's Word, but in reality most of them follow the "Christian" patterns of the community to which they belong.

We must listen to God. We must submit to God's tests. We must be anxious for God's approval. God must teach us how to move through this life with the serenity and the tension of someone who lives primarily with him.

REFLECTIONS

How do you react to the advice in the last paragraph above? Reflect on that, and then frame a prayer around what you need to say to God.

Real Estate

GENESIS 25:7-11

*His sons Isaac and Ishmael buried him in the cave of Machpelah.
. . .There Abraham was buried with his wife Sarah.*

—*Genesis 25:9–10*

Abraham was seventy-five years old when he departed from Haran (Gen. 12:4). He walked with the Lord for one hundred years. Then he was buried in the cave of Machpelah.

Every funeral is a test of our faith. What we see argues against what we believe. We see the rule of death, while we confess the reign of Christ. Yet it is the surprising testimony of many Christians that their faith was strengthened when they buried their loved ones. Most of us grow faster in faith at a funeral than at a wedding. Maybe one of the reasons is that when we are compelled to surrender what we love, we fall into the arms of God.

Abraham's funeral was a peculiar test of faith. God had promised him the land of Canaan. When he had lived in Canaan for a hundred years, he left some heaps of stones called altars. The only piece of real estate to which he held title was a graveyard for his wife and himself.

The urge to possess some real estate appears to be strong in all human beings—at least the ones we know. The fun and pride of ownership may well be among the nicest joys God gives people. But we must not overrate the importance of our temporary ownership of a house or some land.

What is "real" estate, anyway? People say it's something you can lay your hands on, set your feet on, get a price for, or dig a grave in.

What is "real"? What Abraham saw with tear-filled eyes. The promise and presence of God is the only reality you can hold on to, even when you come to the end of the road.

REFLECTIONS

How do we know if we're too attached to the "real estate" we own?

Laughter

LUKE 1:26-38

"Blessed is she who has believed that the Lord would fulfill his promises to her!"
—*Luke 1:45*

There will always be two kinds of laughter around the birth of Christ, which is the center of our faith and the heart of the Bible. The cynical laughter of unbelief continues—like bad music. May God have mercy on those who laugh loudly or smile politely at the story of the virgin mother and child. But the other kind of laughter, about the fulfilled promise, also continues to resound.

This laughter is an echo of the sound that was first heard in Abraham's tent, where two old people gazed at their baby. "Isaac," they said. "Laughter." God has done the impossible.

The promise of a son, so often repeated to childless Sarah, came to Mary in the fullness of time. Again, it was a human impossibility: "How will this be since I am a virgin?" But when the angel had spoken to Mary about "the power of the Most High," she bowed in faith and received the blessing. Mary sang a psalm before she sang a lullaby: "My soul glorifies the Lord, and my spirit rejoices in God my Savior."

Mary's relative was Elizabeth, who was too old to have a baby. Therefore God showed her that he is God and that the salvation God brought into the world is exclusively his work. So Mary sang and Elizabeth laughed. And Zechariah—well, he couldn't believe at first that such miracles would happen so long after the days of Sarah and Abraham. But when God allowed him to speak again, he joined the chorus of song and laughter, praising God, who had kept "the oath he swore to our father Abraham."

We continue to carry our crosses along the highway of faith. Some day the joy that began in Genesis 25 and the laughter that is so rich in Luke 1 and 2 will resound without end, "when all flesh shall see the token that God's Word is never broken."

REFLECTIONS

Read Mary's song (Luke 1:46-55) and make it your own song of joy to the Lord.

Three Hundred and Sixty-Six

MATTHEW 6:25-33

"Can any one of you by worrying add a single hour to your life?"
—*Matthew 6:27*

If you read this page on the date for which it was written, you will read it only once in four years. This is the day that makes every fourth year longer than the normal ones. Today we add one cubit—if not to the span of our lives, then to the span of this year.

It doesn't really make any difference how you count your days. You may do it by the Julian calendar or by the Gregorian calendar, or you may count by the cycles of the moon. We cannot really add or subtract from the days God has measured out for us.

Our days are numbered.

But it does make a big difference what you mean by this confession. Some races and religions believe that fate rules people's lives. They will expose themselves to danger and do other irresponsible things, saying that if their god wants them to die, they cannot stop him, and if their time is not yet up, they'll get away with it.

Christians also believe that their days are numbered. But when they say this, they don't fear their fate but trust their Father. And they couple their belief in a sovereign God with a conviction of human responsibility. God is not fate but Father, and we are not puppets but people.

The fact that we have a limited number of days allotted to us by an all-wise God has a double influence on our lives. We don't spend our days in anxiety. We live responsibly and take normal precautions, but we are not going to worry about all that could possibly happen, for we know that nothing can happen without the will of our heavenly Father.

Second, we use our days wisely. We receive them gratefully and dedicate every one of them to the service of the Lord, knowing that this service of the Lord will continue after we have fulfilled the number of our days on earth.

REFLECTIONS

Bring whatever makes you anxious and worried to the Lord, who has numbered your days and who loves you always.

Sharing the Suffering of Christ

If we hope to be raised with Christ, we must also be ready to share his suffering. The devil is still free to attack.

daylight

The King

PSALM 72:1-11

"Where is the one who has been born king of the Jews?"
—*Matthew 2:2*

The big surprise of the gospel is that the promised King of Israel lived as a slave and died as if he were a criminal. This gospel is no less amazing if we give it much thought. At the same time, the gospel of the suffering King casts light on the lives of those who believe in Jesus Christ. For the present, those who belong to this King must share in his suffering.

To appreciate anew this big surprise of the gospel, we must try hard to imagine the godlike power of an ancient king. When we think of a king, we tend to imagine a government official who is very important but is still a human being like the rest of us. But those who lived under the shadow of ancient thrones knew better: before the king all mortals either bow or perish. They weren't so sure that the king himself was human.

Our ignorance of absolute monarchy is a handicap in Bible reading. Why? Because the heart of the Old Testament is the promise of a mighty King. And the core of the New Testament is the message that Jesus is this perfect ruler.

If Jesus is really the ruler promised in Psalm 72, the New Testament should describe how the governors of the world bow before him and how all people lay their treasures at his feet. But—as you know—the big surprise is that Jesus had to hang on a cross before he came to sit on a throne; Jesus was the slave of all before he became Lord of all.

Today—at least in the so-called free world—Christians may worship their King, for all people are guaranteed the freedom to worship as they choose. We are grateful for that freedom, and we must be ready to defend it. However, we must not make the mistake of thinking of Jesus' kingship in terms of modern tolerance. As a matter of fact, it is with Jesus as it was with the ancient kings: either we bow down or we perish.

REFLECTIONS

What are the implications for you of thinking of Jesus as King?

The Murderer

MATTHEW 2:7-18

> *When Herod realized that he had been outwitted by the Magi, he was furious, and he gave orders to kill all the boys in Bethlehem and its vicinity who were two years older and under. . . .*
>
> —*Matthew 2:16*

Nobody realized the absolute power of the newborn King—except the devil. Through Herod, his willing agent, the devil moved in for the kill. But God moved faster.

The devil "was a murderer from the beginning" (John 8:44). Long before Herod's time, the Pharaoh of Egypt tried to kill all the male children of God's people, as the devil's agent. That time Moses, the deliverer of Israel, escaped the massacre. He was nursed, protected, and educated right in Pharaoh's palace. Oh, the humor of God! And in Herod's attack on the male children of Bethlehem, the Savior escaped. History was not being repeated; it was being fulfilled.

The scene in Bethlehem is heartrending. Wailing mothers hold their dead babies. Powerless fathers sob in silent rage. Who will take vengeance on the mean murderer of God's people?

As if he wants to bring all the sorrow of God's people into one picture, the writer reminds us of Rachel, another weeping mother in Bethlehem. She died there in childbirth, and she called her son a child of sorrow (Gen. 35:18).

The whole history of God's people has been written in blood and tears. The attacks of the devil and the judgments of God have gone over them. Their mothers weep and refuse to be comforted. Where is the deliverer?

But now the word of comfort is announced: Dry your tears, mothers of Bethlehem. Take courage, daughters of Zion. The city of David has given birth to the Son of David. The Savior lives. God has come to fight the battle of his people. The time is fulfilled.

Weeping may tarry for the night, but joy comes with the morning (Ps. 30:5). Jesus is coming to save his people. And he will take all our sorrows upon himself!

REFLECTIONS

Reflect on the cost of your salvation, and then give thanks.

The Battle

DEUTERONOMY 8:1-8

Jesus answered, "It is written: 'People do not live on bread alone, but on every word that comes from the mouth of God.'"
—*Matthew 4:4*

Here is the record of the devil's meeting with the King of Israel. The battle is on. The stakes are "all the kingdoms of the world and their splendor" (Matt. 4:8). The absolute rulership of the world is in the balance.

However, the battle is not to be fought by pitching power against power. The test is obedience. God's kingdom comes when God's will is done. The devil is conquered when the Father is obeyed.

The devil has been very successful in seducing humankind. Adam failed his Maker. Israel too failed the test. The forty years in the wilderness had but one purpose: God "tested" them to see whether they would keep his commandments or not. He "humbled" them and fed them with manna to show them that "people do not live on bread alone but on every word that comes from the mouth of the LORD" (Deut. 8:3).

This remains a basic test for all God's children. All of us must learn that we don't yet have life when we have something to put into our mouths. We live only when we trust and obey what comes out of the mouth of the Lord.

Now Jesus follows same course Israel took as he attends the school of God. He walks the way God's people walked. For forty days Jesus wanders through the wilderness. Then the tempter comes. "First things first," the devil says. "You need to eat. If you are the Son of God, have the Father prepare a table before you. Command these stones to become loaves of bread."

But Jesus is not going to use his power to save his life. He is going to use this power to be obedient unto death. Therefore he says: "Even if my Father wants me to go hungry, I will obey." It is better to be obedient and go hungry than to have bread and sin.

REFLECTIONS

How might the last line of this reading apply to your life today?

Another Attack

MATTHEW 16:13-23

Jesus turned and said to Peter, "Get behind me, Satan!"
—*Matthew 16:23*

Only the demons and the devil could recognize the King of the world in the man Jesus. Sometimes ordinary people did recognize the Christ, but only if they received assistance from heaven. For example, Simeon in his old age knew by the Spirit that the baby in Mary's arms was the promised King (Luke 2:27). And the wise men from the East were led to Bethlehem by God's direction (Matt. 2). Now Peter recognized Jesus. But it took more than "flesh and blood." The Father in heaven had told him.

Peter expressed the true dignity of Jesus in a statement that has become the model confession of the church of all ages: "You are the Messiah, the Son of the living God."

Right after this climax, "Jesus began to explain to his disciples that he must . . . suffer many things." Then all hell broke loose, for the devil also knows this secret about our King: that he will redeem his people by suffering.

Hell can break loose through the concern of a dear friend as well as through Herod's infanticide. This time Peter himself, the man of the great confession, is the devil's agent.

He says: "Never, Lord, never!" To Peter's mind, it is impossible that the King must suffer and the deliverer be oppressed. But Satan is speaking through Peter. The devil sees his kingdom totter, as he sees Christ preparing himself for obedience unto death.

Jesus says, "Behind me, Satan. Get out of my way. I want to deliver my people at any cost." No friend or foe is going to stop him on the road of obedience.

REFLECTIONS

Does the devil still use similar methods to tempt us off the road of obedience?

The Last Attack

MATTHEW 27:32-44

> *"He saved others," they said, "but he can't save himself! He's the king of Israel! Let him come down now from the cross, and we will believe in him."* —*Matthew 27:42*

Jesus is hanging on the cross. The road of obedience is the road of suffering. Now he is in the last phase, the bitter phase.

The devil despairs, but he does not give up. The persistence of the devil is great; it is surpassed only by the persistence of the Holy Spirit.

Through Herod the devil tried to snuff out the life of the holy baby. In person the devil tried to bring Jesus to disobedience in the wilderness. Through Peter he tried to stop the Messiah on his way to the cross. And now, at the cross, Satan still shoots his arrows.

The ignorant crowd is shouting: "He saved others, but he can't save himself!" The devil puts drops of poison into their words. It is a taunt, a provocation. Little kids know how to taunt each other: "You can't get me. . . ." "You wouldn't dare. . . ."

What a temptation, this provocation by the crowds! "Come down now from the cross, and we will believe in you." Forgive the jeering crowds. They don't know what they are shouting. But God knows it and the devil knows it. Jesus hears the tempter's voice.

Angels and demons have joined the crowd. They watch the spectacle people cannot fathom. There are dimensions present here, a depth people cannot see unless God has opened their eyes and their heart.

The middle figure on the hill hangs writhing with pain.

The devil's attack is fierce. It hurts more than Jesus' nail-pierced hands. But he remains on the cross. In his heart Christ renews the oath to the Father, "If I am to save others, I cannot save myself. Away from me, Satan. Since I must save others, I shall not save myself."

It wasn't the nails that kept Jesus on the cross but his love.

Bless the Lord, bless your Lord, O my soul.

REFLECTIONS

Give thanks and praise that Jesus stayed on the cross out of love for you.

MARCH 6

We Are Under Attack

REVELATION 12:1-6, 13-17

> *When the dragon saw that he had been hurled to the earth, he pursued the woman who had given birth to the male child.*
> —*Revelation 12:13*

The victory of Christ does not mean that the armies have laid down their weapons. The war continues with undiminished fury. What, then, is the benefit of Christ's victory? "The dragon saw that he had been hurled to the earth." In other words, the devil has been thrown out of the driver's seat. But Jesus, the "male child," has gone from earth to heaven. He moved from the place being governed to the seat of government. He is in the control center. He was "snatched up to God and to his throne" (v. 5).

The devil is still free to attack, but he can never again gain control. The control belongs to Jesus. For "to us a child is born, to us a son is given, and the government will be on his shoulders" (Isa. 9:6).

The dragon spends his fury on the woman who has borne the male child. She is the daughter of Zion, the weeping woman of Bethlehem. She is the mother of the people whose history is written in blood and tears. She represents God's people, the church of all ages.

Don't think for a minute that since Christ has been under attack, those who follow him will go scot-free. That would be contrary to everything Jesus predicted. In faith we know today that Jesus is Lord, but we don't see it yet. We must live by faith and act out of faith. That means that we obey our Lord without fear, for the authority belongs to God and his Messiah (v. 10).

Hope in the Lord. He will provide. We will be carried on an eagle's wings (v. 14). Keep God's commands and bear testimony about Jesus (v. 17).

"Since I must fight if I would reign, increase my courage, Lord; I'll bear the toil, endure the pain, supported by thy Word" (Isaac Watts).

REFLECTIONS
Sing or say the words above from Watts's hymn as your prayer.

The Army

EPHESIANS 6:10-18

Put on the full armor of God, so that you can take your stand against the devil's schemes. —Ephesians 6:11

Nobody can be a soldier—let alone an officer—without training. And an army without discipline does not have a ghost of a chance. Training and discipline are essential to the survival of the church of Christ.

Yet not all that many church members today are interested in training and discipline.

When we think of training, we generally think of children and young people. Certainly we should start when we are young. However, far too many people not only start but also quit while they are still young. As a result, the church becomes childish.

Fighting the devil takes a man or woman of God.

In industry, job training continues until retirement. Otherwise the business suffers from inefficiency. The requirements in the school of God are no lighter. Training must begin when we are babies, and it must continue until we are called home.

When we think of discipline, we should remember that in an army every soldier must know and obey orders without *if*s or *but*s. It is time that we do the same in the spiritual army, or we'll lose the battle. We must clearly know and simply obey the orders of our Lord. And we must stop having those "interesting" religious debates. We must end those interminable sessions in which we discuss our problems. We are at war!

The authority of Christ's orders is beyond dispute. But too many of Christ's followers don't even know what the orders of our Commander are. And as soon as these orders are clearly spelled out, they come with their *if*s and *but*s.

If we do not put on the "full armor of God," that is, the spiritual weapons and protection God supplies, we cannot possibly stand in the "day of evil" (v. 13). And that day is right now.

REFLECTIONS

What kind of spiritual training are you receiving? Would you describe yourself as a disciplined man or woman of God?

Faith Under Fire

JAMES 1:12-21

"Lead us not into temptation, but deliver us from the evil one."
—Matthew 6:13

It is impossible for any Christian to escape the battle. Those who confess the Lord have to face the enemy. Faith is always under fire. If this is so certain, why does the Lord teach us to pray that we be kept from temptation? Because only fools rush in where Christ himself feared to tread.

Christians have good reasons to pray for deliverance from temptation. We know our own weaknesses. Spiritually immature Christians are like little children who think that war is a game. But mature Christians pray that they will be kept from temptations, and they work hard to stay away from them. Christians do not try to find out how close they can get to the dragon. Instead they stay as far away from the dragon as possible.

God does not tempt us to evil (James 1:13). The devil is the tempter. Yet God leads our lives. And it is to God that we pray "Lead us not into temptation." Therefore, although we do not desire the battle, we will not rebel either when our general leads us into contact with the enemy. We know very well that a general does not bring his troops under fire to have them killed; he does so because it is the only way to victory and peace.

Thus we pray to be kept from mortal combat. And we are certainly not going to seek it. But if it pleases our Father in heaven to bring us into the hardships of spiritual warfare, we trust that even this experience will be for our good. And we hear Scripture say: "Blessed are those who persevere under trial, because when they have stood the test, they will receive the crown of life" (James 1:12).

Christians avoid confrontations with the enemy: "Lead us not into temptation." But when they have to endure warfare, they receive the power to persevere.

REFLECTIONS
In what areas is your faith likely to come "under fire"?

Servants

JOHN 13:12-20

"The Son of Man came not to be served, but to serve. . . ."
—*Matthew 20:28*

In our language the word *service* is linked with business. "Good service is good business." The price for "professional services rendered" is usually quite high. But we never seem to feel that the word *service* is completely out of place on an invoice that demands payment.

Our habit of connecting service and business makes it hard to understand biblical language. In the Bible the word *service* means the kind of work a slave did for his master. He didn't get paid for it.

Just as we have trouble untangling "service" and "business," the Jews had trouble bringing the words *servant* and *king* together. A servant was a slave, and service was the work of the slave. But a king was someone before whom even masters bowed in slave-like obedience.

So when the king said, "I came not to *have* servants but to *be* a servant," all the values of the Jews were overturned. If we could bring ourselves to look at Jesus with new eyes, we would receive a similar shock. And this is exactly what we must try to do. We must always try to see him anew, as he really is according to the Bible. Our environment and upbringing may have distorted the image of Jesus.

This Jesus who came to serve rather than to be served is now calling all people to be his followers. Obeying Jesus' call means more than cleaning up our language and getting rid of bad habits. It means a total conversion of attitudes.

Service is the work rendered by a slave or servant. One may not expect to get paid for serving one's Lord. And if anyone feels "above" this life of service, he or she is outside the realm of Jesus. On the other hand, it is only in a slave-like, humble, obedient life that we suddenly discover the greatness of Jesus' company.

REFLECTION

What does being a "servant" of God look like in your life?

Ransom

MATTHEW 20:20-28

"The Son of Man did not come to be served, but to serve, and to give his life as a ransom for many." —*Matthew 20:28*

Jesus' life was service, and in his death he gave everything. Jesus' life is the pattern for us. His death sets us free to follow that pattern.

Jesus' death was a "ransom." We read the word *ransom* in the newspaper when someone has been kidnapped. "The kidnappers are demanding a ransom of $200,000. If they don't get it, they will kill the banker's daughter."

A ransom is the price to set a prisoner free—usually a prisoner who is doomed to die. In return for the ransom, a captive receives both life and freedom.

Since Christ has given his life as a ransom for those who believe in him, we are no longer under the power of the arch-criminal. We have a new Master. We may now live in the house of our Father. But we must live by the rules of his house, the patterns of the One who came to serve, not to be served.

Jesus said that he gave his life as a "ransom for many." *Many* does not include everyone. He died for his own. In saying this, Christ did not mean to emphasize that some people would not share the benefits of his death. His point was rather that he would go to his death as "one for many."

War stories are usually gruesome, and war must not be glorified. But there are some heroic tales that can inspire us. In every war, it seems, some brave soldier throws himself on a grenade just before it explodes, catching all the fury of the explosion in his own body and saving the lives of all those around him.

That's the meaning of "one for many."

Jesus' life of service is our pattern. By his death he set us free to follow that pattern.

REFLECTION

Imagine that you are among those soldiers whose life was spared when a friend fell on that grenade. What would your reaction be? What does that suggest about your reaction to Christ giving his life for you?

Following Jesus

MARK 8:27-38

"Whoever wants to be my disciple must deny themselves and take up their cross and follow me." —*Mark 8:34*

When Winston Churchill became prime minister of Great Britain, he promised "blood, sweat, and tears." Yet, never before has a nation rallied to the support of its leader as the British people did in their finest hour. They accepted Churchill and his challenge, because they knew of no other road to victory.

When Christ comes to us with his call to discipleship, he demands self-denial and gives us a cross to bear—"blood, sweat, and tears." We must accept him and his challenge, for there is no other road to victory. All other saviors will lead to defeat.

Self-denial and cross-bearing are two parts of one action for a disciple of Jesus. The meaning is best understood when we look at Christ himself, who refused one way of life and deliberately chose the way of love and obedience.

To deny oneself and bear one's cross involves much more than declining a certain pleasure and putting up with an inconvenience. Some people think they have performed an act of self-denial when they decline a piece of cake at a party. And some people think that they are bearing the cross of which Christ spoke when they go through the trials common to the human race—instead of the troubles Jesus reserved for his followers.

Just what self-denial and cross-bearing mean cannot be explained in a few words. We cannot learn it in one lesson. It is a way of death and a way of life at the same time. Let's not say too soon that we know it. There is so much to learn on this journey of the disciple! So many old things must be unlearned, and so many new things must be acquired! We should not say that we know all about it before we have seen it all.

REFLECTIONS

Reflect on what "denying yourself" and "taking up your cross" means for you personally today. Then ask God to help you do both.

Peter Follows Jesus (1)

MARK 1:14-20

"Come, follow me," Jesus said, "and I will send you out to fish for people."
 —*Mark 1:17*

This was the day on which the father of Simon and Andrew lost both his sons to Jesus. And father Zebedee's sons, James and John, also left the fishing business. What a beautiful way to lose your children!

What makes a person decide to follow Jesus?

We might as well ask what made Abraham decide to leave his country and go to the unknown land of Canaan. It's always a word that comes to us in the form of a command. "Follow me." But there must be more. After all, the word comes to many. And yet one person stays, while another leaves his nets and follows Jesus.

It is faith in Jesus that makes the difference.

Those who follow Jesus are convinced that Christ is the way, that Christ is the *only* way. They have come to the conclusion that they cannot afford to disobey the call. They do not lose when they go; they are lost if they stay put. It is faith in Christ that makes one a follower of Jesus.

That's the way it was with the salesman who sold pearls. One day he saw a pearl that caught his fancy so irresistibly that he just couldn't be happy anymore without it. So he sold all his other merchandise in order to acquire that pearl of great value (Matt. 13:46).

It's true, of course, that the apostle has told us to stay in the situation in which we were called and serve the Lord there (1 Cor. 7:20, 24). Some unfortunate things have happened to a few people who misunderstood the call to conversion as a call to become a preacher. But unless you have experienced the call of Jesus as the big change in your life, you have not yet obeyed his call.

Christ has freed us from so many things that used to hold our interest! For us, it's Christ or nothing. The road may be rough and the Master may have little visual appeal in the worldly sense. But we believe.

"Lamb of God, I come."

REFLECTIONS

As your response to Jesus' call, sing or say the words of the old gospel song: "Just as I am with one plea / but that thy blood was shed for me / and that thou bidd'st me come to thee / O Lamb of God, I come, I come" (Charlotte Elliott, 1836).

Peter Follows Jesus (2)

MARK 14:66-72

"You were also with that Nazarene, Jesus," she said. But he denied it. "I don't know or understand what you're talking about," he said. . . . —Mark 14:67-68

There came a day in Peter's life when he could not follow Jesus anymore. Certainly he loved the Master. In the garden, when the rabble attempted to lay hands on his rabbi, Peter had drawn his sword. Narrowly missing a skull, he had cut off Malchus's ear. Don't say that Peter did not love Jesus. But Jesus was so different: he rebuked his friend, and he touched his enemy with healing hands.

Now Peter was a part of the scene in the courtroom and the courtyard. From the yard Peter could see Jesus. There was blood on his face, and he was silent, meek. In a word, Jesus looked like a lamb who was brought to the slaughter.

Peter's heart was in turmoil. How could he identify with a king who was so meek? How could he follow someone who suffered so much and accepted it as if it came from God himself?

The servant girl said, "You were also with that Nazarene, Jesus." But Peter denied it: "I don't know or understand what you're talking about." Peter moved, so that he stood closer to the exit. When the servant girl saw him standing there, she told the others: "This fellow is one of them." Again, he denied it.

And a third time someone asked him if he followed Jesus. Fear and frustration gripped Peter. He swore that he did not know Jesus.

Then the rooster crowed.

It was dawn—the dawn of Good Friday. The King was going to become a Lamb. Outside the gate stood Peter. He was crying like a child.

But in such tears is a glimmer of hope. All unfaithful Christians, all of us cowards are brought back by the way of repentance to the Master's cross.

REFLECTION

When have you found it difficult or embarrassing to admit that you are a follower of Jesus?

Peter Follows Jesus (3)

JOHN 21:15-19

Then [Jesus] said to [Peter], "Follow me!" —*John 21:19*

When Jesus died, nobody felt more miserable than Simon Peter, for Peter had lost his Master twice—once by death, along with the others, and once by denial. "I don't know him; I don't belong to him." That's what Peter had said.

Peter's restoration took place in three steps. First, the angel said to the women: "Tell his disciples and Peter . . ." (Mark 16:7). In other words: Peter, the news is for you, too. You still belong!

The second step came when Jesus himself appeared to Peter. We don't know what was said in this meeting. It was a private conversation. We only know that it happened (Luke 24:34; 1 Cor. 15:5).

The third step was the official restoration. Perhaps the stage was set to remind us of the night when Peter denied his Lord. In the gray morning light, there was again a charcoal fire. There were three questions, and again Peter had to state three times his relationship to Jesus.

In answer to Christ's questions, Peter declares his love and loyalty. But he is much less sure of himself. The third time Peter is "hurt" by Jesus' questions.

And how did it all end? It ended with the same words with which it had started: "Follow me." But now these words have much more meaning. At first Peter was an eager novice. Now he is scarred, and he has been restored—through fear and faith and repentance. "Lord, you know all things; you know that I love you."

Everyone who has followed Christ for a while feels the way Peter felt. We learn to expect less of ourselves and more of Christ. We know that the road of discipleship brings suffering, and that only his grace is sufficient to keep us going. Whenever we look at Jesus, sometimes tired or bewildered or uncertain, he simply says to us, "Follow me."

REFLECTIONS

As led by the Spirit, confess your weaknesses and sin to God, and be restored by his invitation "Follow me."

Peter Teaches (1)

1 PETER 2:18-25

> *To this you were called, because Christ suffered for you, leaving you an example, that you should follow in his steps.*
> —*1 Peter 2:21*

Once Peter acted as a tool of the devil when he tried to keep Jesus from suffering. But in his first letter, Peter has become an instrument of the Holy Spirit, explaining the suffering of Jesus and teaching all of us how to stay on the path of the suffering Lord.

The suffering of Jesus has two sides. Peter mentions them in one breath. The suffering is *for you*, and the suffering is an *example*.

For you means that he suffered on our behalf. This suffering may not and cannot be repeated. It is the once-for-all suffering for sin.

The other side of Jesus' suffering is the suffering that must be shared by all who follow him. The life of Jesus is an "example" that must be copied. It is the path of a guide through unknown territory. Therefore we must "follow in his steps."

Not one of us is independent enough to live for him- or herself. We are all followers. Children have their heroes, teens have their idols, grown-ups have their ideals. Every day we are under pressure to live according to this or that pattern. The pressure comes from neighbors, from relatives, and through whatever we see, hear, or read. In countries where mass communications are in the hands of commercial powers or governed by political powers, people's ideals are shaped—and certainly influenced—by these powers.

Christ comes to all people in all countries with a new and revolutionary pattern of living. Softly and tenderly, yet firmly and emphatically, he says to everyone, "Follow me." He does not want any of us to simply copy the way of life of the people among whom we are living. He wants us to stop and think and listen to him. And we must pray. "Teach us your way, Lord—your way!"

Christ suffered for us. And he gave us an example we should follow—in his steps.

REFLECTIONS

"He (Christ) does not want any of us to simply copy the way of life of the people among whom we are living." Is this a temptation for you? What might you be tempted to copy from the lifestyles of people around you?

Peter Teaches (2)

1 PETER 4:12-19

Dear friends, do not be surprised at the fiery ordeal that has come on you to test you, as though something strange were happening to you. —*1 Peter 4:12*

Do not be surprised and don't think it strange when suffering comes over God's people. There is much more reason to believe that something strange is going on when the church has peace than when it is under fire.

If our Christian way of life is generally accepted, it's time we took a critical look at it. Christ was "despised and rejected," and we claim to be his followers.

According to the Bible, the suffering of God's people is normal. Peace and quiet are abnormal—although desirable. We have never been promised rest and triumph in this world. Whatever we receive along that line is more than we may expect. Christians who are experiencing peace and relative prosperity are living under very unusual conditions—for Christians, at any rate. They must make good use of the opportunities that such peaceful times present. And they must watch and pray lest they and their children get accustomed to the soft life.

The Christian faith is bound to go through fire, says Peter, for at least three reasons. Everything that is worthwhile must be tested for endurance and genuineness. Therefore the Christian faith needs to be tested by fire.

Second, Christ has taught us that the only way to the glory of his kingdom is the road of obedience and self-denial. So it is inevitable that Christians experience struggles in themselves and opposition from others.

Third, if we are to experience the fellowship of Christ in this life, we have to share in his suffering. "If you are insulted because of the name of Christ, you are blessed." Suffering for Jesus' sake is a source of joy—a joy that is very unworldly and very profound.

May those who must suffer today experience the fellowship of the One who was crucified. And may all of us be sure that we are still in his company.

REFLECTION

What might "getting accustomed to the soft life" be like you for you and your family?

Prayer for the Executioners

LUKE 23:32-38

"Father, forgive them, for they do not know what they are doing."
—Luke 23:34

It was not "the sweet hour of prayer that calls me from a world of cares." It was the hour when the ugly pain started. Jesus was hanging on a beam. His hands were nailed to a crossbeam. His body twitched in searing pain.

Some people use a special "religious" tone of voice when they talk about the cross. Actually, a cross is a primitive tool for torturing and killing a criminal. While he was on the cross, Jesus prayed.

"Father," he prayed, for his faith did not waver. Some of us believe in the Father as long as we are happy and secure. When things happen to us that aren't nice or that hurt us, we wonder if we still have a Father in heaven. But in this horrible hour, Jesus said, "Father . . ."

Jesus asked his Father to forgive the executioners. He did not scream for help. That would have been natural. He did not cry for revenge. That would have been understandable. Instead Jesus asked his Father to forgive the ignorant hangmen.

"Forgive them, for they do not know what they are doing." Ignorance is not bliss, nor is it innocence. Yet throughout the Bible, ignorance is a ground on which we plead for forgiveness. There is a willfulness that is beyond forgiveness.

Most people are still as ignorant as the Roman soldiers who carried out the execution. They don't know that it was *our* sin that put him there. *We* crucified Jesus.

Now *we* must pray. We must ask God not to judge the ignorant and worldly people who don't know what they have done—to God, to Jesus. And we must earnestly pray that the Father will teach us how to show them what God has done—there, in Jesus, on the cross.

At this cruel and sacred place, every person must learn to kneel and thereby be delivered of his or her ignorance.

REFLECTIONS

Frame a prayer of your own "at this cruel and sacred place."

The Servant Is Like the Master

ACTS 7:51-60

Then he fell on his knees and cried out, "Lord, do not hold this sin against them." —Acts 7:60

People are interested in stories of martyrs. Books about martyrs were bestsellers during the Middle Ages. Today a publisher's chances are better with a biography of a prostitute than with the tale of a Christian martyr. Nevertheless, all sects and many churches are still too interested in their own martyrs, saints, and heroes.

The Bible is very sober about this matter: the death of the apostle James is mentioned in less than a sentence (Acts 12:2). We have not been told where and how Paul and Peter died. If we knew, we would build a dozen churches and a score of shrines; millions would make pilgrimages to the place of their death. But the Bible is just as opposed to this sort of thing as people tend to be in favor of it.

So it seems strange that we are told about the death of the first martyr, Stephen, in considerable detail. But when we look closely at the account, we are struck by the parallels between the death of Jesus and the death of Stephen. Suddenly we understand why the Holy Spirit wants us to know the story of the first martyr. Stephen's death is a declaration that "a disciple is not above the teacher . . . it is enough for the disciple to be like the teacher, and the slave like the master" (Matt. 10:24-25, NRSV). Jesus really meant it when he said, "Whoever does not take up their cross and follow me is not worthy of me."

Stephen was treated as Jesus had been treated. The servant's prayer was the prayer of his master. There is no higher honor for the disciple than to be like his or her teacher.

Leaders and martyrs must be honored only insofar as they teach us true discipleship. But Christ himself sets the pattern for our lives. To him we give glory in death.

REFLECTIONS

What is the Spirit teaching you from this account of the first martyr?

Good Night

LUKE 23:44-49

Jesus called out with a loud voice, "Father, into your hands I commit my spirit."   *—Luke 23:46*

While they were stoning him, Stephen prayed, "Lord Jesus, receive my spirit."   *—Acts 7:59*

The last words Jesus uttered are similar to a prayer some children still pray when they go to bed: "Now I lay me down to sleep, I pray the Lord my soul to keep."

The cross—what a deathbed! What a strange place to say goodnight. Yet it is the only place where we can learn how to die.

Jesus is our teacher in all areas and at all times. He has showed us how to live; he will teach us how to die. When we have learned how to live, we must not be afraid that we won't know how to die. The Teacher will be there.

Ever since Jesus' death, the dying of Christians has been called "falling asleep." Even the violent death of Stephen, when the rocks cracked his skull, is called "falling asleep" (Acts 7:60).

A Christian surgeon returned to the Lord through the prayer of a child. Six-year-old Johnny was very ill, but he didn't know it. The doctor and the nurse came to get him in a desperate attempt to save his life by surgery. They wheeled his bed from the children's ward to the operating room. The doctor was very fond of the boy. "Now I am going to give you a prick in your arm, and then you are going to sleep," he said.

"Am I going to sleep?" asked Johnny.

"Yes, you are."

"But then I must first say my prayer."

The little boy worked himself up on his knees, closed his eyes, and folded his hands. While God, the doctor, and the nurses listened, he prayed, "Now I lay me down to sleep, I pray the Lord my soul to keep."

Johnny never woke up. He really did "fall asleep." But that night the doctor whispered: "Father, into your hands I commit my life."

REFLECTIONS

What is your only comfort in life and in death?

My Master Is My God

MATTHEW 28:16-20

> ". . . in the name of the Father and of the Son and of the Holy
> Spirit . . ."   —Matthew 28:19

The death of Jesus and the death of Stephen are much alike. The Holy
Spirit told us the story of Stephen's death to show us how disciples can
learn from their teacher. Stephen had learned from Jesus how we must
pray: "Lord, do not hold this sin against them." And Stephen had learned
how to die: "Lord Jesus, receive my spirit."

But there is one important difference between the last words of Jesus
and the last words of Stephen. Jesus prayed to God his Father: "Father,
into your hands I commit my spirit." Stephen spoke to Christ: "Lord
Jesus, receive my spirit." Jesus prayed to God the Father; Stephen prayed
to God the Son.

What we meet here is not just a problem. Problems can be solved. We
have come to the greatest mystery of the Bible—the being of God himself!

Throughout the Old and New Testaments, we are taught to believe in
the one and only God of heaven and earth. At the same time, the name
of Jesus (especially "Lord Jesus"), is used freely when the only God is
addressed. Yet we are never allowed to think of God as more than one;
any hint in that direction is rejected.

There is much about God's existence that we do not understand. We
must confess that the God to whom Jesus prayed and the God on whom
Stephen called are the same God, for God is one. And Jesus was both
truly God and truly man.

You and I are not the first ones who are perplexed by this difference
in unity. Throughout the centuries, believers have struggled to put this
mystery into words. And although words aren't quite capable of saying
who God is, the church has finally formulated its faith in the holy Trinity or Three-Unity. God exists in three persons—Father, Son, and Holy
Spirit! Yet God is one.

This teaching is not an addition to the Bible. It is a reverent reflection on
what the Bible tells us about God. You come to the teaching of the Trinity
when you think deeply about the moving prayers of Jesus and Stephen.

REFLECTIONS

What questions would you like to ask God about God?

Prisoner of Christ

ACTS 9:10-20

"I will show [Saul] how much he must suffer for my name."
—Acts 9:16

Saul agreed to Stephen's death sentence. He was eager to wipe out the Christian sect. And he was willing to go to Damascus to get prisoners for the Sanhedrin. In fact, he volunteered for the job.

The Christians fled and prayed, "Lord, save us from the hands of Saul of Tarsus."

Then the living Lord met Saul on the road to Damascus. Saul did not take any prisoners in Damascus. Instead he himself was led into the city as a prisoner of Jesus Christ.

Ananias had to announce the gospel of grace to Saul. By this gospel Saul would be saved and would be able to save many others. The Lord had a program ready for Saul: "I will show him how much he must suffer for my name."

It sounds as if the Lord wants to get even with Saul. Saul has brought suffering to the Christians; from now on, he must suffer for Christ.

If this is our understanding of the Lord's words, we have forgotten that he calls everyone in the same way ("Follow me") and on the same terms ("Take up your cross"). True, he does not have the same program for all of his followers. He made Paul more useful than any of us. Therefore, the load Paul had to carry was bigger than the load most of us carry.

Suffering for Christ is not exceptional, and being useful to Jesus is not reserved for the few. Both suffering and usefulness belong to the ordinary Christian lives to which all of us have been called. It is also normal that the load of suffering gets bigger as the extent of service is increased. To the same degree, the joy deepens and the fellowship becomes more intimate when the suffering of Jesus becomes real in the lives of his followers.

God's programs for us are different, but discipleship is basically the same. For each of us the Lord prescribes more glory and more suffering when we identify with his name.

REFLECTIONS

In what way(s) would you like to be more "useful" to your Lord?

Sing While You Suffer

ACTS 16:25-34

About midnight Paul and Silas were praying and singing hymns to God, and the other prisoners were listening to them. —Acts 16:25

The two inmates who were locked up in the inner security cell seemed no different from the other prisoners sent down by the Roman magistrates. Their garments were torn off their backs and they looked a mess. Maybe they had received a few more blows than usual. But for the most part, they were just prisoners, as far as the jailer was concerned. "He put them in the inner cell and fastened their feet in the stocks."

Around midnight, however, it became abundantly clear that these inmates were messengers of Jesus Christ.

In prison everyone is accustomed to obscenities. You cannot arouse anyone by cursing. But these two men began to pray and sing hymns to God. That was highly unusual.

Apparently, Paul and Silas did not think this was the time to preach a sermon on repentance and faith. Instead they expressed their own faith and joy in prayer and song. There is a time for preaching and a time for giving a testimony.

"And the other prisoners were listening to them." These miserable men, who spent their days waiting for death or release, sat up. It was as if light was streaming into that dreadful place. The angels must have begun singing too. In the act of worship, heaven and earth are always united.

Then God moved his finger. Everything trembled. The chains broke, and the doors fell off their hinges.

Before the night was over, the jailer and his family were also praying and singing hymns to God. God's angels must have sung their most joyful hallelujahs.

What is the secret that makes Christians laugh through their tears and sing while they suffer? The secret is not a thing but a person. The secret is Jesus.

REFLECTIONS

Can you think of a Christian you know who "sang" his or her way through suffering? What impact did this have on you?

Kingdom and Suffering

ACTS 14:19-23

"We must go through many hardships to enter the kingdom of God,"
[Paul and Barnabas] said. —*Acts 14:22*

When the early missionaries gained converts in the towns where they presented the gospel, they would come back to encourage the young Christians and tell them bluntly that they must "go through many hardships [tribulations] to enter the kingdom of God." They presented this message as a general rule. They did not say: "Some of you may have to suffer, and others will live happily ever after." They made it very clear that there is no painless path to glory.

Today's missionaries have told us how many people in Islamic lands, in China, and elsewhere suffer tribulation when they become disciples of Jesus. Yet we must not think only of them. The rule also holds for us. The suffering is not incidental or historical; it belongs to the way of salvation. This suffering cannot be avoided and it must not be evaded. Why is suffering inevitable for us?

- We are going to be the target of Satan. He will try his devilish best to make us unfaithful to Christ.
- We will stand up for the name of Jesus. Therefore we will be despised, ridiculed, and persecuted by others—often by those who are closest to us.
- We must deny ourselves. Our old, sinful self will die a slow death. That will hurt too.
- We learn to love as Jesus loved. That makes us very vulnerable. Love brings pain.

Once we have discovered that our call to the kingdom involves us in suffering, we must avoid two mistakes: we should not try to reason this teaching away by some "interpretation," and we should not suddenly try to become martyrs by stirring up opposition. Orthodox Christians are inclined to make the former mistake; sectarian Christians will make the second. All we have to do, really, is examine ourselves and look critically at our lifestyles, asking ourselves if we are identifying with Jesus. And the gospel of suffering will make itself plain.

REFLECTIONS

In what way(s) do you suffer because you are "identifying with Jesus"? If your life is currently free from suffering, should you be concerned or just give thanks?

The Sorrow of God

PSALM 81:6-16

> *"If my people would only listen to me, if Israel would only follow my ways..."* —Psalm 81:13

There is a tremendous amount of suffering in the world. It's everywhere and it reaches everyone. Just thinking about it makes a person suffer more.

There is physical pain and there is mental pain. There is suffering that can be removed, and there is sorrow that is irremovable because it belongs to the lot of humanity. There is suffering we bring on ourselves by error, bad judgment, or transgression, but there are also disasters that cannot be foreseen or prevented.

It seems impossible to sort it all out. One might try to classify the different kinds of sufferings, and yet, somehow, all sorrow seems to be connected by a network of roots underneath the soil of our existence. Humanity is hurting all over. The wounds were there long before we were born.

The Bible reveals a sorrow of which we remain ignorant as long as we are preoccupied with our own suffering and our world's woes. It is the sorrow of God. God's lamentation is at the top of this page: "If my people would only listen to me..."

The whole Bible is the story of God seeking and people hiding. God asked, "Adam, where are you?" And Adam hid himself. It is one long story of a Father who looks down the road, day after day. He sighs, "My son, when are you coming home?"

God's sorrow explains our suffering. Deep down, all our pain is because we lost God. Religion—the search for God—is not merely an escape for the weak, as some have said. Not one of us is strong enough to survive if we don't find God. By losing God, we lost our authentic environment.

Our only hope lies in a complete reunion with our God. Our sorrows will all be plucked up by the roots only when heaven and earth are reunited. Then we will have reached the fountain of healing. And God will wipe away all tears.

REFLECTIONS

Have you thought much about the sorrow of God? What causes God's sorrow? How does it explain our own suffering and sorrow?

The Sorrow of Christ

MATTHEW 23:37-39

"Jerusalem, Jerusalem . . . how often I have longed to gather your children together, as a hen gathers her chicks under her wings, and you were not willing." —Matthew 23:37

God's sorrow over his runaway children was so severe that he came down to find them and bring them home.

God came to us in Jesus Christ. Jesus is not merely one of us who points to God as the way out. Jesus came from God, and he himself is our way out.

In Jesus Christ, God came to seek and save what was lost. Of course God first looked for his son Israel, for Israel was the one on whom he had spent so much love, the one to whom he had spoken so often.

After all those years of calling, seeking, and pleading, Christ spoke the sorrowful words: "Jerusalem, Jerusalem . . . how often I have longed to gather your children together . . . and you were not willing." And still the people did not understand. Their faces remained blank when they saw the tears of God in the eyes of Jesus.

Humanity is not suffering under a heavenly arch of cold blue steel, as some philosophers have thought. God's sorrow is revealed in his Word. And heaven's compassion became flesh and blood in Jesus' words and deeds. He has cried out for us, but so few have answered.

This is the sorrow of love. Those who do not love do not know this sorrow.

Parents know it. Children never fully realize what is in the hearts of their parents until they have children of their own. Yet much parental pain is downright worldly. It is hurt pride. It may still be noble, but it is not Christian. Christian sorrow springs from Christian love. It is of one piece with the love and sorrow of God and Christ.

The worst pain Christian parents suffer is when their children leave God. Whatever else their children may possess or become, that pain is not healed. By the same token, the joy of Christian parents whose children walk in the ways of the Lord is deep and lasting. Nothing is right if we aren't right with God. But everything will be all right if we only cling to God.

REFLECTION

What does the "sorrow of love" mean? How does this phrase describe "the Man of sorrows," Jesus Christ?

The Sorrow of the Christian

ROMANS 9:1-5

I have great sorrow and unceasing anguish in my heart.
—*Romans 9:2*

The sorrow of God and the sorrow of Christ were reflected in the sorrow of Paul: "I have great sorrow and unceasing anguish in my heart." It almost sounds like exaggeration. Paul feels that most people will have trouble understanding his pain. Therefore he places himself under a solemn oath (v. 1). He speaks the truth in Christ. He does not lie, and his conscience, ruled by God's Spirit, is witness. Then he tells us the reason for his anguish: his own brothers and sisters reject Jesus Christ!

We must be aware that the call to follow Jesus Christ, when obeyed, will bring us suffering. But it also will give us a joy that's deeper and better than any other pleasure. Yet with the new joy comes a new kind of suffering.

We will suffer for many reasons. But the deepest level of our suffering is this one: we share the *sorrow* of God as soon as we share the *love* of God.

All love brings pain. Those who wish to be without pain should keep their lives free from love. If you don't care for anybody, chances are that you won't get hurt unless your own sweet little self is hurt. But if you happen to love your wife, her pain will go through your own soul. And if you are one of those who share in the love of God, you will feel something of God's sorrow whenever you see sin or a sinner.

Some people talk about the love of God as if it were kindness at a distance: "Someone upstairs loves you." There may be some truth in this crude saying—as long as we realize that we remain strangers to that kindness of God until he himself has moved into our hearts. God's love does not remain "upstairs." We know God's love only when his Spirit has moved into us (Rom. 5:5).

Once the Lord has moved into us, it is impossible for us to remain indifferent when he is angry, to hate what he loves, or to love what he hates.

REFLECTIONS

When have you felt something of the "sorrow of God"? What enables you to feel this sorrow?

Sharing His Suffering

PHILIPPIANS 3:1-11

I want to know Christ—yes, to know the power of his resurrection and participation in his sufferings. . . . —*Philippians 3:10*

Isn't that a strange order? To know Christ, the power of his resurrection, and participate in his suffering? I thought that as soon as we have the resurrection power of Christ in our lives, we are past the stage of suffering and begin a glorious life!

Not so. The life of glory begins once we have attained "the resurrection from the dead" (v. 11). And that, according to Paul, is still in the future.

Knowing Jesus Christ is the aim of a Christian. We get to know him—better and better—when we are united with him in faith. Our union means a oneness in Jesus' death and resurrection. By his death Jesus has delivered us from the burden of sin, and by his resurrection he has introduced us to a new life that comes to us through the Holy Spirit.

As soon as we receive this new life, we are introduced to the fellowship of Christ's suffering. His suffering is not the same kind of pain everyone feels. It's a particular kind of sorrow shared only by those who belong to Christ.

Before we knew Christ, we were not moved by human need the way we are now. Before we knew him, we could say, "Let every person be happy in his or her own way." Now we know that there is only one way of life and every other road leads to death. Before we knew Christ, we would get excited about things that can hardly stir us now. Since we know Christ, we have lost burdens that weigh heavily on those who do not know him. We got rid of the burden of sin, and most of the ordinary worries that plague ordinary people have been either taken away or significantly reduced. But we have also received new burdens of which the non-saved are ignorant.

Whoever receives the Word of the Lord becomes engaged in the work of the Lord. It is a feast to have the resurrection power of Christ in your life. But it also introduces you to the suffering of Christ.

REFLECTIONS

What burdens have you been able to lay down because you know Christ? What "new burdens" have you picked up?

Completing Christ's Suffering

COLOSSIANS 1:21-29

Now I rejoice in what I am suffering for you, and I fill up in my flesh what is still lacking in regard to Christ's afflictions, for the sake of his body, which is the church. —Colossians 1:24

Let's take part in the greatest thing that's going on in the world today—the coming of the kingdom of God.

It's true that only the King can bring the kingdom. But it pleases him to work through us. It's true that only Christ has suffered for us. But it pleases him to complete his suffering through us.

Our suffering is not a payment for sin. Of course not! Jesus said, "It is finished," when he died on the cross. Our whole lives rest on the finished work of Christ. But our whole lives are also given shape by the unfinished task he has laid upon us.

This missionary task will also be completed by the living Lord. Christ himself will strengthen feeble Christians, and he will make their enemies harmless. Yet he works through our mouths and pens and pocketbooks. He reaches out through our hands. His compassionate heart has been transplanted into his church. The lifeblood of his Spirit pulsates through his congregation. And the hearts of Christians suffer with the afflictions of Christ.

All the strongholds of Satan must be captured. That can be done only by the power of God's Spirit. But no such stronghold is taken without painful labor on the part of Christian workers. People are not led to the Lord or kept with the Lord without the toil and tears of Christians who give of themselves until it hurts.

This price of suffering must be paid in full before the kingdom comes. The Bible talks about this Christlike suffering as if there is a quota that must be filled before the end can come, as if there is a total cost of discipleship that must be expended before all bow down before Jesus.

There is no greater joy or usefulness than to be involved in the suffering of Christ. He brings the kingdom through the life and death of his followers. Then he will say for the second time: "It is finished and complete."

REFLECTIONS

"There is no greater joy or usefulness than to be involved in the suffering of Christ." Reflect on how that sense of joy and usefulness is found in your congregation, and in you.

Cross and Crown

ROMANS 8:12-17

> *... if, in fact, we suffer with him so that we may also be glorified with him.* —Romans 8:17, NRSV

If in our spiritual journey we have paid little attention to the suffering that belongs to all followers of Christ, we had better correct our mistake quickly. After all, the Bible goes so far as to call suffering with Christ a condition for being glorified with him.

We should not overlook the words *with him*. The Bible does not say that the reward for suffering in this life is glory in the next. That would take us back to the old salvation-by-works heresy. Our crosses never save us. Only the cross of Christ has that power. But the Bible does say that we must identify with Jesus today if we are to be in his company tomorrow: "If . . . we suffer with him so that we may also be glorified with him."

The great surprise of the New Testament is that the promised King of Israel lived as a slave and died on a cross. The obedient Son of God placed himself under the Father's law—first a cross, then a crown. In doing so, he had to reject all the shortcuts to glory recommended by the devil and even by Jesus' own friends.

Anyone who wants to identify with Christ must follow this unchangeable law: first the cross and then the crown. In its present existence, the church is a church under the cross.

The Christian church is not the place where suffering is past because the Spirit is present, as some seem to think. The purpose of the Spirit is not to take away our cross but to give us the power to bear that cross.

Nor is the church an institution through which people can buy themselves some eternal life insurance, as even more seem to assume.

The church is the company of people called by Jesus Christ. They live "with him" or "in him." Whatever they plan, they plan with Christ; whatever they do, they do with Christ; whatever they hope to be, they want to be in Christ. For them to live is Christ and to die is gain. "With him" they suffer; "with him" they will be glorified.

REFLECTIONS

What does it mean to you to be "in Christ"?

The Pains Have Started

ROMANS 8:18-25

> *We know that the whole creation has been groaning. . . . Not only so, but we ourselves, who have the firstfruits of the Spirit, groan inwardly. . . .* —*Romans 8:22-23*

Suffering is universal. No home is passed over, and no life will be without sorrow. The apostle says that not just people but the whole creation is groaning. That includes the animals—and maybe even the plants.

God's people live and work in this present world, even though, in the language of the Bible, they really belong to the future world, the new world God is creating. We live in the present world, but we do not belong to it.

Already we have received "the firstfruits of the Spirit." This is only the first fruit. The whole harvest is not yet in. We have been given the down payment but not yet the whole of the inheritance.

A new principle, one that cannot be found anywhere else in the old world, is already present in God's people. It is the gift of the Holy Spirit. The Spirit is the foretaste of the new country, the first power from the other side, from God, and the Spirit is already here.

Now the suffering of Christians has become more acute than the suffering of other creatures. As long as a person's experience is limited to the present world and the present misery, she tends to accept what she finds here. She gets accustomed to it. She even gets used to sin.

But the church has the Spirit, the beginning of the new life and the new world. Therefore we cannot possibly be satisfied with the old world and the old life. Everything and everyone is groaning, but we groan louder. Everyone is looking for something better, but Christians know where to look for it.

Only the church can interpret the dream that suffering humanity is dreaming. Christians know that the groaning of the present world is the birth pain of the coming age. The message of the church is a tiding of hope: the pain may be severe, but it is the kind of pain that precedes the coming of new life. When these pains begin, the new day is very close.

REFLECTIONS
How do verses 18-25 give you hope when you are suffering?

For a Little While

1 PETER 5:6-11

> *And the God of all grace, who called you to his eternal glory in Christ, after you have suffered a little while, will himself restore you and make you strong, firm and steadfast.* —*1 Peter 5:10*

We have been called to glory—not to suffering. The suffering is the stretch of road we have to travel before we reach our destination.

We will reach the eternal glory after we have "suffered a little while." Why is the time of our suffering spoken of as a little while? First, because it is only a short period compared with the "eternal glory" to which we have been called. Just as the pain of childbirth is forgotten when the child is born, and just as the patriarch Jacob found seven years' work for Rachel as short as a few days (Gen. 29:20), so the overwhelming joy of eternal glory makes our present suffering but "a little while."

At the same time, God is assuring us by these words that we will not suffer beyond measure or beyond endurance. "A little while" means that God has set certain limits. Suddenly it will be over. Then we will admit that it wasn't too long.

We are also comforted by the reminder that it is "the God of all grace" who calls us. Not only are we called by grace—and not because we were worthy of the call—the God who calls gives us grace for every circumstance during our time of suffering. Therefore he is "the God of all grace." His grace will see us through. God himself will restore, establish, and strengthen us. Peter, who gave us this assurance, knew very well how we still need the gracious arm of God to lift us up and hold us fast after we have obeyed the call to take up the cross and follow the Master.

The road leads to eternal glory. We cannot say much about that. Glory is the radiance of God's being and the enjoyment of his presence. Imagination fails us. No doubt it will be better and richer than we can foresee. It will be the complete absence of all suffering, because it will be the full presence of God himself.

After you have suffered for "a little while," you'll see it.

REFLECTIONS

Read verse 10 to yourself several times and be open to its wonderful promises. Then give thanks and praise to the "God of all grace."

Psalms

Although we sing the songs of the new covenant in the church of Christ, we still have much to learn from our ancestors who lived under the old covenant. We must learn to sing their songs as well.

daylight

Blessed Are the Righteous

PSALM 1

> *They are like a tree planted by streams of water. . . . Not so the wicked! They are like chaff that the wind blows away.*
> —*Palm 1:3-4*

According to the songbook of God's people, righteous people are blessed. The tune of worldly people goes "Blessed are those who are smart, and three cheers for those who have made it!" Some modern Christians sing "Blessed are those who are saved" or "Happy are those who go to heaven." But Psalm 1 is more profound: Blessed are those who are upright before God.

Enduring happiness is for people who live according to the will and the Word of the Lord. They do not "walk in step with the wicked" or "stand in the way that sinners take," and they do not sit in "the company of mockers" of religion. On the contrary, they practice their godliness constantly. Day and night their hearts are turned to God, just as the needle of a compass insistently turns to the north. They do right not merely because they have to but because they *want* to: their "*delight*" is in the law of the LORD.

In order to live the righteous life, a person must be born of the Spirit and washed by the blood. We know that even better than the ancient singer.

We, who sing the songs of the temple as we sit in the church of Christ, have much to learn from the fathers who lived under the old covenant. What a clear and concrete view of life and death! They did not say that believers would begin to live when they went to heaven, and that unbelievers would be punished in the hereafter. For them, the issues are decided here and now. The righteous person lives; the wicked person is dead. Either you are a tree or you are chaff.

"Blessed are those who do not walk in step with the wicked." Such persons are truly alive! They look like a tree on the riverside, loaded with fruit. As for the wicked, they are nothing but chaff. God's wind will blow them away.

REFLECTIONS

In what ways do you feel "blessed" by God?

God's Messiah

PSALM 2

> *[The Lord] said to me, "You are my son. . . . Ask me, and I will make the nations your inheritance. . . ."* —Psalm 2:7-8

Perspective enhances the truth. As long as you are a party to a quarrel, you cannot hear the silly things you say and see how foolishly you are acting. Looking back, painfully, many years later, you see clearly what a fool you were. A husband-wife squabble is always embarrassing for a third party; it would be the same way for the husband and wife—if only they could see themselves in perspective.

If human perspective enhances the truth of our folly, how silly people who rebel against God must look from the perspective of God's throne. From such a distance, the angry ants look silly. "The One enthroned in heaven laughs; the Lord scoffs at them."

The psalm promises that these disobedient and rebellious people will eventually be brought into line by God's Messiah. Therefore all little kings are advised to bow before God's King. Otherwise he will dash them to pieces like pottery.

Jesus is this Messiah. He did not seem like a fearful ruler when he was born in Bethlehem—and certainly not when he was killed near Jerusalem. But God raised Jesus from the dead. "You are my son," God said. "I will make the nations your inheritance."

Today Jesus holds ultimate power. All of us are at his mercy—in the most literal sense of the word. To reject him or try to ignore him is not only a grave sin, it is stupid. Be wise and take heed, all people. Bow or perish!

The means by which Christ brings the nations to their knees is the Word of the gospel. The gospel is the good news about God's love. Only those who cannot be won over by the story of God's love are bound to meet with the rod of his anger. Viewed in the proper perspective, what choice do we have?

REFLECTIONS

What picture of God does this psalm give you?

Keep Me Alive

PSALM 6

> *Among the dead nobody proclaims your name. Who praises you*
> *from the grave?* —*Psalm 6:5*

The man who wrote Psalm 6 was in great trouble; he was in fear of losing his life. God should not allow him to die, he said, for in the kingdom of death (called "Sheol" in some Bible versions) nobody remembers God or praises him.

His way of praying shows what he believed concerning life and what he knew concerning death. He knew that the purpose of life is praising God. We live for the glory of God. But in death our voice is muted. The song has ended. Therefore he wanted to go on living. "Let me live," he begged. "Then your praise will be prolonged."

Before we say that this man did not know what we know about death, why not admit that he possessed a truth about life of which we need to be reminded? The psalm-singer says that living is praising God; that's why death is to be feared and hated. Christians, however, have spoken so many soothing words concerning death that they sometimes seem to forget that death is a fearful enemy of God and of the human race. As a matter of fact, some Christians talk about death as if it's the time when the song of praise begins! Such a view betrays a misunderstanding of dying, because it does not see the truth about living.

If the writer of Psalm 6 could have heard that Jesus rose from the dead on the third day, he would have said: "Hallelujah! Now God's praise is continued, for life is continued."

He did not know about the resurrection. We do, because we are living in the age in which Jesus is building his church. And Christ promised that the "gates of Sheol" or the "powers of death" would not prevail against his church.

The church is built on the resurrection. Therefore we are no longer afraid that death will be the end of the song. But a person can be comforted by the conquest of death only when he knows the purpose of life.

REFLECTIONS

Suppose you, like the writer of this psalm, were in danger of losing your life. What reason(s) would you give to God to prolong it?

So Small and So Great

PSALM 8

> *What are mere mortals that you are mindful of them, human beings that you care for them? [Yet] you have made them a little lower than the heavenly beings. . . .* —*Psalm 8:4-5*

If someone were to take your picture from the top of a twenty-story building while you were walking in the street, you would look like an ant in the jungle. But if your picture were taken while you yourself stood on that building, the photo would show you towering over the other buildings with the city beneath your feet. Everything depends on the angle. From one angle a person is puny; from another perspective he or she is impressive.

The Bible wants us to look at people from both angles. People are very small—and they are very great. People are small with respect to what is above them. But they are great because of all that God has placed under them. Projected against the skies, people are puny, but in their workshop (the earth), people are king. God has placed everything beneath their feet.

Therefore, when we hear someone boast, we should visualize the person against the expanse of the skies or against the mountain ranges of God's greatness—and we should shudder. Why? Because a mere human has exalted him- or herself.

On the other hand, we should also shudder when we see a person who has become a slave of that which God entrusted to him or her—a farm, stocks and bonds, machines, material. People were made a little less than God. But they become pitiful beggars when they are reduced to the slavery of things.

We must learn to look at people the way the Bible does. And we can be the kind of people God wants us to be only when Jesus has taught us once again how to be men and women in God's world.

Before the sovereign God, we are small. We eat out of his hand and live by his grace. Nobody has a right to make his or her own rules, and it takes more than human power to keep the rules of God. At the same time, those who have been redeemed by the Lord may never fall into the slavery of people and things. They are princes and princesses in God's palace.

REFLECTIONS

Try turning verses 4 and 5 into a prayer of your own, reflecting both your "smallness" and your "greatness."

Peace and Order

PSALM 9:11-20

> *Strike them with terror, LORD; let the nations know they are only mortals.* —*Psalm 9:20*

Peace in the world depends on order. The order that ensures peace requires that God be recognized as sovereign and that people know their place. "Strike them with terror, LORD; let the nations know they are only mortals."

This is a prayer for peace and a prayer for the kingdom. "Peace," as the word is used in the Bible, is order—a situation where everything is right. Therefore the Bible says, "God is not a God of disorder but of peace" (1 Cor. 14:33). God hates chaos and requires order.

The kingdom of the Messiah is a kingdom of peace. But his kingdom is more than those peaceful pastoral pictures. The kingdom of peace is a new order in which God is worshiped, people love each other, and things are neither worshiped nor loved but used. That's the right order; that's peace.

We will have no peace until people fall in line with God's order. The nations must know that they are but humans—and that God is God.

Pride is the father of sin. Pride is not merely excessive bragging. Everyone can recognize that sin. Ordinary pride is much harder to recognize. It is the refusal to bow before God. This pride damns the lives of people, even those who are otherwise good and civilized. They don't know that they are only human beings.

Humility is the opposite of pride. It is the only door through which we can find God. Therefore children can find him while the wise are left in the dark.

God's way of teaching humility to the human race is a divine humor that moves both people and angels. Humanity fell into sin because it wanted to be like God. But we were lifted from the pit when God became like one of us—a human being. The way to the new world of peace-by-order begins in Bethlehem, with the Baby!

All the proud races of humanity must come here and bow down at the manger. Only then we can find our place in the blessed order of the kingdom of God.

REFLECTIONS

Take time to bow in humble silence before our great God. Then ask God to help you "walk humbly" before him in your day-to-day living.

Tyranny of Lies

PSALM 12

> *Everyone lies to their neighbor; they flatter with their lips but harbor deception in their hearts. . . . And the words of the LORD are flawless.*
> —*Psalm 12:2, 6*

This psalm invokes God's judgment on the wickedness of words. All kinds of sins of the tongue are mentioned—lies, which are statements that are contrary to the facts, as well as flattery, which means that things are said not because they are true but because someone likes hearing them.

A sinful society lives under the tyranny of lies. The lie has destroyed any and every form of fellowship. We can't trust anybody anymore.

The abuse of words did a great deal of harm in the days of David, but the damage caused by this evil has now increased a thousandfold. We are bombarded by words every living hour. But these words often don't mean what they say. We live under a barrage of lies fired at us on the Internet, in the newspaper, on radio talk shows, and on television. Words are supposed to be simple servants that help us communicate. But today people have made the abuse of words a fine art, disguising what they mean, confusing their hearers, coaxing people along, impressing them. The government does it; so does the attorney, the student, the teacher, the salesperson, the reporter. And sometimes the preacher does it.

The Bible says that the most difficult part of Christian renewal is the taming of the tongue (James 3:8). Our yes must mean yes and our no must mean no. There is no room in the New Jerusalem for those who love and practice falsehood.

When words have become so cheap that a promise is just a mouthful of words, we must rediscover what it means that the "words of the LORD are flawless," or, as another Bible version puts it, "the promises of the Lord are pure."

REFLECTIONS

Do you personally find that "the most difficult part of Christian renewal is the taming of the tongue"? What has helped you to be a truthful person?

Doubt and Trust

PSALM 13

> *How long, LORD? Will you forget me forever? . . . But I trust in*
> *your unfailing love. . . .* —*Psalm 13:1, 5*

Four times David says to God, "How long?" He says it because God seems to have forgotten him. The Lord hides his face. He does not take away the pain, and he allows David's enemies to be exalted. "How long?"

If you have never said to God, "How long?" you probably don't take his promises very seriously. After all, God has said that he will hear our cries. Evil will perish, he promised, and those who hope in God will be exalted. When we knock, he will open; when we seek, we will find. And the coming of the kingdom is at hand. How long?

Waiting is an essential feature of Christian living. Not the kind of waiting we do in waiting rooms, where we try to kill time by paging through magazines. Waiting is characteristic of our lives because we work and live by the strength of *promises*, always expecting God to do what he promised.

When we cry, "How long?" we have become impatient. There may also be doubt in our hearts. Does God really care? Is he really listening? Will he come?

Doubt is as old as Psalm 13. Nobody needs to worry that she is especially wicked just because she finds doubt in her heart.

Doubt must be expressed, and then it must be opposed. It may be expressed as freely as it is in this psalm. And it must be opposed by faith. Faith is always fighting doubt. Faith says, "I trust God even in the dark. I believe that if he delays his coming, it must be because he is going to give me even more than I asked for."

It may be common to have doubts, but anyone who nurses his doubts is a fool. A cold is a common illness in many parts of the world, but it is still considered an illness. Doubt must be overcome, and trust must take its place. The psalm ends with a note of trust in God: "But I trust in your unfailing love."

REFLECTION

What doubts have you had (or do you now have)? What, in the face of your doubts, sustains your faith?

Atheists and Other Sinners

> *Fools say in their hearts, "There is no God." . . . There is nobody who does good, not even one.* —Psalm 14:1, 3

Fools do not take God into account. "In their hearts," the center of their beings, they deny that God exists. The actions of fools are consistent with the direction of their hearts. They are corrupt; they do abominable things; they are no good. Just as faith in God is necessarily accompanied by good works, so unbelief is bound to hatch a brood of evil. When the tie with God is broken, people will fall from one wickedness into another. Not automatically and not always individually, as we see people doing, but gradually and by generations, as *the Bible* sees people.

It looks as if this psalm is going to be an attack on the atheists. "The Lord looks down from heaven on the human race to see if there are any who understand, any who seek God." With serene majesty God looks down on little atheists.

But read on, for God is looking at us too. "*All* have turned away, *all* have become corrupt; there is nobody who does good, not even one." Instead of attacking atheists, the psalmist tells us that in the eyes of God, *all* people are equally sinful.

That's how Paul read this psalm when he argued that not only wicked people but *all* people need the gospel. In Romans 3 he concluded that all of us must stop dividing humankind into "good guys" and "bad guys," atheistic sinners and religious do-gooders. We are *all* sinners.

We are not allowed to feel good about God's anger against the fools who deny him. Just when we are ready to agree with God, we are reminded that "there is nobody who does good, not even one."

In such a situation, the Old Testament cries in the words of our psalm: "Oh, that salvation for Israel would come out of Zion!"

And the New Testament gospel says: "give him the name Jesus, because he will save his people from their sins" (Matt. 1:21). There is nobody who does not need to be saved from his or her sins. Not even one.

REFLECTIONS

Before we can know the height of God's grace, we must know the depths of our own sin. Reflect on your need for a Savior, and then give thanks for Jesus.

Supreme Joy

PSALM 16

You make known to me the path of life; you will fill me with joy
in your presence, with eternal pleasures at your right hand.
—Psalm 16:11

Careful parents and pastors often warn young Christians that the Christian life is not all joy and happiness. It involves self-denial and unexpected pain. The Christian life demands a new obedience that goes against the old grain. It isn't easy to be a Christian.

Such warnings are necessary. Especially in a time when everyone is busy seeking self-fulfillment, the expectations of young Christians may be quite wrong. Warnings are in order when success-oriented writers and speakers present Christianity as the best of all possible ways to total happiness. Our ideas of total happiness must also be converted and transformed.

Yet too many warnings may have the wrong effect.

Christ does make us happy. And God is our joy. David already knew that our God does not only give happiness, but is what he gives: "apart from you, I have no good thing."

The rich and happy vocabulary of Psalm 16 becomes even more meaningful when we read it under the lamp of the New Testament. This way of life, along which the psalmist moves from one surprise to another, is really Jesus. Verse 10, which says that God will not abandon us to the realm of the dead, actually tells about Christ's resurrection. Jesus is the path of life—straight to the joy of the Father (Acts 2:25-31).

So Psalm 16 does give us a vision of Jesus as the source of our happiness. We'd better drink it in. Jesus is the path of life. He is not only the way that leads to life but also the path along which life is enjoyed. This is life. His presence is our life. And therefore we are "filled with joy" and have an infinite future "with eternal pleasures" at God's right hand.

Frankly, we have no right to discourage the most optimistic Christian. Indeed, this life is full of joy, and it's going to get better yet.

REFLECTIONS

Reflect on a recent time when you really experienced the joy of God's presence.

Lamentation

PSALM 22:1-11

My God, my God, why have you forsaken me? —*Psalm 22:1*

This is the lament of a righteous person. He has trusted in God all his life: "From my mother's womb you have been my God." And now God has let him down. God has surrendered him to his enemies, to the beasts, to the demons. He calls them bulls, lions, dogs, wild oxen.

This is the worst trouble God's children can experience. They have staked their lives on the reliability of God. They never resorted to deceit or violence. Instead they said, "We trust in our God." But they seem to have trusted in a God who is unable to help.

Therefore it is not the violence or ugliness of these beasts or demons that hurts so much; it is the mockery of the enemies that cuts to the heart. "He trusts in the LORD; let the LORD rescue him." It is the pain of such remarks that wrenches the cry from his mouth: "My God, my God, why have you forsaken me?"

Jesus was a righteous man. He clung to God from the day he was born. "I must be in my Father's house," he said when he was twelve years old. And when he was somewhat older he said, "My food is to do the will of him who sent me." But Jesus' obedience to God led him to a cross.

While he was hanging on the beams, Jesus thought of Psalm 22. The whole psalm became his psalm. God had surrendered him to his taunting enemies. (Were they people, or beasts, or demons?) "He trusts in God. Let God rescue him now if he wants him, for he said, 'I am the Son of God'" (Matt. 27:43). While the sun was darkened, Jesus sang his lamentation with and for God's people: "My God, my God, why have you forsaken me?"

However, when Jesus had uttered this cry, his suffering and ours was nearly over, for the lament of Christ is not merely the voice of one of God's suffering children. It is also God's answer to our cries.

REFLECTIONS

When, if ever, have you felt "forsaken by God"? How was your trust in God restored?

Easter Joy

PSALM 22:22-31

I will declare your name to my people; in the assembly I will praise you. —*Psalm 22:22 (Hebrews 2:12)*

All of Psalm 22 is a song of Jesus. The first part is his lament on the cross. The second part is his song on Easter morning.

When the first light of that Sunday morning shone on the open tomb, the people of God were still weeping. "We had hoped that he was the one who was going to redeem Israel," said one of them (Luke 24:21). *We had hoped. . . .* That's what we always say when our hopes have been dashed and our expectations appear to have been ill-founded. As far as this disciple knew, God had forsaken Jesus. The enemies had triumphed. And death—again—had the last word.

But Jesus was alive! God had raised him up. When all seemed lost, all was gained. When sin and death seemed to conquer, they were conquered. God changed our tears to laughter. God never lets his children down. Now we know it, once and for all.

On the evening of that first day, Jesus appeared "in the assembly" of believers. He began to teach us a new song. The new song is not fundamentally different from the old one. The new is the old fulfilled. "Everything must be fulfilled that is written about me in . . . the Psalms" (Luke 24:44). He teaches us to sing Psalm 22. Yet that psalm sounds even richer when we sing it after Easter.

On Easter Sunday Jesus began to gather the congregation of God. By his Word and Spirit he has been doing that to this very day. "All the ends of the earth will remember and turn to the LORD, and all the families of the nations will bow down before him, for dominion belongs to the LORD and he rules over the nations" (Ps. 22:27-28).

Jesus has endured the suffering of his brothers and sisters—all the way to death. By so doing, he fulfilled the first part of Psalm 22. But now he is gathering the assembly founded on the event of his resurrection. By so doing, he fulfills the last part of Psalm 22 as well.

REFLECTIONS

Reread verses 22-31 aloud in a way that expresses your own prayer of joy for what Jesus has done and is doing.

Trust the Shepherd

PSALM 23

> *The LORD is my shepherd, I lack nothing.*   —*Psalm 23:1*

During its journey through the ages, this psalm has stilled more pain than all our doctors, and it has given more peace to the human race than all the wisdom of the world.

It was composed by David, who used to be a shepherd himself. While he was caring for his sheep, it occurred to him that he, David, also had a shepherd. Thus he composed the opening line of his poem: "The LORD is my shepherd." Since the Lord is the best possible shepherd, he added the confession: "I lack nothing," or, in the phrasing more familiar to many, "I shall not want."

If you think of the Bible as a great musical composition, you could say that here, in Psalm 23, the shepherd motif is struck for the first time. From here on it is replayed in ever richer variations.

Every Christian remembers how Jesus took up the shepherd motif. Not only did he tell the unforgettable story of the lost sheep that was carried home by the shepherd, he also declared: "I am the good shepherd," thereby telling us that the true shepherd of David and of Israel stands before us in the person of Christ.

The climax of the shepherd's psalm comes in Revelation 7. Here, near the end of God's great composition, the familiar strains are played once again. But notice the final variation: "For the Lamb at the center before the throne will be their shepherd" (Rev. 7:17). Now the shepherd is also a Lamb. He himself has gone through the valley of the shadow of death. And the words "I lack nothing" are also infinitely enriched. Now the choir sings: "Never again will they hunger, never again will they thirst. . . . And God will wipe away every tear from their eyes" (Rev. 7:16-17). Their needs have been fulfilled completely. They will lack nothing.

So we keep singing this psalm of confidence, until the last sheep in God's weary flock have found their final rest.

REFLECTION

What does it mean to you that the Lord is your shepherd? Can you honestly say, with David, that you lack nothing?

The King Enters

PSALM 24

> *Lift up your heads, you gates; be lifted up, you ancient doors, that the King of glory may come in.* —*Psalm 24:7*

In the first part of this psalm, the earth and its fullness lie still, as if waiting for the master. Then comes the question: Who may ascend the mountain of the LORD? Where is the pure one who may enter the palace of holiness, the city of the sovereign God? And in the third part we hear people singing enthusiastically because the "King of glory" enters his dwelling.

We cannot be sure at what occasion this song was composed (or even at what feast it was sung), and we can only guess what people were thinking when they used all these different images. But a Christian who reads this psalm is inclined to think that it was composed to celebrate the ascension of the Lord Jesus.

He ascended into heaven. The first phase of his work was accomplished. With "clean hands and a pure heart" he ascended to the dwelling of his Father. He did so for our benefit. We remember and believe that he has triumphed. Sin cannot enslave us anymore. Death cannot harm us any longer. Our Jesus is Lord. He is exalted on the throne, received by the Father, hailed by angels, adored by his people. "Lift up your heads, you gates; be lifted up, you ancient doors, that the King of glory may come in."

Psalm 24 is a celebration of the ascension. He who loves us also rules us. Jesus is on the throne. Mercy and might are now in one hand. Now he is able to do what his loving heart desires. It's like having your father as the ruler of the country, or your brother as a millionaire. But the truth is bigger and better.

Now the second phase of Jesus' work, his heavenly ministry, is underway. Heaven and earth are being reunited. As a matter of fact, they are one already in Jesus Christ. Our body is in heaven; his Spirit is on earth.

Open the gates! Open your hearts! The earth and its fullness will see the glory of the Lord.

REFLECTIONS

What does it mean to your life today that Jesus is now on his throne in heaven?

Praying for Forgiveness

PSALM 25:1-7

*Do not remember the sins of my youth and my rebellious ways;
according to your love remember me, for you,* LORD, *are good.*
—*Psalm 25:7*

The songbook of God's people is also their prayer book. As we read the Psalms, God teaches us how to worship and how to pray.

In the first seven verses of Psalm 25, we find a model prayer uttered on an ever deeper level. First the psalmist prays for deliverance: "Do not let my enemies triumph over me." Then he asks for guidance: "Show me your ways, LORD, teach me your paths." And finally he prays for forgiveness: "Do not remember the sins of my youth and my rebellious ways."

He is deeply conscious of the number and weight of his sins. He does not hide them from God or from himself. "The sins of my youth" are the sins so easily committed. Youth can be a careless time, a time when passions are strong. But the end of youth does not mean the end of sinning. Therefore he adds, "and my rebellious ways," meaning the deliberate, sinful acts of the mature person.

Those who are closest to us do not know the number and weight of our personal sins. We might even try to hide them from ourselves, constantly pushing them to the edges of our consciousness. We shouldn't do that. We should face them honestly and confess them privately to God.

"Do not remember my sins," the psalmist asks. And he adds: "Remember me." Have no regard for the sins, but please regard the sinner. And he bases his plea on God's goodness: "For you, LORD, are good."

"According to your love remember me." The criminal who was crucified next to Jesus prayed a similar prayer: "Remember me!" And he was heard.

With equal fervor and even greater trust, we may ask that God's love will disregard our sins and restore the sinner. And we base our plea not on God's goodness in general but on the greatest manifestation of God's goodness: "for Jesus' sake, remember me."

REFLECTION

Pray the first seven verses of this psalm as your personal confession of sin.

Seeking God

PSALM 27

Thou hast said, "Seek ye my face." My heart says to thee, "Thy face, Lord, do I seek." Hide not thy face from me. —Psalm 27:8-9, RSV

Even a quick reading of this passage, taken from the Revised Standard Version of the Bible, shows that there are two quite different parts to this psalm. The first part is a song of confidence; the second relates to a hard struggle. Some students think that Psalm 27 really consists of two songs that were later sewn together. This may be, but other explanations are possible. The shift from confidence to struggle is not so strange; in fact, it is typical of those who live their lives with God. Confidence and struggle, praise and fear, are only a breath apart.

In the first part the writer speaks boldly *about* God because in the second part he struggles *with* God. We can speak for God only when we have a place where we speak with God. All who are truly great know how to be small before God. We can be strong in public only when we wrestle in private.

Two voices are heard in the poet's prayer struggle. God's command is, "Seek my face." The second voice is an echo of God's voice in the believer's heart: "Thy face, Lord, do I seek."

Prayer is always an answer to an earlier utterance. Prayer is not a human cry into thin air; it is our answer to a Word from the other side— a Word of God.

The command is "Seek my face." The response is "Thy face do I seek." But this is followed immediately by the words "Hide not thy face from me." This is the insistent plea of the seeker who knows that God has every right to turn away from the sinner who seeks him. But the psalmist is encouraged by God's voice. "You have told me to seek. Now allow me to find." Those who find are those who continue to seek.

"Thy face, Lord, do I seek." The purpose of real prayer is not merely to get this or that from God but to have God himself.

REFLECTIONS

How do you go about seeking the face of God in your everyday life?

At the Teacher's Feet

PSALM 32

I will instruct you and teach you in the way you should go. I will counsel you with my loving eye on you. —Psalm 32:8

No wonder the church of Christ loved this psalm so much. It spoke of the blessedness of forgiveness long before justification by faith in Jesus was fully revealed. Martin Luther used to say that Paul could have written this psalm. Paul certainly did love this psalm (Rom. 4:6-8).

Psalm 32 says clearly that God forgives by grace, and that sins must be confessed before they can be forgiven. These basic truths, with which every Christian is familiar, were known before Jesus was born.

In the last part of the song, a teacher begins to speak. The teacher may be a father, a mother, an elder, a rabbi, or a pastor, but the voice is really the voice of God. God usually talks to us through people he has chosen for that purpose. This teacher says: "I will instruct you and teach you in the way you should go." Now that you have confessed your sins, now that you have been forgiven, you must learn to live wisely. "I will instruct you."

The teaching is not made up solely of information that must be received; it also includes a way of life that must be learned: "I will teach you in the way you should go." Neither is the instruction a kind of impersonal mass communication: "I will counsel you with my loving eye on you." Some of us remember very vividly when the teacher made us sit in a desk right at the front of the classroom. "I want to keep an eye on you," she said. We didn't appreciate it at the time, but it was certainly good for us.

God's instruction of forgiven sinners must be taken seriously. The usual place where God instructs us in the way we should go, the place where he gives us his personal attention, is the church. Therefore we must be faithful and diligent in our participation in the life of the church.

Every day forgiven sinners need personal tutoring in the way of wisdom. Who is your teacher?

REFLECTIONS

What do you need to ask God to teach you?

On Assuming Office

PSALM 40:1-8

> *Then I said, "Here I am, I have come—it is written about me in the scroll. I desire to do your will, my God; your law is within my heart."*
> —*Psalm 40:7-8*

This is what King David said when he assumed the office of king of Israel. He was Israel's second king. Saul, the first king, had been deposed by God. Saul had thought: "As long as I give sacrifices to God, I can get away with disobedience." But the Lord said: "To obey is better than sacrifice" (1 Sam. 15:22).

When David assumed office, he said: "Sacrifice and offering you did not desire. . . . I desire to do your will, my God; your law is within my heart."

It almost seems that David went too far to the right, whereas Saul had gone too far to the left. After all, nowhere does God say that he is opposed to offerings. God gets angry when people live disobedient lives while trying to pacify their God with sacrifices. He hates the smell of those offerings, as he said repeatedly through the prophets.

But David's words were actually a prophecy. This prophecy was fulfilled when another King accepted his assignment. When Christ came into the world, he said, "With burnt offerings and sin offerings you were not pleased. Then I said, . . . 'I have come to do your will, my God'" (Heb. 10:6-7).

These words do not only reflect the truth David learned, namely, that offerings without obedience are unacceptable to God. They also point to the further truth that sacrifices and sin offerings cannot bring God and people together. Only the atoning death of Jesus could do that. All the sacrifices could not do what Jesus has done once for all.

Now Christ has also made it clear what the relationship between offering and obedience is. Jesus was so faithful to his oath to do God's will that he became a sacrifice to God. His sacrifice was his obedience, and his obedience led to the sacrifice. Today Christ qualifies God's children to assume their offices. They live a life of obedience: "Your law is within my heart." And this total surrender to God is the only sacrifice the Lord desires.

REFLECTIONS

Can you say, with David, "Your law is within my heart"? How is this evident in your life?

Self-Exhortation

PSALM 42

> *Why, my soul, are you downcast? Why so disturbed within me?*
> *Put your hope in God. . . .* —Psalm 42:11

In order to live the life of faith, a person must engage in *self-exhortation* from time to time. You and I must say to ourselves, "Why are you downcast? Put your hope in God."

Some people assume that you have a mental problem if they hear you talking to yourself. They may be correct—if you are the only one you can talk to.

It's not strange at all to talk to your own soul. There are always two in every human breast. One says, "I want," and the other says, "I cannot." One hopes and the other despairs. Even the most mature and integrated Christian adult has to argue with a pagan voice in the depth of his or her being.

Christians must exhort their own souls to live by faith. Before we can speak the Word to others, we should ask for God's strength to keep our own lives under control and set our own spirits at peace. We cannot condemn the disobedience to God in the world around us if we have not learned to condemn the unbelief and rebellion in our own hearts.

A good deal of Christian living must be spent in calling our very selves, our souls, to an awareness of the spiritual realities to which we are naturally blind.

Christians must exhort their own souls to live by faith. It's ridiculous how we can slide into a rut of lackluster living—we who have been chosen by God to share all the riches of his Son! "Why are you sinking, my soul? Take hold of your God!"

We have been assured that God values us more than a flock of birds. Yet not one bird dies without God's permission. How, then, can we sit and worry until we are sick and useless?

Speak to your soul.

Hope in God! For life and death, for bread and butter, for forgiveness and salvation, hope in God!

REFLECTIONS
What do you need to say to your soul today?

God, My Exceeding Joy

PSALM 43

Then I will go to the altar of God, to God, my joy and my delight.
                                                    —Psalm 43:4

Psalms 42 and 43 belong together. Actually they are one song, one cry for intimate communion with God. The writer must have been in exile; oppressed by enemies, banished from his people—and especially from worship of God. He could not go to the temple, the visible dwelling of God.

What passion this man had for God! How he thirsted for communion with the source of his life! For him, faith was not something he possessed in addition to many other faculties; faith in God was the basic function of his being.

The Bible is a difficult book—and not just because it comes from another culture and through ancient languages. It is difficult because it is so utterly God-centered. The people in this book are God-possessed and God-addicted. Such feelings and such behavior make us ill at ease. We'd rather meet "normal" people.

Chances are, however, that the "normal" people whom we call our friends are mixed up when it comes to religion. Very likely they belong to the masses of people who try to fit God into their ordinary lives. But according to the Bible, we must fit our ordinary lives around our faith in God.

If we suddenly discovered that we have it all wrong, would we have the courage to let our lives become unhinged and transformed? That's what conversion is!

We cannot know God or enjoy him unless he is given the place in our lives that fits him. If God is not our all, we'll end up with nothing.

For the people in the psalms (and, let's hope, for all of us—most of the time), God is the highest good. We join them in honoring God, loving God, enjoying God. As long as we are with God, life is good. But without God there is no life.

Such people also long for the pleasure of the future encounter: "Then I will go to the altar of God, to God, my joy and my delight."

REFLECTIONS

Where do you find yourself today: trying to fit God into your ordinary life, or trying to fit your ordinary life around your faith in God? Ask God for the grace to make him your "joy and delight" every day.

Impatient Crossbearing

PSALM 44:17-26

> *Yet for your sake we face death all day long; we are considered as sheep to be slaughtered.* —Psalm 44:22; Romans 8:36

The people of God live under the cross until they are translated to glory. That was already the case in the Old Testament. But the Old Testament saints did not take their beatings lying down. They refused to accept a situation in which the wicked flourish and the righteous get kicked in the teeth.

There were always some sanctimonious preachers among them who would say, "You suffer because you have secretly sinned." When Job's friends said that, he denied it. The singers of Psalm 44 did not accept that explanation either. "We had not forgotten you; we had not been false to your covenant" (v. 17).

No, they said, we have not sinned. *God* is sleeping! "Awake, Lord! Why do you sleep? Rouse yourself! Do not reject us forever!"

We live in different times, because we live in the New Testament. When we read about people who thought that their Lord was sleeping, our thoughts go to the disciples on the lake in the storm. The Lord was sleeping, and the disciples panicked: "Master, Master, we're going to drown!" (Luke 8:24). Christ did sleep, but it was not because of any lack of interest in the disciples. He was giving them an opportunity to exercise their faith.

We know that the Lord is present and that he "neither slumbers nor sleeps." We also know a little better than did our Old Testament brothers and sisters why God's people are now under the cross. We must suffer with Christ if we are to be glorified with him. And although we use their very words for our present situation ("we are considered as sheep to be slaughtered"), we add, "In all these things we are more than conquerors through him who loved us" (Rom. 8:36-37).

God is never absent, and the Lord never sleeps. The cross must be carried, but we have already won—"through him who loved us."

God forbid that we lose the holy impatience of the old saints. We should cry long and loud for God's final action: Maranatha! Maranatha!

REFLECTIONS

When have you felt the impatience described in verses 20-26 of Psalm 44? Have you expressed these kinds of feelings to God? Should you?

A Mighty Fortress

PSALM 46

God is our refuge and strength, an ever-present help in trouble.
—Psalm 46:1

This is a song of faith. The faith is focused on God, who was, who is, and who is coming. He *was* as the Creator (vv. 2-3). Therefore the upheaval of nature need not be feared, though the earth give way, waters roar, mountains quake. This planet belongs to God; God made it. This God is in the history of his people (vv. 4-7). Their city may be attacked, but God is with her. The church may feel the pinch, but she will not perish: "God is within her, she will not fall." Faith rests in the God who was and is and who is coming (vv. 8-11). In the last fearful events of world catastrophe, faith hears the footsteps of the coming Lord and welcomes the arrival of the kingdom of peace.

A mighty fortress is our God! God himself (not thoughts about God or gifts from God) is the only solid and everlasting support on which his people rely.

Many scientists warn that the earth is getting warmer and that the eventual result of this warming will lead to dramatic climate change and the flooding of coastal cities. And we can all observe that our earth regularly gets beaten by hurricanes, earthquakes, and other natural disasters. But faith rests in the God who *was*. The Creator upholds what he has made.

The city of God, the church, is under attack as much as ever before. As Martin Luther wrote: "Did we in our own strength confide, our striving would be losing." But the right Man is on our side.

As for the future, it seems that historical events are now taking place with accelerated speed. These swift changes (within every area and often within one generation) are unnerving, yet comforting. All human supports must fall away. But God is coming. Soon the last tumult will be over. The final broadcast will be interrupted, and the last bomb will have exploded. Then God will disarm all of us: "Be still and know that I am God."

REFLECTIONS

Sing or say the words of Martin Luther's hymn "A Mighty Fortress Is Our God."

Quiet with God

PSALM 62

Truly my soul finds rest in God; my salvation comes from him.
—*Psalm 62:1*

"For God alone my soul waits in silence," says another translation of verse 1. David's soul is still and waits for God alone. By saying that, David gives us an inkling of a struggle that has taken place. But now he has turned to God. He has received inner strength. Now he wants all of us to become quiet with God.

That's why he says, "Pour out your hearts to him" (v. 8). He wants all of us to pray. Not simply: "Let's say grace and get on with the business." No, he says: "*Pour out* your hearts" and find silence with God.

This is not just a psychological truth to the effect that we must "unload" and "find release" for pent-up emotions. It is a *religious* truth. A burdened heart must be emptied before God before it can experience quiet.

We find silence and relief with God, says David, because from God comes our salvation; our hope comes from him. Now that we have unburdened, God will take care of us. Trust in the Lord. Do not expect it from people, because "the lowborn" and "the highborn" are together "only a breath" (v. 9), a puff of air. We must expect all good from God alone.

Theoretically we agree. God must do it. All our solutions come from him. Yet our schedules don't allow much time for prayer. We run and race and talk endlessly with people of high status and people of low status. Even in our work for the church and the kingdom we resemble the always-busy Martha more than Mary, who sat quietly at the feet of Jesus.

We must give a practical demonstration that we know the true value of people, the true value of prayer, and the reality of the peace God gives. That peace does not forbid us to work hard, but it shows up in the way we live and work.

From where does our help come? We must not answer that question by reciting a memory verse. We must answer it through our conduct.

REFLECTIONS

Are you experiencing the peace that comes from "pouring your heart out to God"? Does your busy schedule give you enough "quiet time" with God?

Blessing Has Purpose

PSALM 67

> *May God be gracious to us and bless us . . . so that your ways may*
> *be known on earth.*   —Psalm 67:1-2

Have you ever heard or said a prayer in which God was not asked to bless something or someone? It's unlikely.

Bless is the all-purpose word for our desires in prayer. We ask for God's blessing on things, plants, people, and whatever and whomever we pray for. Bless the food, bless Dad and Mom, bless the garden, homework, schoolwork, teacher, pastor, president, and prime minister.

Suppose we were pressed to explain what we mean by the "blessing" we ask for. Few of us would have more than a vague notion.

Of course it's right to ask for God's blessing, for on that blessing all people and things depend. God's blessing is his favor. The opposite of God's blessing is God's curse. When God blesses someone or something, he is gracious to that person or thing. When God curses someone or something, he turns away from that person or thing; he withdraws his favor. The blessed person finds life's fulfillment. The cursed one is lost and miserable. The blessed land is fruitful but the cursed land is the desert, the badlands.

This psalm asks for God's blessing on Israel. "May God be gracious to us and bless us." But the purpose of the blessing is also mentioned: "so that your ways may be known on earth." If Israel is richly blessed by God, the whole earth will say, "Praise the God of Israel."

The purpose of God's blessing is—ultimately—God's glory. The psalmist does not merely ask for God's blessing because God's favor is so pleasant and prosperity feels so good. His reason for asking is to make God's name known: "May the peoples praise you, God; may all the peoples praise you."

Lord, bless all your people; bless everyone who reads this page. May those who are married have happy marriages and healthy children; may those who are single be blessed with loving friends and companions; may all flourish and have vigorous lives—so that your name may be known in their city and your glory by all who see them.

REFLECTIONS

Offer a prayer of your own along the lines of the one above, asking God for blessings so that his name may be known and glorified.

Gifts from on High

PSALM 68:15-20

When you ascended on high, you took many captives; you received gifts from people. —Psalm 68:18

When he ascended on high, he took many captives and gave gifts to his people. —Ephesians 4:8

You can see the mighty conqueror returning home after the battle. He leads a host of captives, gives a victory parade, and displays the spoils, while the people of the homeland applaud and cheer.

This victory parade refers to God's triumphs in the Old Testament and in the New Testament. In Psalm 68 the Lord subdues nations that did not honor him. These peoples now pay him homage, while God receives their gifts.

But in the New Testament, the victory parade refers to Jesus' ascension into heaven. The battle is finished and he returns to the Father. Christ displays his power when he returns to heaven. He has conquered the evil powers. They are still alive, but they are in chains. They are Christ's captives: "When you ascended on high, you took many captives."

The text in Ephesians says not that the Victor *received* gifts from people but that he *gave* gifts to people. The victorious Christ is now in a position of power from where he can help his people who are still on the battlefield. "And he gave gifts to his people."

In general these gifts stand for the Holy Spirit that Christ gave his people after he had won the battle. And in particular these heavenly gifts are various kinds of power and spiritual support that the Lord gives his church.

The heavenly gifts assure not only the survival but also the victory of God's people. When we, members of the church of Christ, look at ourselves and at each other, we have no hope. We are always divided, and we are frequently disloyal to our Lord. But our strength comes from above, where Christ is. Christ has the armories of God at his disposal. From his endless resources he gives gifts to you and to me. With his supplies, we can endure this lengthy battle. Thanks to his gifts, we shall overcome.

REFLECTIONS

What gifts have you been given to use in God's service?

Prince Shalom

PSALM 72:1-11

In his days may righteousness flourish and peace abound, until the moon is no more.   —*Psalm 72:7, NRSV*

In this prayer we are asking for the kingdom of the prince of peace. Jesus Christ is the prince of peace. We are asking that his kingdom may come.

Notice how the words *righteousness* and *peace* are used. They are parallel words. They mean about the same thing. When you do righteousness, you do what is right. But if you do right, you will find that you cannot keep "peace" with everybody. For instance, if one is to do right to the needy, their oppressors must be crushed (vv. 12-14). And only when justice or righteousness is done to the needy will there be peace. Peace is the state of affairs in which everything is right!

Some Christians think that we may pray this prayer only for the coming of the "spiritual" kingdom of the Lord Jesus. This is a sad mistake. We cannot speak about Jesus today without working for the kind of society that belongs to the prince of peace. The Lord Jesus would not recognize you as one of his own if you weren't committed to the kind of righteousness and peace he died to establish.

All of us must live and work as followers of Jesus Christ, subjects of the prince of peace. For us, politics and evangelism work towards the same goal—the revelation of the kingdom of God. You cannot have peace with God while you quarrel with your wife. And you cannot share in the righteousness of God while you oppress the needy or protect the oppressor. If you are totally committed to Jesus, you are committed to a totally new order.

The new order is coming. We are commanded to pray for its coming. But only our works can show how eagerly we want it to come.

We who belong to Christ must fight battles in our hearts and in the factory. We have to proclaim peace in our homes and in our cities. But we are on the winning team.

REFLECTIONS

Pray that God will help you bring peace to your workplace, your home, and elsewhere in your world.

God and the Gods

PSALM 82

> *God presides in the great assembly; he gives judgment among the "gods."* —*Psalm 82:1*

The "gods" in this psalm are judges and rulers in the present world. Actually there is only one ruler in the present world—our sovereign God. All people are equal before their Maker. Nobody has anything to say over anybody else unless God has given him or her a little bit of *God's* authority.

So all parents, teachers, bosses, but especially judges, kings, queens, and lawmakers hold some authority that they received from God. And those who have the say-so over others are called little gods, because they are to a few what God is to all.

The little gods remain responsible to the one and only God. All the little gods will one day be called on the carpet. This happens in Psalm 82. God will say, "What did you do with the authority I entrusted to you? Did you give justice to the weak and fatherless? Did you rescue the weak and needy from the hand of the wicked?"

Power is abused by those who have totally forgotten where they got it from. Actually, power is a borrowed good; it is a possession that we have only for a little while, and for which we must render account. Power may be used only in the Spirit and according to the Word of him who has all power—God! Therefore the church should issue warnings to the tyrants in the East and the manipulators in the West. God is going to settle the accounts. All nations belong to him. That includes China, the United States, Canada, Iraq, Israel, and every other nation in the world. "Rise up, O God, judge the earth, for all the nations are your inheritance."

Christians have a double duty with respect to the authorities: we must respect and obey them for the sake of him who gave them this power. And without fear we must tell them to exercise their God-given rights according to God's own rules: they must give justice to the weak and maintain the rights of the afflicted.

REFLECTIONS

In what ways can we realistically encourage our national leaders to give justice to the weak and oppressed?

The Universal Church

PSALM 87

Indeed, of Zion it will be said, "This one and that one were born in her. . . ." —Psalm 87:5

Many people—one-third of Americans, according to a recent *USA Today* survey—believe in astrology. It's amazing and sickening. Respected newspapers that can hardly ever find anything "newsworthy" in the work and message of the Christian church would not dare go to press without the so-called horoscopes of their readers.

Astrology says that a person's fate was fixed by the stars at the time of her birth. A similar fatalism is expressed by those who think that parenthood and birthplace determine what we are and limit what we might become.

God is giving a roll call of the citizens in his holy city. Some people are from Babylon, others from Philistia. Both groups are archenemies of Israel. The hatred between them and the people of God is old and deep, and it would seem to be incurable. Blacks from Ethiopia (Cush) are acknowledged, as are seafarers from Tyre. But all these people go through the temple doors. And they are all counted as born in Jerusalem, cradled in the city of God. Never mind the stars, never mind the cities and countries they hail from. The springs of their lives are in Jerusalem.

The vision of this psalm is fulfilled in the one worldwide church of Jesus Christ. This church confesses the miracle of its existence in the hymn "Elect from every nation, yet one over all the earth, her charter of salvation, one faith, one hope, one birth."

By incorporating us into Christ, God has opened our lives to new possibilities of growth that are unknown to the natural mind. We are people whose common allegiance is no longer determined by natural birth but by spiritual birth. We form a new family. We have one Father, and we are each other's brothers and sisters.

The old divisions are stubborn; yet they lose meaning in the church. As citizens of God's kingdom, all of us hold the same birth certificate. We are all traveling on one passport in the same direction—the New Jerusalem.

REFLECTIONS

How do you experience the diversity and unity of the church? Give thanks for the worldwide family of God!

Praise the Lord

PSALM 103:1-5

Praise the LORD, my soul; all my inmost being, praise his holy name. —*Psalm 103:1*

Let us exhort ourselves to praise God, for it is even better to praise than to pray. And praise will outlast our petitions. When the last petition has been granted, we will still thank and praise our God.

Let's praise the Lord and come with thanksgiving before him. Guided by Psalm 103, we look with surprise at the presence of our God. God has not forsaken us but encircles our lives with his loving-kindness. Praise the Lord, my soul. Do it with the *total* person: "*All* my inmost being, praise his holy name."

Forget not "all his benefits" but call them to mind. Our first thought is of God's grace: he "forgives all your sins." God has removed what was between him and us. Our sins are forgiven; life has begun. Praise the Lord, my soul.

Then bless the Lord for life itself. Don't take it for granted. Thank God you are alive. Praise him for health, for renewed strength, for the miracle of returning energy. Health and healing are not nature's laws; they are God's own gifts. Thank God for the gift of a new beginning, fresh vitality for the whole person, day after day. The eagle's pinions have grown again. The everlasting arms have carried us. Praise the Lord, my soul.

We realize our complete dependence on God. We admit that we are entitled to nothing and have received everything. Our "normal" lot consists of sin and sickness and death. But God forgives our sins, heals our diseases, and redeems our lives from the pit. He crowns our lives with steadfast love and mercy. Instead of being left in the misery we deserve, our lives are redeemed, enriched, and renewed. Every day God's faithfulness continues and his mercy is new. Praise the Lord, my soul.

Thanksgiving is better than prayer, although there is a time for both. In prayer I come to God with empty hands, praying to be filled. But in thanksgiving I bring something to God. I may give what I first received.

REFLECTIONS

Let this psalm and this reading inspire your own heartfelt praise to our gracious God.

In God's Covenant

PSALM 103:6-18

> *As for mortals, their days are like grass. . . . But from everlasting to everlasting the LORD's love is with those who fear him . . . with those who keep his covenant. . . .* —Psalm 103:15, 17–18

What thrilling word pictures the Bible uses to describe the grace of God! God's grace is as great as the heavens are high; sin is removed as far as the east is from the west; God's compassions are tender as a father's love for an erring child. After God's grace is revealed in Jesus and his love in his own Son, we are instructed again to measure "how wide and long and high and deep" is the love of God in Christ Jesus. None of us will understand its magnitude by ourselves. We must make an effort to grasp "together with all the Lord's people" the extent and the character of the love of Christ that "surpasses knowledge" (Eph. 3:18-19).

After the psalmist has spoken of the grace of God for sinful people, the picture changes. People are not only sinful, they are also weak. "Their days are like grass." To be sure, there may be beauty and excellence in human life, but it is short-lived—"like a flower of the field." A person's life is soon gone and forgotten. Human life is not only sinful but also very fragile. And it is so short.

However, in this grass-like, flower-like existence, we have come to know the grace of God's covenant, his "everlasting love." Our short and unsteady lives are overarched by the rainbow of God's mercy. This arch spans "from everlasting to everlasting."

God has made a covenant with us and with our children. It is this relationship to the everlasting God, the covenant of grace, that makes life meaningful. Without it, life is grass and flowers. Here today, gone tomorrow. Without covenant life, there is no meaning in human history.

Therefore, if we are to experience real life, we must keep God's covenant. And if there is one thing all of us must remember, it is "obey his precepts."

REFLECTIONS

Try saying what being in God's covenant means to you. Then give thanks.

The Closing Song

PSALM 103:19-22

> *Praise the* LORD, *all his works everywhere in his dominion. Praise the* LORD, *my soul.* —*Psalm 103:22*

If you were brought up in a Christian, perhaps Calvinistic, home, you must have been told often that we live for the glory of God. Your parents said it about play and work, about plants and animals, even about eating and drinking. It's all for God's glory. That's why the world exists. That's the reason people are on this planet. We heard it so often.

We did not dare say it, but to some of us this idea that God has ordained all things to his glory seemed a sort of almighty selfishness. Then we were ignorant. Now we know that God's design is his almighty love.

We are now beginning to understand—a little. We have found that the rare moments when people are genuinely happy are those in which they can spontaneously say, "Praise the Lord, my soul. Let all that is in me adore you." These are the moments in which we have nothing to ask. Our cup is simply overflowing. We bring thanksgiving to God.

The rule is deeply written in human life: we must be unhappy until we find our joy in God. You can see this rule confirmed in the lives of complaining people who are endlessly busy with themselves. As soon as they begin to care for someone else, a bit of a song comes into their lives—the first hint of healing. It is the age-old rule that a person who lives for himself is seeking joy where it can never be found.

Nobody lives unto himself and nobody dies unto himself. Neither people nor angels are independent enough for this kind of life. But I do not live for my neighbor, nor was my neighbor created for me. All of us have been created for God. And it is only when we give ourselves to God that we also find each other. All of life's goals are reached when all places and all people bless the Lord.

Life will end around a throne. The closing song is a doxology. And the art of living is learning the song of glory while we are on our way.

REFLECTIONS

Recall the last time you spontaneously praised the Lord. Are you learning "the song of glory" while on your way to glory?

Christ's Heavenly Ministry

Christ's ministry did not end when he ascended to heaven. The second phase of his work is his heavenly ministry, which he conducts today from the throne of God.

daylight

Christ Is Living

ACTS 1:1-5

> *After his suffering, [Jesus] presented himself to them and gave many convincing proofs that he was alive. He appeared to them over a period of forty days and spoke about the kingdom of God.*
> —*Acts 1:3*

Jesus Christ is living. We know it because the apostles met him after his death. They saw him repeatedly during a period of forty days. They spoke to him, they touched him, and they ate with him. Moreover, he instructed them about the kingdom of God.

The dead are forgotten sooner or later. But the living cross our paths. You may meet the Lord today, for Jesus is alive. Contact with the living Lord is not only possible but unforgettable. Christ is living and he gives life. Fellowship with him is more profound and more enduring than any other relationship.

An old hymn loved by many Christians has this refrain: "You ask me how I know he lives? He lives within my heart." Blessed are the people who have this knowledge. When the living Christ has given us life, we know from experience what Scripture means when it calls Christ the life-giving Spirit (1 Cor. 15:45).

Yet we should not stake the truth of the resurrection on the experience in our hearts. All of us must admit that we have black days when it seems that Christ is dead. Our own heart is not the most reliable witness to the fact that Christ is living.

When asked how we know Christ lives, we answer that we know it primarily because Jesus showed himself alive to people who knew that he had died. In the plan of redemption, forty days were set aside to prepare witnesses to Christ's resurrection. These witnesses became the foundation of the church.

We must not say that we will believe in a living Christ *after* we have experienced his power. The order God has set is that first we must believe and then we will see. Once you have believed the report of the witnesses, you will also experience that Christ is living.

REFLECTION

How do you know that Christ is alive today?

Scriptural Knowledge

LUKE 24:36-48

Then he opened their minds so they could understand the Scriptures. —*Luke 24:45*

During the forty days between Jesus' resurrection and his ascension to heaven, he appeared to his disciples. They could not doubt that he was the same person whom they had known so intimately before his death. They were even allowed to see the scars of his crucifixion to help them believe.

Yet things were different. The blessed closeness they had experienced before had ceased. Jesus did not live with them anymore. Jesus appeared, and they did not know where he came from. He disappeared, and they did not know where he went.

Notice the change in the relationship between Christ and his disciples. True, the familiar tones of tenderness remained. Just think of the way he said "Mary," and "Tell my brothers," and "Peace be with you." But he was majestic. He was transfigured. Christ was at the other side of sorrow and death. And in the disciples we see traces of deeper awe. They say little else but "Master" and "my Lord and my God."

Nevertheless, the disciples became better acquainted with Jesus Christ during these forty days than ever before. During this period he "opened their minds so they could understand the Scriptures." For the first time they began to understand the necessity of his death. They could see that Christ's death was an offering to God, and that the resurrection was God's way of saying that the sacrifice was accepted. The disciples were given a clearer vision of Christ during these occasional appearances than when he was with them day and night. As they listened to the Bible, their communion with Jesus was closer than it had been when they saw him and touched him daily.

Knowledge of Jesus is not dependent on walking where Jesus walked in Galilee and in Jerusalem. Our communion with the risen Lord depends on the measure in which the Scriptures have been opened to us.

REFLECTION

Ask the Spirit to "open the Scriptures" for you as you read them this month.

The Gain of His Going

JOHN 16:1-11

"Very truly I tell you, it is for your good that I am going away."
—*John 16:7*

When Jesus said, "Now I am going to him who sent me," the disciples were sad. They were deeply attached to their Master. But they did not have a deep insight into the nature and scope of his work.

The disciples are a good illustration of the fact that we always misunderstand God's purpose unless we have the Holy Spirit. Only then does God's purpose become our goal. Before Pentecost the disciples merely added to the sufferings of Jesus. After Pentecost they became God's coworkers. A person cannot work for God unless God's Spirit is in him or her.

Therefore it was so very good and necessary that Christ go from earth to heaven—from the battlefield to headquarters. As soon as he had received the powerful position at God's right hand, he was able to give the Spirit to his own. Without this power we remain as aimless as an unattached wheel. But through the Holy Spirit, God's will becomes our will and God's aim becomes ours.

There was an earthly ministry of Christ, and there is a heavenly ministry of our Lord. When he was about to complete his earthly ministry, Jesus prepared his disciples for the second phase. He knew that he would soon be elevated to the throne. And from the throne of God he would send that awesome power called the Holy Spirit, the Comforter or Advocate who wins people for God's cause. According to the divine order, the Holy Spirit would come only after Jesus had gone to heaven.

After the ascension, a new phase in the redemptive work of Jesus began. Christians who are forever hankering for his earthly presence, who talk romantically about Capernaum and the Sea of Galilee, are insensitive to God's progress. We are now better off, and we are now further down the road. It was for our good that Jesus left. But without the light of the Spirit, we can never know how good it is for us and for the world that Jesus is in heaven.

REFLECTION

When you think of Jesus, where do you usually picture him: on earth, walking the streets of ancient Jerusalem? In heaven? At your side? Some other place?

He Must Continue

JOHN 20:11-18

Jesus said, "Do not hold on to me, for I have not yet ascended to the Father. Go instead to my brothers and tell them, 'I am ascending to my Father and your Father, to my God and your God.'"

—*John 20:17*

Mary of Magdala (Luke 8:2) loved Jesus very much. Jesus had done so much for her. No wonder she is at the tomb very early in the morning to finish the embalming. Now she has found the grave open and his body missing. She is utterly confused.

Mary is blind, physically because her eyes are filled with tears, and spiritually because she does not yet believe his resurrection. That's why she speaks to Jesus as if he were the gardener. But when Jesus says her name as only he can say it, the light breaks through the clouds. With a cry of joy she falls at his feet. She must have thrown her arms around the Lord's knees and held him tightly, as one who reclaims a precious possession.

Then the Lord says that she may not hold on to him. Mary does not understand it yet, but things are not the way they used to be. It's going to be better than it was. Jesus is now entering the second stage of his great work of redemption. He is ascending to the Father.

Mary must let go of Jesus, but she may do something for the Lord. And this is only her first little job. In the second stage of the Lord's work, Christ is going to use those who love him in many ways and for many tasks. The message he gives Mary already indicates what he has accomplished by his death and resurrection: the disciples are his "brothers." His God is their God, and his Father is their Father.

But the whole purpose of the Lord's future work, the whole scope of his heavenly ministry, cannot possibly be clear to Mary. She knows that he lives, and she has heard that he must continue his work.

Really she does not have to worry. She may be just a little disappointed that she may not hold on to him now, but Christ is going to a place where he can forever hold on to Mary—and to all those who love him.

REFLECTIONS

In what ways might we still try to hold on to Jesus, as Mary did?

Ascension

LUKE 24:44-53

*Then they worshiped him and returned to Jerusalem with great
joy.* —Luke 24:52

Nearly everyone on our continent knows something about Christ's birth.
Traditionally it is remembered at Christmas. Very few know that the
church has also set aside a day to remember the day when Jesus left the
earth. Very few ever celebrate the ascension.

We are neither surprised nor angry that Christmas attracts more
attention than Ascension Day. That's because of all the festivities connected with Christmas. You couldn't miss Christmas even if you wanted
to. But we should be disturbed about the disregard of Christ's ascension
within the church.

Why is there so little Christian joy about the ascension? There should
be great rejoicing! His descent from heaven marks Christ's humiliation,
but his ascent to heaven stands for his exaltation. Christ's birth was the
beginning of an earthly life that ended in death. But his ascension was
the beginning of a heavenly reign that will end with a complete victory.
What should the church be celebrating?

Once there was a rich man who left twenty-seven unfinished projects.
He showed interest in the beginning, but he paid no attention to the
development of the projects and was unconcerned about their completion.
Many Christians resemble that man. They love the start, but they lose the
thread of the development and are unconcerned about the completion.

Don't we know that Christ's coming to earth and his going to heaven,
as well as the promise of his return, are so many stages in the mighty
movement of God to usher in the kingdom? And if this divine project,
which is full of the love and power and wisdom of God, does not hold our
attention, what else could possibly be worthy of our interest?

The ascension of our Lord is one of the resting points of our Christian
faith and the solid reason for our hope in a bright future. Rejoice! The
Lord is King!

REFLECTION

Reflect on your own attitude toward Ascension Day and the reasons you
have to make it a day of genuine celebration.

End and Beginning

ACTS 1:6-14

> *In my former book, Theophilus, I wrote about all that Jesus began to do and to teach until the day he was taken up into heaven. . . .*
>
> *—Acts 1:1-2*

Luke's first book is known to us as the Gospel of Luke. According to his own words, this first volume of Luke's writings is a record of what Jesus "began to do and to teach." Thereby Luke implies that his second book continues the story of what Jesus did and taught after he was "taken up into heaven."

The first book dealt with Jesus' earthly ministry. This ministry began in a manger and it closed with the ascension. The second book deals with Jesus' heavenly ministry. This heavenly ministry began with the ascension, and it is still going on today as you read these words. That's why Luke's second book (Acts) begins with a more detailed account of the ascension as it describes the unfinished heavenly ministry of Jesus.

Some Christians seem to think that only the gospels (Matthew, Mark, Luke, and John) contain the acts and teachings of Jesus. Perhaps the so-called "red letter" editions of the New Testament have strengthened that notion. It would be a grave error, however, to think that Jesus speaks only in the gospels, while the book of Acts and the epistles tell us what Peter, Paul, and John were doing and teaching. Such an idea would show that we do not understand the relationship between the earthly and heavenly activities of Jesus Christ.

It is the claim of the New Testament that Jesus, after he had completed his earthly ministry, ascended to the throne of the world. From there he continues his work of redemption. The way he continues his work is different from the way he acted during his earthly ministry. But it is Christ himself who continues to work and teach. The works and words of the risen Lord are revealed to us in the part of our Bible that follows the gospels.

First we must know who the Lord is—what he did and what he does. Then we can understand what the Bible is and what the church is.

REFLECTION

Have you thought of the books of Acts as being about Jesus? What difference might this make for your reading of this book?

The Ground That Holds My Anchor

HEBREWS 6:13-20

> *We have this hope as an anchor for the soul, firm and secure. It enters the inner sanctuary behind the curtain, where our forerunner, Jesus, has entered on our behalf.* —*Hebrews 6:19-20*

A ship encounters rough weather far from the shore. It lowers its anchor. While the anchor chain is unwinding, the crew says a prayer that the anchor may take firm hold down in the invisible depth.

This picture is used in our reading from Hebrews. But our anchor does not go down into the invisible depth. The chain reaches into the invisible height. It reaches "behind the curtain," right to the most holy place, the presence of God, "where our forerunner, Jesus, has entered on our behalf." The anchor of our faith lies in the hands of Jesus. His presence with the Father is the ground that holds my anchor. The finished work of Jesus and the ongoing work of our Lord is the only solid ground on which all of our hopes rely.

There's going to be rough weather ahead. We will be tossed and beaten. However, if we have set our hope on the finished work of Jesus and on his present position of power with the Father, we will remain anchored, firm and secure. The certainty of our faith—that everything will work out for good and that, in the last day, we will not be shown up as fools but as victors—lies in Christ's being with the Father. He is the ground that holds our anchor.

A naturalist spotted the nest of a rare bird ten feet down a steep cliff. He said to a boy: "You can earn twenty dollars if you go and get me an egg out of that nest." "I'll do it, sir," the boy replied, "but I want a rope around my middle and I want my father to hold the other end of the rope." Why did the boy want his father to hold the rope? Because he knew very well that his father would never let go. The father would be his anchor.

What is the bottom of our faith? Who is holding the rope? What is the ground that holds our anchor? Millions of people have no sure reliance. But if your anchor is Jesus—his finished work and his present position—you cannot be lost.

REFLECTIONS

What does this reading say to you about your faith, especially when you run into "rough weather"?

The Apostolic Witness

ACTS 1:15-26

> *Therefore it is necessary to choose one of the men who have been with us the whole time the Lord Jesus went in and out among us, beginning from John's baptism to the time when Jesus was taken up from us. For one of these must become a witness with us of his resurrection.*
>
> *—Acts 1:21-22*

Here we have Peter, who is regarded by many Christians as the head of the "Apostolic College," setting forth the qualifications and task of an apostle. What makes an apostle, according to Peter? The qualification is personal knowledge of Jesus' earthly ministry. If you were not there *at that time*, you can be a Christian but you can*not* be an apostle. And what is the work of an apostle? To witness to Christ's resurrection. It's as simple as that.

Later generations have developed complicated theories with respect to the apostolic office. People thought that not only the faith but also the job of the apostles had to be transmitted through the generations. It seems to me, however, that the qualification and task of an apostle could not possibly be passed on to others. Why? Because the apostles had to be eyewitnesses of the fact that Jesus is living. That is why their Master appointed them, and it is very clear from the New Testament that that is how they understood their task.

We should be very careful how we use the word *witness*. It is true that all of us have been appointed by God to bear witness to his power to forgive and redeem. But we should not forget that in the Bible, *witness* is mostly a legal term. In court cases, not everyone who has an opinion about the matter is allowed to be a witness, only those who have seen and heard. The witness is expected to give a simple and straightforward account of the truth, the whole truth, and nothing but the truth. Her personal ideas she may keep to herself, but her witness account is essential to the truth.

Thus the apostles have entered into the courtroom of the world, stating what they have seen and heard. In doing so, they have laid—deep and firm—the foundation of the church in the historical fact of the resurrection of Christ. And all the men and women who "bet their lives" on the truth of this witness are members of the apostolic Christian church.

REFLECTIONS

How does knowing about the apostolic witnesses strengthen our faith?

What Is Christianity?

1 CORINTHIANS 15:1-11

For what I received I passed on to you as of first importance: that Christ died for our sins according to the Scriptures, that he was buried, that he was raised on the third day. . . . Whether, then, it is I or they, this is what we preach, and this is what you believed.
—*1 Corinthians 15:3-4, 11*

Too often Christianity is presented as a set of truths—spiritual, moral, or intellectual.

But Christianity is first of all a set of historical facts: Christ died for our sins. He was buried. He arose. He appeared to the witnesses. If Christianity were a set of moral truths, the apostles should have been moralists. If Christianity consisted of deep spiritual truths, the apostles should have been gurus, examples of spiritual elevation. If Christianity were a set of intellectual truths, the apostles should have been sages, and we should all become scholars.

But the apostles were men who entered into the arena of the world with their testimony to certain facts: "We know it because we saw it. We saw him crucified. We saw his grave. We knew he was dead. Then we saw him alive. We touched him; we heard him. And we, sinners who are telling this to you, went with him to the top of Mount Olivet. And we saw him go up into the skies. We saw it with our own eyes. Do you believe us or not?"

Christianity has many things to offer—a system of truth, a new and radical love, a new view of people and their world, unequaled spiritual experiences, and so on. All of these have been put forward as the essence of Christianity by teachers who were gripped by one aspect or another. And indeed, none of these can be neglected. But the whole of the Christian faith rests on the simple proclamation of the great facts of redemption: Christ came and lived and died for our sins; he was buried and rose again. This is what the apostolic church of all ages preaches. On these facts every believer's faith is founded.

A person may be lacking in the application of the Christian faith to the whole of life and still be a Christian. But to deny the basic facts would be to exclude yourself from the Christian church.

REFLECTIONS

How would you explain "the basics" of what you believe to someone who is not a Christian?

Twelve and Twelve

REVELATION 21:9-14

> *Then they cast lots, and the lot fell to Matthias; so he was added to the eleven apostles.* —*Acts 1:26*

While the disciples were waiting in Jerusalem after the Lord's ascension and before the coming of the Holy Spirit, they elected an apostle to take the place of Judas the traitor.

Many Bible students have criticized the disciples for this action. Their use of lots has been frowned upon by Christians who think there are better ways of finding God's will in important matters. Many critics have said that God disapproved of the choice of Matthias, and that God himself chose Paul as the twelfth apostle. It should be noted, however, that Paul never counted himself among "the twelve," although he insisted that God chose him to be an apostle (1 Cor. 15:5-9). And the Scriptures give us no ground whatsoever for condemning the action of the apostles in completing their number.

Their Lord had left them, and the Spirit had not yet come. During these ten days, the disciples did two things: they persisted in prayer, and they expressed their faith by the election of Matthias. They trusted that their Lord would finish his work. He would "reign over the house of Jacob" (Luke 1:33). He would restore his people Israel. Not only did they trust Jesus to finish his work, they also began to understand their role in the work of Christ. Now it became plain why there had to be twelve apostles. God's people had been founded on twelve tribes; they would be rebuilt on twelve apostles appointed by the Messiah.

The apostles are ready and waiting for the One who will rebuild Jerusalem according to his unfailing promise.

In Revelation 21 we have the vision of the finished work of Christ's Spirit: the radiant beauty of Jerusalem. The twelve names of the sons of Israel are on the gates, and the names of the twelve apostles are on the foundations.

With faith and impatience like that of the apostles, we take our assigned places in God's program, always praying: "Lord and Builder, hurry the work!"

REFLECTIONS

What does the connection between the "twelve" of the gospels and the "twelve" of Revelation tell you about the Bible? About God?

Power Coming

JOHN 1:29-34

For John baptized with water, but in a few days you will be baptized with the Holy Spirit. —*Acts 1:5*

John the Baptist stood on the borderline of two worlds. He was the last prophet of the Old Testament. "All the Prophets and the Law prophesied until John" (Matt. 11:13). As the last one in the row of the prophets, he alone could stretch out his hand and say: "There he is! Behold, the Lamb of God." He concludes the row of all who pointed forward, and he touches the fulfillment of all their prophecy.

When John spoke of the newness that the Messiah was going to bring into the world, he used to say that the Christ would baptize with the Holy Spirit. In this way he explained how his own work was related to the work of Christ. Baptism with water is a necessary counterpart of baptism with the Spirit. We must do away with the old if the new is to enter.

At the same time, John explained that his own work was inadequate—by saying that he could only baptize with water, while the coming One would baptize with the Holy Spirit. After all, what is the advantage to a person and the world if the old is washed away but the new is not received? It is not enough that sins are forgiven if we still remain powerless to do good. The world is not really benefited by the removal of some old sores. What we need is a new power. Not only must we leave the old and crooked path—by repentance and forgiveness—we also need the power to move to a new way, a new future.

No person and no product on earth can supply this new direction. The best intentions of the best people fail because we just don't have the strength to live a different life and the might to create a better world.

But Jesus Christ has that power. He comes to redirect the life of human beings. He not only forgives our wrongs, he also enables us to do what is right. During his earthly ministry, he bore our sins in the flesh. But when he went to heaven, Christ sent the Holy Spirit. Through him a new power comes to the old, tired world. At last, raindrops are falling in the desert.

REFLECTIONS

Do we sometimes tend to downplay the work of the Spirit in our theology and in our lives? If so, why? What happens when we neglect the Spirit?

Ten Days of Waiting

LUKE 11:5-13

> *. . . stay in the city until you have been clothed with power from*
> *on high.* —*Luke 24:49*

God is a God of order. Anyone can observe God's order in creation. First the bud, then the flower, then the seed. The order of the seasons is fixed by divine wisdom. There is order in redemption: the facts of Christ's birth, suffering, death, resurrection, and ascension form an irreversible order. And there is order in the way we receive Christ's benefits: we must hear before we can believe, and we must be born again before we can be mature in Christ. God insists that in the church all things be done "in a fitting and orderly way" (1 Cor. 14:40). Even the resurrection from the dead has order: "Christ, the firstfruits; then, when he comes, those who belong to him" (1 Cor. 15:23).

In the order of God's plan, there had to be forty days between Christ's resurrection and his ascension. During those days, the witnesses were prepared for their task. For forty days, the Lord convinced the apostles that he was alive, and he gave them further instruction about the kingdom of God. But why did God decree a ten-day waiting period between the ascension and the coming of the Spirit?

Christ had told his apostles to tarry in Jerusalem. According to Acts 1:14, "they all joined together constantly in prayer." Ten days of waiting were ten days of prayer. Only then were they "clothed with power from on high."

We Christians constantly tend to forget that God is the source of our strength. We are as busy as all people. We feel that we need leadership and intellect and organizers and planning sessions—until we suddenly realize that we lack power. The kind of power Christians need is not the power of intellect, money, or organization; it is "power from on high." It is the lasting lesson of the ten days: unless we are willing to wait for the Lord and pray for the power from on high, we will accomplish nothing.

REFLECTIONS

What does "waiting for the Lord" look like in your life?

MAY 13

The Coming of the Spirit

ACTS 2:1-13

> *All of them were filled with the Holy Spirit and began to speak in other tongues. . . .*
>
> *"We hear them declaring the wonders of God in our own tongues!"*
>
> —*Acts 2:4, 11*

We are only people of flesh and blood. We cannot know the presence of the Spirit of God unless the Spirit uses signs our human senses can discern. So when God the Holy Spirit came to dwell in his people, he was pleased to show his presence in ways people could observe.

First is the sign that the ear can hear—the sound of a rushing wind. Then the sign that the eye can see—the candle-like flames on all God's chosen ones in the upper room. However, the most convincing sign of the presence of the Holy Spirit is the speech of these people. It seems that all the age-old barriers between the nations have been broken down. One message is heard in all languages. It is the story of the wonderful works of God. One name is proclaimed by every tongue. It is the name of Jesus.

To this day the Spirit chooses many signs to show his presence. It is entirely up to the Spirit to choose the signs. The signs of the Spirit on that first Pentecost (the sound of wind, the tongues of fire, the speech) have never been repeated, as far as we know. Even the sign of tongue-speaking is different from this first Pentecost, when one message was understood in every tongue.

However, there is one sure sign by which we can always determine the Spirit's presence or absence: the Spirit makes the church speak of Christ and causes people to tell the wonderful works of God. This is the token of the presence of the Spirit, and this is the sign of life.

Wherever the Spirit is present, the church speaks with boldness and clarity of its Savior and Lord. Today the name of Jesus is praised in all parts of the world. Everywhere on the globe, the Spirit gives life to people by touching human hearts. And. wherever this happens, people have something to say about the wonderful works of God. If the Spirit is in us, it is not only possible but inevitable that we give glory to Christ.

REFLECTIONS
Where do you see evidence of the Spirit's presence?

The Last Days

ACTS 2:14-24

"In the last days, God says, I will pour out my Spirit on all people."
—*Acts 2:17*

We are living in the last days. In Scripture the entire period of time between the ascension of the Lord and his return in glory is called the last days.

The Bible teaches that this period of time is marked by two features: the people of God will be more richly blessed than ever before, and they will be more severely oppressed than ever before.

The sum of all God's blessings is the indwelling of the Holy Spirit. This is the Old Testament promise for the "last" days, which has now been fulfilled.

When God says that in the last days he pours out the Spirit on all people, the word *all* must not be understood in an absolute sense. When speaking of the Holy Spirit, the Lord Jesus himself said that "the world" cannot receive him (John 14:17). *All* means that the Spirit comes not to the select few, as in the former days, but descends on Jews and Gentiles, men and women, girls and boys.

Since God is now not only *above* us but also *for* us and even *in* us, we live in closer communion with the everlasting God than anyone in former days. If we are spiritually poor today, we have nobody to blame but ourselves. The heavens have been opened and our Savior has gone in. The gates have opened and the Spirit has come down. Now we live under an open heaven. The Spirit's comfort is here, and only our blindness can make us miss it. If we lack the power of the Spirit, it is because of our unbelief. We are now surrounded by God. Every day of our lives we stand in the sunshine of the grace of Jesus Christ, the warmth of the love of God, and the fruitful fellowship of the Holy Spirit.

We must now enter into the full wealth of these last days. Ask for all of it, and it will be given you. Today every ordinary Christian can have the power of God.

REFLECTIONS

To what extent do you sense that "we are now surrounded by God"? Ask God today for the full power and comfort that only the Spirit can provide.

The Spirit's Sermon

ACTS 2:25-36

"Therefore let all Israel be assured of this: God has made this Jesus, whom you crucified, both Lord and Messiah."　　　*—Acts 2:36*

We are inclined to think that Acts 2, the chapter on the first Pentecost, should explain who the Holy Spirit is, what the Spirit does, and how the Spirit works. However, what the first sermon on the first Pentecost explains is not who the Spirit is but who Jesus is. And that is exactly the whole aim of the Spirit: to tell us who Jesus is for us. Unless the Spirit tells us, we will never know.

The last words of Peter's sermon form the thrust of the Spirit's spear aimed at the heart of Israel. "All Israel"—the priests, the rulers, and all the people are summoned by this proclamation to acknowledge Jesus. For Jesus is *Lord*, the One who, according to the psalmist, would share God's glory. And the prophet declared that whoever called on *Jesus'* name would be saved. Moreover, Jesus is *Christ*. The Jewish word for Christ is *Messiah*. Jesus was the One for whom the Fathers hoped and Israel longed. But Israel had opposed its Lord and crucified the Messiah. The barbs on the spear shaft are in those three words *whom you crucified*.

In this speech the apostle Peter rose to the full height of his great commission. Without fear he proclaimed the lordship of Jesus and accused his nation of the crime of the crucifixion. A few weeks before, the same man had cowered before the saucy tongue of a servant. There is no other explanation for the change than the fact of the resurrection and the coming of the power from on high.

Let us firmly believe what the Spirit can and will do. All of us should quit being impressed with the power of thought and the power of money and the power of people. In answer to our prayers, God will grant us the power of the Spirit. He will impress on us that Jesus is the only Lord. And when that fact has fully entered our consciousness, we will live without fear, in sheer dependence on God's favor in Christ Jesus.

REFLECTIONS

As you feel led to do so, pray for an increased presence of the Holy Spirit in your life, particularly in those areas where you sense you are weak.

Joining the Church

ACTS 2:37-42

> *"Brothers, what shall we do?" Peter replied, "Repent and be baptized, every one of you, in the name of Jesus Christ for the forgiveness of your sins. And you will receive the gift of the Holy Spirit."*
> —*Acts 2:37-38*

When they had heard the gospel, many people replied: "What are we to *do*?" Whenever the call of the gospel has penetrated our hearts, we are bound to ask: What is my duty with respect to Christ? What am I to *do*? Unless our conscience reacts in such a way, we have been superficial listeners. People who hear the gospel year after year but have nothing to say except that it was a good or a bad sermon have never really heard the Spirit speak.

"Repent!" Repentance begins when we are sorry for our sins. Repentance takes hold of us when our hearts turn away from the former love and practice of evil and turn to God and Christ.

"Be baptized!" Christian baptism is the visible expression of our relationship to Christ and Christ's to us. All Christians agree that baptism is the door through which we enter into the fellowship of those who belong to Jesus Christ. Christians differ on the question whether the sons and daughters of believers should be baptized. The record does not indicate whether the children of those who repented and believed were received into the new fellowship. In view of verse 39, I think it is unlikely that they were excluded.

The forgiveness of sins is connected with baptism and repentance. Forgiveness is by grace but not by ritual. The water of baptism makes visible what Christ gives to those who repent and believe.

The gift of the Holy Spirit is for all Christians. The Spirit gives a new kind of life to all repentant sinners when they turn to Christ. You cannot be baptized in Christ without being baptized in his Spirit, for where the Lord is, there is his Spirit.

All these requirements and benefits of church membership are as real today as they were when Peter made his proclamation.

REFLECTIONS

Frame a prayer around each of the requirements and benefits of church membership found in today's Scripture and reading.

Communion of Goods

ACTS 2:41-47

They sold property and possessions to give to anyone who had
need. —*Acts 2:45*

Christians have been quick to point out that the Bible teaches the right to
private property. Correctly so. Even the early experiment of the believers
in Jerusalem in sharing goods did not blunt their sense of the God-given
right of possession. The apostle Peter himself said that people did not have
to give away their possessions: "Didn't it belong to you before it was sold?
And after it was sold, wasn't the money at your disposal?" (Acts 5:4).

Indeed, there is a deep difference between materialistic communism
and the Christian view of property. The communist says, "All yours is
mine," while the Christian says, "All mine is yours." These viewpoints
are radically opposed.

Some Christians believe that the members of the early church made
a mistake in sharing their possessions—a forgivable error, to be sure, in
view of the first thrill of the new life, but an error nevertheless. They
remind us how the apostle Paul had to take up a collection among the
converted Gentiles for the poverty-stricken church in Jerusalem. "That's
what you get," they say, "if you don't keep something for a rainy day, if
you spend it all as soon as the Holy Spirit is poured out."

However, we should be able to say something more positive than that
this sharing was not materialistic communism. And the common-sense
remark about a rainy day does not sound very convincing to those who
are standing in the rain of the Spirit.

There is a lasting lesson and an abiding norm in this practice of the
early Christians. When the Spirit of God moved these people to sell
their possessions and distribute the proceeds among all those who had
need, God himself was teaching the church of all ages that Christians
must forever be more concerned about each other than about their own
possessions.

REFLECTIONS

How are you putting people ahead of your possessions?

Where to Look

ACTS 3:1-12

> *Peter looked straight at him, as did John. Then Peter said, "Look at us!"* . . .
>
> *"People of Israel, why does this surprise you? Why do you stare at us as if by our own power or godliness we had made this man walk?"*
> —*Acts 3:4, 12*

Members of the church of Christ spend much time staring at each other. When they gather for worship, many people cannot see Christ because they see too much of each other. And in many conversations of Christian people, the talk is focused on preachers and other leaders as a safe substitute for a focus on Christ. People look too much at each other. We would benefit greatly from more upward focus.

When Peter said to the man who was lame, "Look at us!" it was to fix his attention on the fact that he and John were only men—and poor men at that. They wanted him to understand that if he were helped, it was not because Peter and John were there but because the Lord was living.

When the crowd had gathered, eager for a sensational miracle, Peter said they were staring at the wrong people. "Why do you stare at us?" The person who was really at work there was the same one they had denied before Pontius Pilate (v. 13). This healing was nothing more than the ongoing ministry of the living Jesus.

"Acts of the Apostles" is a poor title for a book that describes what the Lord Jesus did from the throne. Acts is about Jesus, just as Luke's first book is a record of what Jesus did before he ascended to the throne. So please don't read the book of Acts thinking, "I wish we had such heroes in the church." Instead, think, "This is the kind of Lord we have in the church."

There are at least two ways of looking at the church. The usual way is the wrong way. It takes faith to see how "the Son of God, through his Spirit and Word . . . gathers, protects, and preserves for himself a community chosen for eternal life" (Heidelberg Catechism, Answer 54).

If our eyes are wide open to what the Lord is doing, we join the former man who was lame in his praises to God. But if we merely stare at each other, we form a society as good and as bad as any other.

REFLECTIONS

What kinds of things happen at church that might tempt us to look more at people than at Jesus?

The Spirit Is Fire

ACTS 5:1-11

When Ananias heard this, he fell down and died. . . . At that moment she fell down at [Peter's] feet and died. —Acts 5:5, 10

Pentecost means that God the Holy Spirit came to dwell in his people. From that day on, the God of Israel and the Father of Jesus no longer lives in a locality defined by a tent or by walls but in the congregation of Jesus Christ. The people of God form the temple of God.

We must be deeply aware of this truth. And we must always fight the tendency to make church buildings more and more heavenly at the cost of church people, who become more and more worldly. God resides in his people. We are God's temple.

The Old Testament already said that when God comes to his temple, he will be like "a refiner's fire and launderer's soap." And "who can endure the day of his coming?" (Mal. 3).

That's why God's coming to his people, as described in Acts, shows not only his power to heal but also the terror of his judgment. Not only do we see the lame man leap (Acts 3), we also see liars fall dead. When the Holy One has moved in, whatever is unholy must be burned out.

The church has always wanted God to reveal his presence among us in the same way he revealed it in the early days. We do not quite know what we are asking. We long for that miraculous, almost delirious power. We tend to forget that when God reveals his might, he does so for the glory of his name. We forget that God's might brings judgment and salvation. That's a rule without any exceptions.

It was not really such a big sin, the lie of Ananias and Sapphira. It was certainly not "blasphemy against the Spirit" (Matt. 12:31). They lied because they were concerned about their own name. They stole from the glory of God. A small sin by our standards. But when we live on holy ground, every sin must be burned away. Nothing unholy may enter the temple of the Lord. We cannot take salvation seriously if we do not take sin seriously.

REFLECTIONS

When, if ever, have you felt something of "the fear of the Lord"?

Jesus and His Church

ACTS 9:1-9

"Saul, Saul, why do you persecute me?"   —*Acts 9:4*

I have used the word *church* quite frequently this month. This word cannot be avoided when we think of the heavenly ministry of Jesus. The church is the people among whom Christ is present by his Word and Spirit after his ascension. Jesus loves these people and he identifies with his church.

The Lord did not say to Saul: "Why are you persecuting my church?" What he said was: "Why do you persecute *me*?" Jesus identifies with his church. An attack on the church is an attack on Jesus.

Saul, who was later named Paul, thought that Jesus was dead. He thought that the disciples were spreading a new teaching, a teaching dangerous to the Jewish faith. Actually, it was the living Lord who was continuing his own work through his Spirit and by his followers. When Saul lifted up his hand against the Lord's followers, the Lord stayed his hand and changed his life.

Any husband jealously defends his wife, or he is no husband at all. "If you touch her, you touch me." The Scriptures say that the unity between husband and wife is but a shadow of the unity between Christ and his church.

This means that every other human organization is well advised to keep its hands off the church. Let nobody abuse any function assigned to him within the church by Christ. The Lord will guard his rights as owner and lover: "If you touch her, you touch me."

What a comfort! And what an obligation! Anyone who comes close to us, to the members of Christ's body, enters the presence of the living Lord.

Our highest ambition is to be counted with the people of God. God's cause is our cause, and his will is our command. Christ's Father is our Father, his enemies are our enemies, and his home will be our home. We identify with Christ because he has made us his own.

REFLECTIONS

In what ways do you identify with Christ?

Grieving the Spirit

EPHESIANS 4:25-32

> *And do not grieve the Spirit of God, with whom you were sealed for the day of redemption.* —*Ephesians 4:30*

We can insult a stranger, but we can only grieve someone who is close to us. To grieve means to cause pain or sorrow. This is the grave responsibility of a love relationship: a son can bring more joy to his mother than any stranger can, but he can also hurt her more than any other boy. Due to their unique and intimate relationship, a husband and his wife can bring more happiness to each other than anybody else this side of heaven—but they can also cause each other more pain than anything or anybody this side of hell.

Closer than a son to his mother and closer than a wife to her husband is the Holy Spirit to the children of God. That's why Paul tells us not to grieve the Spirit.

How do we grieve the Spirit?

We grieve the Holy Spirit whenever we go against his purpose: to devote our lives to the glory of God. He wants to write the glorious name of Jesus throughout our days. And when we do not want that, when we suppress the Spirit and insist on writing our own name and doing our own will, we grieve the Spirit of God.

We grieve the Holy Spirit if we do not want to read the Bible, for it is *his* book. We hurt the Spirit of God if we do not care about the church and its mission, for the church is *his* temple and its mission *his* work. We cause pain to God's Spirit if we do not want to pray, for *he* came to teach us how to say, "Abba, Father."

Here we sense what sin is for a Christian. It is not merely breaking a rule in the book. It means grieving the Holy Spirit, hurting the heavenly Father.

We, who are so sensitive—perhaps overly sensitive—to the hurt caused by those we love, must be more sensitive to the hurting love of God's Spirit. And we must praise the superhuman patience of God, who has not divorced us from his Spirit.

REFLECTIONS

If you grieved the Spirit in some way that's now obvious to you, bring it to your forgiving Father in prayer. And praise God for being so patient with all of us sinners.

The Sealing of the Spirit

2 CORINTHIANS 1:18-22

He . . . set his seal of ownership on us. . . .

—*2 Corinthians 1:21-22*

We must not grieve the Holy Spirit, for in him we are "sealed for the day of redemption" (Eph. 4:30). God has sealed us by giving us the Spirit (2 Cor. 1:22). We have received the Spirit as God's seal.

A seal is a mark of ownership. Today people are still finding ancient jars and vessels with the seal of an owner who lived long ago. In a similar way we place our name or stamp in a book to mark it as our property. Not only the sealing of things but also the sealing of persons is common in the Bible. The best example is the sealing of the 144,000 in Revelation 7. It means that God puts his mark of ownership on them. He writes his name on them. They are his. Therefore they may not be hurt in the last judgment.

Also, baptism "in the name of" the Father, the Son, and the Holy Spirit is a kind of marking of a person as the property of God.

When God redeems a person, that is, when he *buys that person back*, he pays with the price of his Son. We were redeemed not with gold or silver "but with the precious blood of Christ" (1 Pet. 1:18-19). After paying so dearly, God does not want that person to get lost again. He seals that child not by a visible mark but by giving the Holy Spirit as a constant companion. In that way we are "sealed for the day of redemption."

Maybe it takes more power to *keep* a person with Christ than to *bring* him to Christ. At least, that's the way it often looks to us. At first there are so many good intentions, but we fail to fulfill them. There are so many brand-new feelings, but they evaporate.

Where is the staying power, the strength to hold on and stick it out? The Holy Spirit is that power. The Spirit makes the lordship of Christ real in our lives and establishes us in an everlasting relationship to our heavenly Father. He cannot and will not disown us. He marks us as God's own—now and in the last day.

REFLECTIONS

Where in your life, right now, do you especially need the staying power of the Holy Spirit, the "strength to hold on and stick it out"?

The Spirit as Guarantee

2 CORINTHIANS 5:1-5

Now the one who has fashioned us for this very purpose is God, who has given us the Spirit as a deposit, guaranteeing what is to come. —2 *Corinthians 5:5*

The Spirit here is called a "deposit." In everyday language we would call it a down payment. By making a down payment, we mean to say that we are going to complete the transaction. So when we put money down on, say, a house, we are telling the seller that we are a serious buyer. The down payment is a kind of guarantee that we'll live up to all future obligations.

The Holy Spirit is God's initial fulfillment of all his promises. God is going to give us a new and better life in a new and better body on a new and better earth. That's the extent of his promise. Most of it is still in the future. But one installment has already been paid: the Holy Spirit has come. This down payment is God's guarantee that all the rest is coming.

The Holy Spirit is the connection between this life and the life to come. It is the one gift in the present world that has come from the future world. That's why the Spirit cannot possibly feel at home in the present world. He is "otherworldly." He is constantly at war with the present lords and the present powers. Restlessly the Spirit strives to bring all thoughts and words and actions under the dominion of the Lord of lords, the King of kings.

By the Spirit we have the beginning of the future, and through the Spirit God prepares us for the future. When we finally come to God's new world, it will be a new kind of existence, an existence quite different from what we have now. But whatever we have already received from the Spirit of God goes with us.

For the present we have the treasure of the Spirit in an earthen vessel. That is to say, our whole environment and our whole persons have not yet adopted the tone and color of the kingdom. In fact, sometimes we almost despair of seeing the kingdom become real. But the Spirit himself is the guarantee. God does not stop with the first installment.

REFLECTIONS

How is the Spirit preparing you for the future, when you finally come to God's new world?

Between Two Comings

TITUS 2

> *For the grace of God has appeared . . . training us . . . to live sober, upright, and godly lives in this world, awaiting our blessed hope. . . .* —*Titus 2:11-13, RSV*

We live between Christ's coming in grace and his coming in glory. These two great events, one past and the other future, determine the way in which we live "in this world."

The grace of God in Christ has appeared already. God's grace did not "appear" only to "disappear" again; it continues to instruct or train us in living. And the glory, although it has not yet appeared, is already attracting us. That's why it is called "our blessed hope."

The grace of God teaches us how to live in the present. It is "training us . . . to live sober, upright, and godly lives in this world." The words *sober, upright,* and *godly* describe three aspects of our Christian behavior. *Sober* is a description of our personal ethics. *Upright* says how we behave in relation to our neighbors. And *godly* is a form of life that results from fellowship with God. None of these virtues is acquired by self-development. It is the "grace of God" that "trains" us to live in a sober, righteous, and godly manner in this present world.

Let's pay special attention to the word *sober.* The word recurs in this chapter (vv. 2, 4, 6, 12) and throughout the New Testament. *Sober* is the opposite of drunk or intoxicated. In this present world, everyone is in danger of becoming intoxicated by the things of this world. When we are sixteen, we are under the influence of different things and powers than when we are sixty. But the effect of the powers is equally intoxicating. Love, popularity, and possessions can make a person drunk.

We are trained, by the grace of God, to remain sober, that is, to retain a sense of direction in the midst of all the attractions, diversities, and adversities of the present world. The Spirit of Christ won't let us forget that we live our lives between the coming of grace and the coming of glory.

REFLECTIONS

What does "sober" (in the sense used in this reading) look like in your life?

Christian and the Spirit

ROMANS 8:9-11

> *And if anyone does not have the Spirit of Christ, they do not belong to Christ. But if Christ is in you, then even though your body is subject to death because of sin, the Spirit gives life because of righteousness.* —Romans 8:9-10

The New Testament teaches that anyone who is in Christ has the Holy Spirit. Those Christians err who think that they first have to believe in Christ and later will receive the Holy Spirit as a higher rung on the ladder.

It's true that some Christians are closer to Christ than others, and some are more yielded to the Spirit than others. "Having the Spirit" is not the same as "being filled with the Spirit." If we are made alive by the Spirit we haven't necessarily learned to walk by the Spirit.

But nobody can be in Christ unless he or she has the Holy Spirit. In fact, the only sure way of finding out whether people have the Spirit is to ask them what they think of Jesus Christ (1 Cor. 12:3; 1 John 4:2).

Sometimes the Bible uses the names of Christ and the Holy Spirit interchangeably. That happens in the part of Romans 8 we just read. "The Spirit of God in you" or "Christ in you" stands for the same reality. It means that we have gone over from a state of death to a state of life. To be sure, our "bodies" are still subject to death. Our present form of existence is not yet beyond the reach of sin and misery. At the same time we are alive. That new life comes to us from Christ, who died and rose again. The new life is in us through the Holy Spirit.

It is this daily living and daily dying that makes the Christian life so intense and sometimes so difficult. We must never be satisfied with what we have, spiritually, for as long as we are in this body we have not yet arrived. There is always more to unlearn and to learn. We must lose more of the old self so that we may gain more from God.

However, let's not confuse each other by separating the work of Christ from the work of the Spirit. Growing up in Christ and living by the Spirit is the same thing. And it's worth everything.

REFLECTIONS

"We must never be satisfied with what we have, spiritually." What does this mean for you personally?

Variety of Gifts

ROMANS 12:3-8

> *For just as each of us has one body with many members, and these members do not all have the same function, so in Christ we, though many, form one body. . . .* —Romans 12:4-5

The exalted Lord Jesus has given many gifts to his church. In a few Bible passages we find lists of these gifts: prophecy, speaking in tongues, healing, serving, teaching, and so on. These lists are not identical, and they are not exhaustive. They are not intended to be a complete inventory of the spiritual possessions of the early Christians.

The gifts differ considerably. To our mind they also differ in nature: "speaking in tongues" makes us think of a sudden overpowering by the Spirit, but when the gift of administration is mentioned, we tend to think of a natural ability. And when Paul includes even church officers in the list (Eph. 4), we are more apt to think of human appointment than of heavenly equipment. But the Scriptures want us to know that all these gifts are endowments of Christ. They come from heaven because they come from the Lord. They are heavenly graces or *charismata* that the Lord, or the Spirit, freely gives.

All these gifts, as varied as the functions of a human body, have but one purpose—building the body of Christ. They have no value in themselves. They become valuable when they are used. And the most valuable gifts are the ones that are most suitable for building the church of God.

We may not be proud of our gift or jealous of the grace given to another (v. 3). Certainly we may never make our special gift a standard for being a Christian. Nobody may say: "Since I speak in tongues and you don't, you are not a Christian." Or, "Since I am a teacher and you are not, you do not belong to the body." These special gifts of the Holy Spirit are given by the Lord according to the need of the hour, according to the prayers of Christians, and according to his sovereign pleasure. A measure of discussion is required so that we may know how to ask. Yet Christ's gifts must not be discussed too much. They must be used.

REFLECTIONS

What special gifts has Christ given you? How are you using his gifts to build up the body of Christ?

Abiding Gifts

1 CORINTHIANS 13

> *And now these three remain: faith, hope and love. But the greatest of these is love.* —*1 Corinthians 13:13*

The Lord Jesus gives many special gifts to his people. These gifts are richly varied and sovereignly bestowed. Yesterday we read about them.

However, next to these *special* gifts of the Holy Spirit there are also certain abiding gifts the Spirit gives to *every* Christian. These are faith and hope and love, sometimes called the three gifts that "abide" ("So faith, hope, love abide," RSV). *Abiding* gifts are gifts that endure, that remain.

The special gifts may never be used as a criterion for being Christian. Nobody may say, "Since you do not speak as I speak or teach as I teach, you are not a Christian." But of the abiding gifts it may be said, "If you don't have these, you aren't a Christian." A Christian has faith and hope and love—these three.

Faith is the means through which we receive Christ and all his benefits. Although it is a human activity, it is a gift of the Holy Spirit. That's what makes us so grateful and so humble about having faith in Christ.

Hope is the same thing as faith—but with a view to the future. It is the expectation of things to come—the kingdom, the great change, the completion, Christ himself. A church that does not live in expectation is no church.

"But the greatest of these is love." By faith we receive him, and by hope we stretch ourselves out to him, but in love Christ himself is present among us. Wherever there is Christian love, the presence of God has become a reality.

The value of all gifts must be measured by their usefulness for church-building. No wonder, then, that love is the greatest. Love is the cement that unites the members. Love is the Spirit of Christ putting us in his service for the glory of God and the benefit of others.

Next to these three gifts, a church and a person may possess other gifts. That is not only common but necessary. But faith, hope, and love—these three abide; and the greatest of these is love.

REFLECTIONS

Pick one of the three abiding gifts and reflect on its meaning for your life as a Christian.

The Stature of Christ

COLOSSIANS 1:15-20

He is before all things, and in him all things hold together. And he is the head of the body, the church; he is the beginning and the first-born from among the dead, so that in everything he might have the supremacy. —*Colossians 1:17-18*

It is impossible to exaggerate the importance of Jesus of Nazareth. In our process of getting to know him, we usually begin with his earthly ministry. Then we must learn to make the connection between his earthly ministry and his heavenly ministry. The same Jesus who was robbed of his clothes and executed on a cross is the One who broke the dictatorship of the prince of this world. We must learn to know him as the One who is now in charge of God's armories. We must believe and experience that he can supply every need of ours, far above what we can pray or desire.

But when we have said this, we have not yet said enough. We must learn to make a connection between Jesus and the world as it existed long before he entered it as a baby. He was "before all things." He existed with God long before his earthly ministry. When the almighty speech of God created the universe, Christ was the heart and harmony of that order. Apart from Christ, the harmony of the created order disintegrates, loses coherence, is void of meaning. For "in him all things hold together." The implications are far-reaching: Jesus, who is the heart of the cosmos, is also the head of the church.

Christ, this divine person, entered into creation when it was falling apart. From the side of the Creator he came to the side of the creature. In his earthly ministry, he allowed the disintegrating forces of sin and death to spend themselves on him. By his death he turned the tide. And he emerged as the new "beginning." He gave the whole world a new direction. Leaving the tomb and entering glory, he represented a new creation, a whole reordering of life in which Christ has supremacy.

Please don't say this is too difficult. It is so tremendously profound that it's worth an hour's meditation, a life of devotion, an eternity of praise.

REFLECTIONS

Perhaps this Scripture and reading opened some new windows for you on who Jesus is and what he did. Meditate on it for a while—you don't have to put in a whole hour, but let its far-reaching truths sink in. Then praise God.

Total Warfare

2 CORINTHIANS 10:1-6

The weapons we fight with are not the weapons of the world. On the contrary, they have divine power to demolish strongholds. We demolish arguments and every pretension that sets itself up against the knowledge of God, and we take captive every thought to make it obedient to Christ. —2 Corinthians 10:4-5

Here is a description of the nature and power of preaching. The word of the gospel is in the first place a call to repentance and an announcement of salvation in Christ. That word has the power to bring about conversion and salvation because it is the Word of God.

But the gospel is more than the call for repentance and faith. It is also the power to prick the balloons of human reasoning and the artillery that wrecks the forts of human pride. In fact, the gospel will not only expose the folly of human-centered thought, it will take these thoughts captive to obey Christ.

Christians have not always paid attention to the wider implications of the gospel. Too often they have regarded the gospel as a message through which peace was restored between the soul and God. They have not always sensed its power to affect the thought patterns that rule the university and the ideas that shape the struggle in the field of labor relations. We must be aware that our attitudes towards sex and money, science and warfare, have everything to do with our faith in Jesus Christ as the beginning of a new order of things. And this reordering of thoughts and attitudes is brought about by our listening to the gospel.

When Christian warriors enter these different fields and areas, they must not switch weapons. In academic life they will be tempted to rely on logic; to lean on oratory when they turn to politics; to think in terms of worldly power when in business. But "the weapons we fight with are not the weapons of the world." The reordering of thoughts and attitudes is brought about by the Word of God.

Just as the original creation was made by God's speech, so the new order is called into being by the Word of Christ. This gospel must be proclaimed by God's people—not just *extensively*, that is, over the whole earth, but also *intensively*, to every part of life.

REFLECTIONS

Pick an area of your life such as working or parenting or studying or using your leisure time. How could the transforming power of the gospel be more evident in that part of your life?

He Has the Keys

REVELATION 1:9-18

> *When I saw him, I fell at his feet as though dead. Then he placed his right hand on me and said: "Do not be afraid. I am the First and the Last. I am the Living One; I was dead, and now look, I am alive for ever and ever! And I hold the keys of death and Hades."*
> —*Revelation 1:17-18*

We are all going to die. Unless Christ returns within the next hundred years, all the readers of this page will have died. Perhaps you find this thought appalling. Maybe it is an unnecessary reminder. But nobody can deny that it is realistic.

Death is our constant companion, although we never get used to him. When people speak of death as their friend, they are not quite healthy anymore. Death is our enemy (1 Cor. 15:26), whatever else we Christians have to say about him. Thank God, we can say more.

Death is a dark curtain, and nobody can see through it. It is a high wall, and nobody can look over it. The older we get, the greater the number of people we used to know who have vanished behind that curtain. Nobody has returned.

Only one man went that way and returned. His name is Jesus. He now crosses our paths because he is in the land of the living. He comes to us while we are still on our way. And he laid his hand on John's head, an infinitely gentle gesture. "Do not be afraid. I am the First and the Last. You have to die, but I was dead and I live. When you have to go through the gate, do not be afraid. I have been there. And I have the keys."

Jesus speaks as the One who has conquered death in death's own realm. And he has every right to speak that way. He is forever beyond the dominion of death, but death is not outside Christ's dominion. That's what he means when he says: "I hold the keys." His authority extends behind the dark curtain.

As far as we can see, the righteous and the unrighteous leave this life through the same gate. They disappear behind the same wall. But we have heard the Word and received the Spirit of Jesus Christ. Therefore we walk our way with confidence. Even when we have to take that last step, we hear his voice: "Do not be afraid. I hold the keys."

REFLECTIONS

Reflect on your own attitude toward death. What are you afraid of? What comforts you?

The End of Christ's Ministry

1 CORINTHIANS 15:20-28

Then the end will come, when he hands over the kingdom to God the Father after he has destroyed all dominion, authority and power. For he must reign until he has put all his enemies under his feet. —*1 Corinthians 15:24-25*

This month we have been reading and thinking about the heavenly ministry of Jesus. Finally we want to observe that this heavenly ministry has a goal. When that goal has been reached, Jesus' ministry will cease.

The goal of Christ's work is the kingdom of God. For that purpose he came to earth, and for that goal he works from heaven. When that kingship of God is fully established, God the Father will receive all honor. He will be "all in all" or everything to everyone. Then Christ himself will cease his royal work like a general who retires after the campaign is over.

When Jesus Christ transfers the kingdom to the Father, he will have destroyed every dominion and every authority and every power; that is to say, he will have destroyed all the forces that are still resisting the sovereignty of God. One of those evil powers is mentioned by name—death. Christ will take care of this enemy as the last item on his agenda.

The Bible does not explain how the different powers in this world ever got into evil hands. But we know that they are in the wrong hands, and we also know how we will get rid of evil. Jesus has done it by his earthly ministry, and he is doing it by his heavenly ministry. Christ is reestablishing God's power throughout the cosmos. The end will be upon us when he says to his Father: "Now all things are yours. The whole cosmos is subject to you."

Then there will be rest—eternal rest. A Sabbath without end. An enjoyment of the goodness of God without boundaries or limitations. No sin, no pain, no battle. At last we will be free, and finally we will have rest.

Christ is in command until the battle is over. Let's be loyal to him. It can't last long anymore.

REFLECTIONS

Reflect on what "an enjoyment of the goodness of God without boundaries or limitations" might be like. Then read 1 Corinthians 2:9 and give thanks.

Grace Must Flow

Once we receive God's grace, we become channels through which grace reaches others. We are saved by grace only if we know for what purpose we are saved.

daylight

Saved by Grace

EPHESIANS 2:1-7

It is by grace you have been saved. —*Ephesians 2:5*

We must know *if* we are saved, and we must also know *how* we are saved.

When the question "How were you saved?" is asked, we must not give such unimportant answers as, "By meeting that person," or "By undergoing that surgery," or "By listening to that preacher." These details may be important for our personal files and friends, but such answers should not be the topics for speeches, books, or songs.

When the question "How were you saved?" is asked, we should all be able to answer: "By grace!" That's an important answer. And a worthy topic for a speech or a book or an eternal song.

"By grace" means that we did not save ourselves. *God* saved us through Jesus Christ. With Christ I died, and with Christ I arose. That's how I was saved, and that's how you were saved—or you are not saved at all.

"Grace" is God's unmerited favor. We did not get what we deserved. In fact, we got exactly the opposite of what we deserved.

"By grace" means that salvation is free—not cheap, of course, but a gift nevertheless. God's way of salvation makes a joke of all human efforts and all do-it-yourself religions. We are saved by grace, through faith in Christ—or we are lost.

If you have to explain to someone what you mean by the grace of God, you find yourself talking about Jesus. You can't help it. Why? Because God's "great love for us" (v. 4) has been completely revealed in the saving work of Jesus Christ.

We were saved because Christ represented us in his death and in his resurrection. Grace wiped out our sins on Good Friday, and God's grace "made us alive with Christ" on the first day of the week.

REFLECTIONS

What does it mean for your daily living that you are "saved by grace"?

Renewed by Grace

EPHESIANS 2:4-10

> *For we are God's handiwork, created in Christ Jesus for good works,*
> *which God prepared in advance for us to do.* —*Ephesians 2:10*

Saving people from death and hell is not God's ultimate plan. It's too negative. The good works of new lives was God's objective in giving us Jesus.

Urban renewal begins with the tearing down of slum dwellings. But the purpose of the job is the erection of new houses. Fields are not merely plowed to kill the weeds. The harvest of a new crop is the goal of the farmer.

So when we speak of God's saving grace, it is not enough to talk of the misery that was removed. We need to say something about the newness that has come. God did not do all his saving work merely to snatch us from the fire. God wants to change us so that we will bear the image of Christ.

You must not only know *that* you are saved and *how* you are saved but also *for what purpose* you were saved.

God's love removes all the debris of the old and dying city. That happened at Golgotha. But the power of God's grace is really seen in his creation of a new humanity in Christ. The resurrection was the beginning of all that is new and good.

Grace saves and transforms selfish human beings into new people who produce good works. And that's the aim of God's grace. It takes a lot of hard work on the farmer's part to remove the weeds. He does not work so hard because he hates the weeds but because he loves the crop.

"For we are God's handiwork, created in Christ Jesus for good works, which God prepared in advance for us to do." God is the workman, and we are his products, his "handiwork" or "workmanship," as some Bible versions say. And when this architect-workman started his gracious work, he had a design in mind that he "prepared in advance." God's objective was the good works of a new people.

REFLECTION

How is God's renewal project going in your life? What signs do you see of the newness God is looking for?

Funnel and Flow

GALATIANS 5:1-6

> *For in Christ Jesus neither circumcision nor uncircumcision has any value. The only thing that counts is faith expressing itself through love.* —*Galatians 5:6*

The first readers of the letter to the Galatians argued about the question "What must we do to show that we are really a part of God's people?"

One group said that if a person really wanted to be a member of the people of God, he should keep Moses' laws and submit to the rite of circumcision.

People still argue about the question that bothered the Galatians. True, there aren't many who would say that *real* Christians should keep all the laws God gave through Moses. But many would say that *real* Christians must accept regulations and believe "revelations" that have come through recent prophets, leaders, and teachers.

In fact, there is real danger today that we or our children may be led astray by human additions to the gospel of Jesus Christ. Therefore we must stress the simplicity of the gospel and emphasize the heart of the matter. Once we are in Christ Jesus, circumcision means nothing and uncircumcision means nothing—it has no value. The only thing that counts is faith expressing itself through love.

All of us carry some baggage from one tradition or another. And countless vendors on Church Street try to sell us more than we can carry. Now we must remember that the only thing that counts, in Christ Jesus, is to have a faith that is active in love.

Faith is the funnel through which we receive the grace of God in Christ. Faith is nothing but empty and open hands, humble and contrite hearts. Once grace is received, it flows through us in works of love. And love is the power to do God's will. Faith is the funnel, while love is the goods we receive and pass on.

A childlike acceptance of the grace of God (faith) and a lifestyle that expresses the Spirit of Christ (love) is the mark of those who belong to the people of God.

REFLECTIONS

Offer a prayer reflecting the thoughts of this reading, especially the last sentence above.

Pass It On

MATTHEW 18:23-35

> *"Shouldn't you have had mercy on your fellow servant just as I had on you?"*
> —*Matthew 18:33*

Here is a simple story to instruct us in the truth that grace must flow on and on. Jesus told the story.

This particular man lived and worked at the court. His many connections made it easy to borrow money, and he took out hundreds of thousands of dollars. But the good living ended when the day of reckoning came. He could not pay. He fell on his knees and begged his master for mercy. And his master forgave him his huge debts.

Immensely relieved, he walked out. Then he met another servant who owed him ten dollars. He showed no mercy but insisted on full payment. He had the debtor put in prison until such time as someone would put up the money.

Then the king became very angry: "Shouldn't you have had mercy on your fellow servant just as I had on you?" Throw him in jail! For the unforgiving, there is no forgiveness.

We have not been forgiven if we cannot forgive. "For if you forgive others when they sin against you, your heavenly Father also will forgive you. But if you do not forgive others their sins, your Father will not forgive your sins" (Matt. 6:14-15).

Grace cannot be retained by those who are unwilling to pass it on. Love is not real if it does not become evident in deeds.

The master gives the unforgiving servant to the jailers to be tortured, and Jesus says that's how God will treat us unless "you forgive a brother or sister from the heart." That's a harsh statement—the loving Jesus speaks of torturers. But don't forget his exact words: the torture is for those who are anti-forgiveness.

Christ's words aren't a real threat to those who stand in the blazing generosity of their heavenly Father. Forgiven! All is forgiven! We are free from guilt and torture, debts and death.

REFLECTIONS

When have you learned how important it is to forgive someone who offended you?

Much Received, Much to Give

LUKE 7:36-50

"Therefore, I tell you, her many sins have been forgiven—as her great love has shown. But whoever has been forgiven little loves little." —Luke 7:47

While Jesus was eating in the house of Simon the Pharisee, a woman who had once been a prostitute wandered in. She walked around the table at which the host and his guests were reclining—they were reclining on couches, with their bare feet away from the table—and stopped at Jesus' feet. There she could not restrain herself. She became very emotional. She cried, letting the tears drip on Jesus' feet. Then she wiped his feet with her hair and anointed them with a costly ointment.

Simon the Pharisee did not get emotional about Jesus. In fact, he had not even shown Jesus the courtesy due an honored guest.

In this room—as in many rooms—there are two reactions to Jesus. One person is coldly indifferent. The other cannot control her feelings of gratitude and adoration.

The Lord explained this event with the help of a story: A person who has been forgiven a debt of $500 will show more gratitude than a person who has been forgiven a debt of $50, won't he? Even Simon the Pharisee agreed to the truth of this saying. Then Christ said: "This woman has been forgiven much because she loved much."

Let's make sure we read that correctly. Her love is not the *reason* why she is forgiven; her gratitude is *proof* of her forgiveness. It is true that Jesus' final word to her is: "Your sins are forgiven," and "Your faith has saved you." But he did not say, "Your *love* has saved you." Her display of love was a fruit of forgiveness. Otherwise she could not be the illustration of Jesus' story that when you are forgiven much, you love much.

Sometimes we are painfully struck by the cold reaction some people have to Jesus. They certainly don't get emotional about him. And their gifts are cheap. We must understand, then, that the gifts we offer him are in proportion to the forgiveness we received from him.

REFLECTIONS

How would you describe your relationship with Jesus? To what extent are you open and demonstrative about him?

Consistent with the Gospel

GALATIANS 2:11-16

When I saw that they were not acting in line with the truth of the gospel . . .   —*Galatians 2:14*

The truth of the gospel is that we are all sinners and we must all be saved by grace. Otherwise we cannot be saved. As soon as we say or think that we are better than someone else, we are not "acting in line with the truth of the gospel."

The apostle Peter ("Cephas," as Paul always calls him) was having dinner with his friends from Jerusalem. They were sitting at their own little table, eating their own kosher foods. That made them feel very much at home. Eating *with* non-Jewish people was still difficult for the Jewish Christians. It went against everything their fathers and mothers had taught them for two thousand years. Eating the foods that the Gentiles themselves ate was even more difficult. So these Jewish friends huddled together—for old times' sake and because they did not want to rock the boat.

Peter "stood condemned," and Paul told him so. Either you believe the gospel of grace, or you try to be justified before God by foods and works and Old Testament rites. You cannot accept the Christian gospel, which puts all people on the same level, and then act as if you belong to God's elite.

With one stroke the gospel removed all distinctions we make between good and bad people; we are all under sin. And salvation is only by grace. There just isn't any other way.

In our relationships to fellow believers, we must make allowances for differences in behavior, and we must tolerate different opinions about certain matters. But if we know what it means to be saved by grace, we will raise our voices loudly against any practice or teaching that would undercut the gospel.

All pride and prejudice is gone. We must look at people and live with people in terms of the gospel of grace. If we bring back even the least bit of the old distinctions, we are not "acting in line with the truth of the gospel."

REFLECTIONS

What "distinctions" between people do we sometimes introduce in our relationships with other Christians?

Christ in Me

GALATIANS 2:15-21

> *"I have been crucified with Christ and I no longer live, but Christ lives in me."* —*Galatians 2:20*

Salvation is a very personal matter. Yet you cannot possess it privately, outside the church of the redeemed.

When it comes to salvation, it is not always easy to find the right balance between the personal and the communal. But it is certainly true that nobody is saved by a *general* knowledge of sin and grace. We must know sin and salvation personally. If we don't, we know neither one.

Usually Paul talks about *we* and *us* and *ours* when he speaks of salvation. But here he becomes personal. He talks about *I* and *me* and *mine*.

"I no longer live," he says. Do notice, however, that when he tells how he was saved, he speaks of the cross that stood on Golgotha. "I have been crucified with Christ." There the old power was broken, and he became free to serve God.

The new life is described in this way: "Christ lives in me." That's the redeemed state. Anyone who was included in Christ's death and resurrection can say something about this new impulse: Christ is in us. That does not mean that the "I" disappears. You keep your personality. Paul still talks about "the life I now live in the body." But this life is lived unto God. Paul lives it "by faith in the Son of God, who loved me and gave himself for me."

Everyone who knows the self-giving love of the Savior knows this new kind of life. "He loves me!" Yes, he loves you too. But now allow me to say: "He loves *me*!" He gave himself for sinners, yes, thousands of them, but now allow me to confess: "He gave himself for *me*!"

Christ dominates my life. He rules my inner being. A friendly guide may help you out of the maze of the city to the expressway and then say: "From here on you're on your own." But that's not the way Christ saves. He saves to renew. He stays in us to reach for others. Grace flows through us because Christ lives in us.

REFLECTIONS

Reflect on how Christ loves *you*, died for *you*, and lives in *you*. Then give thanks.

God's Kind of Love

MATTHEW 5:43-48

"But I tell you, love your enemies and pray for those who perse-cute you, that you may be children of your Father in heaven."
—*Matthew 5:44-45*

The ability to love is evidence that Christ dwells in us.

However, the kind of love that the Bible calls "the fulfillment of the law" (Rom. 13:10) is a very special, child-of-God love.

Matthew 5:43-48 gives us one reason why it's different from other types of love. It makes no distinctions among people.

We all love our own mother. We love her because she is our mother. And we love our friends because they are our friends. These types of love also have their source in God, for God is the source of all goodness. But these types of love are common among both Christians and non-Christians.

"Christian love" is something special. It passes through us and goes out to others, not because of what *they* are but because of what *we* are. We don't love others because they are kind or pretty or members of our club; we love them because we are children of the heavenly Father. Therefore we can even love enemies.

This is the way God loves. There are many people in his world who have insulted him beyond measure. But instead of burning them up, God permits them to eat his food, and he lets his sun shine on them. God does that not because *they* are good but because *he* is good.

When we are children of the Father, his love begins to flow through us to others. The world is not able to create this kind of love. It is not made on earth; it was made in heaven. When people see it in Christians, they see a little picture of the greatness of our loving Father in heaven.

It is marvelous to be the object of God's grace. But it is even better to become a channel of his grace. This is God's design: his grace must flow, his love must show.

REFLECTIONS

Who are the people in your life you find it difficult to love or even care about? Pray for grace to let God's love flow through you to them.

Knowing the Lord

1 SAMUEL 2:12-17

*Eli's sons were scoundrels; they had no regard for [did not know]
the LORD.* —*1 Samuel 2:12*

Everyone who loves has been born of God and knows God.
—*1 John 4:7*

The sons of Eli were scoundrels, "worthless men" (RSV). Usually it is said that they were so ill-behaved and godless because their father was too soft. It is true that Eli was not strict enough (1 Sam. 3:13), but that does not yet explain why his sons were godless. No doubt Samuel was a much better disciplinarian, but Samuel's sons did not walk in the ways of the Lord either (1 Sam. 8:3).

The sons of Eli did not *know* the Lord. Our TNIV text and other translations say "they had no regard for the Lord." That's just what "not knowing the Lord" means, of course. But the Bible could simply say of a person who steals from God's offerings and commits deeds of immorality in God's house: "He does not *know* the Lord."

These two young men had been exposed to religious instruction. They were the sons of the high priest! If they were living in our days, we would say that they had gone to Sunday school and Bible class and church services. But they did not know the Lord.

Here we feel our inability to teach anyone the knowledge of the Lord, for "knowing the Lord" is a personal thing. If we don't have a personal relationship with God, we cannot know him.

Knowing the Bible is a condition for knowing the Lord. And ignorance of God is most commonly related to lack of Bible knowledge. But it is conceivable that someone could memorize the Bible without knowing the Lord.

"*Everyone who loves* . . . knows God." This does not mean that "a lover" or "a warm personality" or anyone like that has the true knowledge of God. What the text means is that the life and love of God flows through his children. We know God only when we have experienced his love. And when we have experienced God's love, we ourselves are able to love.

When we give evidence of Christian love in our own lives, we know God.

REFLECTIONS

How can others tell that you "know the Lord"?

The Grace of Giving

MATTHEW 6:1-4

"Then your Father, who sees what is done in secret, will reward you."
                                                    —*Matthew 6:4*

Giving money has always been an essential part of the practice of piety. We must not only do it, we must do it rightly.

Our Lord emphasized secrecy when we give money. It is an act of worship. It must be done because we love God. But if this act of godliness is observed and praised by people, the action ends where it started—on earth, before people. It never reaches God. "You did it to be seen by people? Well, people are saying that you're terrific. So you have your reward."

When we give it, it must be unseen by others and unrecorded by ourselves. That line about the left hand not knowing what the right hand is doing means that we should keep no record of our good deeds. Some people therefore conclude that you may not use your gifts as income tax deductions. That's nonsense. The Lord's point is that we may not attempt to figure out the credit points we gained with *him* because of what we have given. If we remember our good works too well, we are living by works and not by grace. Some people will spend fifty dollars in a restaurant without giving it a second thought. But if, in a moment of emotion, they give that amount to charity, they feel righteous for weeks. We must give our money because we love God. Then we should not make too much of it, nor should we think much about it.

God is not only the origin of the grace of giving but also the end. The grace that flows from God and through us returns to him in the form of dollars. That's the beauty of giving when it is done rightly.

Money given is not money wasted. "Your Father will reward you." But this will happen only when the money is given in the right way. The art of giving is difficult. The giver has numerous opportunities to "steal the show." If that happens, the giver loses the prize. Our gifts must be flowers of grace presented to God.

REFLECTIONS

What can you apply to your own giving from this Scripture and reading?

Sacred Secrecy

MATTHEW 6:5-15

"But when you pray, go into your room, close the door and pray to your Father, who is unseen. Then your Father, who sees what is done in secret, will reward you. —Matthew 6:6*

Jesus stressed secrecy when he taught us how to give money. In the case of prayer, he is just as emphatic. It's a matter between God and the one who is praying: "Go into your room, close the door and pray to your Father, who is unseen, but who sees what is done in secret."

Public and communal prayers have a place in Christian living. This the Bible clearly shows us. And there can be great beauty and encouragement when many are united in a prayer uttered by one. But anyone who has led in such prayers also knows about the pitfalls. The one who is praying must be heard by those for whom he is praying. The danger is great that he thinks more about the audience on earth than the audience in heaven.

Prayer is first and last a secret matter. It is talking with the Father who is in the secret place, the Father who sees the secrets of our lives. We cannot be Christians unless we have private prayers.

Every life has a private side. Our respect for persons includes respect for their right to privacy.

The worldly attack on privacy continues in full strength. On television you see and hear interviewers who have no consideration for the honor and privacy of the person they are questioning. Certain magazines and Internet sites do nothing but pry into the private lives of well-known people. This kind of journalism sells well because it gives people an obscene pleasure to get into the private lives of public figures. They always hope that the private side is a shady side. But couldn't the private side of a person's life be the sacred side?

Privacy is also under attack in the church. People are made to think they have to share the most private elements of their spiritual existence. This promotes neither faith nor honesty. Jesus' words are sobering. Close the door, and speak secretly to your Father. Have no other audience than God.

REFLECTION

What opportunities do you have in your day for private prayer? If you don't have a regular time set aside for private prayer, make a plan to include it each day.

Secret Fasting

MATTHEW 6:16-18

". . . so that it will not be obvious to others that you are fasting, but only to your Father, who is unseen. . . ."   —*Matthew 6:18*

You don't hear much about fasting these days, except from those who are on a diet. People on a diet fast for health reasons or perhaps in order to be seen by others.

Other forms of fasting are intended as a protest against injustice. The avowed purpose is publicity. Secrecy would spoil it. This fasting has no religious goal.

In the Old Testament, God prescribed fasting for a few occasions. But in the New Testament period, we are not bound by these "ceremonial laws." Nevertheless, fasting did play a role in the life of Jesus and in the religious experience of the early church. The Bible always assumes that those who take their relationship to God seriously will fast in some form.

Fasting is the denial of legitimate things for the purpose of religious concentration. The Bible does not prescribe it, and churches may not prescribe it. If it is not done voluntarily and without attracting attention, it loses its value.

There is always reason in the church to warn against asceticism. Watch out whenever people are afraid to enjoy what God has given us to enjoy. The gospel of grace may be in danger.

But there is also reason to warn against a spiritual laziness, an obesity and sluggishness that can afflict Christians. Christians on the North American continent are too preoccupied with food and drink and clothes; they are too much distracted by sports and games and all their "recreation." We must deny the temporary gifts voluntarily in order to be richer in faith and hope and love.

Nobody may ask for anything beyond what the Lord has commanded. But in a time of indulgence there is reason to suggest that we receive too little from heaven because we give up too little on earth.

REFLECTIONS

Have you ever considered fasting as a spiritual discipline? Why or why not?

Faith and Action

MATTHEW 7:24-29

*"Therefore everyone who hears these words of mine and puts them
into practice is like a wise man. . . ."* —Matthew 7:24

In the Sermon on the Mount (Matthew 5-7), Jesus said many difficult
things. The church has had long discussions about the question how we
should interpret these sayings. Some say that Jesus preached these radical
commandments in order to make us feel guilty: when we feel guilty, we
will turn to Christ and ask for the grace of forgiveness.

Others say that Jesus gave the rules in the Sermon on the Mount only
for those who are advanced in Christian living. But other commentaries
on this sermon try to interpret Jesus' words in such a way that an ordinary
Christian "can live with them."

However, the Lord Jesus seemed to have had a different idea. He said
that there are only two kinds of hearers or readers. Some hear and do,
while others hear and don't do what they are told. The person who obeys
is wise, but the person who does not do what Jesus said is a fool.

The purpose of grace is obedience. Grace does not mean that you're
OK and I'm OK, and everything is all right because God loves us all.
Grace means, indeed, that God accepts sinners. "Just as I am without one
plea . . . I come." You may come and I may come. But once I am in his
company, he does not leave me "just as I am." He teaches obedience.

Some people say, "God loves you," and they paint smiles on their faces,
as if to say that now all the lights are green. But the love of God never
means a go-ahead for sinners. Once you experience God's love, you can
never be the same again.

Only fools think that you may listen to Jesus without doing what you
hear him say. And fools, in God's book, are people who do not really
believe. Therefore they do not act. But a wise person is a God-fearing
person who has been taught by the gospel how to obey the law.

REFLECTIONS

Jesus tells us to be hearers and doers of the Word. What does that look
like in your life?

To Each the Same

MATTHEW 20:1-16

"Those men who were hired last worked only one hour . . . and you have made them equal to us who have borne the burden of the work and the heat of the day."   —*Matthew 20:12*

You would get into a lot of trouble if you treated your employees the way this farmer did. He paid the people who worked for one hour just as much as those who had labored a full day—and a full day used to be more than eight hours.

Here Jesus was teaching us something about the kingdom of heaven (v. 1). He was not proposing a fair labor contract.

Christ was telling us that the latecomers ("the last") shall be frontrunners ("the first") in the kingdom. Indeed, the Gentile latecomers have replaced the Jewish frontrunners.

Jesus' story speaks especially to those of us who have been at work in the vineyard for some time. Some of us have "borne the burden of the work and the heat of the day." We worked hard. Of course we know that we were received into the kingdom by grace, but we are also aware that grace must produce fruits of obedience. We showed obedience. By now we have quite a record. Some fellow Christians regard us highly. We've acquired jobs as managers and supervisors. In fact, sometimes we wonder what the vineyard would look like if we had not been working in it from sunup to sundown.

Along comes someone new to the kingdom who isn't even dry behind the ears. This newcomer makes all the baby sounds of one who has just been born again. Do you know what the Master pays him? A denarius. And do you know what we old-timers get? A denarius.

Yes, grace produces obedience, and this obedience is also rewarded. But the Lord is now giving us a public relations lesson for kingdom workers. There is to be no envy and no pride of seniority. All of us must be deeply convinced that we are in this kingdom by grace. Without this conviction, we do not belong here at all.

And grace is still the opposite of merit.

REFLECTIONS

"The older I get, the more I realize it's all by God's grace." Are you finding this to be true? How do you keep the focus on God's grace and off your own merits?

The Lord's Supper

MARK 14:22-25

> *. . . Jesus took bread, and when he had given thanks, he broke it and gave it to his disciples. . . . Then he took the cup, and when he had given thanks, he gave it to them. . . .* —Mark 14:22-23

God's grace comes to us through his Word. If we believe it, we receive it. It is possible for God's Word to bring grace into our lives, for the Word comes with the power of God's Spirit. God's Spirit brings to our hearts that which we hear with our ears.

As a further favor, our God strengthens our faith through the Lord's Supper. Here he assures us of his grace in a very direct manner. When we receive a piece of the bread, Christ says that he has given his body for us. He wants us to eat that bread and believe that he so loved us that he died for us. Then we must drink the wine or grape juice. Thus we do not only hear, we can even *taste* that God has forgiven our sins because Jesus shed his blood for us.

We must believe that this has happened for us, once for all. We don't have to pay for our sins, and we will not be punished for our sins. That *has happened*. It does not happen in the Lord's Supper. The Lord's Supper assures us that it has happened once for all on Golgotha. We *remember*, we believe, and we rejoice.

Something is also happening during the supper. We eat a piece of bread, and we drink a sip of wine or grape juice. It's a sort of a meal. Ordinarily we eat foods and drink fluids in order to live and to do our work. But now Jesus is feeding us with himself. His power comes to us through his Spirit. He makes us strong so that we can live and do the work to which he has called us.

When we observe the Lord's Supper, we look *back* and remember Golgotha. We look *up* and see the living Lord who is now giving us all we need. We look *around* at all the other sinners Christ has saved and given us as brothers and sisters. And we look *forward* because the Lord wants us to believe that our communion with him is forever, and that he is preparing an even greater feast.

REFLECTIONS

How does the Lord's Supper strengthen *your* faith?

Grace Makes Beautiful

1 PETER 3:1-6

> *Your beauty should not come from outward adornment. . . .*
> *Rather, it should be that of your inner self, the unfading beauty of*
> *a gentle and quiet spirit, which is of great worth in God's sight.*
> —*1 Peter 3:3-4*

Peter says this to Christian wives whose husbands resisted the grace of God. "Don't preach to them," he advises. "Just show grace by your behavior." Their husbands had heard the *word* of grace. Now they had to see the *work* of grace.

God's grace does not only flow *through* us, it also does its work *in* us. God's grace gives people an inner beauty. Frequently people who have opposed the gospel will surrender to it when they see the effects of grace in a beautiful person.

Today we are all exposed to many lies about beauty. We must pray especially that our daughters and sons won't believe the lies. May God's grace teach them to cultivate the inner beauty that is imperishable. Grace makes beautiful. And the beauty of grace has more power than words.

Beauty conquers by its own power. It does not have to scream for attention. Beauty is never loud.

Some of our witnessing to the grace of God must be verbal and, if not loud, at least articulate and unmistakable. But most of our witness should be unintentional. And it will have a winning power of its own, for beauty conquers people quietly, modestly, irresistibly.

But it does not always work that way. There are women of great inner beauty who do not actually win those whom they love to Christ. And there are some quietly beautiful Christian congregations whose winning power seems to be nil.

But the Bible says that this inner beauty is precious *in the sight of God*. God looks at these people. God sees what his grace has done and rejoices in it. Of these people he says, just as he once said of creation, "That's beautiful." And God determines to keep these jewels forever.

REFLECTION
Pray along the lines suggested in today's reading.

Fighting Blocks Grace

1 PETER 3:7-12

Live considerately with your wives . . . since you are joint heirs of
the grace of life, in order that your prayers may not be hindered.
—*1 Peter 3:7, RSV*

First Peter spoke about husbands who were not converted when their wives became Christians (3:1). But here is a much happier situation. In this case both husband and wife are heirs of God's promises. They are both Christians. And since they are joined in marriage, he calls them "joint heirs of the grace of life."

"Live considerately with your wives." Perhaps it was the rude background of these recent converts that made the warning necessary. Peter means that husbands must show tenderness and understanding. Peter himself was married.

Joint heirs have joint prayers. Biblically speaking, it is unthinkable that two Christians who are married to each other should not pray together. Yet every now and then I meet an older Christian couple who have not learned to pray together. And now they find it too awkward to get started. But they must do it! It's not yet too late to bring in some of the treasures they almost missed.

However, when the tender harmony of a married couple is broken, the prayers are "hindered" or "blocked."

The apostle could have mentioned other bad results of marital disrespect. Marital troubles have a host of bad consequences. But he mentions the worst: it will block the flow of grace.

Notice carefully what Peter is saying. He does not make the comment you probably have often heard: "If you have problems, you should pray together." He says: "Don't cause problems; otherwise you cannot pray together."

The Bible does not regard prayer as a last resort for human beings, an effort to get done with God's help what they could not manage on their own. Prayer is the door through which we receive God's grace. And without grace we simply have no life.

Therefore, husbands and wives must live in such a way that they can always pray together.

REFLECTIONS

What do you think of the perspective this reading gives to marital troubles? How does the reading relate to your own prayer life? Do the principles discussed in this reading apply to other relationships as well as marriage?

Stick Your Neck Out

1 PETER 3:13-17

Who is going to harm you if you are eager to do good?

—1 Peter 3:13

The grace of God makes us quiet and modest, but also passionate for what is right. God's grace restrains us from being loud and self-assertive. But God's Spirit does give us a zeal for righteousness.

Christians must have strong convictions about right and wrong. For us it is not enough to hold the opinion that crime does not pay. That's TV morality. We must be deeply persuaded that righteousness pays everlasting dividends.

When you believe in God, you must dare to stick out your neck for what is right. Whatever is right and true and good comes from God. Therefore the pursuit of righteousness, truth, and goodness is from God. It is carried on through God, and it leads to God. Why be timid if you walk in the way of God himself?

Some kids keep mum when crimes are committed in school. They are nice kids. They believe that crime doesn't pay. But they don't believe that righteousness pays either.

There are still plenty of "good citizens" who do not participate in crime. But they don't believe it is their business to start a crusade for righteousness either.

The lukewarm attitude of decent but unbelieving citizens is understandable. Their main concern, after all, is to mind their own business. That's the scope of their calling. But Christians are cut out of a different cloth. We have been addressed by God. He has laid his hand on us. He has put his Spirit in us. If we are ever lukewarm about right and wrong, truth and falsehood, we are denying our Lord.

God wants and creates people who do right for no other reason than that it is right. And if we are hurt while we are doing right, we are not really harmed. The only time we suffer real evil is when we do evil or refuse to do right.

REFLECTIONS

What might "sticking your neck out for God" look like at work? At a game? At school? With your friends?

Stewards of Grace

1 PETER 4:7-11

Each of you should use whatever gift you have received to serve others, as faithful stewards of God's grace in its various forms.

—*1 Peter 4:10*

A steward, in Bible times, was someone to whom the master had entrusted the care of his household and business. Often the steward was appointed because the master had to be away for an extended period of time. But even when the master was around, he might appoint a trusted slave as a steward. The steward was in charge of the supplies. He had to feed the household from his master's stores. Joseph had that kind of job in the house of Potiphar (Gen. 39).

When the Bible says that we must be faithful stewards of God's grace, it means that we must be diligent in distributing to God's household the gifts drawn from God's storehouse. God's household is the church. The household lives on the grace that God supplies. By this "grace" we usually mean the forgiving favor of God, the favor that saves and strengthens God's people. It comes to us through the Word and by the Spirit. And God has appointed stewards for bringing these heavenly supplies from the storehouses to the household.

But the storehouses of God are filled with grace in various forms—all kinds of gifts from God. Each member of the household gets one or two of these gifts, for which he or she must be a "steward."

In God's household, one person does not have access to all of God's gracious supplies. Each is a steward for "whatever gift you have received."

We might say that the household of God does not live on one meal cooked for all: God's children are fed by a potluck supper, where the varied gifts are carried in by each to the benefit of all.

We are told that *each* has received a gift. But since we are stewards, these gifts aren't really our own possessions. We are responsible to God for them. God wants the whole household of faith to benefit from what's entrusted to us. God's gifts of grace must flow on and on.

REFLECTIONS

How can the gifts God has given you be used to benefit the household of faith?

Grace Descends

1 PETER 5:1-5

All of you, clothe yourselves with humility toward one another, because, "God opposes the proud but shows favor [grace] to the humble and oppressed." —1 Peter 5:5

Grace, like water, runs to low places. The deeper you bow, the more you receive. But for those who live in high places, it's hard to get.

Throughout the Bible we read that God scatters the arrogant and sends the rich away but fills the hungry and exalts the lowly. The prayer of the humble one is the only window through which the grace of God can shine.

However, we must practice humility not only before God but also toward one another. "All of you, clothe yourselves with humility toward one another."

Humility is not a gesture that we make now and then. It is a garment in which we are clothed for the duration of our pilgrimage.

In this respect the Christian community presents the greatest possible contrast with worldly society. Christians don't climb over each other; they bow down to each other. They don't envy each other; they rejoice with each other.

And those Christians who have been appointed as shepherds over God's flock should remind each other not to behave like successful executives in a worldly business. Together they are little shepherds or pastors who are awaiting the return of the chief Shepherd, to whom the flock belongs. When he comes, they will get their promotion—no sooner.

The chief Shepherd himself lived and died in service. He humbled himself to the depths of our shame. And only after he had finished it all was he crowned with glory. The people of God must live and work on earth in the shadow of his cross until the day of coronation.

It is Christ's custom to lift only those who are low and to give crowns only to those who have been bearing a cross. Therefore we must remain uncrowned in this life. And we must live in places low enough for grace to reach us.

REFLECTIONS

"Christians don't climb over each other; they bow down to each other." How do you (could you) "bow" to other Christians?

Grace Unites

ACTS 4:32-37

All the believers were one in heart and mind. No one claimed that
any of their possessions was their own, but they shared everything
they had.   *—Acts 4:32*

The Holy Spirit is the sum total of the grace God gives to us when we believe in Jesus. All the riches of Christ—forgiveness, renewal, the pledge of the future, yes, the love of the Father himself—are poured into our hearts when we receive the Spirit.

And this grace must flow from one person to another. The Spirit immediately unites us with those who are in Christ and urges us to communicate the gospel to those who are outside of Christ. These are not only commandments given to the new community of believers, they are pressures that come from within. This is how the Spirit's own nature is revealed.

The early Christians were "one in heart and mind." They had been radically renewed and united.

"They shared everything they had." The natural attitude toward earthly possessions was changed by the coming of the Spirit. It was no dictator's rule to the effect that all that's yours is mine. No, it was pressure from within that made them say, "All that's mine is yours."

The Christian community's way of life is not the same at all times and places. It changes. There's nothing wrong with the changes, although some Christian groups appear to be frightened by them. Countless leaders have tried to stop the clock or even set it back. That's not only silly, it's sinful. It's an insult to think that the Holy Spirit can work in us only if we arrange for an agrarian setting on a communal farm.

God himself is in control of the world and the changes in society. God works in today's church with the same power he has always used. All who have the Spirit are one in heart and mind. And all who are possessed by him change their attitudes toward earthly possessions. They learn to put the fellowship first.

REFLECTIONS

How have you experienced "the community of saints" and the fellowship of believers?

The Wrong Fidelity

ACTS 5:1-11

Peter said to her, "How could you conspire to test the Spirit of the Lord?" —*Acts 5:9*

This early death penalty for a lie in the Christian community must serve as a lasting deterrent: we who live by God's grace, who form the temple of the Holy One, must not carry anything unclean into God's presence. The Spirit guards the temple that was cleansed by grace.

The sin of Ananias and Sapphira was of minor proportions, as we measure sin. It was not greed. They made a big donation (which they didn't have to do), but they made it look bigger than it really was. They lied and thereby detracted from the honor of God. Husband and wife both agreed to the deed. Although Sapphira had a separate chance to confess, she stuck to her husband in sin and shared his punishment.

We must love the truth more than our wives or husbands or anyone else. There are moments when one person has to say to the other: "No, honey, we can't do that."

Too many are more loyal to a person they love than to the truth. The law recognizes this—that's why husbands and wives are disqualified as witnesses in court in a case that involves either one of them. They would protect each other anyway.

Children learn that too. When the telephone rings and Dad says, "If that's Mr. Jones, I'm not home," junior will say, "Sorry, Mr. Jones, my dad is not home." He is loyal to his dad. Together they lie.

God wants us to be more faithful to the truth than to bonds of family or friendship. If you really love your family or friends, you will do all you can to keep them from sinning.

We should have so much love for each other that we can muster the courage to keep each other from sinning.

For the sake of keeping peace, some have conspired to "test the Spirit of the Lord." Don't do it! It's better to risk a fight in the family than a battle with God.

REFLECTIONS

What happens in our relationships if we put ties with family or friends before the truth?

Waiting on Tables

ACTS 6:1-7

Choose seven men from among you who are known to be filled with the Spirit and wisdom. We will turn this responsibility over to them. . . . —*Acts 6:3*

Since the Christian community is united in heart and mind, it shares its possessions. That's how it started. Times may change, but the norm remains.

The members of a congregation must always have a common confession and a united song because they are one in heart and mind. And they must always have their offering plates, budget envelopes, money drives, and all the rest, for their attitudes toward possessions have been sanctified by the Spirit of God.

In the earliest Christian church, the one in Jerusalem, the resources of the congregation were pooled and "daily distributions" were made. The seven men who were appointed to "wait on tables" had to see to it that nobody was forgotten. Even if only one was in need, all would be at fault.

Situations have changed considerably. Some things have changed for the better. The position of widows, for instance, has vastly improved. It's true that they still deserve special attention because they receive the Lord's special concern, but they aren't as dependent anymore as they used to be. Other things have not changed for the better. Some Christians have too much and give too little.

The basic principles that governed the earliest church must be upheld today. By the ministry of the Word, the doors of the kingdom are opened. By the ministry of prayer, the power of God's grace is released. And through the distribution of tangible goods, grace flows between Christian people.

This last part of the threefold ministry is as essential as the first two. Offerings must be received, carefully administered, and properly distributed.

The congregation must always see to it that people who are "full of the Spirit and wisdom" are busy making sure that the flow of grace among God's people is not blocked.

REFLECTIONS

Review some of the ways your congregation uses its offerings to benefit others.

Grace through a Seamstress

ACTS 9:36-43

She was always doing good and helping the poor. —*Acts 9:36*

The community of Christ does not make a big distinction between material and spiritual services. Both come from the divine source, and both aim at God's glory. It's all spiritual service, for one Spirit uses both.

The responsibility for mutual assistance is not limited to the officials of the church. All those who are reached by God's grace must be used to make God's grace flow.

Our gifts are not equal, and our usefulness is not the same. Dorcas was a woman who had the gift of helping—in the greatest possible measure. She was "*always* doing good and helping the poor." She was not one to content herself with making a thing or two for a needy person now and then. No, doing good works was a way of life for her. She was "full" of good works, as one Bible version puts it.

What a blessed woman! When we think of the many widows who exhibited the fruits of her love (the hats, the shawls, the dresses), we see a picture of a thank offering richer than the showbread that was lifted up to God in the tabernacle of the old covenant. These are the humble and honest thank offerings in the new temple.

The Christian church has a strong tradition of devoting a few hours of the first day of the week to the ministry of the Word and the service of prayer. Why don't we establish an equally strong custom of setting aside part of that day for the ministry of "doing good and helping the poor"? We would not want to limit the performance of such deeds to Sunday. Works of charity can be done at any time. But things that can be done at any time tend to be done at no time.

We thank the God of grace for all the quiet people who faithfully perform acts of love and mercy. We thank God for the grace that shows through the activity of their hands. And we trust that God will raise them up to live with him forever.

REFLECTIONS

Name some people in your congregation who faithfully and quietly perform acts of love and mercy. Give thanks for "the grace that shows through the activity of their hands."

All of the Message

ACTS 20:17-27

"Therefore, I declare to you today that I am innocent of the blood of everyone. For I have not hesitated to proclaim to you the whole will of God." —*Acts 20:26-27*

When God says to a wicked person, "You will surely die," but God's prophet fails to pass that warning along to him or her, the prophet will be guilty. "Those wicked people will die for their sins, and I will hold you accountable for their blood." This is what God said in Ezekiel 3:18-21.

God loves sinners so much that he wants them to be converted. He does not want sinners to die.

Some ugly rumors say that God kills people by throwing them into hell. But the biblical truth is that people themselves are hell-bent and self-destructive. And God will do anything to prevent people from killing themselves. He even went so far as to send his own Son to his death in order to save those who hate God! Moreover, God has warned his people, his church, and their pastors that he will punish them if they don't get his message out to all runaway sheep.

The Christian church is not sufficiently aware of its responsibility. It does not remind itself often enough that God requires the blood of those who perish from those who fail to speak. New Testament messengers may not forget this Old Testament warning. Paul did not forget it.

"I am innocent of the blood of everyone," said Paul, "for I have not hesitated to proclaim to you the whole will of God." By the "whole will of God," he means all of God's revelation. He has not watered down the truth, and he has not been one-sided. When we present half-truths, we aren't doing God any honor, and we aren't doing people a favor.

If you have a remedy against cancer while cancer patients are dying all around you, you are guilty of murder because you didn't help. It's no excuse to say that you were always kind to the dying. You did not show the one kindness that was really important. You withheld what could have saved them.

It is difficult and embarrassing to warn people of dangers they don't see. But it must be done. Those who despise the Son of God's love will perish.

REFLECTIONS

Review how your congregation attempts to reach out to nonbelievers in the community. Pray earnestly and regularly for God's blessing on these outreach efforts.

Content and Package

ACTS 20:28-38

"Now I commit you to God and to the word of his grace. . . . I have not coveted anyone's silver or gold or clothing." —*Acts 20:32-33*

Many pastors who leave a church have borrowed these words of the apostle Paul for a farewell speech or sermon: "Now I commit you to God and to the word of his grace." But there aren't many who have stressed the words that follow this text: "I have not coveted anyone's silver or gold or clothing. You yourselves know that these hands of mine have supplied my own needs and the needs of my companions."

It would be a shame for a regular congregation not to provide a living for its pastor. Paul himself was used by God to lay down some rules in that respect. The fact remains, however, that there is a close relationship between the message and the behavior of the person by whom it is presented. If we tell people that *God* cares for them while it is obvious that *we* couldn't care less, the message becomes unbelievable.

There are plenty of religious racketeers in North America. They must be exposed and rejected, for they dishonor the church of God. They don't care for the sheep; they want to fleece them.

You and I are the packages in which the grace of God is presented to people. We will always be inclined to say, "Please don't judge the content by the package." We don't call people to the church of Christ because *we* are so good but because *Christ* is so good.

Nevertheless, we must watch out that we don't resemble the Pharisees of whom Jesus said that you should listen to their words but not act according to their deeds. We have plenty of right to say that we carry the treasure of the kingdom in the earthly vessels of our present lives. But God's Spirit is powerful enough to show more of Christ through more of us.

The Spirit will give us so much grace that our total behavior supports the whole of the message.

REFLECTIONS

How do you react to being "the package in which the grace of God is presented to people"? Ask for a rich measure of God's grace so that more of Christ is seen through us, his people.

The Spreading Flame

ACTS 28:17-24

He proclaimed the kingdom of God and taught about the Lord Jesus
Christ—with all boldness and without hindrance! —Acts 28:31

From Jerusalem to Rome—that's the story of the book of Acts. It begins
in Jerusalem, where the flame was lit. At the end of the book, the fire is
spreading through the capital of the empire.

The last few lines of the book give us the information that Paul lived
for two whole years in the city of Rome at his own expense. But these
closing lines have a message that goes beyond this information.

First, the content of the message is restated here. The message concerns
the "kingdom of God." This was originally a Jewish hope. The oppressed
looked forward to the coming of the Lord to overthrow the foreign rulers
and establish the righteousness of his kingdom on earth. The hope for that
kingdom was kept alive by the prophets in the darkest hours of Israel's
history. Now Paul preaches that kingdom as having come in Jesus.

That's why the phrase *proclaiming the kingdom* is joined with *teaching
about the Lord Jesus Christ*. The kingdom is no longer a vague and future
hope. The kingdom is opened and can be entered by believing in Jesus,
who is the Messiah and the Lord. By believing in him we enter it.

Preaching the kingdom and teaching about Jesus are not two unrelated topics on the church's agenda—as if you have to go to a prophecy
conference to hear about the kingdom and to a revival meeting to learn
of Jesus. The kingdom is proclaimed when Jesus is presented. And when
Christ is presented, the kingdom is opened.

Second, the last lines of Acts tell us about the triumph of the Word
of God. Paul preached and taught "with all boldness and without hindrance." What a closing note of victory! The Word goes on. It conquers
the world for the kingdom.

The greatest thing happening today is the coming of God's kingdom
and the teaching about the Lord Jesus Christ.

REFLECTIONS

Use the Heidelberg Catechism's explanation of what we mean when we pray
your kingdom come (Answer 123) as your prayer today: "Rule us by your Word
and Spirit in such a way that more and more we submit to you. Keep your
church strong, and add to it. Destroy the devil's work; destroy every force
which revolts against you and every conspiracy against your Word. Do this
until your kingdom is so complete and perfect, that in it you are all in all."

Supplied and Supplying

JOHN 7:37-39

"Whoever believes in me, as Scripture has said, rivers of living water will flow from within them."   —*John 7:38*

This is the promise of Jesus and the experience of thousands: thirst is satisfied when you believe in Jesus.

All of us are born thirsty. And all of us go through life trying to satisfy our thirst. Some try to satisfy their thirst by vulgar means, while others try more refined and cultural means. People try money and what it can buy, power and what it will yield, and sexual satisfaction in many forms.

But there is no thing and no person in this world that can fill the vacuum and quench the thirst. The longed-for possession does not supply what it was expected to give. A man cannot give it to a woman, and a wife cannot satisfy her husband's deepest desire. We were created for God. Only in God can we find what we seek—what all of us seek.

Jesus has come into our world to bring us the water of life. Pagans dreamed of such a man. The thirst is universal; everybody dreams of fulfillment, which is always beyond our horizon. The Jewish people were hoping for such a liberator who would fulfill the longing of the ages. Jesus has come to bring us the water of life.

Drinking what Jesus offers means believing what he claims to be. That's the humble act by which we bow down and drink the water.

Then we find that he not only satisfies our thirst but also gives us life within ourselves. Where there was first a vacuum we receive a power. The Bible calls it "living water from within." It means that those who came to Jesus to have their own thirst quenched are now able to offer the living water to others. The objects of God's grace become his vehicles of grace.

The grace, or the life, or the Spirit of God, quenches our deepest thirst. Only it—only God—can enter deeply within us and turn our thirst into a fountain. Then God works through us and extends the cup to thousands who are dying.

REFLECTIONS

What is your "deepest thirst"? How can God satisfy it? Has he satisfied it?

Indwelling Grace

JOHN 14:18-24

Jesus replied, "Anyone who loves me will obey my teaching. My Father will love them, and we will come to them and make our home with them." —John 14:23

To love Jesus means to obey him: "Anyone who loves me will obey my teaching." Love for Christ, like love in marriage, is a very practical thing. It consists not of speeches but of deeds. Or, if speeches are called for, they are tolerable only if they are consistent with actions.

A person who is attached to Christ in this way of love-through-obedience experiences the grace of God ever more richly in her life. She feels a continual trust in God's grace. In fact, God lives in her!

We learn to think of God in three persons: Father, Son, and Holy Spirit. We think of God in that way because that's how the Bible reveals the one eternal God. We think of God the Father as the One above us, as the creator and ruler. We think of God the Son as the One who is for us, the mediator. We think of the God the Holy Spirit as the One who is in us.

However, the three are one, because there is only one true God. And although the Bible teaches (usually) that it is the Holy Spirit who comes to live in us when we receive the grace of God, here Jesus says, "We—the Father and I—will make *our* home with them."

The everlasting God makes his dwelling place in us if we love Jesus Christ. The thought is so rich that it almost scares us.

The almighty God, who once lived in a golden temple so that his people could come to him, has now chosen to live in my fellow believers and in me. What grace! And what a noble obligation! Now we are the place where people must find God.

This teaching states once and for all the deepest reason why grace must flow through us to others, once we have believed in Jesus.

REFLECTIONS

"The everlasting God makes his dwelling place in us if we love Jesus Christ." Think on that stunning truth and its implications for your life.

Fruit-bearing

JOHN 15:1-11

> *"This is to my Father's glory, that you bear much fruit, showing yourselves to be my disciples."* —*John 15:8*

Think of an orchard or vineyard. The owner arrives to look for fruit, because that's the main interest of the fruit farmer. Lots of fruit makes the owner happy; it says that he is a good farmer. When there is no fruit, the owner trims back the branches with a pruning knife. If there is still no fruit, he cuts branches off.

Being fruit is, of course, a figure of speech when applied to people. Just as a fruit farmer works on his trees, God, the Owner of the orchard, works on people. God's aim is to harvest as much fruit as possible. He uses the knife only to get a richer yield. Only if no fruit appears after all this work does God cut the branch away. To be cut off means that God no longer tolerates you as someone who belongs to the people of God.

We cannot bear fruit unless we belong to Jesus. "Apart from me you can do nothing." Only when God's grace is known to us and God's Spirit is in us can we do works that God approves. These works are the fruits that please the Father.

We bear fruit when we suffer without growing bitter, when we do good deeds without taking credit, when we obey even if it is costly, when we confess Jesus even if it makes us unpopular, when we follow Christ even when he leads us where we do not choose to go.

Bearing fruit is impossible for those who are outside of Christ. But it is nothing spectacular for those who have received new life from Jesus. When a Christian fails to bear fruit, something has gone wrong, and it's time for serious self-examination.

God does not work in vain. When God has sent this powerful grace that changes our lives, God will also reap the fruits he has caused to grow.

An old catechism says that it is *impossible* for those who are implanted into Christ by a true faith not to bring forth fruits of thankfulness.

REFLECTIONS

When God looks at you, what fruit does he see?

The Gospel According to Paul

Paul's letter to the Romans is the Christian gospel, the "power of God that brings salvation to everyone who believes." The gospel of righteousness by faith, as presented by Paul, clarifies the way of salvation revealed in the Old Testament.

daylight

Gospel Power

ROMANS 1:8-17

I am not ashamed of the gospel, because it is the power of God that
brings salvation to everyone who believes. . . .   —Romans 1:16

God gave us much of the New Testament through the apostle Paul. And the fullest statement of the gospel, as Paul preached it, is in his letter to the Romans. Romans is the gospel according to Paul.

The letter was written a long time ago, in the year 58. At that time Rome was the capital of the Roman Empire. The emperor himself lived in Rome. But he and most other important Roman citizens were not aware of the small group of Christians in their city who one day received a letter that would outlast the empire. God had determined that this one little letter would have a greater influence on human history than all the Roman armies.

The church of God in Rome sat down to read the letter. "Paul is coming to Rome," they exclaimed. "And here he writes the gospel as he preaches it."

This small Christian church in Rome would soon be in big trouble. The emperor and the other important people in their city were about to take note of these Christians. They would not tolerate them serving Jesus as Lord instead of Caesar. They would throw the Christians to the lions. But the empire would not defeat the Christian faith. Christianity would win the empire—because the gospel is the power of God that brings salvation.

Whenever Christians have scored victories in the course of history, a rediscovery of the gospel in *Romans* was usually the secret of their strength. A careful reading of Romans will always bring the church fresh insight and give new power to those who represent Christ in this world.

We are "not ashamed" to recommend the reading of Romans. It is the Christian gospel, "the power of God that brings salvation" to everyone who reads and believes. By means of this letter, the saving power of God gets to work here and now, wherever there is faith.

REFLECTIONS

What concerns and anticipations do you bring to reading and studying the book of Romans?

Filthy Sinners

ROMANS 1:18-28

God gave them up. . . . God gave them up. . . . God gave them up. . . .   *Romans 1:24-28, NRSV*

You and I are not to judge those who prefer to live like pigs. They themselves will be the first ones to tell us that their way of living is none of our business.

God is their judge—and ours. God is also the great voice who addresses them in starlight, in dewdrops, and in the depth of their (human!) being. Certainly, they have heard God. But they did not want to listen. Therefore they are "without excuse" (v. 20) when God judges them.

Damnation and salvation are not only future, they are also present—although neither one is *fully* present. Some people are already walking revelations of God's wrath (v. 18), just as others are already experiencing God's power for salvation (v. 16). The beginnings of both are here and now.

When people suppress the inner voice of which everyone is conscious, the road to hell begins. When they succeed in shutting off the voice of God, they begin to listen eagerly to the voice of their own lusts. Finally they attempt to rewrite God's laws for living: they set their own standards for their own lives. Then the words "God gave them up" are fulfilled before our eyes.

In the year 58, when Paul wrote these words, and in the year when you are reading this page, thousands of people are racing to hell. They began by suppressing the truth God has revealed to all. They follow through by disobeying God's laws that are written in creation itself. When they do what they "like," the Word is fulfilled and God "gives them up." God no longer withholds or restrains them but allows them to have what they wanted all along.

Only the gospel has the power to pull pigs from the mire. It's hard to believe how far God has gone to save filthy sinners. But when Christ hung on the cross, the Word was fulfilled: "God gave him up for us all" (Rom. 8:32).

REFLECTIONS

Do we have an obligation to bring the gospel to people who are "filthy sinners"? Why or why not?

Decent People

ROMANS 2:1-11

So when you, a mere human, pass judgment on them and yet do the same things, do you think you will escape God's judgment?
—*Romans 2:3*

In chapter 1 of Romans we read about people who sank to the depth of idolatry and immorality. But the world is not made up only of people who live like pigs. As long as we have some form of society, most people have to live fairly decent lives. Romans chapter 2 is addressed to decent people who condemn filthy sinners.

The gospel operates with a new understanding of sin. God is not interested in whether you are a bad sinner or only a moderate sinner. God condemns you because you are a sinner.

That does not mean that all the different kinds of sin are equally bad. Robbing a bank is still worse than dreaming about it. But both the robber and the dreamer are sinners.

It isn't robbery or adultery that makes us sinners. We commit robbery and adultery because we *are* sinners. All lechery, thievery, and lying are symptoms of an evil that is in all of us. And until the Bible points it out, we don't even recognize this evil within us.

Our sin is that we don't love God above all and don't love our neighbor as ourselves. Sin is missing the mark. It is not being what you are supposed to be by God's design and calling.

All people (nearly all) can recognize certain deeds, such as murder and theft and whatever else is considered immoral behavior, as sins. Christianity explains that we don't *become* sinners by such sinful deeds; we do such deeds because we *are* sinners.

In the light of the gospel, all our traditional distinctions between good people and bad people disappear. "You, therefore, have no excuse, you who pass judgment on someone else" (v. 1).

God places all of us under the conviction of sin so that all of us may know that we need Jesus.

REFLECTIONS

How convinced are you that you are a sinner? Why is this so important to recognize?

Jews Are Guilty

ROMANS 2:12-24

You who boast in the law, do you dishonor God by breaking the law?
—Romans 2:23

Please don't become weary of God's instruction concerning sin. This whole first part of Romans is intended to show us that the gospel of Christ is the only hope for us and for all people. All false supports must be knocked out of our hearts. All other doors must be closed. Then we will rely on Christ alone, and we will enter through the door that God has opened.

This time we learn that the Jews fall under God's judgment.

Ever since the state of Israel was established in 1948, many speeches have been made and books have been written about a "special standing" the Jews have with God. And most of those making the speeches and writing the books are Christians.

That's why it's doubly necessary to read this passage, which says that outside of the gospel there is no salvation for the Jews. In order to be saved, the Jews, as well as the rest of us, must burn all credit cards and trust in Jesus alone.

Non-Jews cannot be saved by their heritage either. Paul himself wrote how he had to go through a process of disposing of everything he once thought might give him credit with God—his pride of race and background, his arrogance because of his religious education, his reliance on work and zeal for God's cause. At one time he thought he had all of this going for him. Then he discovered that he had to discard it all and desire nothing except to know Jesus Christ (Phil. 3:4-11).

The Jews were inclined to "boast in the law." They were the proud possessors of revelation. Paul argues that they broke the law, even by obvious transgressions.

Possessing God's revelation is a real temptation for the Jews and for all who stand in a religious tradition. It does not guarantee anything. What counts is doing. Not *having* the book but *obeying* the Word is the purpose of life. The failure to *do* must drive us to the gospel. For only the gospel gives us power to obey.

REFLECTIONS

How can being a solid member of a religious tradition be dangerous to our salvation?

Brotherhood in Misery

ROMANS 3:9-20

Therefore no one will be declared righteous in God's sight by observing the law; rather, through the law we become conscious of our sin. —Romans 3:20

Now comes the conclusion of the teaching of the first part of Romans: "In the court of God, the law is not your advocate but your prosecutor. You Jews, as well as the whole world, are liable to God's judgment. God's revealed will, the law, will not help you get credit with God. On the contrary, the law spells out your penalty and increases your sin."

The teaching of sin as the introductory part of the gospel equalizes all people. All of us are accountable to one Judge, all of us are sinners. No one has good reason to look down on anybody else. To be sure, we differ in that some are worse sinners than others. There is a difference in quantity, but there is no difference in quality. We are all sinners.

All the masks are now removed. Every mouth is stopped. All are silent and sinful in the sight of God.

The frightful reality of sin has been revealed. It appears to be much more than the bad behavior people observe and discuss. Sin is a power that jails us: "Jews and Gentiles alike are *all* under the power of sin" (v. 9). And nobody can escape from this prison in which all of us are inmates. We cannot set ourselves or others free.

Some people are fond of talking about "the brotherhood of man." They think that people aren't so bad, really, and that we could achieve peace and unity if we would only try hard enough to be "nice."

In view of Romans 3:20, we must admit that we, with all thieves, cannibals, and murderers, share in a solidarity of sin. This is our "brotherhood," if you will. No Orthodox person can survive because he is Orthodox, no Jew because he is a Jew, no politician because he is nice. But this brotherhood in misery is not a creed that comforts us. It makes us look for an escape. "Foul, I to the fountain fly; wash me, Savior, or I die."

REFLECTIONS

How does God's law function in your life?

This Is the Gospel

ROMANS 3:21-31

> But now apart from the law the righteousness of God has been made known, to which the Law and the Prophets testify. This righteousness is given through faith in Jesus Christ to all who believe.
> —*Romans 3:21-22*

"But now . . ."

Here is the big turning point. *Now* means after God acted in Jesus Christ. Salvation hour has struck. And things will never be the same again.

"The righteousness of God has been made known." *Righteousness of God* refers to the way in which people can be right with God. This way was not discovered by people but was *made known* by God. And it is righteousness *apart from law*. This means that we receive it without works.

This is news. It was not told or revealed before Jesus' coming. Nevertheless, the Law and the Prophets testified to it; the Old Testament Scriptures pointed forward to this great event as with an outstretched finger. But *now*, in the fullness of time, the righteousness has been revealed.

The way to get right with God is "through faith in Jesus Christ." Christ is the content of God's revelation of righteousness. He took our condemnation, and we received his righteousness. Faith in him makes us righteous. *Faith* means that we give up trying to do it ourselves; we rely entirely on the work of Jesus.

This is it. It is amazingly simple and simply amazing. And it is for everyone, for "all who believe."

Not only does the revelation of God's righteousness serve to show the lostness of all people: "all have sinned" (v. 23), it also fills the need of all people by means of the one great gift—Jesus Christ. We are "justified freely by his grace" (v. 24). This is the gospel. Here all the weary roads of humanity end. And here we find a new beginning.

Now we must place all our trust in Jesus. In him God has given us what we could not find. In Christ God came to us when we could not and would not come to him.

REFLECTIONS

We should be willing and able to tell others the "good news" (gospel). Try phrasing that good news in your own words.

On Your Account

ROMANS 4:1-8

However, to anyone who does not work but trusts God who justifies the ungodly, their faith is credited as righteousness. —Romans 4:5

The gospel is new. It was revealed with the coming of Christ—no sooner. However, "new" in the Bible means that the "old" is fulfilled—not abolished. When we buy a new car, the old one goes. But when God brings a *New* Testament or a *new* covenant or a *new* commandment or a *new* earth, the old is fulfilled in the new, as the seed is fulfilled in the plant or the child in the mature person.

Thus the gospel is not a complete break with the Old Testament. In fact, Paul shows that the gospel of righteousness by faith clarifies the way of salvation that was revealed in the Old Testament.

The relationship between God and Abraham was not an employer/employee relationship. If it had been, Abraham would have had rights and earnings. Instead, God came to Abraham with a promise, and Abraham had to respond with faith. For us the situation is essentially the same. We must respond to God's promise by faith.

Righteousness was obtained and is obtained by believing—not by working. When God *credited* righteousness to Abraham, it was not because Abraham had earned enough merit points or because he was really righteous. The righteousness was credited or imputed to Abraham when he *believed*.

And that's the way justification by faith works. We are not justified because we are good. God justifies the ungodly. The goodness of Christ is imputed to them when they believe. The merit points of Christ are written on the account of believing sinners by the God who justifies the ungodly.

Justification is not something that occurs within us; it is a legal work of God. God gives us the credits of Jesus. Christians are living off someone else's righteousness. When I look at myself, I cannot see if justification has really happened. I must look at Christ. In him I am righteous—by faith.

REFLECTIONS

What does it mean to you to be "justified by faith"? What difference does believing this key teaching make in your life?

Father of All Believers

ROMANS 4:9-12

> *And [Abraham] received circumcision as a sign, a seal of the righteousness that he had by faith while he was still uncircumcised. So then, he is the father of all who believe but have not been circumcised. . . .*   —*Romans 4:11*

What Paul says here about Abraham and his children sounded revolutionary to Jewish ears.

Abraham did not receive righteousness when he was circumcised. He was righteous before that, says Paul (v. 10). Paul makes it sound as if Abraham was a Gentile when God counted him righteous. Gentiles were the uncircumcised.

But Paul based his argument on Scripture. Genesis 15:6 says that Abraham "believed the Lord; and he credited it to him as righteousness."

Circumcision followed much later, in Genesis 17:24, as a sign and seal of the blessing that Abraham already possessed. Abraham was righteous not by circumcision but by faith.

Once Abraham is seen in this perspective, his fatherhood is enormously extended. All Gentiles are his children as long as they *believe* as he believed, for righteousness is not by circumcision but by faith.

At the same time, the fatherhood of Abraham is restricted. He is not the father of the Jews just because they are circumcised. He is the father only of those among the Jews who believe as he believed. Why? Because Abraham is not the father of the circumcised; he is the father of *believers*.

This is not just a clever finding of the apostle Paul to make his ministry to the Gentiles acceptable and defensible; it's the way God has fulfilled his promises to Abraham. Righteousness is not by circumcision but by faith. And God counts the children of Abraham not according to their Jewish heritage but according to faith. Anyone who counts differently is out of step not just with Paul's interpretation but with God's history of salvation.

Abraham and his children are righteous by faith. And only believers may claim Abraham as their father.

REFLECTIONS

You are a son or daughter of Abraham. How is this possible? And what does it mean to you?

Peace

ROMANS 5:1-5

Therefore, since we have been justified through faith, we have peace with God through our Lord Jesus Christ. —*Romans 5:1*

Self-righteous people have no use for the gospel of peace. They have no fear of God because they have no knowledge of themselves. Smug people cannot be afraid of God—simply because they are self-satisfied.

We don't have to fear for the salvation of those who are still afraid of God. For them there is hope. But tremble for those who cannot even be afraid anymore. They are self-righteous.

May God spare us the peace of the self-righteous!

As soon as people know they are sinners, they lose peace. They are dissatisfied and become afraid of God. But for people who fear, there is hope. At least they have an inkling of their unworthiness, even if they have not yet learned the worth of Christ.

It is true that many people fall into the rut of self-accusation. This can be deadly. In some Christian circles, self-depreciation is considered piety. It is learned and cultivated and endlessly prolonged. But it is not real piety. Rather, it is a subtle way of having other people think or say we aren't really as bad as we ourselves believe.

God does not want us to continue in self-accusation. He wants us to put our faith in Jesus Christ. If we trust that what Jesus has done is sufficient also for us, we have peace with God. And peace is a relationship of favor and friendship.

When we trust in Christ, our fears disappear. We are still "no good" in ourselves. But Christ is good. By faith in Christ, peace is established between God and us. The more I look at Christ, the better I can live with myself. If God has accepted me, I may also accept myself in Christ.

First I have peace with him. Then I get peace within.

Peace is never smugness, for it is based not on self-satisfaction but on the satisfaction of Christ.

REFLECTIONS

Do you have peace with God? With yourself? How do you know?

Love

ROMANS 5:6-11

But God demonstrates his own love for us in this: While we were still sinners, Christ died for us. —Romans 5:8

It is important to have a good hold on the basic teachings of the Bible. For instance, we should be able to show from the Bible what justification by faith means. And we should be able to state this doctrine in our own words to friends.

This fundamental teaching is always in danger of getting lost. That's why we should have such a hold on it that even when learned people and smooth talkers present a different doctrine, we stick to justification of sinners by faith in Jesus Christ. We must hold on to this gospel not *as if* our lives depend on it but *because* our lives depend on it.

False teachers aren't hard to find. There are lots of them around. That's why we need people who can discern sound doctrine. We need them as badly as we need unpolluted air.

However, the devil does not leave us alone when we have become soundly orthodox. Whenever our knowledge of Christian doctrine increases, we are also exposed to new dangers.

One of these dangers is that we may begin to think that our salvation rests on the right theory of the atonement and the correct understanding of justification. We begin to think that we are saved because we are able to point out where other Christians go wrong. The subtle devil will try to have us shift our confidence from Christ to teachings *about* Christ.

Then we must take time to reflect on Romans 5:8. We are saved not because we have the right theory of justification but simply because God loves us. And since God loved us, Christ died for us. He did not give his life for us while we knew him and loved him; he did it "while we were still sinners."

Certainly we should be able to say a few things about the cross: the *why* and the *how* and the *for whom*. But we must also be able to say nothing—merely be silent and look, just look at the cross. The cross is God's lasting assurance of his love for miserable sinners.

REFLECTIONS

Which do you need more: to learn more about key teachings like justification or to "merely be silent and look at the cross"?

One for Many

ROMANS 5:12-21

. . . Adam . . . is a pattern of the one to come. —*Romans 5:14*

How can all of us be saved by the death and resurrection of one man?

We can understand how this is possible when we think about Jesus Christ as the representative, the one who acts on behalf of the many.

The idea of representation is not strange to us. All of us know how the acts of a parent affect the whole family, for better or for worse. From the Old Testament we know examples of kings whose acts were decisive for the nation. Today's giant corporations are ruled by a few who decide for the many. But Adam's deeds decided for all humankind. And Adam is the best example you can use to show the extent of Jesus' work as one who represented many.

Adam stands at the beginning as the cause and origin of sin. In Paul's words, *sin* is a power that *came in* through the door called Adam (v. 12). Adam could have said: "I am the door; through me the ugly power entered."

Sin and death *came in* through Adam but *spread* to all, "because all sinned" (v. 12). Here Paul does not mean that all people are sinners because all people commit sins; he means that "all people sinned when Adam sinned." By his one representative act, Adam decided for all. All people sinned and died in him.

This is the perfect illustration of the one who represents the many: Adam "is a pattern of the one to come." Adam was the door through which sin and death came in to ruin us. But Christ is the door through whom grace and life come pouring in on all who are "in him."

Paul talks about Adam in order to clarify the one decisive act of the other man, Jesus. He teaches us the concept of representation so that we may be completely assured that the lot of the many was decided by the deeds of the one. The only ground for our salvation lies in the decisive acts of Jesus.

It's not what you or I have done but what Christ has done that brings us justification and life.

REFLECTIONS

Some people will object and say "it's not fair" that we must suffer the effects of sin just because of Adam and Eve's disobedience so long ago. How would you answer this objection?

Dead and Raised

ROMANS 6:1-11

In the same way, count yourselves dead to sin but alive to God in Christ Jesus. —Romans 6:11

From the very beginning of the preaching of the gospel, some people have objected that grace is dangerous. If all the emphasis is placed on the works of Christ, what happens to our works? And if the law of God and the sins of people merely serve to show the greatness of God's grace (Rom. 5:20), why should we live beautiful lives? "Shall we go on sinning so that grace may increase?" (v. 1). Or, as the Heidelberg Catechism puts it, "But doesn't this teaching make people indifferent and wicked?" (Question 64).

People become "indifferent and wicked" only when churches are peddling cheap grace. It will never happen as long as the churches preach the gospel. The accidents happen only when teachers are selling and people are buying grace without Christ—the gift without the giver.

According to the Christian gospel, the one represents the many. But let's not forget that the many are incorporated into the one. So those who believe in Jesus Christ are no longer Adam-people but Christ-people. We form a new body under a new power—a saving and renewing power.

Whatever happened to Christ happened to those who are in Christ. He died, so we died. He arose, so we arose, for we are embodied in Christ. "You are baptized, aren't you?" says Paul. "Well then, unless your baptism was merely playing with words and water, you share in the death and resurrection of Christ, for baptism shows the reality of our union with Christ."

From now on, you must "count yourselves dead to sin but alive to God in Christ." You must do so by exercising your faith.

Baptized Christians are in Christ. Therefore we are dead to sin. Sin has no claim on us any longer. Christ died, didn't he? And I am in Christ, am I not? So, what's past is past. And the new has come. With him we arose to a new life dedicated to God and governed by the Spirit. This new life begins not with a feat of strength but in the facts of faith.

REFLECTIONS

What does it mean to you to be "in Christ"?

The Price of Freedom

ROMANS 6:12-23

> *Do not offer any part of yourself to sin as an instrument of wickedness, but rather offer yourselves to God as those who have been brought from death to life. . . .* —*Romans 6:13*

In verse 11, the apostle told us that the battle is won. He says, in effect, "Look, it's past, it's over; you did die and you have been raised." But then in verse 12 he tells us to wage the war, to keep on fighting: "Don't let sin reign in you."

That's exactly what it means to live the new life of faith. The gospel declares that everything is finished and done. We are in Christ, and therefore we have died and have been raised. We have been punished for our sins in Christ, and we have begun the new life in Christ. The old dominion of sin has been broken. Now we live for God in Christ Jesus.

The gospel gives us this good news as a message that we must believe. But it also passes on the message in the form of a command: "Do not offer any part of yourself to sin . . . but rather offer yourselves to God." Every aspect of who we are and how we express ourselves—our bodies, our minds, our thinking, our talking, our doing—must be dominated by our new Master, not by the old one.

This is both a message and a command. If you believe the message, you will obey the command. And by obeying the command, you show your faith in the message.

The gospel declaration that we are in Christ Jesus is not a magic formula, for the other side of the coin is the gospel's command. Faith is followed by fight. From now on we may not allow the devil to use us as "instruments of wickedness." Rather, our whole being is devoted to God.

This is the tension of the new life. The tension itself is a sign of the presence of the new life. We are always fighting—or else we are not believing. And we will win, because Christ has won. We stand and fight by his power.

The price of our new freedom is constant vigilance. Pray and watch every hour. Our lives must show who is really Lord. And he must have his way with us.

REFLECTIONS

How do you experience the "the tension of the new life"?

A New Covenant

ROMANS 7:1-6

So, my brothers and sisters, you also died to the law through the body of Christ, that you might belong to another, to him who was raised from the dead, in order that we might bear fruit for God.
—Romans 7:4

We are free from the power of sin, as Paul teaches in chapter 6. We are also free from the power of the law, as he goes on to tell us in chapter 7.

Paul begins with an example from the field of law. He picks his example very carefully, because he wants to bring out two points: that we are set free from a law relationship and that we are free to enter into a new relationship.

This is how his argument goes:

- Law can apply only to people when they are alive (v. 1).
- The law for marriage ceases to be in force when one of the marriage partners has died (v. 2).
- As long as your spouse is living, you break the law when you give yourself to another; but after the death of your partner, this law no longer applies (v. 3).
- With our death "through the body of Christ," we are no longer under the law but ready for a new relationship (v. 4). We are going to be married to Christ by his Spirit. This is the new covenant.

This seems an elaborate way of making a point. And it raises questions about widows and widowers (it doesn't seem very nice to say that they are freed from the old law of marriage). But Paul isn't really concerned with marriage. He has his mind on what God did in Jesus Christ.

Paul is telling us that "under the law" our lives are unfruitful. We cannot obey even one of the commandments. But when "you have died to the law" in Christ, you can enter a new life of fruit-bearing for Jesus.

Nearly every day we meet people who were brought up in Christian homes, who know what's right and what's wrong and what they should do. But they don't *do* it. They know the law, but they don't know Christ. It is only in the new relationship, by the blood and the Spirit of Christ, that we can bear fruit.

REFLECTIONS

What would your life be like if were you were still living "under the law"? How would you describe your life under your new relationship to Christ?

Religious Despair

ROMANS 7:14-25

I know that good itself does not dwell in me, that is, in my sinful nature. For I have the desire to do what is good, but I cannot carry it out. —Romans 7:18

All human beings are religious. And "religion" is a human activity—not to be confused with the way of faith in the gospel.

Only God knows how many people take up religion as a way of salvation. But it will never work. True religion is a *fruit* of salvation. Human religion cannot save a soul.

There are bad religions: astrology is cold, Baha'i is like a tossed salad. All the self-development religions are pipe dreams—popular, expensive, and futile. But good religions don't work either: social work does not save, and memorizing Bible texts does not do the job.

North Americans devote about as many hours to religion as to keeping pets, and they invest almost as much money in dog food as in missionaries. But Romans 7 has taught us once and for all that religion does not save.

Why not? Because even the good that God has given to human beings is wasted on them. Even his holy law cannot bend us into a different kind of life. In fact, the more we learn about God's perfect will for our life, the more we experience our own wretchedness.

That's a frightful picture. But it's true. And we know it's true—not only because the Bible says so but because we have experienced it. Countless people get involved in religion for their temporal and eternal salvation. They may be more admirable than those who turn to liquor, but their pain and guilt are worse.

Only God can save a person. God *is* our salvation. God comes to us through Jesus Christ, and God brings us the power of the Holy Spirit. That's a new beginning none of us invented.

God—and God alone—can save. The most heroic efforts of the noblest people can only *will* what is right. They can never accomplish it.

Every religious pilgrim has to discover this anew.

REFLECTIONS

Reflect on how you learned or are learning that only God can save, that nothing you could do would make a difference. Then give thanks for what God has done for you in Christ.

Fulfilling the Law

ROMANS 8:1-11

> *For what the law was powerless to do because it was weakened by
> the sinful nature, God did by sending his own Son in the likeness
> of sinful humanity to be a sin offering. And so he condemned sin
> in human flesh, in order that the righteous requirement of the law
> might be fully met in us, who do not live according to the sinful
> nature but according to the Spirit.* —Romans 8:3-4

The law requires that we love God above all and our neighbors as ourselves. The tragedy is that we cannot do this. Even if we know God's
will, that does not make us any more able to do it. The *knowledge* of what
is right does not make people do the right. If we could print the Golden
Rule on all the billboards of the country so that all people could read the
will of God, it would not cure the country. The law is "weakened by [our]
sinful nature." We just cannot do it, no matter how hard we try.

However, for those who are "in Christ Jesus," there are two tremendous benefits. First, there is no condemnation for them, because Christ
has borne their condemnation. Second, in Christ Jesus they receive power
to do what they could not do. The requirement of the law is fulfilled in
them. They begin to love as they ought.

In other words, if we are in Christ Jesus, we share in his death and in his
resurrection. In Jesus' death, God has condemned us for our sins. He condemned sin in the flesh of Jesus. That has happened. There is now no condemnation for those who are in Christ Jesus. God will not punish us twice.

But the second benefit is equally important. We also share in Christ's
resurrection power. That power comes to us by the Holy Spirit. From
now on we do not live "according to the sinful nature but according to
the Spirit."

With Christ we pass from one state of being—"the sinful nature"—
into another—"the Spirit." First we had only human strength, which is
no strength at all when it comes to doing the will of God, but now we
have God's strength—the Spirit.

We may and we must walk in the new reality of the Spirit. We must
and we can do the will of God. That does not require our best efforts. It
requires faith. Let the Lord take over.

REFLECTION

Think of an example from your life of letting the Lord take over.

God's Adopted Children

ROMANS 8:12-17

*And by him we cry, "Abba, Father." The Spirit himself testifies
with our spirit that we are God's children. Now if we are children,
then we are heirs—heirs of God and co-heirs with Christ. . . .*
—Romans 8:15-17

In a time when so many families are falling apart, we thank God for the
many Christian parents who adopt children.

An adopted child has the full rights of a natural son or daughter. To
a Christian family, such an adopted child is a constant reminder of what
all Christians are in God's family—by grace and by rights.

All of us have become members of God's family by his grace. We have
no natural rights. Only Jesus Christ is God's *natural* Son. We are what
we are by God's love through Jesus.

Now we may—and must—behave as God's children in every way. We
must unlearn certain things like "living according to our sinful nature."
That's the way people outside of God's family live. Living this way is not
becoming for those who call God their Father.

Unlearning the old ways goes faster when we learn the new way. The
more we concentrate on learning the new way of God's household, the easier
it is to drop the old habits. The more we love God, the less we care for sin.

In an adoptive family, the new spirit in the child is developed by the
love that flows from the parents to their child. Likewise, the source of
our conversion power comes from our Father himself. It is the Father's
Spirit who teaches us to conform to Jesus. That's not our natural way of
living, but the Spirit of God overpowers our lives with his love. And then
things melt in us, and other things grow in us.

Sometimes we still find it hard to believe that God has really adopted
us to be his children. But the Spirit assures us. He teaches us to thank
God as our Father for all God is and all God has given.

The Spirit and the Word even tell us that everything Jesus has is now
ours. Why? Because we have the full rights of sons and daughters in
God's family.

REFLECTIONS

What does being an adopted child of God mean to you? Reflect and then
give thanks to your Father.

Undying Hope

ROMANS 8:18-27

For the creation was subjected to frustration . . . in hope that the creation itself will be liberated from its bondage to decay and brought into the freedom and glory of the children of God.
—*Romans 8:20-21*

We have been made to live—not to die. Although nothing is more common to the present life than death and dying, death is unnatural.

All that has breath hates death. People and animals fight for life, even at the portals of death. Death is accepted only by unhealthy people—by some philosophers who have rationalized the irrational or by ordinary people who are too sick and tired to go on.

When the creation is true to character, it wants to live. No creature submits willingly to corruption and death. And since we cannot deny our origin, we continue to hope. We know that all is subject to frustration, but we bang our heads against the bars in hope.

We keep hoping, amidst the tombstones, that somehow a new world may come, that somebody may someday invent something. Creation hopes for what it knows not. And thereby it testifies to the fact that it is the unwilling prisoner of decay.

Christians share this hope and understand this hope. The yearning for life and the groaning in prison are intensified in us because we, of all people, know about the new life and the new world. We have the beginning of the new world now. The firstfruit of the new country is in our hearts. It is the Holy Spirit. Already the first grapes of the promised land are tasted by the pilgrims. The first flowers of paradise are in the church of Jesus Christ.

When Christians hear the groaning of creation in this prison of decay, and when they hear on every side the song of hope God has laid in all his handiwork, they are confirmed in their faith that the new world is coming. We are now able to explain to our fellow sufferers why there is pain and why they keep hoping. And we are the vanguard of all who hope and pray and work for a better country.

Christians are the guides to that country. By God's grace they know where the renewal comes from, where it begins, and how it will be completed.

REFLECTIONS

Reflect again on what gives you undying hope in a world that's subjected to frustration and futility. How would you explain your hope to an unbeliever?

The Golden Chain

ROMANS 8:28-30

And those he predestined, he also called; those he called, he also jus-
tified; those he justified, he also glorified. —*Romans 8:30*

Let's begin with the "call." God calls a person by means of the gospel, addressing that person by his Word and Spirit. God tells him or her to repent and believe the good news about Jesus Christ.

Very likely God's call has come to you. That call may have come through a parent or a preacher or a teacher, but you knew that it was almighty God himself who laid his hand on you and said, "You are mine."

God never calls anyone by accident, offhandedly, or casually. People might do that. We sometimes say one thing today and forget about it tomorrow. But consistency, faithfulness, and reliability, which are so scarce among people, are the everlasting qualities of God.

Therefore, when God called us, this call constituted one link in a golden chain of events that stretches from everlasting to everlasting.

"Predestined . . . called . . . justified . . . glorified." That is the golden chain. Both ends of the chain are fastened beyond our horizon. One end is called *predestined*: it means that before we knew God, God knew us. Before we decided, God decided. Before we loved God, God loved us. This link of the chain is anchored in eternity.

The next two links can be known and experienced in time. They are God's call and his acquittal: *called* and *justified*. God says our names and then gives us our part in the righteousness of Christ.

The final link is forever fastened to the former ones. It is our reception to *glory*. Although this final link is again beyond our horizon, it is as sure as God himself.

So the call of the gospel has come to you. You are sure that it came from God himself. And your whole life has been taken up in the sovereign work of the Redeemer. No "accidents" can happen along the way. Without a doubt, God will lead you to his final goal.

REFLECTIONS

How does the imagery of "the golden chain" make you feel when you apply it to yourself? Be sure to express those feelings to the One who predestined you, called you by name, justified you, and who will one day glorify you!

Assurance

ROMANS 8:31-39

If God is for us, who can be against us? . . . Who will bring any charge against those whom God has chosen? . . . Who then can condemn? . . . Who shall separate us from the love of Christ?
—*Romans 8:31, 33–35*

Romans 8 is the chapter on the work of the Holy Spirit in the lives of God's children. So it closes with a beautiful song of assurance: "We know . . ." "I am sure . . ." "I am convinced . . ." These things we can say only by the Spirit of God.

Faith does not close our eyes to the realities of the opposition. Our spiritual environment is full of obstacles to faith, and countless forces want to drive us away from God.

But now faith hurls its challenges at the environment in which we live. In the assurance of God's power, we say, "If God is for us, who can be against us?" The gospel says that God is for us. And since God has come to our side, we have no fear. Let them come! God is for us! So who can be against us?

And who will bring any charge? We challenge the prosecutor. That's not only the devil but also, at times, our own heart. We are justified by faith, and it is from the position of faith that we challenge our deadly opponents. Even if my thoughts, my guilt feelings, and the devil himself should line up and poke fingers and shake fists, I cry into their faces that it is God who justifies. Even if my conscience accuses me, and even if the devil laughs, I say, "It is God who justifies! Who can condemn?"

And who shall separate us from the love of Christ?

We don't want to sound overly confident. By nature we are afraid of what is coming tomorrow. There are heights to travel and depths to go through. There are powers to face that suck our lifeblood. There are people and powers we fear by nature.

Now we line them up—all these powers and principalities. We don't underestimate them for a minute. But we confess and are persuaded that there is one power that is stronger than the power of money or the power of sex or the power of the devil. And that is the power of God's love. Nothing and nobody will be able to separate us from the power of God's love.

REFLECTIONS

Complete your own "I am convinced that" statement, citing the worries or concerns that sometimes threaten to separate you from Christ's love—but never will.

Transformation

ROMANS 12:1-2

Do not conform to the pattern of this world, but be transformed by the renewing of your mind. Then you will be able to test and approve what God's will is—his good, pleasing and perfect will.
—*Romans 12:2*

We must now think about the new style of living to which Christians are called. According to verse 1, it consists of surrender to God in perfect obedience.

When we give ourselves to God, we live quite differently than those who live for themselves. A lifestyle that is consistent with self-surrender to God is one that does not "conform to the pattern of this world." *This world* means whatever and whoever is still outside the redeeming movement of the Holy Spirit.

Paul does not describe the shape and fashion of the present world. We are all acquainted with it. We are supposed to see through it. We are not allowed to conform to it. The life of the old world—that is, the present world—is lived for the present and not for the future. God has no place in this kind of life. It is lived for self and for pleasure. It tries to avoid difficult questions and ultimate issues.

We are called to a new style of living in the broad patterns of our lives as well as in the details of living, our everyday behavior. Instead of imitating secular patterns, Christian living must proceed from inner renewal. "Be transformed by the renewing of your mind."

The renewal begins in our *mind*, the center of our conscious existence. It is the new principle that the Holy Spirit created in us when we were born "from above," or born again. Now this transformation must be worked out in our total behavior, so that all of it is pleasing to God.

This transformation of our existence into a new style of living is, of course, a lifelong, full-time job. And the last parts of the big job will not be finished until the Lord has completed his work with us. But don't use the size of the job as an excuse for postponing action. It's not enough to say that it's a big job; the question is how we are coming along right now.

The proof of the pudding is in the eating. The test of conversion is a new style.

REFLECTIONS

What pressures do you feel to "conform to the world"? Where do you see progress in your "transformation"?

The New Community

ROMANS 12:3-13

> . . . *we, though many, form one body, and each member belongs to all the others.* —*Romans 12:5*

Speaking of a new style of living (vv. 1-2) leads to a discussion of life within the church (vv. 3-13).

We do not develop a new lifestyle all by ourselves. We learn to live a new life within the new community God created in Christ Jesus—the church of Christ. Here the Spirit gives gifts to each person, so that everyone may contribute to the growth of all.

Today many Christians seem to combine a zeal for Christ with a disregard for the church. According to Paul's gospel, this is a contradictory attitude. We are saved and renewed only when we are *embodied* in Christ. And this body of Christians must accept, help, esteem, and love each other because they are one in Christ. Just as the members of the human body cannot live apart from the body to which they belong, so Christians cannot live the new life apart from the new community.

The New Testament does not view Christians as separate individuals who come together to form a body, a unit. The New Testament teaching starts with the unity of those who are in Christ. Individuals are never more or less than "members." And each believer must have a sober estimate of his or her function within this body.

The gripes and griefs we may have about the church are no excuse for separation. Often they are indications of our own shortcomings and reasons for more and better service "according to the grace given to each of us" (v. 6).

In our individualistic age, all Christians need the reminder that the new life in the fellowship of the church is just as much a part of the New Testament gospel as the teaching concerning the new life itself.

God knows the weaknesses of our fellow church members as well as we know them, and God knows our faults better than we do. All of us must pray that we will receive more of God so that we have more to give to others—for the health and growth of the community that lives for the age to come.

REFLECTIONS

What does being part of the community of believers mean to you? Consider praying as suggested in the last sentence of the reading.

A New Weapon

ROMANS 12:14-21

Do not be overcome by evil, but overcome evil with good.
—Romans 12:21

The gospel transforms us and teaches us a new lifestyle of surrender to God (vv. 1-2). This new way of living is learned within the new community—the church of Christ (vv. 3-13). The Bible gives directions on how to live with each other within the church. Its main message is that we must love each other. But in our relationships with those who would harm us, we must also use that new weapon of love.

The Christian life is first and last a life of love. This love comes from God, is revealed in Christ, and becomes ours by the Holy Spirit. It goes through us to others, and it is the best assurance that we are children of God.

Christian love is new and redeeming. It is desperately needed in our world where even natural affection has a hard time surviving.

"Do not be overcome by evil." Evil is a power that overcomes everyone who does evil—also the person who counters evil with evil. If we avenge ourselves, evil has scored a double victory: first we were the objects of evil, and then we became the subjects of evil. Both my adversary and I used the weapon of evil. Evil won.

"But overcome evil with good." Christians place good over against evil. While every "natural" person pitches evil against evil, Christians use a new weapon: they attempt to overcome evil with goodness.

Although many will smile at the very suggestion, Christians will practice this rule. They'll use the new weapon of love and goodness because they believe in the power of God.

But what if good does not prove to be stronger than evil? Shouldn't we refrain from wasting goodness on those who are evil? No! It is better to be a fool for God than to become a victim of evil. We are victims of evil only when we practice evil—not when we suffer for the cause of goodness.

REFLECTIONS

What form does evil sometimes take in your daily life? For example, have you been treated with hostility or prejudice or rudeness? What would a response of love and goodness look like in one or more of those situations?

God and Government

ROMANS 13:1-7

Let everyone be subject to the governing authorities, for there is no authority except that which God has established. The authorities that exist have been established by God. —Romans 13:1

It has always surprised students of Romans that this section about worldly governments is in the book about the new life and the new world.

In this section we are reminded that God controls our world while working out his plan of salvation. One of the ways in which God exercises his government of the world is through governments: "For there is no authority except that which God has established."

Today hardly anyone can read the principle that all authority is from God without raising a series of *but*s and *however*s. It seems too sweeping and too simple. And it is simple. These seven verses do not include a discussion of all the issues that could be raised with respect to government, such as accountability, obedience, and disobedience.

The basic principle is simple and straightforward: God rules through governments. Governors are God's servants for the benefit of citizens. Citizens must obey those who govern because it pleases God to rule us through them. For Christians, obedience to government is a matter of reverence for God. If this basic principle is not honored, society becomes impossible.

The Christian community will make no progress in Christian living if it refuses to honor God by obedience to the government. This obedience must show in the way we talk about our elected leaders, obey traffic laws, and fill in tax returns. If we cannot honor God in these little things, God cannot use us for the big things.

Here, then, is a general rule: "There is no authority except from God, and those authorities that exist have been instituted by God." Our obedience is grounded in a teaching that does not allow for exceptions.

Criminal opposition (not legitimate opposition) is rebellion against God. By their obedience to their governments, God's children show respect for God.

REFLECTIONS

What are some specific ways you try to show respect to "governing authorities"?

Love and Law

ROMANS 13:8-10

> *Love does no harm to its neighbor. Therefore love is the fulfillment of the law.*
> —*Romans 13:10*

We learn right behavior toward our neighbors only after we have experienced how God has conducted himself toward us.

God has loved us. Eternal love set all God's saving work in motion. God revealed the fullness of love in giving his Son for sinners. And God keeps us in his own love by the gift of the Holy Spirit in our hearts.

Now it's our turn to give. But whatever we give we must first receive. We cannot produce the kind of love the Bible talks about. We don't have this love. That's why we could not keep the law, for the law wants us to love. And we cannot give what God requires until God himself has given us what he is asking of us.

"Love is the fulfillment of the law." We have not yet done what God commanded if we refrain from murder and hatred. The law is fulfilled by *loving*. It is not enough to refrain from stealing what belongs to another. We must learn to share in love what God has entrusted to us. And love is learned from God. When we know God's love in Christ and when it is ours by the Spirit, we begin to love.

That's why boasting is out of place in the Christian life. What we give to our neighbor, we have received from God.

Some people misunderstand the Bible's teaching on Christian love. They think love has replaced the law, and that love is a feeling in your heart you must now follow as the rule for Christian behavior.

However, lawless love is not of the Spirit, just as loveless law is not of God. What the law requires can be given only in love. And the only ones who can render this obedience are those who have received new life and love through Jesus Christ.

Only after we have believed the gospel can we begin to fulfill the law. The more we know of God's love, the better we can obey God's law. For of him and through him and unto him are all things—even our own obedience.

REFLECTIONS

Think of an example of love without law and law without love. How would you describe the right relationship between love and law?

Daytime People

ROMANS 13:11-14

Let us behave decently, as in the daytime. . . .

—Romans 13:13

God made daytime and nighttime. Daytime is for work and play. Night-time is for sleep. Children learn this rule. When they don't go to bed on time, they are cranky in the morning. Since nobody tells grownups when they should go to bed, they often stay up too late. Then they don't perform very well the next day.

The Bible has based a figure of speech on this rule of God. But by *daytime people* the Bible does not mean those who go to bed on time or get up on time. Daytime people are those who got up when the *Son* began to shine!

On the clock of God's redemptive history, the hour to "get up and live" struck when Jesus performed his mighty acts of salvation.

Daytime people are those for whom salvation has come in Jesus Christ. They don't live in darkness anymore. People who live in darkness are those who don't know Christ. By their behavior they make it obvious that they don't know Jesus.

This passage of the Bible was once used by God to convert Augustine, a great leader in the early church. He lived in darkness—a wild nightlife—but he was converted and became the most influential teacher of the church.

The same words that converted him tell us to live as *daytime people*. Our moral behavior should be able to stand the bright light of day.

In the second half of verse 13, Paul mentions the things that are done by the children of darkness: *carousing* and *drunkenness*, *sexual immorality* and *debauchery*, *dissension* and *jealousy*. The first two words have to do with drinking parties, the second two are words for sexual immorality, and the third pair always go with such immorality. They are the exact opposites of Christian love.

The sins committed by the people of darkness are reminiscent of Roman night life. But the same words could be used to describe the darkness that has descended on much of our culture.

As *daytime people*, let's have nothing to do with these sins.

REFLECTIONS

What do you think—is it getting harder or easier to be daytime people? What in our society lures people—including Christians—towards the darkness?

Free

ROMANS 14:1-12

You, then, why do you judge your brother or sister? Or why do you treat your brother or sister with contempt? For we will all stand before God's judgment seat. —Romans 14:10

Parents regulate all things for their young children. But when children grow up, they have to make their own decisions. In fact, a big part of education is teaching children to make their own decisions.

Compared with Old Testament times, New Testament believers have to make many decisions for themselves. God treats us like growing children. God has made us free, and Christians must learn to use their freedom responsibly. We may not force each other to a certain kind of behavior in areas in which God has given us freedom.

Many church members want the ruling bodies of the church to make their decisions for them. And some unwise pastors and church assemblies attempt to enforce rules that the Lord has not laid down. Christians must stand in their freedom, and church leaders may not demand more than the Scriptures.

We are never free, however, to forget the Lord. God is our judge. This we must constantly remember. We must live in such a way that our conscience convinces us that God approves of our actions. We are never free to disobey. Freedom is curbed by obedience.

Freedom is also tempered by love. When we decide what we will do and what we will not do, we need to consider not only our personal responsibility toward God but also our responsibility toward our fellow Christians. Our actions may never become harmful to others—by example or by challenge.

Our main obligation toward the fellowship of the church is to make others stronger. Our concern for fellow believers must be so strong that we are willing to give up certain rights. Why? Because love for fellow believers is more important than the rights of any individual.

We need wisdom if we are to grow up as free and mature Christians. We need to keep in mind all the principles: God alone is our judge. His will is the only law. Christian freedom may not be violated. Love is the greatest.

REFLECTIONS

Try applying the principles mentioned above to a specific issue involving Christian freedom that you (or your church or denomination) are facing.

When in Doubt, Abstain

ROMANS 14:13-23

> *But those who have doubts are condemned if they eat, because their eating is not from faith; and everything that does not come from faith is sin.*
> —Romans 14:23

We must do all things in the conviction that we are doing right before God. When we lack that conviction, we must abstain.

That's different from saying that we can do anything—as long as we "can't see anything wrong in it." That phrase we hear too often. People always say it defensively: "If you can't prove I'm wrong, I'll go ahead and do it."

We ought to be more serious about living with the gift of freedom. Jesus Christ has set us free from the power of sin and the power of the law. He has given us peace with God. Now we must use that freedom responsibly. And at all times we must retain our peace with God.

After all, the basic rule of Christian living is that we live by faith. Whether we eat or drink, live or die, we are the Lord's. This tie with God, which is called *faith*, must be preserved at all costs. So Paul did not tell the "weak" members that they should eat what he considered to be legitimate food (v. 14). Instead he told them that they must "keep the faith" (v. 22). Whenever they think they cannot do a certain thing and keep faith in God at the same time, they should not do it.

The biblical principle is that "those who have doubts are condemned." Why? Because "everything that does not come from faith is sin."

The blessedness of our lives is never in the things we see or eat or do or buy but always in our relationship to God. If that relationship is broken, all things turn to ashes. Any fun, any gain, any day, anything for which we cannot honestly thank God is not of faith. It is sin; it comes between God and us. It can never be a blessing. It is a curse. The principle is that we should abstain when in doubt.

But any fun, any feast, any gift, any purchase, and any relationship that is "from faith" is good. God must be praised and thanked for such things because he is the source from whom all blessings flow.

REFLECTIONS

What kinds of things might you abstain from because you could not honestly thank God for them?

God's Ongoing Work

ROMANS 15:14-21

I will not venture to speak of anything except what Christ has accomplished through me in leading the Gentiles to obey God by what I have said and done. . . .   —*Romans 15:18*

God is using us to win others and bring them to the obedience of faith.

When this happens, we must be careful not to take any credit. *If* we are going to speak about it at all, we should follow Paul's example and talk only about "what Christ has accomplished through me."

The work of Christ did not come to a close with his ascension. When Paul speaks of Jesus as the subject of his missionary work, he is not using a pious phrase. He is simply stating the reality of Christ's ongoing work— "what Christ has accomplished through me." Jesus' work is not limited to what he did while on earth; today he continues his work through us.

The dignity and nobility of the Christian life and the Christian church is precisely that we are tools of God. The gospel that was proclaimed by the apostles and that we are studying in Romans takes on flesh and blood in today's believers. God uses Christians to make other people bow before him.

The question is not whether Christ is alive. He is! The question is not whether he is working. He is! The question is whether Christians are making themselves available as willing tools for Christ's ongoing mission.

How many of us are able to tell "what Christ has accomplished" through us to win others?

If we take the time to answer this question, we should reply as members of the body of Christ, the church. The Christian mission has countless aspects. It includes works of mercy to assist the needy, Christian political activity, training Christian teachers, translating the Scriptures, ministries in countless institutions, sending workers abroad, and much more.

Christ uses all the members of his church in this one grand work. "Join me in my struggle by praying to God for me," said Paul (v. 30). God uses all members of his church to bring all people to obedience.

How are you being used?

REFLECTIONS

Reflect on how God is using you in his ongoing mission. Pray for a willingness to work for the Lord as opportunities are provided.

Shalom

ROMANS 16:17-20

The God of peace will soon crush Satan under your feet.
—Romans 16:20

When he comes to the close of his letter, the apostle thinks of the congregation of Christ—how it is surrounded by evil forces and false teachers (vv. 17-18). But then he encourages the church and himself by pointing at the work God is doing: "The God of peace will soon crush Satan."

Often the Bible calls God by the gifts he gives. For example, God is called the "God of grace" and the "God of comfort" and the "God of encouragement." Why? Because God is the source and origin of these gifts that flow to us. Here Paul calls him the "God of *peace*."

When we call God the "God of peace," we mean more than that we have peace with God through our Lord Jesus Christ. We also mean that God is the God of *shalom*—an old Hebrew word that most believers have learned again.

Shalom is peace and prosperity, wholeness and healing, harmony and rest. It is the peace of God's kingdom. The "God of peace" is the one who brings the kingdom.

God brings this shalom of paradise, this everlasting kingdom, by crushing Satan. "The God of peace will soon crush Satan under your feet." This statement refers back to the first promise God made when he punished people and cursed the serpent (Gen. 3:15). That promise is now being fulfilled.

The serpent (Satan, or the devil) is the great disturber of the peace. Once he is crushed, shalom is established. By the work of Jesus Christ, the devil has received the decisive blow. Today this battle goes on. Soon it will be over.

"The God of peace will soon crush Satan *under your feet*." God does the crushing, but he uses the shoes of his church. Through us, the Lord fights to make peace in the world. God does it, but he does not do it without us.

"Soon" all evil will be defeated. The ancient foe is about to be crushed. Then it will be *shalom*, my friends. Shalom!

REFLECTIONS

How do you see the church—your church—fighting to make peace in the world?

The Obedience of Faith

ROMANS 16:25-27

> *The mystery . . . is now disclosed, and . . . is made known to all the Gentiles, according to the command of the eternal God, to bring about the obedience of faith.* —*Romans 16:25-26, NRSV*

At the close of his letter, Paul repeats a phrase that he also used at the beginning: "the obedience of faith." He started out by saying that he was appointed to bring the gospel to the Gentiles "to bring about the obedience of faith" (1:5). He closes by praising God for this gospel, the good news that was hidden in God until it was revealed in Jesus. Now this good news is being made known to all nations, "to bring about the obedience of faith."

Apparently "obedience of faith" is the objective of gospel preaching. When the hearers have listened well, or when the readers have read rightly, the result of the confrontation with the gospel is "obedience of faith."

This is a strange phrase, for it seems to bring together two things that are often contrasted in Romans. Paul has told us so often that salvation comes by hearing and not by doing, by promise and not by law, and by believing and not by working. Nevertheless, we can also say that the whole purpose of preaching the gospel is to bring all people to "the obedience of faith."

The gospel is not a new law. It aims at *faith* in the hearer. But faith includes the recognition that Jesus is Lord. Therefore faith can also be described as obedience, that is, "obedience of faith."

The gospel is always message and command at the same time. The Word of the gospel says to us, "You are a new person in Jesus Christ." That's the message we are to believe. Then it continues, "You must live as a new person in Jesus Christ." That's the command. If we believe the gospel, we will obey the command. And only our obedience to the command shows that we have believed the gospel.

The mission of God, which he fulfills through his servants, aims at "obedience of faith" among all nations. That's why God revealed the gospel and gave us Paul's letter to the Romans.

REFLECTIONS

As you end this study of the book of Romans, you may want to pray the words of its final verse: "to the only wise God be glory forever through Jesus Christ! Amen."

God's Last Word

The letter to the Hebrews explains that what God says to us in Christ is God's last word. Nothing more is hidden; God has said it all.

daylight

God's Last Word

HEBREWS 1:1-4

> *In the past God spoke to our ancestors through the prophets at many times and in various ways, but in these last days he has spoken to us by his Son. . . .*   *—Hebrews 1:1-2*

The New Testament divides history into two parts—the days before Christ and the time after the coming of Christ.

In both time periods God addressed his people—his Word was heard through human mouths. The difference is in the instrument God used. In the old days God spoke "through the prophets." The word *prophets* is used in the widest sense, so that Moses as well as David and Isaiah are included. But in these last days God has spoken to us "by his Son."

You and I are living in the last days—and God has spoken to us by his Son. The letter to the Hebrews explains that what God has said to us in Christ is indeed God's last word. Every chapter emphasizes this central fact.

In what sense is God's message in Christ the last word?

First, it is the last word because it is God's deepest Word. It is not just the truth; it is *all* of the truth. Now God has told us "all his heart." Nothing remains hidden. God has said it all.

Some people are afraid that there are dark and hidden facts about God, "things you never know," things that might fill us with fear or suspicion. But that is simply not true. God has told us everything we need to know about him by means of Christ, his only Son.

Second, what God has said in Christ is the last word because it is God's final word, the last will and testament. We should not expect any further revelation.

Somehow we always want to look for a new revelation that is more exciting than the one we have already. Many religious cults and sects thrive on this expectation.

But don't be confused by the deceivers who claim to have a more recent revelation. If we know what God has done and said in Christ, we have God's last word for the last days.

REFLECTIONS

What are some implications of Christ being God's last word? Try completing this statement: "Because Christ is God's last word, I . . ."

The Hardest Question

HEBREWS 2:1-4

. . . how shall we escape if we ignore so great a salvation?
—Hebrews 2:3

In days of old, God spoke from Mount Sinai through Moses. God did not just tell the people what they had to do; he also set down the penalties for those who refused to obey his voice. Every transgression received its just retribution.

The New Testament does not have a criminal code. But this does not mean that those who disregard the "last word" of God will escape without penalty. For those who neglect Jesus, the punishment will be beyond description: "How shall we escape if we ignore so great a salvation?"

The contrast is between *then* and *now*, between *they* and *we*. If *they* could not escape the penalty for every breach of the law, how shall *we* escape if we neglect the gospel of the Son of God? After all, we are living in the last days and have received God's last word.

Note that the Bible does not say, "If we *reject* salvation." It says, "How shall we escape if we *ignore* salvation—such a great salvation?"

The majority of those who are not saved will be lost "simply" because they have not paid attention to the gospel of the Son of God. They have not openly rejected God's last and loving word, but they have shamefully ignored it and neglected it. More people perish by disregarding the gospel than by opposing God's Word.

The Bible has answers to our most perplexing problems. If a person has committed such a vile sin that even his or her friends have turned away, the Bible still shows a way out and Christ is still a healer. If a person has degenerated so far that even his or her mother despairs, God can open a whole new perspective of regeneration.

But there is one question that remains, even in the Bible. No one knows the answer, and even God is silent: "How shall we escape if we ignore so great a salvation?"

REFLECTIONS

How can apathy toward Christ and our salvation creep into a Christian's life? What might "ignoring" our salvation look like?

How We Got the Gospel

ACTS 1:1-8

> *This salvation, which was first announced by the Lord, was confirmed to us by those who heard him. God also testified to it by signs, wonders and various miracles, and by gifts of the Holy Spirit distributed according to his will.* —Hebrews 2:3-4

What we know as the New Testament is God's last word for the last days. But how did we get the gospel of God in this written and printed form? The book did not fall from heaven. It has a history.

It was "first announced by the Lord." What Christ said and did was God's good news to people. This was the first form of the gospel.

Not only did Christ proclaim his message and fulfill his mission, he also prepared for the church of the future. He saw to it that faithful witnesses would tell the world what he had said and done. These witnesses were mainly the twelve apostles who had been with him since the beginning of his ministry. And it was to these apostles that Christ showed himself alive after he had risen from the dead.

These witnesses carried their report into the world. And while they did that, "God also testified to it by signs, wonders and various miracles, and by gifts of the Holy Spirit." In this way God was underlining the truth of what the apostles were saying.

For instance, through the apostle Peter, God made a lame man leap (Acts 3) and punished a liar with death (Acts 5). God even brought a dead woman back to life (Acts 9). Thus God proclaimed loudly that the message of the apostles was reliable.

Then came the third stage. The apostles died, but the believers were very careful to adhere to the apostolic teaching. They needed the great message in a permanent form. God provided for that need by preserving both the church and the apostolic record.

The report of the apostles who were witnesses to Christ was written down under God's care. It is the New Testament. This is the last word for the last days. No one who clings to it can go wrong. And no one can survive if he or she ignores it.

REFLECTIONS

God took great care to make sure we got his message. What does that tell you about God? About us? About God's message?

Christ Our Brother

HEBREWS 2:5-13

So Jesus is not ashamed to call them brothers and sisters.

—*Hebrews 2:11*

A respectable person may have an unrespectable brother. This can be very embarrassing for the respectable one. Never ask, "How is that brother of yours, the one who used to be in jail?" Our decent friend is ashamed of that brother and would rather not talk about him.

But there is amazing comfort in Hebrews 2:11: the Son of God is not ashamed to call *us* his brothers and sisters!

The eternal Son of God saw the rebellion on our planet. He saw you and me bowed down and wounded. We were in the prison of our sins, thoroughly unrespectable. Then he said something like this to his Father, "Father, those creatures of yours are lost and dying. I want to go and share their lot. I want to live their life, and I want to die their death. I want to become their brother so they may become your children."

That's how Christ became our trailblazer. He walked ahead of us, right through the jungle of our misery, through sin and death and hell, and opened a path to the Father. With great joy he stood before the Father again and said, "Here am I, and the children God has given me" (v. 13).

Jesus Christ is not ashamed of us.

If we absorb this truth and then recall the occasions when we were ashamed to be associated with Jesus, we groan under a burden of guilt.

If we reflect on the fact that Jesus is not ashamed to call us brothers and sisters, how can we ever again prefer the company of the rich and the popular? No, since Jesus unashamedly embraces us, we count it our highest honor to identify with the least of his brothers and sisters.

Once we know how unworthy we are of Christ's love, we will never be ashamed of each other.

REFLECTIONS

Jesus calls you his brother or sister. What does that mean to you?

Flesh and Blood

HEBREWS 2:14-18

Since the children have flesh and blood, he too shared in their humanity so that by his death he might break the power of him who holds the power of death—that is, the devil—and free those who all their lives were held in slavery by their fear of death.

—Hebrews 1:14-15

We are only people. The Bible calls us beings of flesh and blood. That expression reminds us that we are weak and mortal. For flesh and blood, no desire is stronger than the desire to live, and no fear is greater than the fear of death.

We try hard to cover our fears, but we are never quite successful. Death is our constant companion. But we never get used to him. We "cannot live with him." In order to live a "normal life," we must suppress the knowledge that death is only a breath away.

We don't have to try so hard to cover our fears. Our desires for life and our fears of death rightfully belong to flesh and blood. We are not being sinful if we don't want to die; we are being human. And even God does not ask more of us than that we be perfectly human.

The eternal Son of God became a Son of man. He shared in our flesh and blood, and he shared our human nature. He existed as we exist with a desire to live and a fear of death.

But *his* existence and *his* death have made a great difference for *our* existence and *our* approaching death. Jesus has not taken death away. Flesh and blood must still die. But Jesus has made death his own tool. For all who trust him, Christ has taken the fear out of dying.

Since Christ has lived our kind of life and died our kind of death, things have changed. Through death, Christ has destroyed him who had the power of death—that is, the devil. That triumph has changed our flesh-and-blood way of living. Death is not the cave where the devil's prisoners go. It's a narrow passage through which we go to be with Christ.

Now Christ begins to make our lives free from fear and full of faith. And when the last day comes, he will give us the full assurance that we will move nearer to him.

REFLECTIONS

How does Christ becoming "flesh and blood" help you face your own death?

The House of God

HEBREWS 3:1-6

> *Moses was faithful as a servant in all God's house. . . . But Christ is faithful as the Son over God's house. And we are his house, if indeed we hold firmly to our confidence and the hope in which we glory.* —Hebrews 3:5-6

The letter to the Hebrews constantly compares the old covenant with the new covenant to show that the new is better than the old.

This time the comparison is between Moses, the mediator of the old covenant, and Christ, by whom we have entered the new covenant. The point is, Moses was great, but Christ is greater.

Both Moses and Christ are called "faithful." Moses was faithful as a *servant*, and Christ as a *Son*. Moses was faithful *in* God's house; Christ, as the Son, was faithful *over* God's house.

Israel is called a house or household of God, and the church of the New Testament is also called a household of God. The two are compared with each other. The conclusion is that it is greater to be a member of the church ruled by the Son than to be a member of the people who were taught by Moses, God's servant.

Today the importance of the Jewish people is loudly proclaimed by many Christians. But the writer to the Hebrews says that the house of God in the New Testament is better than the house of God in the Old Testament. Why? Because Jesus is more than Moses.

The Hebrews to whom he was writing were Jews who had accepted Jesus as the Messiah. The writer was telling them that by moving from the household of Moses to the church of Christ, they moved from the lesser to the greater. And they will remain the household of God only if they continue in the freedom and hope God has now given them in Christ.

The Bible wants us to acknowledge the riches of the church of the New Testament as compared with God's people under the old covenant. We should realize anew that Christ and his household belong together. You cannot have the one without belonging to the other.

REFLECTIONS

The writer tells the Hebrews (and us) that we are the house of God. What does that mean to you?

Daily Encouragement

HEBREWS 3:7-14

But encourage one another daily, as long as it is called "Today," so that none of you may be hardened by sin's deceitfulness.
—Hebrews 3:13

God has now spoken his last word for the last days. There is nothing more important than that we hear and obey that word. In Old Testament days, many of those who heard his Word were lost nevertheless. That must be a warning to us: "See to it that none of you has a sinful, unbelieving heart that turns away from the living God" (v. 12).

Since our path is dangerous and sin is deceitful, Christians must live in a fellowship that exercises a watchful care over its members. Within this fellowship, Christians should "encourage one another daily." We need daily stimulation to faith and good works. We need it ourselves, and we owe it to each other as a daily payment of love.

This is the biblical norm for the life of Christian churches. We hardly ever realize how far we have departed from this norm and how much we have adapted ourselves to the demands of modern ways of living. Instead of "encouraging one another daily," countless church members take one hour a week to sit in a big building in order to be "encouraged" by a preacher at a distance. Then they are "busy" until next Sunday.

Avoidance of Christian fellowship shows that we are not aware of the seriousness of God's last word, nor of the reality of sin's deceit.

The Bible says, "Encourage one another daily, as long is it is called 'Today.'" *Today* is the time of God's grace—the period during which God speaks in Jesus Christ. As for our personal lives, it's obvious that "today" cannot exceed our lifetime. But the writer has another crisis than our death in mind when he says that "today" is right now: "that none of you may be hardened by sin's deceitfulness." Hardening begins with a reduced sensitivity of conscience and ends with a total inability to hear and do God's Word.

We must stand firm, and we must stand together. Faith must be warmed by fellowship. Otherwise the devil takes his toll.

REFLECTIONS
How does the "fellowship of the saints" encourage you in your faith? Give thanks for people who stimulate you to faith and good words.

The Rest

HEBREWS 4:1-10

There remains, then, a Sabbath-rest for the people of God.
—Hebrews 4:9

Sabbath rest is the goal of life. This rest is also the full and final promise to all who hear God's voice *today*.

The work of creation described in the first chapter of Genesis was fulfilled on the Sabbath day. On that day, God and all of creation fully enjoyed the wonder and goodness of it all. In the same manner, the work of redemption will finally be crowned and fulfilled in Sabbath rest. On that day, God and the redeemed world will fully enjoy the wonder of it all.

"Rest" is the enjoyment of God and what God gives. The final rest is the full and uninterrupted joy and harmony of the new world.

The Old Testament people of God were given a picture of Sabbath rest not only in their weekly cessation of work but also in the country granted them as a heritage. The name of the man who led Israel from the desert to the promised land was *Joshua*. In Greek his name is *Jesus*. This old covenant Jesus could bring Israel to a picture of the country to which the new covenant Jesus is leading *his* people. Jesus fulfills everything that Moses and Joshua did. Jesus brings God's people to the promised land.

Today God calls us to learn from the bad example of others. That's very difficult. It's a rare son who learns from his father's mistakes. Yet the new Israel (that's us) must learn from the old Israel.

We are told that thousands of God's old covenant people never entered into the rest of the promised land. They fell in the desert because they did not believe.

Now we are traveling through the desert. Our leader is Jesus. We must stay very close to him and do exactly what he says. We must also stay close to each other. And when the going gets rough, one of us should always point forward: "Look, there is the land of rest!"

REFLECTIONS

How do you get through the "deserts" in your life? What comfort does this Scripture and reading give you for those times?

Sympathy and Help

HEBREWS 4:11-16

For we do not have a high priest who is unable to empathize with our weaknesses, but we have one who has been tempted in every way, just as we are—yet he did not sin. Let us then approach God's throne of grace with confidence, so that we may receive mercy and find grace to help us in our time of need. —Hebrews 4:15-16

Most of us feel, at one time or another, as if others never quite understand our problems. "You don't understand what I have to go through." Perhaps we say that as an excuse for our failures. Or maybe it's an honest expression of the loneliness we experience.

However, we can never say to Christ that he does not know what we have to bear. He was tempted as we are in all points. There is no weakness in us that he does not know, and we face no trouble with which he is not acquainted.

Christ shared our weaknesses without committing sin. He knows what it is to be tired. He has been disappointed in people more than anyone else ever was. He has tasted fear of pain, and the fear of death has made him tremble. He knows how a person can be tempted in all these experiences. But he did not sin.

The point of this text is not to tell us that since Christ knows how hard it can be for us, he'll be quick to forgive us. (Some people say: "When you know it all, you can forgive it all.") No, the point is that since we know Christ has been through it, we must boldly and confidently go to the throne of grace in our hour of trial. He knows. He understands. And he can help.

Not only is Christ profoundly sympathetic and empathetic, he also has tremendous power. He is now on the throne. That's why we go to him without hesitation. We call on him boldly, "with confidence," that is, with faith and daring.

And we do not ask Jesus only for sympathy but also for help. We may ask that his mercy remove our burden. Or to give us power to bear the burden. But the main purpose of our prayers is—or should be—that we be kept from sinning in the hour of our trial, just as Christ did not sin when he was on trial.

REFLECTIONS

What burdens are you struggling with right now? Have you approached the "throne of grace" and confidently asked for mercy and help?

He Saves Those Who Obey

HEBREWS 5:1-10

> *Son though he was, he learned obedience from what he suffered and, once made perfect, he became the source of eternal salvation for all who obey him.*　　　　　　　—Hebrews 5:8-9

When the Bible says that the Son of God "learned obedience," it does not mean that he had to learn *how* to obey. Rather, by all his sufferings, he had to learn the full weight of obedience.

This passage in Hebrews likely refers to Christ's agony in the garden of Gethsemane. There he cried and wept and learned the holy and terrible will of God (Luke 22:39-46). Through his suffering, he learned the full meaning of the word *obedience*.

Then he was "made perfect," which does not mean sinless, for he was already sinless. It means he came to the *goal*; he reached the aim of his work by rendering full obedience in the most trying circumstances.

Now he has become "the source of eternal salvation for all who obey him." The Son's obedience to the Father corresponds to our obedience to the Son. The salvation procured by the obedience of the Redeemer is available to the redeemed who obey.

We must always maintain a proper distance between Christ and ourselves. Christ is our Savior. We are saved because of his obedience, not because of ours. At the same time, we may not imagine that we are so different from Christ that we leave the obedience to him while we continue to be disobedient. You cannot say that you believe in Christ if you refuse to obey him. The Bible knows no faith without obedience.

If someone should come running into a meeting and shout, "Fire, get out!" the only way to show that you believe what he or she says is to obey the command. You believe that there is a fire only when you run to get out. This is how faith and obedience are related as one act of confidence.

We must trust and obey. There's just no other way.

REFLECTIONS

How have you learned to "trust and obey"?

Milk or Solids

HEBREWS 5:8-14

> *In fact, though by this time you ought to be teachers, you need someone to teach you the elementary truths of God's word all over again. You need milk, not solid food!* —Hebrews 5:12

When the author of Hebrews was about to begin an explanation of the priesthood of Christ, he suddenly doubted if his audience was ready for the subject. Certainly they should have been ready: "You ought to be teachers." But they still needed milk, the food of babies, instead of the solid foods mature people eat.

No one will enter the kingdom of God without a childlike faith. But that does not mean God wants us to be childish. All people must be born again, or they will never see the kingdom of God. But that does not mean God wants us to remain spiritual babies.

Too often, education in the Christian church is almost entirely confined to children. Many full-grown people who have developed their intellectual abilities to a high degree have an understanding of the Scriptures on the level of a ten-year-old. They ought to be teachers but they live on a spiritual diet of milk.

Christian education is the need of the hour! The weird sects that have mushroomed all over the world would not have had a chance if ordinary Christian people had known their doctrines. Nearly every new sect is the revival of an old sin.

Of course, none of us ever outgrows the ABCs of salvation. We can never discard the basics, but we have to work with them and build on them. Unless we go deeper and higher, we stand in danger of losing even what little we have.

Education must be taken seriously by the church at large and by each member individually. A weak faith may be caused by any one of a number of factors. Flirting with sin, neglecting prayer, keeping the wrong company, and similar things are well-known causes of feeble faith. But all experienced and godly pastors will agree that the main cause of weak faith is ignorance.

REFLECTIONS

What might you consider doing to increase your knowledge of God and his Word?

The Certainties of Faith

HEBREWS 6:13-20

Because God wanted to make the unchanging nature of his purpose very clear to the heirs of what was promised, he confirmed it with an oath. —Hebrews 6:17

Some Christian people are opposed to the use of oaths in courtrooms. Although I agree that Christians ordinarily do not need to swear an oath (their yes is simply yes and their no means no), the oath before the magistrate is still meaningful.

The oath is an admission that all people are unreliable. Their words are not to be trusted. You are a liar and I am a liar, we are saying, but now we are going to swear an oath: "So help me God." Placing ourselves solemnly before the One who cannot lie, we say, "I promise to speak the truth, the whole truth, and nothing but the truth, so help me God." In this situation, people "swear by someone greater than themselves, and the oath confirms what is said" (v. 16).

But now God swears an oath. That seems totally unnecessary. God's every word is true. Why, then, should he have to confirm that which can stand by itself?

God wants to help us in our weakness. He wants us to believe deeply that his promises are "firm and secure." Through "two unchangeable things" (the Word and oath of God) "in which it is impossible for God to lie," we may be "greatly encouraged" (v. 18).

The main business of the church of Christ is the administration of the Word and the sacraments. This business, if faithfully done, will build the church and serve the coming of God's kingdom. The sacraments (baptism and the Lord's Supper) add nothing to the Word. You don't get anything "extra" from the sacraments that you would not have by believing the Word of the gospel.

The Word and the sacraments are like the promises and the oath of God. God surrounds us by his yes and amen, "an anchor for the soul." Therefore we are greatly encouraged to trust him completely.

REFLECTIONS

What assures you that God's promises are absolutely reliable?

The Last and Everlasting Priest

HEBREWS 7:21-25

Therefore he is able to save completely those who come to God through him, because he always lives to intercede for them.

—*Hebrews 7:25*

The gospel is God's last word, also because it is the news about the last priest who presented the last sacrifice. And this priest lives forever to save forever all who seek access to God through him.

A priest is a person who helps people come to God. All nations and religions have had priests. They would bring people into contact with God by sacrifices, secret arts, rituals, and prayers. The human race has always known that there is a God, and people have universally realized that they need help to be restored to this God.

The author of Hebrews disregards the world religions. He speaks only about the religion of Israel. He surveys the long line of the sons of Levi and the sons of Aaron, and he shows the imperfection of their priestly work. Then he contrasts them with the perfect priest who brought a complete and final sacrifice. This priest is Jesus Christ.

The priests under the old covenant brought sacrifices repeatedly and endlessly. The smoke went up and the blood flowed. Bullocks and goats and lambs. More and more, never enough. The very repetition seemed to say: "Not enough, not enough." But then came the last sacrifice of the last priest, the real priest. "It is finished!" No more the bleating cry of the dying lambs, for the Lamb of God has taken away the sins of the world.

Jesus became our everlasting priest. He does not need to be replaced. The succession of the sons of Levi came to an end. Christ lives forever in the holy place of God to save forever all those who come to God through him. The last priest is the everlasting priest.

By implication, all other priests of all other religions are declared ineffective. All efforts to come to God must fail. We can find God only through the priestly work of Jesus.

REFLECTIONS

Jesus is your everlasting high priest. What comfort and security does this give you?

The Priest-King

HEBREWS 7:26-8:1

Now the main point of what we are saying is this: We do have such a high priest, who sat down at the right hand of the throne of the Majesty in heaven. —Hebrews 8:1

Under the old covenant, the priests were not the only ones who could establish contact between God and the people. There were also prophets and kings—rulers. God used these three "offices" to maintain the traffic with his people.

The prophet spoke *for* God *to* the people. The priest spoke *for* the people *to* God; he led the people to God by means of sacrifices and prayer. And the king ruled *over* the people *on behalf of* God. Without the prophet, the people would not know the will of God. Without the priest, the people would not have the peace of God. And without the king, they could not enjoy the protection of God.

Today Jesus fulfills all these functions for God's people. Jesus has revealed the will of God, he has become our way to God, and God rules us through him.

Christ is our prophet because in these last days God has spoken his last word through him. Christ is our priest because he has led us to God by his once-for-all sacrifice. And Christ is our king because he is seated "at the right hand of the throne of the Majesty in heaven."

All our knowledge of God, service of God, and worship of God is concentrated in Jesus Christ. Outside of him we do not know God, cannot please God, and have no protection by God.

In the text printed above, we are asked to get "the main point" of Christ's priestly kingship. The writer wants us to observe that the great high priest of Christians is exalted above all, that he is not in a human-made building but in the only one that is not an imitation of something better than itself. Moreover, the writer informs us that the old covenant priesthood of Aaron has now been replaced by the "order of Melchizedek." The new has taken the place of the old.

REFLECTIONS

What specific things does Christ do for you as your prophet, priest, and king?

The Two Covenants

HEBREWS 8:1-7

> *For if there had been nothing wrong with that first covenant, no place would have been sought for another.* —*Hebrews 8:7*

If we meet someone who wants to know God, we should give her a Bible. Chances are, however, that she will expect essays about God in the Bible. So we'll need to explain that the Bible is not exactly a book that tells us all about God. Neither is it a book about people. Instead it is a book that deals with the relationship between God and people. They start out together (Gen. 1-2), they lose each other (Gen. 3), but at the end they are together again, forever and ever (Rev. 21).

Then we'll need to explain to our friend that the Bible has two main sections: the Old Testament and the New. We can show her the big section that is called the Old Testament and the smaller section that follows called the New Testament.

The word *testament* means covenant. We can explain that these words stand for the same idea, because both have to do with pledges or promises.

The old covenant is the relationship between God and his people under the laws of Mount Sinai. And the new covenant is the relationship between God and his people through the blood and the Spirit of Jesus Christ.

By this time we may have lost our friend because of all the technical terms we have been using. But have you ever tried to explain baseball or soccer without the use of technical terms? Too bad there are more sports fans than Bible lovers.

Let's make sure our friend remembers that it is the word *covenant* that keeps the whole Bible together. It means that throughout history, God speaks and people must answer. God makes pledges and people must trust and obey. And God's last word comes in Jesus Christ.

Once we get to Christ, we can explain to our friend what the new covenant is. And we will not be able to explain that unless we ourselves know the value of the blood and the power of the Spirit.

REFLECTIONS

Try explaining in your own words how the word *covenant* holds the Bible together.

Blood and Spirit

HEBREWS 8:8-13

> *This is the covenant I will establish with the house of Israel after that time, declares the Lord. I will put my laws in their minds and write them on their hearts. . . . I will . . . remember their sins no more.*
> —*Hebrews 8:10, 12*

Now the new covenant has come, according to the promise of God quoted here from Jeremiah 31:31-34. At that time God said he would bring about a big change in the attitude of his people. Forever and always they had been disobedient and stubborn. But, said God, there will be a new covenant, and then they will do my will not merely because they are told but from an inner conviction: "I will put my laws in their minds and write them on their hearts."

The secret of this big change is the coming of the Holy Spirit. In the new covenant, the Spirit of Christ lives in the hearts and minds of God's people.

But how can the *Holy* Spirit live in *sinful* people?

That is possible because God has first cleansed his people: "I will remember their sins no more." The sacrifice of Jesus Christ is made for the complete forgiveness of all their sins. And all who are cleansed by the blood have the Spirit living in them. The people of the new covenant are forgiven and renewed.

So what is *new* about the new covenant? And what is the last word for the last days? It is this: complete forgiveness through the blood of Jesus Christ and the gift of the Holy Spirit.

Forgiven and renewed! By faith we must take hold of the full wealth of the new covenant. All of the Bible is about covenant living, because all of life is a matter of learning to live with God. And there is progress in the Bible. We are moving toward the day when all our troubles will be over, when there will be unbroken unity between God and us. Already we have come a long way as compared with the old covenant. We don't depend on daily sacrifices and the work of many priests. The one sacrifice of our only Priest is enough forever.

And God's will is no longer a "strange" command to us; it is a law God has written in our hearts.

REFLECTIONS

You are forgiven and renewed. That's the bottom line of the new covenant. Reflect on the richness of this teaching—and give thanks.

An Incontestable Will

HEBREWS 9:15-22

> *For this reason Christ is the mediator of a new covenant, that those*
> *who are called may receive the promised eternal inheritance—now*
> *that he has died as a ransom to set them free from the sins commit-*
> *ted under the first covenant.* —*Hebrews 9:15*

Every person is advised to make a will, even if he or she has little to pass on. The living are greedy, and they can quarrel much over little.

In a will, a person "declares his mind as to the manner in which he would have his estate disposed of *after his death*." That last clause is important. The executor of a will cannot open the will and divide the estate unless he has proof of the death of the testator. Even the Bible says: "In the case of a will, it is necessary to prove the death of the one who made it" (v. 16).

God made a "will" or "testament" or "covenant." Since the Bible writers have one word for all three of these English terms, it does not sound so strange to say: "God made a will." In that will, God promised the "eternal inheritance" to "those who are called." Now the big question is: Are we in God's will? Who exactly are "those who are called"?

We know for sure that Abraham is mentioned in God's will. It was to Abraham that God started to talk about his will (or covenant promise). Moses is also mentioned, of course. And the people of Israel. But you are in there too. And so am I. To us God said, "This is the blood of the covenant" (v. 20). That's the proof that your name is in the will.

In fact, we are much more convinced that we are entitled to the "promised eternal inheritance" than the people in Moses' time. In those days, the will was still contestable. There was no proof that the death had occurred. The opponents of God's heirs, led by their chief, Satan (whose name means *adversary*), were always saying that those whom God had called were not really entitled to the inheritance. But now this matter has been settled. The will of God is now incontestable.

Those who have been called are getting the inheritance, for "he has died as a ransom."

REFLECTIONS

Why are you in God's will? What "inheritance" do you expect to receive from God?

Death Is Final

HEBREWS 9:24-28

> *Just as people are destined to die once, and after that to face judgment, so Christ was sacrificed once to take away the sins of many; and he will appear a second time, not to bear sin, but to bring salvation to those who are waiting for him.* —Hebrews 9:27-28

The writer is using another illustration to show the finality of Christ's death. Now he appeals to a rule with which all of us are familiar. A man is born once; he lives once; he dies once. Then nothing remains but the judgment before God.

All of us are subject to this law, because it is the relentless rule of human existence.

But when the Son of God took on human nature, he had to submit to the same rule. He was born, he lives, and he died once. His death can never be repeated.

When Christ comes back, his coming will have nothing to do with sin, as far as believers are concerned. He will come to receive his own into eternal life. Our sins have been taken away by his death. Just as our own death can never be repeated, so his death was final.

Death is final. In one way, at least, that is a sad and somewhat scary thought. Death is not one event among many but a final event. All the living in this body is then finished. All the things that can only be done while we are among the living must be done by then or they cannot be done at all.

But when the Bible tells us that death is final, the intention is not to scare us but to comfort us. We are asked to believe that the death of Jesus was the full and final payment for all our sins. Therefore we have nothing to fear anymore.

How do we expect Christ to deal with us when he comes in judgment? Do you think he is going to tell the whole universe (and the people in our church!) what dirty sinners we are? No, of course not—not if we have confessed our sins while we were living. He is not going to deal with us according to our sins. He did that when he came the first time. He dealt with our sins in his death. And death cannot be repeated. That's final!

Praise the Lord!

REFLECTIONS

When you think of judgment day, do you have a picture of everyone being told about all your secret sins? Why won't that happen?

The Story of the Curtain

HEBREWS 10:11-22

Therefore, brothers and sisters, since we have confidence to enter the Most Holy Place by the blood of Jesus, by a new and living way opened for us through the curtain, that is, his body.
—*Hebrews 10:19-20*

Do you know the story of the curtain that was hanging in the temple?

The curtain was very heavy and very beautiful. It was hanging there to separate God from the people. It's true that the temple was also a meeting place for God and people. Here they could offer their gifts; here they had communion with God. And here they found forgiveness and new strength. Yet there was always that curtain. The curtain did not suggest "communion." It suggested "separation." The curtain was one big *No Admission* sign. The holy God was telling common people that they had to keep their distance.

Only the holiest man in Israel could approach God's own presence—once a year. The high priest would come, washed and dressed in spotless white, carrying blood. He would sprinkle the blood on the ark to cover the sins of the people and his own sins. Then the heavy curtain would be closed again.

But one day the curtain was torn by the finger of God from top to bottom. It happened on a Friday, Good Friday, just when Jesus died on a hill outside of Jerusalem. When the loving heart of Jesus broke, the temple veil was torn in two.

The closed curtain said "No admission." The torn curtain said "Admission for all those who believe in Jesus Christ."

Now we have "confidence to enter the Most Holy Place by the blood of Jesus." Even the least significant persons may go straight into the holiest place—as long as they believe in Jesus. If they believe, they are washed and dressed in spotless white.

Now we may come to God with boldness. And God comes to us in grace. We may go into the sanctuary, and God comes out of the holy place, making *us* a holy place. The two-way traffic goes through the torn curtain. Christ is the torn curtain.

REFLECTIONS

The torn curtain allows you to come into God's holy presence. Bow before him and give thanks.

The Awesome God

HEBREWS 10:23-31

It is a dreadful thing to fall into the hands of the living God.
—Hebrews 10:31

What a change in the tone of this letter to the Hebrews! In the one paragraph we read the most joyous statement on God's full and final forgiveness. The very next paragraph makes us tremble at the vengeance of God.

This change of tone should not really surprise us. After all, we have heard God's last word. The curtain has been torn. God's heart has been opened. We are now living on holy ground, under an open heaven, in the presence of the almighty God.

In such a situation of love and mutual possession, our bliss is beyond description. But the accidents can be fatal.

Many people know, or will find out, that marriage can be a source of either bliss or misery. Great joy may be possessed in sacred love. But love turns to disgust when the marriage is desecrated.

We have been wedded to God by the new covenant bond of the blood and the Spirit. Therefore we are often overwhelmed with a trembling joy. We know peace. And we have moments of great ecstasy. But all of this can suddenly turn to acute agony when the relationship is desecrated.

The writer is here describing an outrageous sin. He is talking about a person who has accepted the life of his lover and then trampled it underfoot. We call this the sin against the Holy Spirit.

We must reassure sensitive Christians that they have *not* committed this sin. Their very fear shows that they could not have done it.

Nevertheless, the warning is issued to all. A love relationship may never be taken for granted. It must be cultivated. God's love-word in Christ must forever move us to worship and praise, fear and trembling, joy and hope.

REFLECTIONS

What place do "fear and trembling" have in your walk with God?

Faith

HEBREWS 10:32-11:1

Now faith is being sure of what we hope for and certain of what we do not see.   —*Hebrews 11:1*

If you have done any amount of reading in the letter to the Hebrews, you know that the new covenant is far more excellent than the old covenant. But the new covenant is still a covenant. That means that it is a relationship to God based on his Word, to which we must respond by an act of faith.

That's why, in chapter 11, the writer can present a survey of the acts of *faith*. The history of people who acted by faith reaches back to the creation of the world and forward to the church of Christ. At all times God has spoken, and at all times people must respond in faith.

Today, maybe more than ever before, we realize the difficulty *and* the necessity of faith. Science has had a deep influence on our way of living. The scientific method accepts no evidence unless it has been seen, checked, and double-checked. This method is good and necessary in the fields that are appropriate to it. But the certainties of faith are radically different.

Faith simply means we take God at his word and direct our lives accordingly. All the men and women mentioned in this chapter rested on the promises of God; they did not have any visible evidence that these promises would ever be fulfilled. Yet the promises meant so much to them that they regulated the whole course of their lives in the light of these Words of God.

Things that are future ("hoped for") with respect to everyday experience are present to *faith*. Things outwardly unseen are visible to the inward eye of faith. For this reason, men and women of faith do things that may seem astounding, heroic, or foolish to an outsider. But whatever they do makes sense to people who have faith. Faith has its own certainty and its own evidence, for faith takes God's Word seriously. The unbeliever says, "Show me, so I may believe." God says, "Believe me, and you will see." God does not want to be checked. He wants to be trusted.

REFLECTIONS

What words would you use to describe your faith in God?

The Basic Law of True Religion

HEBREWS 11:1-6

> *And without faith it is impossible to please God, because anyone who comes to him must believe that he exists and that he rewards those who earnestly seek him.* —*Hebrews 11:6*

We are going through a crisis of faith. People today are no longer squabbling over minor points of doctrine. They are arguing about the very existence of God.

Honesty requires us to say that doubt about God is not far from any one of us. Honesty also requires that those who deny him should leave the church, for the church is still a fellowship of believers in the God who spoke to Abraham and through Moses, the God who said his final word in Jesus Christ.

God sets the terms of our fellowship with him—we are to approach God "by faith." If we refuse, God cannot be reached. God must be sought by those who believe that he exists, in the expectation that he rewards those who long for him.

We cannot give faith to anyone. We can only say, "If you approach God in the confidence that his Word is reliable, you will be rewarded." We say this "by faith," but we also speak because we ourselves have been enriched by what we found.

Some people deny God's reality. To us they sound painfully arrogant. We know their answer when we tell them that they must begin their search by faith. They do not wish to surrender before they start. Yet it is God who spells out the terms of the encounter. The basic law of all true religion is that there are no approaches to God and can be no knowledge of the everlasting One unless we believe God exists. And the only reward desired by those who seek him is the joy of finding him.

Christians are humble enough to admit difficulties in persevering. Those who seek do find. Yet they find because they always seek. Probably the greatest mystery of a life of faith and prayer is this: in our search for God we come to discover God's search for us. At the very moment when we find, we must admit with a smile that we were found by God.

REFLECTIONS

"In our search for God we come to discover God's search for us." Reflect on how this has been true in your experience.

Believers Are Pilgrims

HEBREWS 11:8-16

All these people were still living by faith when they died . . . admit-ting that they were foreigners and strangers on earth. People who say such things show that they are looking for a country of their own. —*Hebrews 11:13-14*

The author of Hebrews is describing people who had a country promised to them. At the end of their lives, the promised land was still just that—a *promised land.* Yet to them that promise was so sure that they staked everything on it.

These original believers, the patriarchs, used to talk about their lives as a pilgrimage. Abraham said: "I am a foreigner and a stranger among you" (Gen. 23:4). And Jacob spoke of the long course of his eventful life as "the years of my pilgrimage" (Gen. 47:9). "People who say such things show that they are looking for a country of their own."

It's easy to see why these unsettled, tent-dwelling fathers of the nation considered themselves pilgrims. But their historical circumstances are not the complete explanation. They understood life as a pilgrimage because of the nature of their *faith.*

Living by faith always means that the heart is attached to something that is not here. Whatever is here cannot be the "real thing." Seeing and believing are not the same—at least, not yet. More often than not, what we see is a denial of what we believe—and therefore a temptation to our faith. The heart must cling to the promise. Otherwise the pilgrim is lost.

In much of the Christian church, the emphasis these days is on "involvement." The Christian community may not live in isolated enclaves, and the Christian faith may not be focused on a country that is totally unrelated to the country in which we live, here and now. This emphasis is good. Our peculiar problem and constant prayer is to learn how citizens of tomorrow's city must work in today's society.

Believers are pilgrims. The secular city is not our home. Neither will we manage to build a sacred city within the present world. Our faith is fixed on a city of which God is the architect and builder.

REFLECTIONS

"Believers are pilgrims." How has this been true for you?

All Things Are Possible

HEBREWS 11:29-38

> *Women received back their dead, raised to life again. There were others who were tortured, refusing to be released so that they might gain an even better resurrection.* —*Hebrews 11:35*

By faith all things are possible, for faith is complete reliance on the power and promises of God.

The saying "All things are possible if you only believe" has so often been abused by religious hucksters that it's hard for us to know what the Bible means by it. "If you believe," these hucksters imply, "all sorts of nice and miraculous things are possible." And then perhaps we feel guilty for not believing strongly enough—after all, if we believed, more of these good things would be happening to us!

It won't help to argue over whether there is something to faith healing. (There is.) Instead, we must listen more closely to the Bible, where "by faith" has an altogether different ring.

The women who received their dead children by resurrection are described in 1 Kings 17 and 2 Kings 4. The prayers of faith were offered first by Elijah and then by Elisha. Those who were tortured and refused to accept release are people whose stories are told in the books of the Maccabees. The jeers, flogging, chains, and imprisonment (v. 36) were endured by a host of Christian people, including Jesus Christ himself. The horrible tortures mentioned in verse 37 were reportedly suffered by the prophets Isaiah and Jeremiah.

The Bible reports these examples so that you and I will place our trust in God. We must rely on God so completely that the only fear we could possibly have is the fear of being faithless to him. Those who live by faith . . . live!

This is the story of the power of faith. All things are possible!

But this truth of the power of faith is twisted into a caricature when I first say what I want and then "use God" to get what I want. We must not use biblical phrases to turn a biblical truth into its opposite.

REFLECTIONS

Where in your life—right now and in the immediate future—do you especially need to place all your trust in God?

The Better Part

HEBREWS 11:32-40

These were all commended for their faith, yet none of them received what had been promised. God had planned something better for us. . . . —Hebrews 11:39-40

We join hands with the believers of all ages, including all the Old Testament people who hoped in God. Essentially we are all in the same situation. All of us must respond to a Word of promise by an act of faith. Each one may take hold of the promise with the fingers of faith.

But the new covenant is much better than the old one, because Jesus Christ is the fulfillment of the old promise. All these Old Testament men and women, who still serve as examples of what it means to trust in God, did not receive what was promised. But we did, because we know Jesus as Savior and Lord.

Now everything is "better," as the writer to the Hebrews says. We have a "better hope" (7:19) since we are in a "better covenant" (7:22) based on "better promises" (8:6) and "better sacrifices" (9:23). There may be many points of similarity between the covenant life of the fathers and mothers of faith and our relationship to God, but with us everything is "better."

It is not immodest to remind ourselves of this truth. As a matter of fact, it is necessary for us to be deeply aware of the excellence of the new situation as compared with the old. We live and work under the conditions, privileges, and obligations of a *new* covenant.

There is always a pull in the Christian church to return to the Old Testament. Many seem to prefer living under the law to living under grace. Most people love the spectacle of religious ritual and the hallowed atmosphere of temples made by hands. Besides, the laziness of people makes it easy for church leaders to behave as if the church were dependent on their teaching and intercession.

All these factors contribute to make backsliding a real danger and a constant threat. Watchfulness requires not only that we know history but also that we know Christ.

In these last days God has come to us in the Son. In the cross of Christ, the last word has been said about our sins. In Christ's exaltation, the decisive word has been spoken about our future.

REFLECTIONS

Express your thanks to God for the benefits of living under the new—and better—covenant.

Look at Jesus

HEBREWS 12:1-4

And let us run with perseverance the race marked out for us, fixing our eyes on Jesus, the pioneer and perfecter of faith. For the joy set before him he endured the cross, scorning its shame, and sat down at the right hand of the throne of God. —Hebrews 12:1-2

Living a Christian life is like running a race. To run it well, we need to lay aside our sins and the spiritual handicaps that would make progress impossible or hinder us in running. We also need to be encouraged and instructed by the "cloud of witnesses" who "by faith" ran and obtained the prize. Above all, our eyes must be fixed on Jesus.

Jesus is the "pioneer and perfecter of faith." When it comes to faith and endurance, he is the one who has showed us how. It may be true that earlier witnesses (all those mentioned in chapter 11) give us plenty of incentive. But Christ is faith's trailblazer, and he himself ran the race from start to finish. In him faith and endurance have reached perfection.

This time the writer is not talking about faith *in* Jesus but the faith *of* Jesus. If we are to triumph in our contest, we must learn from Jesus how to believe and how to endure. "For the joy set before him he endured the cross." He endured the pain, scorned its shame, and was finally rewarded for his unwavering faith in God. Now he is seated at the right hand of God, having run the race.

The whole life of Jesus was characterized by faith in the Father. He accepted the ordeal of the cross because his Father had prepared it for him. "Not my will, but yours be done," he prayed (Luke 22:42). And in all the taunting, mocking, and rejecting, he was supported by his faith in God.

Jesus' death on the cross was not only painful but shameful. It was a punishment for those who were considered less than human. No Roman citizen could be crucified. Such a cruel punishment would bring dishonor to the Roman name. For Jesus, however, the disgrace was not worthy to be taken into account, for it was a matter of obedience to the Father and of reaching the joy of the end of the race.

Thus Jesus inspires and encourages us to run with endurance, until we share his glory.

REFLECTIONS

What helps you keep your eyes fixed on Jesus?

Discipline

HEBREWS 12:5-11

No discipline seems pleasant at the time, but painful. Later on, however, it produces a harvest of righteousness and peace for those who have been trained by it. —Hebrews 12:11

The worst thing parents can do is to let their children have their own way. The theory of permissive upbringing has produced a shocking number of disturbed youngsters and spoiled brats. The cause of much juvenile delinquency is parental delinquency. Parents who do not discipline their children do not love their children.

God loves his children. That's why God disciplines them. When God administers this medicine, it seems "painful," not pleasant.

Some Christian teachers and writers have taken this to mean that as soon as something hard or painful comes into our lives, we must thank our heavenly Father because it's good for us. But this is not possible or even desirable. The first experience is pain. Pain cannot be effective medicine if we experience it as pleasure.

When grief strikes or pain comes, the first temptation is to lose our trust in God. So the first thing we must do is keep quiet. Silence is the first grace. While staggering under the blow, we should say nothing.

But then, if the discipline is to have its desired effect, we must be "trained" by it. It must be a learning experience. That's what God intends it to be, and we may not doubt God's loving goal.

The "training" does not take place automatically, just as going to school does not guarantee that we learn anything. Some Christians who have suffered much have learned little. Others were "trained" by God's discipline, and the "harvest of righteousness" is there for all to see.

It is impossible to say *what* each of us should learn. Parents know the differences between their children, and they vary the discipline for each accordingly. God, our loving and discerning Father, knows just what each of us should learn.

And countless children of God thank their Father today for what they learned in periods of grief and loss and disappointment.

REFLECTIONS

How should we respond to God when God disciplines us?

God's Fire

HEBREWS 12:18-29

> *Therefore, since we are receiving a kingdom that cannot be shaken, let us be thankful, and so worship God acceptably with reverence and awe, for our "God is a consuming fire."* —Hebrews 12:28-29

The whole material universe will be shaken to pieces someday. Only the unshakable things will survive. The kingdom of Jesus Christ belongs to the order of things that cannot be shaken. And we have received this kingdom. We have been taken up in the eternity of the new order that Christ has established.

Our awesome God will accomplish this. God will destroy the temporary world in order to reveal the abiding city. That's the new country to which God has called us. "Let us be thankful" and worship God. Not only must our offering of worship proceed from a heart of gratitude, it must be *acceptable* in God's sight. In other words, we need a clear awareness of God's holiness.

We need to be thankful, but we also need a deep sense of the true character of God, for our "God is a consuming fire." The One who spoke from Mount Sinai and who has spoken his last word in Jesus Christ is the white heat of purity that consumes everything unworthy of himself.

God will burn up all that is temporal and all that is false.

And anyone who wants to be identified with the temporal and the impure will burn in the same heat.

Our style of living and worshiping will show whether we know God as a consuming fire. If we are truly aware that no impurity and falsehood can exist before him, we will pray and strive to be filled with God's holiness. We will ask to be guided through the world and beg to be kept in the kingdom of Christ Jesus.

We will also learn, reverently and humbly, how to talk about this aspect of God's character. It is not much discussed these days. But it is less than "honest to God" to ignore the fire.

Perhaps there are some people who despise the grace of God partly because Christians have painted such a harmless picture of the Eternal One. Maybe if they had an inkling of the truth, they would listen now, while it is called "today."

REFLECTIONS

How does your style of living and worshiping show that you know God as a consuming fire?

God, Sex, Money

HEBREWS 13:1-8

> *Marriage should be honored by all. . . . Keep your lives free from*
> *the love of money.*   *—Hebrews 13:4-5*

Marriage and money do not belong to the unshakable things that we will take along into the abiding city. The value of sex and money are vastly overrated today. To most of our sensual neighbors, sex and money are the two things that make life worth living. Magazines and conversations focus constantly on these two topics, and the person who is reported to have a lot of both is a celebrity.

Sex and money are legitimate joys in the present world if they are rightly used. Of course it's a sin to use your marriage partner instead of loving him or her. Of course it's a sin to love money instead of using it. But both marriage and money are right and good—if the marriage is honorable and if the money is the servant of the servants of God.

The art of Christian living is to order and direct your life in such a way that first things receive priority while all other things are given their proper place. It's like your house. Fire burns in the furnace, which is its good and proper place. But if the fire eats the furniture in the living room, the whole house is in ruins. If sex and money have their proper place in the house of your life, they add to the joy and warmth of Christian living. But if they are allowed to enter where they don't belong, the fire runs wild and the house is destroyed.

God has assigned our sexual expressions a place. They are good and beautiful in that place: "Marriage should be honored by all." But God "will judge the adulterer and the sexually immoral," even when our society finds such behavior quite acceptable.

Money, like sex, is a gift of God to be used responsibly. But when it becomes the god you love, you cannot keep the faith that sings: "The Lord is my helper; I will not be afraid" (v. 6).

REFLECTIONS

What would you list as the top ten priorities in your life?

The Everlasting Praise

HEBREWS 13:7-17

Through Jesus, therefore, let us continually offer to God a sacrifice of praise—the fruit of lips that openly profess his name.
—Hebrews 13:15

There are two kinds of sacrifices—offerings for sin and offerings of praise. The sacrifices for sin were offered throughout the Old Testament period. But Jesus Christ was the last sacrifice. He died for sin, once for all. No sacrifice for sin will be kindled again in all eternity.

Sacrifices of praise were also frequently offered in the Old Testament period. But we really learned to praise our God only after he had done his mighty works in Jesus Christ. Now the offerings of praise will rise to him forever and ever.

"*Through Jesus* . . . let us continually offer to God a sacrifice of praise." The offering of praise is acceptable to God only through Jesus. In the Old Testament there were many do's and don'ts in connection with the service of offering. The new covenant also has rules. The basic and all-inclusive rule is that offerings of praise must be offered to God *through Jesus.*

The praise comes from the *lips* of those who know Christ. They use their mouths to praise God. Many congregations love to sing "O for a thousand tongues to sing my great Redeemer's praise." But some people aren't even using the one tongue God gave them to sing his praises.

We must not praise God *only* with our lips. "Not for the lip of praise alone, or even the praising heart / I ask but for a life made up of praise in every part." Again, if you are asking for a life made up of praise, you certainly want to offer praise with your lips.

"Let us *continually* offer up a sacrifice of praise to God." The service of praise must go on all the time. It must be uninterrupted. After all, the offering of praise is a *fruit* of what God himself has planted. Generously God has sown; richly God shall reap. God's praise shall never end.

Since Christ has given the last sacrifice for sin, he has given us the Holy Spirit. The Spirit is the flame that kindles the sacrifice of praise.

REFLECTIONS

Reflect on the many things Jesus has done for you, especially as shown in our study of Hebrews. Then "offer a sacrifice of praise to God."

Final Prayer

HEBREWS 13:17-25

*Now may the God of peace, who through the blood of the eternal
covenant brought back from the dead our Lord Jesus, that great
Shepherd of the sheep, equip you with everything good for doing his
will. . . .*   *—Hebrews 13:20-21*

Finally, the writer of Hebrews makes the main elements of his teaching
the content of a prayer. And he lays this prayer on our lips. Most Christians understand that this is the way our Bible reading must have its fruit,
and so they combine times of Bible reading with times of prayer.

But we should also try to make our prayers a kind of answer to what
we have read in the Bible.

As long as the teachings of the Bible show one thing while our prayers
express a desire for something else, we are not in a partnership with
God, a covenant. But when the revelation of God has taught us what to
desire—that is, how to pray—we learn to walk in the way of God.

This union with God, this partnership in a covenant, is a mystery. But
it is no secret when and where this union is established and strengthened.
It happens when the Word of God comes to us and when we turn to the
God of this Word by means of our prayers.

There is much more to it, but Bible reading and prayer is the heart of
it. It's the heart of covenant living.

Covenant living is made possible for us by the blood and the Spirit of
Christ. By his blood we are saved, and by his Spirit we are directed to live
according to God's will, until we come to the eternal city where we will
live in everlasting union.

So let's now make the main elements of Hebrews the content of our
prayer:

> God of peace, in the name of Jesus our Shepherd, whose
> death was approved in the resurrection and whose blood
> is our salvation, equip us with the Spirit, so that we are
> able to do your will. Amen.

REFLECTIONS
Consider making the prayer that ends this reading your morning prayer
for a time, until you know it well.

Exodus

The book of Exodus tells a story of deliverance from oppression. It prepares us to meet Jesus our Liberator and gives us a glimpse of the battle behind the scenes.

daylight

Let My People Go

EXODUS 1:8-14

> *. . . so the Egyptians came to dread the Israelites and worked them*
> *ruthlessly. They made their lives bitter with harsh labor in brick and*
> *mortar and with all kinds of work in the fields . . . .*
> —*Exodus 1:12-14*

Exodus is about the liberation of an oppressed people. For that reason it's been a favorite book among oppressed people of all times and places.

African slaves sang the songs of Exodus on plantations in the southern United States. Workers in sweatshops have compared themselves to the Israelites under Pharaoh; their Moses was a labor leader. The Zionist movement, which led many Jews to resettle in Palestine, made frequent references to the Egyptian oppression.

When we begin reading this book, we should answer these questions:
- For whom is this book written?
- Who are the oppressed?
- Who is Pharaoh and who is the liberator, and what kind of freedom does he give?"

Actually, it's a question of interpretation. One of the basic rules of Bible interpretation is that every verse and every paragraph must be seen in its connection with the other verses and paragraphs. And every book of the Bible must be seen in its connection with all the other books. Otherwise anybody can use any part of the Bible for virtually any purpose.

Exodus is a historical account of the birth of the nation of Israel, an epic in which Moses is the central figure. The story begins in the labor camps. We are told how Pharaoh attempted to enrich the strength of his kingdom while reducing the size of the Jewish population. Then God acted. God forced his will on Pharaoh and gave Israel freedom and a covenant.

Exodus has lasting lessons about tyranny, oppression, and freedom. But we should understand it as only one mighty movement in the whole liberation story of the Bible, an epic in which Jesus is the central figure.

The God of Moses and the Father of Jesus will destroy the tyranny of Satan and of every oppressor. This great God will give his children their freedom in Christ, who is his Son and their Lord.

REFLECTIONS

Recall a time in your life when you felt trapped in a highly unpleasant situation and wanted "out." Then think of what it must have been like for Israel to have been "worked ruthlessly" year after year in Egypt.

The Oppressed

MATTHEW 5:1-10

> *"Blessed are those who hunger and thirst for righteousness, for they will be filled."*
> —*Matthew 5:6*

Who may identify with the people oppressed by Pharaoh and delivered by God?

Exodus isn't the only book of the Bible to describe oppressed people. In the book of Psalms these same oppressed people cry to the Lord. In the prophecies of Isaiah they are promised a helper. In the Sermon on the Mount they are blessed by Jesus. And in these blessings or "beatitudes" they are described most completely.

These people are at the wrong end of the stick in the present world. They are not self-sufficient but poor. They are victims of injustice, but they do not resort to violence. They refuse to accept the status quo—that is, the way things happen to be in the present world. Although well-meaning people have told them that they should try to enjoy life, such as it is, and to "take care of themselves" the way other folks do, they will not conform, and they don't feel at home. They *mourn*.

They are deeply disturbed by the absence of justice. They love mercy, peace, and righteousness. They are strangers in the present system. They hunger for righteousness and thirst for a new life and a better world.

Jesus came to liberate these people. He became their Messiah. He himself walked the path of the meek. He was oppressed by evil, but he broke the tyranny of evil by steady faith and unrelenting obedience.

Jesus, the leader of God's oppressed people, gave them this message: "Blessed, seven times blessed are you, people of God. I know that you don't trust in your own power, your cleverness, the strength of your tongue, or the reach of your money. You hope in God. I now pronounce you blessed! Even if you still go hungry, I declare that your hunger for righteousness will be satisfied. Be faithful. Your eyes shall see God. Yours is the kingdom."

REFLECTIONS

If Jesus were to give you his "blessing" today, what might he say to you?

The Murderer

EXODUS 1:15-22

Then Pharaoh gave this order to all his people: "Every Hebrew boy that is born you must throw into the Nile, but let every girl live."
—*Exodus 1:22*

The brutality of Pharaoh was extreme, but it is not unmatched. History has shown that people are capable of any inhuman act once the devil gets hold of them.

And it is not so hard for the devil to get hold of us. We are all born as sinners. We do not become sinners because we commit crimes; rather, we commit crimes because we are sinners.

This biblical teaching has received much scorn, even from theologians who should know it's true. Especially in an age in which people wear clean shirts and socks every day, you cannot convince many people that we are less than nice by nature.

When people acquire bathtubs and pleasant manners, they are inclined to think that they have grown out of the barbaric stage. But the forms of good living do not keep the devil away. A visit to the British Museum can show you that the Egyptians had all the cultural niceties at the time they drowned the Hebrew boys.

Humanity as a whole has not learned anything from the revelations of evil. We are unspeakably superficial. One generation experiences the raw power of the devil, and their surviving children aren't even interested in knowing about the events, let alone why these events happened. They just want clean shirts, hot tubs, beer, and baseball.

In our personal lives we find it hard to decide whether the ability to forget is a blessing or a curse. Could it be some of both? In each of our lives there is going to be at least one moment in which we see the stark reality of evil. Let's hope that in that moment we become wise.

The next generation may consider us "stuffy" and "killjoys"—even if we tell them only that life is not a joyride for fun-lovers. In fact, the life-and-death issue for all human beings is the struggle between the kingdom of God and the kingdom of Satan. Either we live and die in darkness or we move toward the light.

Christ makes the difference.

REFLECTIONS

When have you seen "the stark reality of evil"? What have you learned from that experience?

The Devil's Panic

MATTHEW 2:1-12

When King Herod heard this he was disturbed, and all Jerusalem with him. —*Matthew 2:3*

Herod's murder of the babies was not an isolated crime. Thirteen centuries earlier, the Pharaoh of Egypt had committed a similar cruelty. The two attacks originated in the same mind—the devil's. And both attacks were aimed at the deliverer of God's people.

Deep in his evil being, Satan knew that the Liberator was going to come. He ordered the murder of the boy babies because he wanted to stop the liberation movement. Pharaoh and Herod were the devil's pawns, although they had interests of their own to defend.

Notice how Matthew 2 says that King Herod was *disturbed*. His throne began to wobble. (He had already killed a few others whom he considered a danger to his throne.) Herod was "disturbed, and all Jerusalem with him." Those who supported his throne also began to feel insecure. Their insecurity was rooted in the devil's insecurity. The devil is insecure because he is afraid. He has only a short time, and he knows it. His doom is sure, and although he does not accept it, he is aware of it.

Therefore the devil is full of panic.

Christians don't panic. They may be impatient or worried, but they don't panic. Faith is the refusal to panic. Panic strikes a person when she loses control, when the bottom drops out of her world, when everything suddenly seems lost.

By faith we know that no matter what happens, the worst cannot happen. Even in the most trying circumstances, we have something to fall back on. The throne of God stands forever. God's plan of salvation is sure. Troubles, yes; panic, no.

Panic gripped Pharaoh and Herod. The devil's servants lose control when the Liberator comes. They slide into a bottomless pit. But God's people have a deep-seated optimism even in the worst trial. Everything and everybody is under control.

REFLECTIONS

What can you take from this devotional that will help you the next time you're facing a potential "panic" situation?

God's Humor

EXODUS 2:1-10

When the child grew older, [Moses' mother] took him to Pharaoh's daughter and he became her son. —*Exodus 2:10*

God's children are not always optimists. The lack of progress in the coming of the kingdom and the losses of the Christian church can fill us with apprehension and sometimes gloom. At times Christians seem to be a negligible minority. Their voices are so muted, their efforts so feeble.

If your head, your heart, and your treasure are in the kingdom of God, you must have reason, every now and then, to complain to fellow Christians and pour out your worries before God.

But we may never jump to the conclusion that the kingdom of God is not coming.

For one thing, it is easier to see sin than to see grace. Evil deeds and evil people make headlines. But according to Matthew 6, good works are a secret business between God and his children. Good works will not make headlines until the last day. That's why the good works of devoted Christians are much more numerous than any one of us will ever know.

Besides, God has a wonderfully quiet way of working. The devil's kingdom makes an enormous amount of noise. The poorest products always need the most advertising. And noise often gives the appearance of power to those who have none. But while the devil has the noise and the headlines, God's crop is growing as quietly as wheat in the field of the world.

When the devil moves in like a roaring lion, we must be on our guard, but we must not be intimidated. The battle is not won by noise.

Think of this: Pharaoh's soldiers were tearing baby boys from their mothers' breasts. The mothers were wailing, the young boys were drowning, and the devil was having his way. But meanwhile, at headquarters, Pharaoh's daughter was playing with a little boy. Pharaoh himself became the adoptive grandfather of Israel's liberator!

The devil may make a lot of noise. But "the One enthroned in heaven laughs" (Ps. 2:4).

REFLECTIONS

Where have you seen God's "wonderfully quiet way of working"? Reflect—and give thanks.

Bethlehem's Tears

MATTHEW 2:13-18

"A voice is heard in Ramah, weeping and great mourning, Rachel weeping for her children and refusing to be comforted, because they are no more."
                                                                —Matthew 2:18

According to an old story, when Herod sent his soldiers to Bethlehem to kill all the boys ages two and under, there weren't any. God had seen to it that in the year Jesus was born and in the year after that, no other boys were born in Bethlehem.

A lovely story. A nice effort to keep Christmas nice.

But Matthew tells us that Bethlehem made him think of Rachel. She was a mother who died in Bethlehem while giving birth to a son (Gen. 35:18). And Matthew was not the only one who thought of Rachel when he saw the misery of God's children. Jeremiah also mentioned her tears when he saw the sons of Jacob driven from their land into slavery (Jer. 31:15).

And yet it is exactly when grief makes it difficult to think of anything else that Israel must listen to the word of prophecy: "But you, Bethlehem . . . out of you will come for me one who will be ruler over Israel, whose origins are from of old, from ancient times" (Mic. 5:2).

The daughter of Zion must now believe that all of Israel will be saved by the salvation of God's Son. All of God's children are saved as long as the Son of God is saved. If he lives, all of us will live. If he escapes the sword, all of us will be free. If he conquers the devil, all of us will be conquerors through him.

We may not deny the sorrows of the earth. But the Word of comfort wants to assure us that earth has no sorrow that heaven cannot heal.

The sorrow of Israel's children will not just be healed in the hereafter; heaven has already come to earth to bring healing. The Word is being fulfilled, and the history of God's people is moving to its climax. When it becomes very dark, a new day is very close.

Weep not, people of God. Remember that the Savior lives!

REFLECTIONS

"Earth has no sorrows that heaven cannot heal." What are the "sorrows," worries, concerns, or fears that you need to bring to "heaven" today?

The Coming of God

EXODUS 3:1-12

> *The LORD said, "I have indeed seen the misery of my people in Egypt. I have heard them crying out because of their slave drivers, and I am concerned about their suffering. So I have come down to rescue them. . . . "* —Exodus 3:7–8

The book of Exodus is the story of the liberation of *God*'s people. *God* delivered them when *he* decided that the time had come.

"I have seen the misery of my people." How could God see it with his holy eyes and yet wait so long? "I have heard them crying out." Why, if God heard those piercing cries, didn't he come sooner?

The waiting of God is the greatest trial of God's people. It is worse than oppression by the enemy. Our greatest fear is not being killed by our enemies but being forgotten by our God.

"Will the Lord reject forever? . . . Has his unfailing love vanished forever? . . . Has God forgotten to be merciful?" (Ps. 77:7-9). God's people have not only thought it, they have said it and shouted it. These cries of near despair are printed in their Bibles.

We are not permitted to know God's schedule. That is none of our business, according to God's express declaration. So writers and preachers should quit their sensational guessing games.

"I have come down to rescue them." God came down when it was his time. God sent his Son "when the set time had fully come" (Gal. 4:4). During his life in the flesh, Jesus often spoke of "his hour." Impatient people heard him say frequently that "his time" had not yet come.

Today we are living by the promise that Jesus will return to rescue us. He will not come too soon, and he will not come too late. He will come at his sovereignly appointed hour.

The only really important question is whether we are ready to meet him. Maybe we should cry louder and pray more. "Come now, long-expected Jesus!"

We don't know when Jesus is coming. But we certainly know *that* he is coming.

REFLECTIONS

What does it mean to you to "live by the promise that Jesus will return to rescue us"?

His Name Is Yahweh

EXODUS 3:13-17

> *Moses said to God, "Suppose I go to the Israelites and say to them, 'The God of your fathers has sent me to you,' and they ask me, 'What is his name?' Then what shall I tell them?" God said to Moses, "I AM WHO I AM."* —*Exodus 3:13-14*

The children of Jacob, or Israel, had been in Egypt for nearly four hundred years. Then God declared that their time of estrangement was finished. He led them to the land he had promised to Abraham, the grandfather of Jacob.

But the Israelites had not had many revelations from God. They hardly knew God. True, they had their traditions and they still feared God, as you can tell from the story of Moses' parents. But they had no frequent voices speaking to them and they had no Bible scrolls.

On this occasion God shows himself to Moses. He must tell the Israelites that the God of their fathers has spoken. Then they will be reminded that God has not forgotten his promises. But from this time on, the Israelites would also know God by a new name—*Yahweh*, explained as "I AM WHO I AM." That name means, I am here and I am alive.

Since God revealed this name when he delivered Israel out of Egypt, the name *Yahweh* is going to be the most sacred name. To all of God's people, the name means that the holy God loves them and is always present to help them according to his covenant faithfulness.

The name *Yahweh* was already used by Eve in Genesis 4:1. Yet it was a name of God not known before the liberation from Egypt.

Many people know the names *husband* and *wife* as labels for two people in a marriage relationship. But it is only when a person enters into that relationship that he or she really learns to say the name. In the moment in which the man and the woman get to know each other, he calls her *wife* and she calls him *husband*. They look at each other with new awareness. They know the meaning of the name.

The Israelites did not know God as *Yahweh* until they had tasted God's faithfulness, seen God's power, and experienced God's redemption. In the same way, the name of God is a mere label to us until we have experienced his salvation. Only when we know Christ and have received the Spirit do we know him by a new name—*Abba*, Father.

REFLECTIONS

How does knowing God as your *Father* in heaven affect the way you pray to him?

Disobedience

EXODUS 5:1-9

> *"This is what the LORD, the God of Israel, says: 'Let my people go. . . .'" Pharaoh said . . . "I do not know the LORD and I will not let Israel go."* —Exodus 5:1-2

The Word of God can be disobeyed—but only by human beings. The sun, the moon, the sea, and the animals obey God's will at all times. When God says, "Rise and wane and build nests and be still," the sun, the moon, the birds, and the sea obey. But *people* can say no to God.

It's a frightening thing to say no to God. And foolish too. We are bound to suffer for it when we dare to disobey the will of the Creator of the universe.

The most frightening aspect of disobedience is that God punishes it by a process the Bible calls "hardening."

God demonstrated this process in the Pharaoh of Egypt. But you may observe this punishment of God all around you, maybe in your relatives.

This process is similar to what happens in the lives of children who are neglected by their parents. They never learn the meaning of *yes* and *no*. They don't know what is allowed and what is forbidden. They've never experienced a firm and loving voice that taught them that a command is a command. So they don't take authority seriously until the police insist that *no* means *no*. By then it is almost impossible to reeducate them. They are *hardened*.

People who refuse to obey God finally *cannot* obey anymore, even if they want to. In the beginning they will not believe; in the end they cannot believe. If we do not seek the Lord "while he may be found," there will come a time when we cannot find him anymore.

It is not up to us to say of any particular person that he or she has been hardened beyond repentance and redemption—only God knows that. But the Bible tells us that there is a connection between disobedience and the punishment of a hardened heart. That should make us obey the Lord with fear and trembling, promptly and immediately.

REFLECTIONS

Are there any parts of your life where Satan is trying to "harden" you against doing what you know God wants you to do?

The Sovereign

ROMANS 9:14-24

> *For Scripture says to Pharaoh: "I raised you up for this very purpose, that I might display my power in you and that my name might be proclaimed in all the earth."* —Romans 9:17 (Exodus 9:16)

Here we plunge into a letter of Paul. He is talking about the fact that Israel had hardened its heart to the gospel of grace. Although this gospel came to the Israelites in the first place, the majority of them rejected it. Their hearts were hardened. When their promised Deliverer finally came to them, they were unwilling to receive him.

Does this means that the Word of God has failed? No, says Paul in verse 6.

Both obedience to the gospel and disobedience to the gospel come from God. Of course, people are responsible for their own actions. That's always true. But people cannot frustrate the plans of God.

People can never put God in the position of saying: "Now what am I going to do? My plans have failed and my goodness was not accepted." That does not happen because God is not merely a spectator watching the world in which we act; God is also the Ruler over us and all things.

When God said to Pharaoh, "Let my people go," he disobeyed God. Then God used Pharaoh as a means to proclaim God's own glory to the world. The same is true of the hardening of Israel. To God, Israel's disobedience is neither frustrating nor final. God uses it as a means for spreading his own glory throughout the whole world. The gospel goes from Jews to Gentiles, from Jerusalem to Europe.

When God sets out to liberate a nation, and when God sends his Son to liberate the world, neither a stubborn Pharaoh nor a hardened Israel will be able to stop the salvation movement. On the contrary, they will serve it!

"Oh, the depth of the riches of the wisdom and knowledge of God! How unsearchable his judgments, and his paths beyond tracing out! . . . For from him and through him and to him are all things"—even the disobedience of his enemies. "To him be the glory forever! Amen" (Rom. 11:33, 36).

REFLECTIONS
Let Romans 11:33, 36 be your own song of praise to our "unsearchable" God.

The Pressure Is On

EXODUS 5:15-6:1

"You have made us obnoxious to Pharaoh and his officials and have put a sword in their hand to kill us." —Exodus 5:21

When God finally visited his people, Moses fearlessly spoke the Word of the sovereign God to Pharaoh, the oppressor of God's people: "Thus says the Lord, 'Let my people go!'" (Ex. 5:1, RSV).

Hearing this, Pharaoh issued his own command. His servants spoke to Israel: "Thus says Pharaoh, 'I will not give you straw . . . but your work will not be lessened in the least'" (v. 10, RSV). They had to produce the same quota of work, and they also had to gather their own supplies.

When God's messenger had spoken his "Thus says the Lord," the countermeasure was announced with the same solemnity: "Thus says Pharaoh" (vv. 1, 10)

The Word of God liberates. However, as soon as it is proclaimed with boldness, the problems multiply. And since the result of Word-proclamation is trouble, people will always be inclined to say to their preachers, "Take it easy. You are going to cause problems. Don't rock the boat."

When God's people as a whole, to whom God has entrusted his message of deliverance, begin to speak that Word with boldness, the enemy will be aroused and the burdens will become heavier. If all of us show the courage to speak the Word and live according to that Word at all times and in all places, we must not immediately expect an influx of new members into the church. We must be prepared, first of all, to face consequences without fear of others or what they can do to us.

This message is exactly the fire Christ came to cast on the earth. "Do you think I came to bring peace on earth? No, I tell you, but division. From now on there will be five in one family divided against each other, three against two and two against three" (Luke 12:51-52).

The proclamation of God's Word puts the pressure on. But "when these things begin to take place, stand up and lift up your heads, because your redemption is drawing near" (Luke 21:28).

REFLECTIONS

About what should the church today say, "Thus says the Lord"? To whom?

Liberty and Oppression

LUKE 4:16-30

"The Spirit of the Lord is on me, because he has anointed me to proclaim good news to the poor. He has sent me to proclaim freedom for the prisoners and recovery of sight for the blind." —Luke 4:18

Jesus said that he came to proclaim freedom for the prisoners. With his coming, the hour of liberation had struck for those who were oppressed. He sounded like Moses speaking to Pharaoh. But Jesus was speaking in the synagogue of Nazareth, his hometown.

And the people of Nazareth reacted to Jesus the way Pharaoh and his servants had reacted to Moses.

This incident should make us realize anew that in the New Testament, the oppressors are not Egyptians or Romans, and the oppressed do not belong to any particular nation. God's people are all those who hope for the revelation of his kingdom. Jesus identifies with them, and they accept him as their Savior.

We must be careful not to "spiritualize" these words against the oppressors to such a degree that the liberation Jesus proclaimed is only religious. The Spirit who rested on Jesus and on all the messengers who went before and after him is the Spirit of justice, the Spirit of love for the needy and the afflicted. The freedom proclaimed is not "only" religious and not "only" social, economic, and political. It covers the whole range. And the oppressors who are attacked are not "only" spiritual powers but also political dictators and other slave drivers and profiteers.

When God's people boldly proclaim the gospel's "Word of liberty," the opposition will stiffen. Within Christian circles it is not uncommon to take the bite out of the gospel by "interpreting" the oppressors and the oppressed, the prisons and the captives, as merely "spiritual" values and issues. But that is unfair to the text and an overreaction to those who believe only in a "social gospel."

The liberating work God began through Moses he now continues through those who represent Christ in the world. By the gospel of the kingdom, God opposes every form of tyranny and establishes a whole new order.

REFLECTIONS

Pray for Christians you know who are actively involved in, say, ministries to prisoners or ministries that seek justice for the poor.

The Last Judgment

EXODUS 11

> *Then Moses, hot with anger, left Pharaoh. The* LORD *had said to Moses, "Pharaoh will refuse to listen to you—so that my wonders may be multiplied in Egypt."* —*Exodus 11:8-9*

The freedom of God's people could not be obtained at the conference table. Finally God's judgments had to take place. After ten plagues the Egyptians were forced to acknowledge the greatness of the God of Israel. Not until the last plague had rocked the nation were God's people free.

What happened to Egypt must happen to our world: there will be no peace for the oppressed until the world has seen the judgments of our God.

The hardening of hearts finally comes to the point where God gives people up. After they have disobeyed and taxed God's patience to the point of no return, final judgment is unavoidable. God is God. Everybody is bound to find that out.

In Exodus 11 Moses leaves the court of Pharaoh, where he has been pleading the cause of God's people. This time he leaves Pharaoh "hot with anger." Moses' anger is worthy of a separate study. When he was younger, Moses relied on his own muscle to bring righteousness to Israel. "He saw an Egyptian beating a Hebrew, one of his own people. . . . He killed the Egyptian and hid him in the sand" (Ex. 2:11-12). But now, as God's ambassador, his voice is God's mouthpiece and his temper reflects God's anger.

"Then Moses, hot with anger, left Pharaoh." God's ambassador has been recalled. He breaks off the peace talks. Pharaoh has gone too far. The last door to peace is closed. Judgment must run its course.

Moses is exhausted. Then God speaks to him. God comforts Moses. He tells Moses that he is now going to answer the one prayer that is always first on the lips of those who know God: "Hallowed be your name."

The ultimate issue of history is not the salvation of people but the glory of God. When Christ has put all God's enemies under his feet, the Lord God will be all in all, everything to everybody.

God will be glorified by the deliverance of his people. But God's name will also be hallowed by the punishment of his enemies.

REFLECTIONS

What kind of situations today should provoke us to anger because God's name has not been hallowed?

God's Fires

REVELATION 16:1-9

Since, then, we know what it is to fear the Lord, we try to persuade people. . . . We are therefore Christ's ambassadors, as though God were making his appeal through us. —2 Corinthians 5:11, 20

In any church or sect where belief in the coming judgment is strong, members are bold in evangelism. At opportune times and at inopportune moments, they urge people to "accept Jesus Christ" as the only way of escape from the coming judgment.

When we know that the fires of God are coming, we have little time to waste. If we are convinced that God's wrath will be poured out, and if we have any compassion in our souls, we will live and talk as God's ambassadors.

Of course we don't go around telling people that God is about to burn them. But at opportune times we will discuss the alienation suffered by people who do not believe in God and are still outside the Christian fellowship. Within our own congregation, we will try hard to exercise this kind of Christian fellowship. And toward those outside of the church, we may engage in what is called "pre-evangelism"—not a direct approach, but a witness with a soft voice, soft drinks, coffee, and doughnuts.

There isn't any one sure method for approaching those who do not know Jesus Christ. The method depends on time, place, opportunity, people, and other variables. Neither does evangelism consist of talk only. It is much more.

The point is that if we really believe that God's wrath will be poured out on all who obstruct the freedom march of the kingdom, most of us should be much more urgent in our behavior than we are now.

The God of peace is also the God of fire. The Lord who loves us and our children is also the God of the tenth plague.

When God recalled his ambassador Moses from the peace talks with Pharaoh, only judgment was left. As long as Christ's ambassadors for peace are talking with today's Pharaohs, the day of grace endures.

But it won't last forever.

REFLECTIONS

Why are we often so timid in our efforts to call people to believe in God?

Passover

EXODUS 12:1-13

"*. . . when I see the blood, I will pass over you.*" —*Exodus 12:13*

The Israelites had been slaves in Egypt for four hundred years when God delivered them. That night they ate their Passover meal. Bitter herbs were on their tables to remind them of their bitter slavery. Unleavened bread reminded them they were in a hurry to leave. For that reason they also ate standing up, staff in hand. But the main course of the meal was the Passover lamb. Their houses were marked by the blood of this lamb. By eating this lamb, they experienced communion with the One who delivered them.

Ever since that night, Passover has been celebrated to remember this deliverance. It is called Passover because the judgment of God "passed over" the houses of all those who had the blood of the lamb on their doorposts.

This great salvation story of the Old Testament points forward to the salvation proclaimed in the New Testament, for God is coming again in judgment. No mansion will be missed, no apartment dwelling will be overlooked, no hut will be skipped. But the judgment will "pass over" all the families who have communion with the blood of the Lamb, that is, all the households that belong to Jesus.

That's the reason you must not remain in your sins until judgment day. God hates sin so much that his Son had to die on the cross to pay for it. So the first thing you must understand is that you are a sinner, and God hates sin.

You must also believe that this judgment on Jesus was designed to save you. You must believe the picture of the Old Testament and the gospel Word of the New Testament, which together say of Jesus: "Look, the Lamb of God, who takes away the sin of the world!" (John 1:29). God loved us so much that his Son died to save us.

Now God invites us to celebrate the Passover in the New Testament sense: we may have communion with Jesus Christ and his people. We escape the slavery of sin and the curse of judgment. We are free to serve our God, and we are traveling to the promised land.

REFLECTIONS

How does thinking of the sacrament of communion as "Passover in the New Testament sense" deepen the meaning of the sacrament for us?

No Old Yeast

1 CORINTHIANS 5:6-8

> *Get rid of the old yeast, so that you may be a new unleavened batch. . . . For Christ, our Passover lamb, has been sacrificed.*
> —*1 Corinthians 5:7*

Christ is our Passover lamb. He was killed for our trespasses. His blood saved our lives. Now we are God's people, free to serve our Lord.

All the old yeast (or leaven) must be removed from the Christian community, says Paul.

He refers to an old custom that is still sometimes observed: Jewish children search the house for old leaven (the parents hide a few pieces of old bread) just before the celebration of the Passover.

We have had our Passover, says Paul. By this, he doesn't mean that we have a feast once a year. He means that we are redeemed once and for all through Jesus Christ.

"Old yeast"—that is, the sins of the old nature—belongs to the time before our redemption. It is the leaven of malice and wickedness. This stuff does not belong in the community that has been saved by Christ.

Since Christ has now been sacrificed as a Passover lamb, it's time we got rid of the old yeast of evil in our lives. Since this is a community that has been redeemed by God, let us search out all malice and wickedness and throw it away.

All Christians know that although we are redeemed, we are not yet sinless. Although Christ has broken the old powers of sin, those powers still do harm among us. In fact, some Christians have said this so often that we have come to consider it "normal" that Christians are sinners and not holy people. But the Bible considers it abnormal.

Those who believe in Jesus Christ as their Redeemer and yet have a lot of old yeast in their lives must immediately throw it out. A Christian is not merely a sinner who has gone straight. And the Christian church is not just the old society patched up. It is radically new.

The old yeast is a foreign substance that does not belong in this body. It's an ugly growth that must be cut out.

REFLECTIONS

Search your heart and life for "old yeast," then ask God to help you get rid of it.

Hope

GENESIS 50:22-26

Moses took the bones of Joseph with him. . . .   —*Exodus 13:19*

God's people live in hope. We are sure God is going to do something in the future, something that our eyes are not yet allowed to see. We are so certain it is going to happen that our present lives are governed by our expectation.

The believers in Israel never gave up hope during their long exile on Egyptian soil. Egypt never became their home, although they lived there for about ten generations.

Joseph knew that Egypt was not his real country, even though he held a high position there. Next to Pharaoh, Joseph had the highest government position in Egypt's political structure. He ruled the country. He was concerned about Egypt. He served its welfare better than most Egyptians. In fact, he was called the savior of the land. Yet Joseph said, "I don't belong here. I share in the promises God made to Abraham, my father's grandfather."

Joseph was not allowed to see the promises fulfilled. He lived and died in hope, and by faith he gave directions for his funeral. His last will and testament showed that he did not doubt the Word of God: "Let me be buried in the promised land."

Some 430 years after he was sold as a slave in Egypt (Ex. 12:40), Joseph's coffin was carried out of Egypt toward the land that was promised to his fathers.

We tend to be impatient people with a short-range view of life and events. We want success and results, and we want them now. But God has a different view of the human race and of us. God sees us as members of a body, links in generations, twigs on a tree. God's purposes ripen while generations pass. His promises are true, but those who fix their hopes on him are carried in their coffins.

God wants us to live in hope. With our lives we make a long-range investment. This present country is not our home, though we serve it well. A future has been promised us. And that expectation determines the way we conduct ourselves.

REFLECTIONS

Thank God for the hope that he gives you and every believer.

Dying in Hope

1 THESSALONIANS 4:13-18

> *Brothers and sisters, we do not want you to be uninformed about those who sleep in death. . . . we who are still alive, who are left till the coming of the Lord, will certainly not precede those who have fallen asleep.* —*1 Thessalonians 4:13, 15*

We do not long for the return of the Lord with the ardor of the early Christians. That's one of the reasons why we are unable to understand some of their problems.

They were so sure that Jesus would display his lordship soon that they were expecting him any time. But after they had lived in this hope for a few years, some of the members of the congregation died. They "fell asleep," the Bible says. That's the Christian word for dying.

Then the Christians who buried their loved ones felt doubly sad. Not only did they experience the common pain of death, they also thought that the departed loved one would miss out on the excitement of Jesus' return. That day was so sure and so close. But now the beloved departed, who had spoken so often of the day of the Lord, would not see it.

Such a problem can exist only in a community where the question is constantly asked: "Will the Lord come today? Will we see him tomorrow?"

We don't live in that kind of a Christian community.

But the Thessalonians should not have worried, says Paul. Those who are still living when Christ returns will have no special privileges. They "will certainly not precede those who have fallen asleep." As a matter of fact, if there is going to be any kind of prominence, the faithful departed are going to have that place. "The dead in Christ will rise first" (v. 16).

And yet it will not be a matter of "They get this and we get that," for all of us, *together with them*, will be caught up by God's irresistible power. It is not true that only those who stay on earth will see the Lord. The meeting place will be "in the air." Then the reunited family will be with the Lord forever.

We certainly hope that our eyes may see him before we die. But if it pleases the Lord to let us fall asleep before his coming, we will nevertheless attend the celebration on Victory Day.

REFLECTIONS

Should we live in greater awareness of the Lord's return? If so, how would we do that?

Now They See It

EXODUS 14:21-31

Israel saw the Egyptians lying dead on the shore. And when the Israelites saw the great power the LORD displayed against the Egyptians, the people feared the LORD. . . .   —Exodus 14:30-31

Twice these verses draw our attention to what "Israel saw."

The eyes of these people had seen horrible things. They had seen their comrades beaten to death by the Egyptian slave drivers. Through their tears, they had seen their boys drowned in the Nile. When their ears heard the words of Moses, their eyes saw only increased oppression as the loads were made heavier by the servants of Pharaoh. The look in their eyes became very painful and very weary.

But now their feet are on the shore, and their eyes see the Egyptians. All the unrighteousness is washed away in God's flood, and they lived to see it!

They see the hand of God, the Lord of Israel, who is also Lord over the Egyptians. The Savior had done a mighty work. In the past they had seen and felt the crushing power of Pharaoh's hand. Now they see "the great power the LORD displayed against the Egyptians."

> Yet he saved them for his name's sake,
> to make his mighty power known.
> He rebuked the Red Sea, and it dried up;
> he led them through the depths as through a desert.
> He saved them from the hand of the foe;
> from the hand of the enemy he redeemed them. . . .
> Then they believed his promises and sang his praise.
> —Psalm 106:8-10, 12

There are rare moments in our lives when we too may see the hand of God—outstanding occasions when we see with our own eyes that God reigns over death and sickness; God converts sinners and brings his enemies to their knees.

But most of the time we live by faith. In his wisdom and for his own reasons, God makes us wait—and wait. When God finally arises, his enemies and ours will be scattered. And Zion will sing her song. We are free! Free at last! Thank God!

REFLECTIONS

Perhaps you've had one of those "rare moments when you saw the hand of God"? If so, what did you learn from your experience?

The Song at the Sea

EXODUS 15:1-10

> *"The LORD is my strength and my defense; he has become my salvation."* —*Exodus 15:2*

Free people sing. That's the only right response to salvation. That's why churches have so much singing. And that's why heaven is full of hymns. "He brought out his people with rejoicing, his chosen ones with shouts of joy" (Ps. 105:43).

The Egyptians were floating to the shore like so many dead fish. The chariots that had threatened to wipe out God's people a little while earlier were invisible, buried beneath the water. And the waves echoed the song of the redeemed.

Maybe you are not as deeply impressed with this first exodus as Moses and Miriam were. Perhaps you would have found it hard to sing and dance because you would have been bothered by the sight and the thought of the dead Egyptians. When you see the dead victims of violence, you might wonder, does anybody ever "win" a war, except those who manage to abolish war?

When we think along these lines, we may be showing some fruit of the progressive revelation of our God. Remember: there is no enlightenment unless it comes from the Light.

The second great deliverance by God, the one through Jesus Christ, was much more excellent than the first one.

In the first exodus, God saved the life of Israel, his son, by killing his enemies. In the second exodus, at Calvary, God saved his enemies by giving the life of his Son.

The last one is overwhelmingly better than the first. In both cases, however, judgment is a necessary part of the "plan of salvation." God's salvation unavoidably involves death and pain—not because God lacks love but because sin is that bad.

Another necessary accompaniment to salvation is the response of the redeemed: God's people sing their song of praise to the One who set them free.

REFLECTIONS

Offer your own prayer of praise to the One who has set you free.

The Song of the Free

REVELATION 15:1-4

[They] sang the song of God's servant Moses and of the Lamb:
"Great and marvelous are your deeds, Lord God Almighty."
—*Revelation 15:3*

Those who overcame the beast stand beside the sea of glass and fire, singing the song of Moses and the Lamb.

The Bible's themes of liberation flow together into one picture and one song. The first exodus with Moses and the second exodus through Christ are now set to one tune. The redeemed of the old and the new covenants praise God in the same words: "Great and marvelous are your deeds, Lord God Almighty! Just and true are your ways, King of the nations."

To our ears there may be a difference between the song of Moses and the song of those who are redeemed by Christ, the Lamb of God. When God made his people free by leading them through the Red Sea, the people sang, "The LORD is a warrior, the LORD is his name" (Ex. 15:3). Once Jesus paid the price for our freedom, we began to sing, "For God so loved the world . . . Love is his name."

Yet we are singing to the same God, the God who works salvation because he loves and executes judgment because he is righteous.

And it is the same enemy who must be crushed: the anger of Pharaoh and the fury of the beast reveal the cruelty of our deadly enemy, Satan. The gratitude of the saved must therefore be shown in lives that are ever more devoted to the Lord Jesus Christ and his people. But the same kind of devotion is to be shown in hatred for the beast and all it stands for.

The God who works salvation is the same God throughout history. The enemy that needs to be defeated is the same enemy. And the song of all the redeemed becomes one chorus, for all must pass through the water and all must be baptized with fire. The saving experiences of God's people are symbolized by the flood, the Red Sea, and our own baptism. They are all acts of judgment and salvation.

Therefore when all the battles have been fought, God's people will forever praise the might of Israel's Warrior and plumb the depths of the love of God.

REFLECTIONS

Praise God using the "song of Moses and of the Lamb" found in Revelation 15:3-4.

For Our Instruction

1 CORINTHIANS 10:1-11

> *Nevertheless, God was not pleased with most of them; their bodies were scattered in the wilderness.* —1 Corinthians 10:5

All of us who were baptized into Christ have had our exodus. We have left the house of bondage and tasted the wine of freedom. All of us are on our way to the promised land. In fact, through the resurrection of Jesus Christ we already share in the new creation.

And now God gives us a serious warning, reminding us what happened to our ancestors:

- *all* were under the cloud
- *all* passed through the sea
- *all* were baptized into Moses
- *all* ate the same spiritual food
- *all* drank from the spiritual rock

Nevertheless, with *most of them* God was not pleased.

Five times God says that *all* were in, and then God excludes *most* of them.

We have no spiritual privileges except those that we enjoy as members of God's people. Christianity is not individualistic. The only way to be saved is to be incorporated into Christ and the fellowship of believers. Yet we may not seek our security in belonging to the fellowship. The security is in Christ, the salvation is confirmed by obedience to him.

Incorporation into Jesus Christ is not a sort of eternal life insurance. People can never sit and rest on their spiritual heritage or be safe because of their present environment. The question is how you and I react to God's favor.

Already we have one foot in the promised land. Now let's keep our eyes on the future, seek God's kingdom, and hate all forms of idolatry. How terrible to be shipwrecked when the harbor is in view! How tragic to be killed when you are almost home after a long journey!

All, all, all—five times *all*. And then: "God was not pleased with most of them." Paul continues: "Now these things occurred as examples to keep us from setting our hearts on evil things as they did" (vv. 6, 11).

REFLECTIONS

In what ways might we "sit and rest on our spiritual heritage"?

The Law

EXODUS 20:1-17

"I am the LORD your God, who brought you out of Egypt, out of the land of slavery. You shall have no other gods before me."
—*Exodus 20:2-3*

If we take careful note of the *time* the law was given, we will also learn what purpose the law is supposed to fulfill in the lives of the redeemed.

The law serves its purpose between the exodus and the promised land. Israel is now in the desert, at the foot of Mount Sinai. The exodus is behind them. They have been redeemed. They were delivered from the house of bondage not by keeping the commandments but by God's grace and might. God took pity on them. They owe their freedom not to their own works but to God's love. Their salvation was the work of God.

Now they are in the desert through which they have to travel to reach their destination. At this point they receive the law as a road map and a guide for the lives of a redeemed people. This law is the covenant pact with their Redeemer. These are the rules for God's people in their partnership with their Lord.

So it follows that the law is never a way of salvation. Yet it's almost impossible to get rid of the human tendency to regard the law as a way of salvation.

The Israelites regarded the possession of the law—or the keeping of the law—as the means by which they would obtain righteousness. Ever since the apostle Paul's letters, all preachers of the gospel must spend a great deal of time explaining that the law is not a way of salvation and that it is not abolished.

The exodus is the salvation. And that mighty act is entirely a work of God. The law spells out the way of obedience. It explains how a redeemed people should now live in gratitude to their Redeemer.

Later, in the New Testament, the meaning of the law is deepened, and the power to keep the law is revealed. But the function of the law is unchanged: by obedience to God's law, God's people honor the God of the exodus.

REFLECTIONS

How does God's law act "as a roadmap and a guide" for your life?

Keeping the Law

ROMANS 8:1-4

> *. . . in order that the righteous requirement of the law might be fully met in us, who do not live according to the sinful nature but according to the Spirit.* —Romans 8:4

The redemption through the cross is greater than the redemption through the Red Sea.

This is because the first exodus broke the power of the Egyptians, while the second exodus broke the power of sin.

Finally it is possible for God's people to do what God requires of them in his law. The new people of God are delivered from the power of the enemy within. Now the power of the Holy Spirit overcomes the weakness of their own flesh, so that the people of God are able to obey their God.

It's all summed up in Romans 8:1-4. We are delivered from the power of guilt because Christ died for us. We are delivered from the power of sin because the Spirit dwells in us.

Once the old covenant people of God had been set free to serve their Lord, they received the laws of God. That was a great privilege, but it became their downfall. Their disobedient hearts were never able to render acceptable service to God in accordance with his laws.

Israel was responsible for its own disobedience. Yet the law served a certain purpose in the plan of God: "The law was bought in so that the trespass might increase" (Rom. 5:20). In other words, God also used the giving of the law to prepare the way for giving Jesus Christ.

Those who have received Jesus Christ have received real freedom. Not only are we freed from death, we are taught how to live! Not only are we forgiven for what we did wrong, we are taught to do right!

And it is all God's work. God delivered us from the burden of sin by giving us Christ and delivered us from weakness in obeying by giving us the Spirit. The Spirit is the power to obey.

Between our exodus and our arrival in the promised land, we live for the glory of God. The exodus—our redemption—was the work of God through Jesus Christ. And our obedience is God's work in us by the Holy Spirit.

REFLECTIONS

"The Spirit is the power to obey." How have you experienced this power?

The Old Covenant

EXODUS 24:1-8

> *"This is the blood of the covenant that the LORD has made with you in accordance with all these words."* —*Exodus 24:8*

At Mount Sinai, God and his redeemed people have their most intimate meeting—the most intimate meeting until the Baby is born in Bethlehem.

God talked to the people: "I carried you on eagles' wings and brought you to myself. Now if you obey me fully and keep my covenant, then out of all nations you will be my treasured possession" (Ex. 19:4-5). God carried the people from Egypt, through water and wilderness. And now, here at Mount Sinai, the covenant is officially ratified.

Moses, the mediator of the covenant, stands between God and the people. From the "Book of the Covenant" (v. 7) he reads God's will. That's the covenant contract, you might say. Then the people make their vow: "We will do everything the LORD has said; we will obey."

The second part of the ceremony consists of blood-sprinkling. Half of the blood is thrown against the altar. (Whatever goes to the altar goes to God.) The second half is sprinkled on the people. "This is the blood of the covenant" (v. 8).

Now the two parties are wedded together by the blood of the covenant. God has elected Israel to be his own people, and the people have accepted God as their Lord. Now it's official: Israel is God's people.

God could have placed his people immediately in the land "flowing with milk and honey." Instead he wanted them to travel through the wilderness.

But they would not travel toward their destination alone. Just as many people go through their lives not as individuals but as couples bound together in a covenant of marriage, so God's people—whether single or married—travel with their covenant partner, God. God is the protector of his people. We can count on God. God has shown already that his love is equal to his power. God's people will trust and obey. The relationship between God and God's people is sealed with blood.

This makes us think of Jesus and of the bond that ties us to the Lord, for the God of the exodus will be fully revealed as the Father of Jesus.

REFLECTIONS

You are not walking alone but are traveling with God, your protector, on your spiritual journey. What does this mean to you?

The New Covenant

1 CORINTHIANS 11:23-32

"This cup is the new covenant in my blood; do this, whenever you drink it, in remembrance of me." —*1 Corinthians 11:25*

The new covenant too was sealed by the shedding of blood. The blood of Jesus Christ was given on the last altar. All of his people must drink the cup of wine as an assurance that they are God's covenant partners.

Just as the people of God in the old covenant were not immediately placed in the promised land after they had been redeemed from Egypt, so the people of God in the New Testament are not taken out of the world when they are redeemed by Christ. They have to travel through this world. But they do not travel alone; God's people are wedded to him by an everlasting covenant.

Our union with God is celebrated and underlined in the Lord's Supper. Just as moments of intimate sharing constitute the strength of a marriage, so the intimacy of the Lord's Supper gives strength to our covenantal way of living.

We will never reach the end of the journey unless our relationship to God is real and our communion with him is constantly maintained. The Lord's Supper—the covenantal meal—is one of the means whereby the Lord himself strengthens us.

Paul underlines the importance of the Lord's Supper by raising an embarrassing matter. He chides the people of the congregation in Corinth for being greedy and selfish (vv. 20-22) when partaking of the Lord's Supper. Because of their unseemly behavior, God has sent his judgment on them (vv. 29-32).

Does the story of sin forever repeat itself, then? Must the people in the new covenant fall by the same kind of disobedience that made Israel lose its place of honor?

Celebrating the Lord's Supper does not merely assure us of God's love and the forgiveness of our sins; it is also an occasion for covenant renewal. God reminds us that he delivered us out of the house of bondage. By eating and drinking, we pledge that we will do whatever the Lord has commanded.

REFLECTIONS

How does the Lord strengthen you when you take communion?

The Golden Calf

EXODUS 32:1-6, 15-20

"These are your gods, Israel, who brought you up out of Egypt."
—*Exodus 32:4*

When we read the story of the golden calf, we can't help but ask, How could they do it? These people had just heard the mighty voice of God: "No other gods before me." "No graven images." And they had responded with solemn words: "We will do everything the LORD has said; we will obey" (Ex. 24:7).

Now, in spite of all their experiences with the living God, they make themselves a dumb idol. How could they ever do it?

We might remind ourselves that this nation of Israel, as it came out of Egypt, was far removed from the worship of the living God. Their knowledge of the will of the Lord must have been very shallow, while their exposure to paganism had been deep and long. The craving for visible gods and tangible leadership was natural to them. This is also the reason why God kept them so long at Mount Sinai. They had to learn God's ways and be organized into a worshiping community by means of the tabernacle.

At this point, Moses had been gone for nearly six weeks. And Aaron—at least in this story—was weak and cowardly. Some Bible students suggest that Aaron and the people did not really intend to make another god for themselves; they wanted to serve the true God by means of this image. In other words, they transgressed the second commandment, not the first. However, there is really no practical difference. It was definitely a sin of idolatry.

At any rate, there's no reason for us to become judgmental. Idolatry is the cardinal sin for all people. Many people profess to be Christians. They worship the true God on Sunday but serve an idol on Monday. How can they do it?

The Israelites would have been lost without a mediator to plead for them. Moses was their mediator. He turned to God with a heart full of love for Israel. He spoke to Israel with a voice filled with the wrath of God.

We, the members of a new covenant, are also dependent on our Mediator. It's the love and anger of Jesus that keeps us from idolatry.

REFLECTIONS

What might "idolatry" look like in our lives?

They Could Not Enter

NUMBERS 13:25-33

> *"But the people who live there are powerful, and the cities are fortified and very large. We even saw descendants of Anak there."*
> —*Numbers 13:28*

Almost two years after the people had left Egypt, they came to the frontiers of Canaan. Then twelve men were selected (one for each tribe) to form a sort of commando group to spy out the land. They spent forty days in Canaan.

When they returned, they brought evidence of the riches of the land. They found grapes of such enormous clusters that they had to be carried on a pole by two men. Yet the majority presented an unfavorable report. Ten out of twelve concluded: "We can't attack those people [of Canaan]; they are stronger than we are" (v. 31).

Joshua and Caleb had a different view. But they did not get a hearing. The people had come so far and had traveled so long that they were totally disheartened. "That night all the members of the community . . . wept aloud" (Num. 14:1).

A tumultuous meeting was held, and the spies reported. Joshua and Caleb tried in vain to encourage the people. Finally the furious mob was ready to throw stones at their leaders. At that moment the blinding light of the glory of the Lord descended on the tent of meeting—which meant that God wished to speak to Moses. Then Moses had to struggle with God for the life of the nation.

The Bible says that the Israelites "were not able to enter, because of their unbelief" (Heb. 3:19). The reason was not the strength of the Canaanites, the fortified cities, or the giant descendants of Anak. It was unbelief.

This is also the difference in the reporting by the spies. There are two ways of seeing things—in the light of faith, and without that light.

The church has been called to possess the earth. If we look at that challenge without the light of faith, the world looks scary and the mission impossible. But faith says that all things and all people will bow before the power of the Lord—even giants and fortified cities.

REFLECTIONS

What are some of the "giants" that threaten the church today—and you as an individual Christian?

The Sign That Saves

NUMBERS 21: 4-9

"Just as Moses lifted up the snake in the wilderness, so the Son of Man must be lifted up, that everyone who believes may have eternal life in him." —John 3:14–15

The regrets came after the punishment. First the Israelites complained about the journey and the food. Then they grumbled about the leadership of Moses and of God. In a moment of disgust, they tossed away all the privileges of being God's own people. They were taunting their Lord, inviting him to cast them off. And it was only after they were dying from poisonous snake bites that they cried to Moses and begged him to pray for them.

"We have sinned when we spoke against the LORD and against you."

Humbled to the dust, the people of Israel cried out to be spared.

God answers in a very remarkable way. Moses is told to make a replica of a serpent and put it on a pole. Then, when people are bitten by a snake and the poison begins to course through their system, they can look at the brass serpent and be healed.

Some five hundred years later, Israelites were burning incense before the bronze serpent Moses made, until a God-fearing king destroyed the object of superstition (2 Kings 18:4).

Within the church, this short and bitter episode in the history of Israel's wanderings might have been forgotten, were it not for the fact that this saving sign became a teaching model in the New Testament.

Jesus himself used the figure of the serpent to clinch his instruction of Nicodemus. First he humbled the ruler of the Jews, and all of us, by declaring that flesh is only flesh and human beings are unable to lay hold on the life that comes from God. And then our Teacher chose the bronze serpent to show that it is up to God to choose the instrument of healing.

"Just as Moses lifted up the snake in the wilderness, so the Son of Man (the Messiah) must be lifted up (on a pole or a cross), that everyone who believes (looks to him as the message from God) may have eternal life in him." So simple and so profound!

All of us are dying and no one has medicine. Then God gives us Jesus on the cross. And all we have to do is look up and live.

REFLECTIONS

Remind yourself to look up to Jesus today and whenever you sense your need for healing from sin, weakness, and lack of faith.

Death of Moses

DEUTERONOMY 34

> *And Moses the servant of the* LORD *died there in Moab, as the*
> LORD *had said.* —Deuteronomy 34:5

Moses had committed a sin that disqualified him from entering the promised land. Numbers 20:2-13 tells the story. Moses lost his patience and did not follow the instructions of the Lord exactly. He was supposed to *tell* the rock that it should yield water. Instead he lashed out at the people—"Listen, you rebels!" Then he *hit* the rock.

Psalm 106 recounts the incident as follows: "By the waters of Meribah they angered the LORD, and trouble came to Moses because of them; for [the Israelites] rebelled against the Spirit of God, and rash words came from Moses' lips" (vv. 32-33).

If the Bible itself presents excuses for Moses, then we had better not sit in judgment on his angry words and deeds. God always counts sin heavier when it is committed by someone who is close to him. Therefore Moses was not allowed to enter Canaan.

As an intercessor, Moses had often caused a change in the Lord's intentions. But all his pleas to be allowed to enter Canaan were turned down flat: God said, "Do not speak to me anymore about this matter" (Deut. 3:26).

In this way God teaches us that he is just in all his ways, and that there is only one perfect Mediator between God and man—the Man Christ Jesus.

The weary wanderings had come to an end. Israel was encamped in the valley of Moab. Here the old leader renewed the covenant between Israel and its God (Deut. 29-31). Moses gave them a song, and he blessed each of the tribes of Israel (Deut. 32-33). Then Moses climbed Mount Nebo, from where God showed him the land of Canaan, which the Israelites were now ready to possess. And Moses died.

No man in the Old Testament was greater and closer to God than Moses. And no man came closer to fulfilling the function of Jesus Christ, both in revealing God's will to people and in interceding for the people with God.

The life of the Old Testament mediator shows us how much we need a mediator. And his death reminds us that only Jesus can do it perfectly and forever.

REFLECTIONS

What can we learn from the death of the greatest man in the Old Testament?

Your Will Be Done

"Your will be done" is not a prayer of resignation; it is a prayer for obedience. We often pray the Lord's Prayer without much thought, but Jesus himself prayed it with blood and tears.

daylight

The Christian's Prayer

MATTHEW 6:5-15

"Our Father in heaven, hallowed be your name, your kingdom come, your will be done, on earth as it is in heaven." —Matthew 6:9-10

Only Christians can pray the Lord's Prayer. Others can say it or recite it, but they cannot pray it. When we pray, we desire and therefore we ask. We work for it too. Our works show the sincerity of our prayers. Only Christians have the desire that the Father's will be done. And their works show that they mean what they say.

The first three lines of the Lord's Prayer have essentially one request. In three parallel petitions, the Father in heaven is asked to finish his work of redemption: "Hallowed be your name, your kingdom come, your will be done." The first line of the prayer is explained by the second line: God's name must be honored by the coming of his kingdom. And what does the coming of God's kingdom mean? That God's will is done on earth as it is done in heaven.

God will be completely honored when the kingdom has come. And his kingdom will be fully established only when all who live obey God's will.

It is tragic and blasphemous that this prayer is widely used for pious recitation and liturgical filling. When he taught this prayer, the Lord warned people not to "keep on babbling like pagans." Yet the prayer he taught as an antidote against "many words" has been rehearsed and repeated throughout the centuries as if it were the best of all incantations.

God is not to be won by incantations. And it was never Christ's intention that we should forever repeat his exact words. Rather, he wants us to use this prayer as a model for all of our prayer life. He wants us to love our Father so much and to long for his kingship so intensely that these desires dominate all our requests. He wants us to pray that our Father's will be done in our homes and towns and churches as it is done in heaven.

REFLECTIONS

In what ways should the Lord's Prayer be a model for our own prayers?

The Decision of Christ

HEBREWS 10:1-7

"Then I said, 'Here I am—it is written about me in the scroll—I have come to do your will, my God.'" —Hebrews 10:7

Jesus spoke the words recorded in Hebrews 10:7 before he was born in Bethlehem. This is the oath sworn by the Son of God in the council of the triune God before he entered the world.

The eternal Son of God saw our planet swinging in space. He saw you and me, bowed down and wounded. He saw our inability to come to him and fulfill our calling. He saw the sacrifices and he noticed the burnt offerings. They were temporary measures, the shadows of things to come. In themselves they were powerless to bring people to God and keep them there.

Then Christ made his decision and announced his goal: "I have come to do your will, my God." The purpose of his life and death is summed up in these words. If you ask why God became a human being and why Christ suffered and died among us, here is your answer: that God's will might be done on earth as it is in heaven.

Christ came to do God's will. And he did it.

According to God's will, he was born in Bethlehem and lived in Nazareth, in Jerusalem, in Gethsemane, and on Golgotha. Then he cried from earth to heaven: "Finished! Now the Father's will has been done on earth as it is being done in heaven. My God and Father, I have done your will, as it is written of me in the scrolls of prophecy."

Christ came to do God's will, and he came to teach the rebels of this earth the road of obedience.

When a teacher has a class of completely unwilling students, he or she hopes for one, just one, who can be a leader among them and bend the behavior of the class from opposition to cooperation. One like that has come into our world, and he has turned the tide.

Now the Son of Man is in heaven, and the Spirit of God is on earth. The followers of Christ are also the sons and daughters of obedience. They have been set free by the Spirit of Christ so that the will of God might be done on earth as it is in heaven.

REFLECTIONS

What new insights does this Scripture and reading give you about Christ?

The Food of the Son

JOHN 4:31-38

"My food," said Jesus, "is to do the will of him who sent me and to finish his work." —*John 4:34*

When a commando unit has landed inside the territory of the enemy, it doesn't go on a sightseeing tour. It has to accomplish its mission and return to the base.

Jesus spoke of his actions in a similar way. He lived to obey the orders of the One who sent him. He had to accomplish a mission. He could not be distracted from his single goal. After doing the will of his Sender, he would go and report to the Father: "Mission accomplished."

On this particular day, Jesus was sitting at the well, tired after a long journey (v. 6). The disciples had gotten food, and they urged Jesus to eat some. But Christ made it clear that he had more important things on his mind. He was intent on doing the Father's will.

The kingdom of God was coming to Samaria! Christ had just offered the water of life to a sinful woman. While he was sitting at the well, Jesus saw a vision of the harvest fields in which his disciples would be the reapers. There was such joy in this contemplation of his Father's will and his Father's work that all other things were unimportant.

When we learn to know this joy of the Lord, we will pay less attention to the things everybody else deems important and more attention to the things that enthralled Jesus Christ.

We are often inclined to make a big fuss about such little things as eating and drinking. But we must learn to distinguish between the things that are really important and the things that are trivial. That's a big part of Christian living. Once we have our priorities straight, doing God's will and sharing in God's work will be high on our list. Then we will also be closer to our Master.

As long as we have not tasted the Master's "food," we don't know him very well.

REFLECTIONS

"We are often inclined to make a big fuss about little things." What "little things" tend to distract you from "doing God's will and sharing in God's work"?

Fellowship of Obedience

MARK 3:31-5

"Whoever does God's will is my brother and sister and mother."
—Mark 3:35

Christians have always called each other *brother* and *sister*. Occasionally the custom sounds somewhat stuffy. Yet its meaning is profound.

Christ himself taught us to think of our fellowship as a household in which God is the Father and we are brothers and sisters to one another. He did not despise natural relationships. One of the few words he spoke from the cross concerned his care for his widowed mother. But Christ did teach that the other bond, the bond of the Spirit, is deeper and more lasting than the tie of blood.

Some have suggested that the Christian custom of calling each other *brother* and *sister* stems from a faith in the general fatherhood of God and the general brother- and sisterhood of all people. However, this has never been a teaching of the Christian church. On the contrary, we teach that the church, as the household of God, is separated from the world to do the will of God. It is obedience to God that creates the ties that bind.

When Christ began to gather his own people, he created a new fellowship. He laid the name of the Father on the lips of his followers, and he taught them that this Father has authority in his house. So the fellowship of Christ's followers may be called the fellowship of those who do the will of God.

Christians make all their relationships secondary to their fellowship with those who obey—with their brothers and sisters in Christ. We would rather break off all other relationships than let go of this fellowship—just as we would rather suffer pain and persecution in our personal life than be disobedient to the will of our heavenly Father.

When the church has become a company of those who find their unity in similarities of race, color, or social status, it has degenerated. It is and must be a fellowship in obedience.

And the church ardently desires the brother- and sisterhood of all people when it prays, "Your will be done, on earth as it is in heaven."

REFLECTIONS
Think about—and give thanks for—the strong ties you have with others in your congregation because of your common desire to do God's will.

Stand Up!

DANIEL 3:8-18

*"If the God we serve is able to deliver us, then he will deliver us.
. . . But even if he does not, we want you to know, Your Majesty,
that we will not serve your gods or worship the image of gold you
have set up."* —*Daniel 3:17-18*

When we pray, "Your will be done," we pray for obedience on earth as it
is practiced in heaven.

These three young men in the valley of Dura did the will of God. They
knew God and his will. They knew God had the power to deliver them
from the fire of the furnace. But they were not sure God would indeed
rescue them from the flames. God might let them burn to death. "But
even if he does not . . . we will not serve your gods or worship the image
of gold you have set up."

God knows our temptation to do what everyone does. If all the others
fall to their knees when the music sounds, it requires much faith and
courage to stand there alone, tall and strong. We all know teens who
would rather die than be different from their peers. But even for grown-
ups it takes a lot of courage to row against the stream. After all, we cannot be sure that we will be kept from suffering when we choose the path
of obedience.

The three men in the valley of Dura said they would be obedient even
if God did not deliver them from the fiery furnace.

Obedience comes first. We do not obey God because doing it means
we are going to come out on top. First we obey. Then we trust in God
for the rest.

A young Christian lived to tell about his experiences in a concentration
camp. He had been helped by the presence of an older Christian man who
had not lived to see freedom. One day he asked his older fellow prisoner:
"Is the war going to last long?" The older man had said: "Nobody knows
how long the war is going to last. To us, that's not an important question.
The only important question is how we are going to live through it."

We don't know how long we are going to be on the battlefield. The
only important issue is whether we dare to stand up in obedience when
every knee bows to the image of gold.

REFLECTIONS
What risks are you willing to take for God?

The Sign of Jonah

JONAH 3

. . . and now one greater than Jonah is here. —Matthew 12:41

Sometimes the Lord can be amazingly insistent that his will be done by very unwilling prophets. Jonah disobeyed God's command. Instead of going east, he went west. Instead of going on a mission tour of Nineveh, he went on a cruise and fell asleep in the cabin of a ship.

Jonah disobeyed but the storm and the wind obeyed God's will. So did the fish. Finally Jonah obeyed God's will too—although reluctantly. He did preach repentance to Nineveh.

It did not seem that Jonah's mission could be carried out. By all human standards, when he disappeared with the fish, that should have been the end of him and his commission. But it was God's will that he come out alive and that Nineveh be converted.

Jesus' mission also seemed to be a failure. He was buried in the earth. By all human standards, that should have been the end of him and his missionary career. But he arose from the grave, and by his gospel the world is being converted.

God willed the salvation of the city of Nineveh. That's why he was so insistent that Jonah obey his command. Behind the will expressed in that command stood the will of redemption. God insisted on obedience because he had compassion on those who were perishing.

Jesus is greater than Jonah. Jesus died in obedience to the Father, and he arose to bring all people to the obedience of faith. Jesus was greater because his heart agreed with God's redemptive will. No sacrifice was too heavy to carry out the will of God. Jesus' heart was moved with compassion when he saw the multitudes. But Jonah despised the Ninevites.

God insists on our obedience, and he desires the conversion of all people. In his good pleasure he has called us to render willing service in bringing all people to the obedience of faith.

REFLECTIONS

What does the story of Jonah tell you about God? About our attitude toward those who don't know God?

No Vacant Houses

MATTHEW 12:22-29, 43-45

"Then it goes and takes with it seven other spirits more wicked than itself, and they go in and live there. And the final condition of that person is worse than the first. This is how it will be with this wicked generation." —Matthew 12:45

After Jesus had taught the multitudes that it was his mission to cast out the old enemy, the devil, he told the people a parable. There was a man with an evil spirit. This spirit was cast out. But since no one else moved into him, and since a demon is always restless, the demon came back with seven other evil spirits to bring complete destruction to this poor fellow. "The final condition of that person is worse than the first." And that's what happens to such people ("this wicked generation"), said Jesus.

Today this type of thing is happening to entire countries and continents. For centuries they have been strongholds of demons and victims of old superstitions. Then the evil spirit is cast out. But what next? Freedom is incomplete when the unholy power is broken. If no new, holy power comes to rule that house, a legion of evil spirits more destructive than the first will take over. And the final condition of that country—or continent, or generation—is worse than the first.

Such things also happen to people individually. A person can belong to different masters, but a person is never a house that can be vacant. He or she is like a store in the business section of the city. The store may change hands, but the business is continued "under new management."

Christ did not come merely to break the power of the devil; he came to establish the kingship of God. He saves us *from* the bondage of sin *to* the lordship of Christ.

If we want to clean our house—and only the most conceited person does not want to get rid of some evil in his life—but refuse to let Christ take complete control, the damage will be progressively worse.

We cannot keep our house clean and empty. It won't work. We can't stay out of the hands of the devil if we are unwilling to fall into the hands of the Lord. Only when we begin to obey the Lord do we stop being a pawn of the devil.

REFLECTIONS

Consider the various aspects of your life—work, leisure, relationships, possessions. In which of these or other areas would you like to give more control to the Lord?

The Price of Obedience

GENESIS 39:1-10

"How then could I do such a wicked thing and sin against God?"
—*Genesis 39:9*

Consider the similarities between the careers of Joseph and Jesus. Both left their father's house, both lived obediently through a state of humiliation, both were exalted to the throne after their time of obedient suffering had ended, and both saved the lives of their people.

These similarities are too striking to be ignored by those who believe that the Old Testament predicts what the New Testament proclaims. But since the New Testament does not even mention the name of Joseph, the eleventh son of Jacob, we must be cautious in our conclusions.

Joseph refused to sin with Potiphar's wife. In our time, in which adultery passes for entertainment and lust is advertised, Joseph is not only scorned for passing up a good time, he is also considered abnormal. At least one psychologist claims he has "established" that Joseph was sexually abnormal because of his intimate love for his father.

We cannot expect the people of this world to understand Joseph, who said, "How could I do such a wicked thing and sin against God?" The children of the present world cannot understand Joseph because they don't know Joseph's God: "How can I . . . sin against *God*?"

How many of us would commit a sin if we could be absolutely sure that we would not be found out by people? And how many sins have we refrained from simply because we lacked the opportunity—or, to put it in Christian terms, because we were spared the temptation? Knowing this about ourselves should make us forever reluctant to condemn anyone else who falls into sin.

Meanwhile, the cynics of the world have another reason to laugh: Joseph's obedience is the start of his troubles. He gets a jail term of at least two years.

But that should not confuse us. Those who are obedient will often be humiliated. To us that's proof we are on the right track, for that's the way of obedience Jesus followed.

REFLECTIONS

Ask yourself the personal questions found in the third paragraph from the end of this reading.

This Kind of Father

MALACHI 1:6-12

> *"If I am a father, where is the honor due me? If I am a master, where is the respect due me?" says the LORD Almighty.* —Malachi 1:6

There was a time when *Father* was a title. Among certain tribes, the chief was called *Father*. Jewish disciples called their rabbi *Father*. And in several church communities, *Father* is still used as a title of respect for the clergyman. The word *pope* comes from *papa*, which is a name for father. In short, *father* used to be a term that suggested feelings of respect for authority.

That's changed over the years. Respect and honor are no longer our first associations with the name *father*. Some fathers act like boys, and some boys like to use their fathers. In novels and films, the father is frequently a comical figure.

And for countless children, *father* is the name of a man who left long ago. There have always been unfaithful fathers and rebellious sons, but their tribe seems to have increased a thousand fold.

This changed father image is bound to have some influence on our use of the name *Father* for God. We believe God's fatherhood means that he loves us and especially that he cares for us. But the name *Father* is not likely to fill us with a deep sense of respect.

God has many great names in the Bible. By his names God tells us who he is. His greatest name is *Father*. This name has been revealed mainly through his Son, Jesus Christ. In fact we must belong to the Son if we are to call God our Father. The name reveals his love to us. But it also retains the old-fashioned notions of respect, honor, and authority.

God is forever the same kind of Father. God's love does not fail, and his authority is unquestionable. Looking at an earthly father is not enough to help us know God, but earthly fathers must look at God in order to know what it means to be a father.

God wants no other children than those who love and obey him with undiminished respect. We use God's name in vain if we call him Father and then refuse to obey him.

REFLECTIONS

When you pray to your Father in heaven, what does that name mean to you?

The Obedient Adam

ROMANS 5:12-21

For just as through the disobedience of the one man the many were made sinners, so also through the obedience of the one man the many will be made righteous. —Romans 5:19

Our fall was due to the disobedience of one; our restoration comes through the obedience of One.

This verse says that the disobedience of the one affected the many, and the obedience of the other one was also rendered on behalf of the many. But we may not say that since "many" is not "all," not everyone is affected. The point of the verse is that the deeds of Adam and Christ are representative.

The daily acts of ordinary citizens like us are not likely to affect the course of world history. But the deeds of a prime minister or a president may affect the country—not because he or she is different from all others but because of the position he or she holds.

There is no position quite like that of father of the human race. That's why the disobedience of father Adam had an influence far beyond any other act of any of his children—not because he was different from any of his children but because of the position he held as their father.

The greatest thing since Adam is the coming of Christ. He was given to us as the "second Adam." And because of that position, his acts have an influence as wide as the human race: his death is our death, his resurrection is our resurrection, and by his obedience sinners are made righteous.

Let's notice especially that we were saved by *obedience*. The battle between Jesus and Satan was not a power struggle to see who was the strongest. The issue in the struggle was whether or not Christ would remain *obedient*.

Neither have we fully done justice to the work of Christ when we say that he suffered and died for our sins. His suffering and death were part of the *total* obedience he gave to God—with all of his person and all of his actions.

Today all people are branches on one of two trees: those who are in Adam are known by their disobedience, but those who are in Christ glory in Christ's obedience.

REFLECTIONS

Offer a prayer thanking Jesus for saving you by being totally and perfectly obedient.

The Burden of God's Will

MATTHEW 26:36-46

> *"My Father, if it is not possible for this cup to be taken away unless I drink it, may your will be done."* —*Matthew 26:42*

In Gethsemane our Savior struggled to unite himself with the will of his Father. It was sheer agony. But when he left the garden, he was ready for the supreme act. He agreed to do God's will, even though it meant that he had to drink the last drops from the cup of God's holy wrath.

From his agony and self-surrender, we learn that praying "Your will be done" means much more than shrugging our shoulders and saying, "If I can't have it my way, let God have it his way."

Looking at Gethsemane, we learn that when we pray, "Your will be done," we should become so united with God's holy purpose that we are prepared to do God's will at any cost.

"Your will be done" is not a prayer of resignation; it is a prayer for obedience. Resignation is "yes" with a sigh. Rebellion is "no" with a shout. But obedience means accepting the present not as it is mapped out in our plans but just as it stands in God's books.

So we must know what we are doing when we begin to pray the prayer Jesus taught. Most people recite the Lord's Prayer without much thought. But Christ prayed it with blood and tears.

We should be fully aware that anyone who prays this prayer about God's name, God's kingdom, and God's will has chosen sides in the conflict that divides the world. From now on, that person is with the minority who places goods and self and everything at God's disposal. Whoever has prayed "Your will be done" is bearing the burden of the Lord.

That's what Elijah did, and he cried in weariness that he was alone. That's the burden Jeremiah was bearing, and he cringed under it. That's the burden under which Jesus nearly collapsed in the garden of Gethsemane.

If there never comes a time in our lives when "doing of the will of God" seems utterly beyond us and absolutely crushing, then it is not the Lord's burden we are bearing.

REFLECTIONS

When have you felt the burden of God's will?

To Go or Not to Go

ACTS 21:7-14

When he would not be dissuaded, we gave up and said, "The Lord's will be done."
—*Acts 21:14*

The apostle Paul was traveling to Jerusalem. He knew that suffering awaited him there, although he did not know exactly what God had in store for him. "And now, compelled by the Spirit, I am going to Jerusalem, not knowing what will happen to me there. I only know that in every city the Holy Spirit warns me that prison and hardships are facing me" (Acts 20:22-23).

Paul's friends did their utmost to keep him from going to Jerusalem. But it didn't help. They could not persuade him to change his mind. He had to go to Jerusalem because it was God's will.

At last his friends gave up: "The Lord's will be done."

Was that resignation? Was that "saying yes with a sigh"?

Perhaps it was, on the part of Paul's friends. They gave in to the inevitable and gave up when Paul's trip seemed unavoidable.

But for Paul it was an active commitment to do the will of the Lord. His going to Jerusalem, "compelled by the Spirit," strongly reminds us of Paul's Master, Jesus Christ. The friends of Jesus also tried to keep him from going to Jerusalem. Jesus knew exactly what was in store for him: ". . . the Son of Man will be delivered over to the chief priests and the teachers of the law. They will condemn him to death and will hand him over to the Gentiles, who will mock him and spit on him, flog him and kill him" (Mark 10:33-34). Jesus traveled to Jerusalem "compelled" by the same Spirit that compelled Paul. In spite of the opposition of his friends, Jesus "resolutely set out for Jerusalem" (Luke 9:51).

Paul follows in the footsteps of Jesus, the disciple learning obedience from the teacher. Like Jesus, he must deny his own desires and do the perfect will of God.

There comes a moment when loving friends must cease their efforts to restrain those who travel by a higher command. That moment comes when it is plain that going is a matter of obedience to God. Then it is proper to say: "The Lord's will be done."

REFLECTIONS

What do you think—when we say "Your will be done," do we usually do so with resignation or with an active commitment to do the will of the Lord?

Struggle and Submission

2 SAMUEL 12:13-23

He answered, "While the child was still alive, I fasted and wept. I thought, 'Who knows? The LORD may be gracious to me and let the child live.'" —2 Samuel 12:22

Many Christian parents, when their child was taken away, have prayed: "Your will be done." That's a Christian prayer. But it's not what this petition in the Lord's Prayer means.

The Lord's Prayer does not teach us to pray, "Help us to believe that all things work according to your holy will." Instead we pray, "Help us to be obedient in a disobedient world." "Your will be done" is a prayer for obedience.

We do need the grace to accept God's decisions—but we don't have to accept them unless they are final.

In this respect we may learn something from David. God had said that his child would die. But as long as there was breath in the sick child, David prayed. For seven days and nights, he struggled with God in prayer.

If we know that the Lord is gracious and full of compassion, we may continue to struggle until God has revealed his will with finality.

The decisions of God are not mysterious forces that operate in darkness, so that all we can do is sit down and say: "What must happen will happen." Often the Lord has allowed the sketches he made to be erased by the prayers of his children. God has given us access to him by means of our prayers. We aren't merely sitting outside the council chamber, waiting for the verdict.

So we must be careful how we advise each other, and we must not be quick to condemn each other. The friends of Job, the friends of Jesus, and the friends of Paul were all wrong in their interpretations of the will of God.

Neither do we always know what to ask. To some God gave faith to ask for a miracle, and they received it. Others knew the will of God in a certain matter and received grace to do that will and live with God's decision.

Once David's child was dead, he rose from his prayer. This, then, was the will of God. Now he knew it beyond a shadow of a doubt. And since God is our Father, shouldn't we trust him?

REFLECTIONS

"Often the Lord has allowed the sketches he made to be erased by his children." Have you experienced this? What convinces you of the power of prayer?

Discerning the Will of God

ROMANS 12:1-2

> *Then you will be able to test and approve what God's will is—his good, pleasing and perfect will.* —Romans 12:2

When we pray "Your will be done," we are asking for obedience on earth to match the kind of obedience that is practiced in heaven. "Your will be done" must not make us think of a secret decision of God Almighty; it is the will of the Father that we, his children, are supposed to be doing.

How do we know what we have to do? How do we know the will of God for our lives?

This question, which no one may dodge, can become crushingly difficult for a serious-minded Christian. We can all agree that we know God's will in general. But how can we be certain of God's will for our worship and work, for the particulars of everyday living, for the choices we have to make and the decisions we face?

To answer this question, Christians have always tended to go in one of two directions. At one extreme are those who leave it to the experts (the church, the clergy) to spell out the will of God. At the other extreme are the spiritualists who receive private revelations of the will of God and know the mind of the Spirit with a certainty no one is allowed to question.

In the new covenant under which we are living, God deals with us as mature children. A certain amount of self-activity is required. Otherwise we would not be mature. We must now "test and approve" what is good and acceptable and perfect in the sight of God.

When God tells us to discern his will in the ordinary things of our lives, we are expected to do more than say that it's not easy. Many people have made this remark and let it go at that.

Of course it's not easy! Neither is it impossible. After all, our minds have been "renewed," and that transformation must show itself in acts of obedience. We no longer can live in the way everybody lives. We ask for the will of God.

And God is no stranger to us. He is our Father.

REFLECTIONS

When you must make a difficult decision with wide-ranging effects, how do you try to determine what God's will is in that situation?

The Love Commandment

MATTHEW 22:34-40

> *Jesus replied: "'Love the Lord your God with all your heart and with all your soul and with all your mind.' This is the first and greatest commandment. And the second is like it: 'Love your neighbor as yourself.'"* —*Matthew 22:37, 39*

It is often said that the love commandment is a summary of the law. This may be misleading. If by *summary* we mean a short saying that catches the essence but fails to give the details, we should not speak of the love commandment as a summary. It is a summary of the law only in the sense in which the sea is the summary of all the rivers. The command to love covers a wider territory than all the commandments.

It is the sum total of a person's duties.

God demands no more and no less than that we love him above all and our neighbors as ourselves. If, starting tomorrow, all people began loving God above all and loving their neighbor as they now love themselves, we would have a new world; the kingdom of God would have come.

We must love God with our intellect, our will, and our emotions. We must love him with our whole being. It is impossible to explain what that means. We must study the lives of the lovers of God as we get to know them in the Bible. Especially the life and deeds of Jesus will teach us what it means to love God.

We are commanded to love our neighbors as ourselves. This means that we must have the same concern for those whom God places on our way as we have for ourselves.

These two commandments are connected. The second is "like" the first. That is to say, when our relationship to God is right, our relationship to our neighbor will also be right. But if we cannot love our neighbor, we do not love our God.

God commands love. God does not merely say: "Go to church and do your work. Be honest and chaste and truthful." He says we should *love*. Nobody can love simply by making up his or her mind to do so. We can discipline ourselves to abstain from many bad things. But we cannot discipline ourselves to do the one good thing that is required—love.

We can only love when the Spirit of Jesus controls our lives.

REFLECTIONS

Frame a prayer around your need to be more loving, asking that the Spirit will control your life more completely.

The Extraordinary Demand

MATTHEW 19:16-22

> *Jesus answered, "If you want to be perfect, go, sell your possessions and give to the poor, and you will have treasure in heaven. Then come, follow me."* —Matthew 19:21

If you were brought up as a Christian, you have often heard the story of the rich young man who came to Jesus. It's an upsetting story for anyone who is somewhat attached to worldly conveniences. There was only one way for that young man to show that he loved Jesus—by giving up everything else.

But every time our teachers and preachers told us this story, they probably gave us a bit of comfort by adding something like: "That does not mean you have to give up everything when you follow Jesus. The point is that your *heart* may not cling to your possessions."

That made us feel immensely relieved. We could follow Jesus—and our savings account was still safe. Of course, that is a form of self-deception, for the only way we can ever find out if our heart clings to our possessions is by surrendering them.

Our teachers and preachers feel called to assure us that life can be very ordinary, even if we are devoted to doing the will of God. In the face of the gospel's extraordinary demands, they still manage to send us home in peace. In fact, you may be sure that many preachers don't believe their own sermons. They would be flabbergasted if people really started to do on Monday what they heard in the sermon on Sunday.

Nobody has the right to say to anyone else that God does not require very much. Neither may we sow any doubts that God gives in extraordinary measure.

The story of the rich young man has a sequel. In answer to Peter's question, Jesus spoke of the generosity of God, who gives back "a hundred times as much" plus "eternal life" to those who surrender their treasures for Jesus (v. 29).

We must listen to Christ. He is reliable. Therefore we must do what he commands and count on his promises. But we may not reduce the Bible and the will of God to the size of "ordinary" Christianity.

REFLECTIONS

How can we be more open to any "extra-ordinary demands" that God may make of us?

Obedience in Ordinary Life

EPHESIANS 5:15-33

> *Therefore do not be foolish, but understand what the Lord's will is.*
> *. . . Wives, submit yourselves to your own husbands. . . . Husbands,*
> *love your wives. . . . Children, obey your parents in the Lord. . . .*
> —*Ephesians 5:17, 22, 25; 6:1*

All Christians are to seek the will of the Lord for their lives. Our teaching and advice may never stand between the voice of God and the conscience of anyone addressed by God. It is very well possible that God would ask of us an unusual deed or an extraordinary sacrifice. If that happens, we can obey cheerfully. We cannot lose if the service is rendered to Jesus. We cannot go wrong if we obey the will of our heavenly Father.

Although we must be alert to the extraordinary things God may ask of us, each of us must obey God first of all in ordinary things.

God demands of us a very usual and ordinary obedience. Married people must love each other according to God's will. Children must obey their parents because God wants it so. Employees must do their job as if they are doing it for God. Employers must do the will of their Master in heaven.

After dinner, a boy went to his bedroom to struggle with God in prayer. He wanted to know whether or not he should volunteer for service in an overseas mission. Then his mother called him to do the dishes. But he failed to recognize that his mother's voice was the voice of God.

Christ does not want us to reduce him and his will to everything that is ordinary and manageable. At the same time, our Lord doesn't lift us out of ordinary life. He teaches us how to live it. The will of God must be done in the living room and the kitchen, in the playroom and the bedroom, in the classroom and the office, at the job and during lunch break. Without ordinary obedience, we are not prepared for extraordinary tasks, should God require them of us.

Many Christians have been rendered unfit for bigger service because they did not obey God's will with respect to their marriage. When we are young, we must first learn to obey God's voice when he tells us to do our homework. Otherwise we won't hear God when he tells us what we should do about the suffering of the world.

REFLECTIONS

How has God taught you how to live your "ordinary life" in obedience to him?

Free Indeed

JOHN 8:31-36

"So if the Son sets you free, you will be free indeed." —*John 8:36*

Although many people are still unwilling to accept the Christian teaching of original sin, few believe any more that a person begins the journey of life in utter freedom. The bad habits that we may have picked up since we were babies do not account for the awful reality of human bondage.

From a distance, two men walking down the street may seem to be moving freely. But when you come close, you suddenly notice that one is handcuffed to the other. At first you didn't see the thin chain binding them together—you had to come closer. So it is with each of us. A closer look reveals that we are chained.

When we pray to do God's will, we also ask God to break our bondage. We cannot run when our feet are tied. We cannot go where God wants us to go as long as there are powers that keep us back.

In principle every Christian has been set free from sin to obey the Father. It is no longer impossible for us to please God, for the Son has set us free.

But the unchaining is also a process. Some of these thin but tough bands are not uncovered until much light from Christ has shone into our lives. For instance, there may be powers in our environment to which we are deeply conformed and accustomed that actually keep us back from being true servants of God.

Pray, then, that the Son may make us free, so that the only thing that counts is doing the will of God.

We are free only when we can obey God with our whole heart. But we still find that our desires to serve God are hindered by other desires. There is still reservation in our love. There is still some unwillingness, even in obedience.

The beauty of the life to come consists in being entirely free to serve. Unreservedly we will be able to give ourselves in love. We will give God our hearts and our all. Our complete freedom will be celebrated in perfect obedience.

REFLECTIONS

What are some of the "thin but tough bands" that might be holding you back from being the kind of Christian you want to be?

A Sense of Mission

JOHN 17:9-19

"As you sent me into the world, I have sent them into the world."
—*John 17:18*

The word *mission* means sending forth. A missionary is one who has been sent to do the will of the sender. Jesus was on a mission for the Father. And Jesus has sent us into the world. So we too are on a mission.

A mother sends her son to a nearby store for a loaf of bread. She tells him to come back right away. But on his way to the store, he meets a friend with a new bike and forgets about his mother who sent him to the store. He forgets that he is on a mission.

Christians resemble that boy. We have been sent by the Master. We are on a mission. But on our way there are so many things that detain us. These things are not necessarily evil, but they become evil to us because they rob us of our sense of mission.

Having a sense of mission does not only mean that we are interested in bringing the gospel to those who do not know Jesus Christ. It also means that others can tell from our way of living that we are under orders by the One who sent us.

We are not at home here. We keep ourselves in readiness to meet someone else. Then we will get to our destination. We are not "of" the world; we have been sent "into" the world to fulfill a mission.

But we are very easily sidetracked. Little things soon become big things, and the really important things are almost forgotten. Like the boy who forgot his errand while he was talking about bikes with his friend, we can forget our mission while we are talking about cars, houses, gas prices, or baseball. Maybe these things are all good and honorable, but somehow the urgency of our mission slips into the background. We forget that we have to report to the One who will ask, "Mission accomplished?"

Only one person could say, "Finished!" And he said it on Golgotha. Since he died, we have peace. Since he lives, he instructs us about our mission.

REFLECTIONS

What is your mission? What kinds of things distract you from it?

God-Willed Prayers

1 JOHN 5:13-21

This is the confidence we have in approaching God: that if we ask anything according to his will, he hears us. —1 John 5:14

If we ask anything according to God's will, he hears us.

The text doesn't say that if our prayers happen to fit with God's plans, we'll get what we want. It does say that Christians can ask with confidence and boldness once they have learned to pray according to God's will. And you and I should know God's will.

Children know their parents' will. That's apparent when we hear them say to each other, "It's no use even asking," meaning that they know their parents cannot possibly allow what the children have in mind.

Asking "according to God's will" means that we are praying for that which God himself desires to give us.

Jesus expressed the same truth in these words: "If you remain in me and my words remain in you, ask whatever you wish, and it will be done for you" (John 15:7). Jesus does not address the words "Ask whatever you wish" to everyone who wants to be healthy, wealthy, and successful. Instead he is speaking to everyone who has Christ's words in his or her heart. Such people will pray according to God's will and will receive what is asked for.

Prayer is not a means of *getting* what we want; it is a means of *becoming* what God wants us to be. And what God wants us to be is also the best we could ever be.

So when we have learned what is good for us and stand committed to God's name, God's kingdom, and God's will, we can also "ask according to God's will," and do so with confidence. When God's name is our chief concern, his kingdom our hope, and his will our wish, we may boldly go and ask for what God has promised. A father would sooner give his son a stone for bread than God would refuse the request of his children.

God wants us to be fully equipped to serve in his kingdom. If we are lacking in any such equipment, it is because we lacked the boldness to ask. To pray for such a thing is to pray according to his will. Ask, and you will receive!

REFLECTIONS

If you followed the advice in this Scripture and reading, would your prayers change? If so, how?

The Only God

ISAIAH 40:12-17

"You shall have no other gods before me." —*Exodus 20:3*

The Ten Commandments stem from a pre-Christian period. They were given by God to the people of Israel. They constituted the core of all the commandments that God gave his people in the covenant of Sinai.

Christ did not abolish these commandments but fulfilled them. That means that his teaching and life have shown the full implications of God's will as revealed in the law in general and in the Ten Commandments in particular.

The Ten Commandments do not give us all that we should know about the will of God for our lives. But they are basic to everything else the Bible has to say about reverence for God and respect for our neighbor.

The first commandment is foundational to all of life and religion: God must be honored as God. God gave this basic rule because humanity's basic temptation is idolatry. Idolatry means that we have a false god in the place of or next to the true God.

All the mysterious powers people encounter in the universe are potential idols—the sun, the moon, the rain, the ocean, growth, fertility, sexual power, beauty, merchandise, money, reason, wisdom. The great lesson God brought into the world through Israel is that God is one. All powers are subject to God. And God does not tolerate anybody or anything receiving the honor due his name.

The same powers still cast their spell over our world. We call them materialism or naturalism or rationalism or hedonism or post-modernism. These powers fight for the place of God in the lives of all people.

Christ came into the world first to reveal the God we worship. We inevitably become like the God we worship. So you can always tell whether a person worships mammon or pleasure or a stern god or a sentimental god or the Father of Jesus Christ. Christ has also come into the world to make all the powers his servants. So we can already devote ourselves totally, together with everything we have, to the service of the King of kings and the Lord of lords.

REFLECTIONS

Think of one thing that you are personally tempted to idolize, something that could become a kind of god to you. Then offer a prayer based on your desire to put God first, ahead of any and all idols or potential idols.

How to Worship God

ISAIAH 40:18-26

"You shall not make for yourself an image in the form of any-thing. . . . You shall not bow down to them or worship them. . . ."
—*Exodus 20:4-5*

God is invisible. And God is unimaginable—outside of Jesus Christ, at least.

Image-making is foolish, but it often happens with the best of intentions. Even pagan people did not mean to say that the (often ugly) image they created was a picture of their god. Instead they meant to say that the power of their god was captured or concentrated in the statue or object. It was a way to get control over their god—a way to handle, manipulate, use the power of their god.

When Christians began to make images, they certainly did not mean to say that the crucifix, for example, had any power. They only intended to remind worshipers of Jesus' love and power. But since all people are inclined to superstition, the symbol soon became identified with the reality it stood for. That's how the church got thousands of holy objects, all regarded with superstitious reverence.

By God's grace, a large part of the church was cleansed of this superstition. But that did not mean Christians were forever safe from sins against the second commandment. The danger of committing idolatry with images is always present.

Ministers and church leaders, for example, are in danger of making their church organization the graven image for which they lay their lives on the altar. And many ordinary Christians have a set way in which they worship God and a time-honored liturgy. Sometimes these forms of worship become more important to them than worship itself. God is caught in the image. The form becomes more important than the purpose. The sound of a certain Bible translation becomes more precious than the message.

But the God who reveals himself as the Father of Christ also determines *how* he will be worshiped. God does not want us to *make* images—God wants us to *be* images, newly created in Christ Jesus. The people God has redeemed are better pictures of the invisible God than anything we could make.

REFLECTIONS

Try restating this commandment in a way that applies to you and how you worship God.

The Holy Name

ECCLESIASTES 5:1-7

"You shall not misuse the name of the LORD your God, for the LORD will not hold anyone guiltless who misuses his name."
—Exodus 20:7

This commandment forbids the use of God's name for magic, false oaths, or other scandalous abuse.

Whenever we take the name of the Holy One on our lips to make ourselves sound impressive, to hurt someone else, or to strengthen an unreliable promise, God "will not hold [us] guiltless."

The abuse of God's name is strictly forbidden. We must always use the name reverently, carefully, and for a valid purpose. So we must not immediately connect this commandment with all those who do not know who God is—and who therefore regard his name lighter than breath. Instead we must think of this commandment first of all in connection with our religious life.

Old forms of magic aren't so common anymore. But politicians and national leaders still use the name of God to strengthen the cause of the country. The combination of national interests with the name of the Almighty should make us tremble. During World War II, the name of God was stamped on the buckle of every Nazi soldier's belt. That was outright blasphemy. But God's name does not belong on the currency of the United States either.

God's name may not be used for the sake of solemnity at funerals and weddings where hired clergymen baptize unholy affairs with Bible texts.

When we attend worship services and use the name of God simply because it's "the thing to do," we use God's name in vain. When we day-dream through prayers, when we focus on the beat of the band or the harmony of the praise team, when we want our worship to be entertaining, we're using God's name in vain. It is the "sacrifice of fools" (Ecc. 5:1).

The intent of the commandment is not to hush up the name of our God. God's purpose is revealed in Jesus: "Repentance for the forgiveness of sins will be preached *in his name* to all nations" (Luke 24:47).

REFLECTIONS
The expression "Oh my God" has become a throwaway line these days—especially on TV and when texting (shortened to OMG). How do you handle this kind of abuse of God's name?

Remember the Sabbath Day

LUKE 6:1-11

"Remember the Sabbath day by keeping it holy." —*Exodus 20:8*

It's very clear what this commandment meant to Israel: the people were not supposed to do any work on the seventh day, which was called the *Sabbath*, the day of rest.

The reasons given in Exodus and Deuteronomy are several. God rested on the seventh day after six days of creation activity. The animals, the servants, and the slaves had to have a day of rest. The Sabbath was also a sign of the covenant God made with his people after the exodus. People who did not rest on the Sabbath day were placing themselves outside the covenant people. That's why violators of this commandment were executed.

It's much more difficult to say what this commandment means for the people of God under the new covenant. Christians are very much divided on this question, and the New Testament sheds little light on the issue. What we do know is that Christians began to gather for worship on the first day of the week almost immediately after the resurrection of Jesus. No wonder. That's when their life began! But Christian leaders did not connect the Christian Sunday and the Jewish Sabbath until many centuries later.

Still, there is common ground on which all Christians can agree.

First, we must guard our life so that it does not become a continuous "workathon." And this responsibility does not apply only to our personal life but to society as a whole. We ought to devote at least one day to the worship of God and to works of mercy, fellowship, recreation, and education.

Second, our participation in the gathering of the church of Jesus Christ is not optional but mandatory. We need it—not merely to survive but to conquer. Such gatherings and opportunities for worship need not be limited to Sundays—in fact, they should not be—but they are most appropriate on the Lord's day.

REFLECTIONS

How do you keep the fourth commandment?

Authority and Obedience

EPHESIANS 6:1-9

"Honor your father and your mother, so that you may live long in the land the LORD your God is giving you." —*Exodus 20:12*

Part 1 of the Ten Commandments deals with our relationship to God. It can be summarized as "Love God above all." Part 2 deals with relationships between people. It can be summarized as "Love your neighbor as yourself."

But the fifth commandment is "in between." It does not deal with the vertical relationship—not quite. And it does not deal with the horizontal relationship—not quite. Our parents stand between God and us. They must be honored and obeyed because it pleases God to place them above us. We obey them not because they are good and wise but because they are our parents. Obedience to them is an act of reverence to God.

"Honoring" our parents is more than "obeying" them. Even when we move away and live apart from our parents as singles or married couples with children of our own, we still have to honor our parents. We never outgrow that obligation.

God commands children to obey, and he gives authority to parents. But authority is never something we hold permanently. It is given to us only for a particular purpose. Ultimately we must give account to God, who gave it.

God has given all forms of authority for the performance of a certain task or service. Parental authority is the most basic of all forms of authority—and the most inclusive. It is also the most demanding. Parents must raise their children in the fear of the Lord and bring them up until they are mature enough to stand on their own and make their own decisions in obedience to God and with a sense of responsibility for their fellow human beings.

This is the biggest job most people get to do in their lifetimes. It can also be the most rewarding. The rewards of keeping this commandment, for parents as well as for children, are received already in the present life.

REFLECTIONS

How do you show honor to your parents? What difference has this made in your life?

Love Your Neighbor

LUKE 10:25-37

"You shall not murder."   *—Exodus 20:13*

God protects people against people in this commandment. In the negative form God says, "You shall not murder." In the positive form he says, "You shall love your neighbor as yourself."

This commandment is rooted in creation. People belong to God because God made them. That's the basis of human dignity (a much-abused phrase). No matter who people are, what they look like, how they behave, what color they are, what houses they live in, or what positions they hold, they are imagebearers of God. Therefore they stand under God's protection.

God protects people not only because he made them but also because he loves them. The devil is a murderer from the beginning, but God loves people. Therefore, says the Bible, a person who hates his brother or sister can never be a child of God but is a child of the devil.

What God demands in the law he gives in the gospel by teaching his people how to form a fellowship. The cement of the fellowship is love. And the community of those who love one another is the restored life— the positive fulfillment of this commandment.

In the Bible, "life" is much more than breathing, and murder is more than cutting a throat. Living means having fellowship with God and with people. Without it, we have no life. All forms of hatred and envy are the seeds of murder. They disrupt the fellowship and they are sown by the devil. Love is what keeps communion and makes fellowship possible; hatred is the opposite of love. Love comes from God; hatred is from the devil. When the final community is revealed as the city of God (Rev. 22:15), the murderers are outside.

God created people to form a community—not to stand over against each other but to be *neigh*bors (people who are "nigh" or "next" to each other). To that end God does not only threaten those who take up the sword but even allowed his own Son to be killed. God did this to teach all of us how much he loves us.

Now we must listen to the story of the good Samaritan, which Jesus concludes with the words, "Go and do likewise."

REFLECTIONS

This commandment is about hatred and love. How does it relate to your day-to-day life?

God and Marriage

GENESIS 2:18-25

"You shall not commit adultery."   —*Exodus 20:14*

God created human beings male and female. Eve was created as a helper suitable for Adam. Not a helper to do little jobs for him, but one who could meet him in his being—his counterpart. These two were so marvelously made by their God and for each other that they were able to become two in one—"one flesh" (Gen. 2:24).

The Bible presents marriage as an institution of God at the dawn of history. Sex and marriage existed before the human race was polluted with sin. As something that comes from God, marriage is good.

As recently as the twentieth century, the story was told that in early times a hairy cave dweller went out to rape a maiden whom he might later swap for a bear's skin—a story still popularized in cartoons and books. But more than a thousand years before Christ, people were telling a different story. They knew that in the beginning there was one man and one woman who were married in paradise.

God's creation of sex and marriage is one of his loveliest gifts to the human race, one of the few remaining flowers of paradise. Rightly used and regarded, marriage can be a source of much happiness. Abused and regarded lightly, it is a well of misery.

The sexual drive and sexual attraction between men and women are gifts created by God. God created these feelings and desires for a purpose. That purpose is marriage. God himself is the guardian of that unity. God intended marriage to be a lifelong union between one man and one woman. Around marriage God has placed his golden ring, and God warns us to keep it sacred.

If people insist on destroying what God has made, they ultimately destroy themselves, for people are bound to suffer when they refuse to do God's will.

REFLECTIONS

Married or single, how would you state this commandment positively as a guide for your behavior?

God and Goods

JAMES 5:1-11

"You shall not steal." —*Exodus 20:15*

We meet our neighbors as people—and we must respect them as such. "You shall not murder your neighbors. Love them."

We meet our neighbors as male or female—and we must respect them as sexual human beings. "You shall not commit adultery. Live clean lives inside or outside of marriage."

And we meet our neighbors in the field of commerce, in the traffic of goods and services. "You shall not steal. You must be a steward of what I have entrusted to you."

God forbids stealing in all possible forms, from pinching the wages of workers to sky-high salaries of executives, from goofing off on the job to ripping off investors, from cheating on exams to cheating on taxes, from looting a bank to looting the earth. God calls theft a crime.

In our society we change our standards with the circumstances. Certain things may be considered crimes or misdemeanors, but if enough people do them, we "decriminalize" that particular offense. Then we "just live with it."

God's law isn't that elastic. And if we consider it our main task to do God's will in the world, we had better watch carefully that we are not "updating" our standards. Does it still make you angry that our society, from high to low, is shot through with thievery, fraud, greed, bribery, usury, and waste? Do you still hate crooks? Do you still believe it is better to be honest and poor than smart and rich?

We had better make absolutely sure what side we're on. Someone said that the frontiers of the church used to be on the mission fields in Africa and Asia. But now the frontiers are right here in the business world. Here we decide whom we serve—God or mammon. And here honest, God-fearing men and women stick out like martyrs, people branded with a cross.

God does not just insist that we refrain from all forms of theft. The Lord wants us to regard our possessions as a trust that we hold only for a little while. The only lasting advantage of having possessions in the present world is that we have a chance to be stewards who are able to do good works with what God entrusts to us for a little while.

REFLECTIONS

Where is your honesty most put to the test?

Taming the Tongue

"You shall not give false testimony against your neighbor."
—*Exodus 20:16*

We can harm our neighbor as a person. Therefore God said: "You shall not murder." We can harm our neighbor as a sexual being. Therefore God said: "You shall not commit adultery." We can harm him or her in the traffic of goods and services. Therefore God said: "You shall not steal." But we can also harm our neighbor by the way we talk. Therefore God said: "You shall not give false testimony."

The direct reference of the commandment is to the courtroom. The witness is asked: "Did you see him steal the diamonds—yes or no?" The witness must speak the truth and nothing but the truth, for the defendant can be killed by the tongue of the witness.

In general this commandment forbids all forms of lying and evil-speaking; it commands us to love the truth and speak the truth in love.

The reliability of the spoken word is the cement of society. But when "yes" probably means "no," and "I don't know" means "I am not going to tell you," the trust is lost and society can no longer exist.

Our worldly society is always at the edge of a total breakdown. And it would not be surprising if the breakdown finally came. Truthfulness is becoming so rare that when you tell the truth, hardly anyone believes you!

The Bible calls the devil the father of the lie. And he certainly has many children today.

James says that the most difficult part of our conversion is taming the tongue. Evil talk has done more harm than knives and guns. Learning to speak with love, with deep respect for the truth, and with a close check on our words before they pass our lips, is most difficult. It requires the gift of self-control and an overhaul of one of the deepest springs in our being.

Our tongues get under the control of love and truth only when the Holy Spirit descends on us. That new power, which showed itself on the first Pentecost as tongues of fire on all who received God, is the Spirit of love and truth.

REFLECTIONS

Try to think of specific situations in which God may be calling you to shine as a person of integrity whom others can trust to tell the truth in a loving way. Then ask God to help you be that kind of truth-teller.

Give Me Your Heart

ROMANS 7:7-20

"You shall not covet your neighbor's house. You shall not covet your neighbor's wife . . . or anything that belongs to your neighbor."
—*Exodus 20:17*

The last of the Ten Commandments shifts the attention from external acts (murder, adultery, theft, false testimony) to inner motives: "You shall not covet." At least, that's how the New Testament interprets this commandment.

Now God forbids and condemns the root of all the former sins—the evil desires in the human heart. The troubles of sinners lie not so much in their outward behavior as in their hearts. Those restless, covetous hearts are the cause of all the unrest and the source of all the wicked behavior.

Christianity is not the only religion that points the finger at this sore spot. Buddhism also teaches that desire is the cause of all sorrow. The solution it offers is the death of desire itself. Psychology, which is a relatively new science, has paid a great deal of attention to this basic human condition. Some psychologists have described people as pots full of evil desires, cravings, wishes, drives, motives, longings. They point out that this whirlpool of desires lies far below the surface of our thoughts and is more profound than our conscious life.

The Bible agrees. But the God who condemns this sinful condition also offers a solution all his own. We are covetous as long as we look left and right, forward and backward. As long as we exist on this horizontal level, we want to possess what can never satisfy us. We will always long for the greener grass and the better deal, always desire to drink deeper—without ever being able to quench our thirst. Our hearts are restless until they find rest in God.

Christianity does not teach that desires must die so that we float into nothing. God himself is the fulfillment of our lives. Our craving hearts must turn to God, who alone can satisfy our deepest thirst. When God fills us with the riches of his love, our deepest need is satisfied. We learn the contentment of the new life and the sanctification of our desires.

REFLECTIONS

When others look at you, do they see a person who is content? What would you say is the secret of being content? (Check Philippians 4:11-13 for Paul's answer to that question.)

On Earth and in Heaven

REVELATION 22:6-13

> *I fell down to worship at the feet of the angel. . . . But he said to me, "Don't do that! I am a fellow servant with you and with your fellow prophets and with all who keep the words of this scroll. Worship God!"* —Revelation 22:8-9

Angels are more excellent than we are because they obey God perfectly. Jesus taught us to pray that we might do the will of God on earth as perfectly as the angels are doing it in heaven.

Angels are also less than we are. That's because we know God better than they will ever know him. They know the splendor of his throne. We know the meaning of his cross.

A child who has been ill for many years sees a kind of tenderness in his parents that may remain hidden from the healthy children in the family. Likewise, we have experienced the Father's heart in a way no angel can fathom.

The angels share in the Father's concern for his lost children. Although they cannot understand the price God paid or his pain in leading us to obedience, they are vitally interested in our doings. When we were created, they sang together. And when a sinner comes home, the angels sing with joy.

Since the Prince of heaven has been with us, our daily prayer is for God's will to be done on earth as it is in heaven. We don't know if the angels share in our prayers. We do know that they have an assignment in God's scheme of things. At God's command they serve to bring us to full and final salvation (Heb. 1:14). If we do God's will on earth, people are bound to oppose us, but the angels will serve us. That's how it was in the case of the Son, and that's how God deals with us.

Angels share in our obedience and our worship. Once the apostle John lost his sense of proportion and kneeled before an angel. Right away the angel said, "If you're going to kneel, I'll kneel next to you." The greatest thing on earth and in heaven is the service of worship. In worship, all who "keep the words of this scroll" kneel—as the equals of angels— before the throne of God.

REFLECTIONS

Praise God that one day you will be kneeling before him—with the angels!

Christ's Full Victory

The great Word from the throne of God is that Jesus saves. The Lamb who was slaughtered directs the whole history of our planet to its eternal goal.

daylight

Beatitude

REVELATION 1:1-17

Blessed is the one who reads aloud the words of this prophecy, and blessed are those who hear it and take to heart what is written in it, because the time is near. —Revelation 1:3

God is the only one who has the power to curse and to bless. All creatures fear his curse, and on his blessing all depend. A blessing of God, such as this one from Revelation, can also be called a beatitude.

This particular beatitude is addressed to the followers of Christ, as they are gathered in the assembly, a kind of church service. One person is standing and reading "The Revelation to John" (which we know as the last book of the Bible) aloud from a scroll. The others are seated and listening. It is the twilight of the day—and the twilight of history.

The church was, and is, assembled around a book—God's revelation. Blessed are these people, says God. Blessed is the one who reads, because he or she *may* read. And blessed are the hearers, because they *may* hear. "Blessed are those who hear it and take to heart what is written in it." The words of the Lord remain in the people of God; their doing is directed by their hearing.

Some people have said—and still say—that we would do well to read the whole Bible but leave the last book closed. That's because many people have been confused by the mysterious images and strange messages that are included in the book of Revelation.

But "the time is near." So not only are we urged to read the words of the prophecy but we are promised God's blessing if we do. Blessed is the reader, and blessed are those who hear and take these words to heart. They are blessed because this is the twilight of history, and in this book is the revelation of what must happen soon.

Blessed is the reader of this page who hears and keeps the words of the book of Revelation. God's beatitude is for you.

REFLECTIONS

Since we'll be studying passages from Revelation this month, take a moment to give thanks for this book and to ask for God's blessing as you read it.

It Must Happen Soon

REVELATION 22:6-16

> *"The Lord, the God who inspires the prophets, sent his angel to show his servants the things that must soon take place. Look, I am coming soon! Blessed are those who keep the words of the prophecy in this scroll."*
> —*Revelation 22:6-7*

The book begins and ends in the same way. Once we have read the beginning and the end, we are sure about the purpose of the writing. We know who is sending the message and to whom it is addressed. The Lord God is sending the message—the same God who spoke through the mouths of the prophets in the Old Testament. He writes to the people who were pictured in the first paragraph of the book—the new covenant people in their assembly. Here these people are called God's servants. And the purpose of the writing is to let the church know what must soon take place.

The beatitude is also repeated: "Blessed are those who keep the words of the prophecy in this scroll." The blessing is pronounced on the book-believing, Word-keeping followers of Jesus Christ. They are the ones who are permitted to know "the things that must soon take place."

These things *must* soon take place. This word should not make us think of some inevitable law of history. Worldly prophets seem to refer to such a law when they say "It's bound to happen" or "What's gotta happen is sure to happen." Please don't think for a moment that there is some sort of historical process according to which things *must* end with a bang or with a whimper.

It *must* happen for the same reason Jesus came in the first place. The same divine will that made it necessary for Jesus to say, "I *must* go to Jerusalem" and "I *must* suffer and die and rise again" makes it necessary for these things to happen soon.

It *must* happen because Christ did not die in vain. It *has* to take place because God is not mocked. It *must* take place because the prayers of God's servants cannot go unanswered. It *must* happen because God is God. Therefore let the earth tremble for what is about to happen.

But blessed are those who hear and keep God's Word.

REFLECTIONS

What is it, do you think, that God says *must* happen soon?

Here Is Your King

REVELATION 1:8-16

> . . . *someone like a son of man. . . . The hair on his head was white . . . his eyes were like blazing fire. His feet were like bronze glowing in a furnace, and his voice was like the sound of rushing waters. . . . coming out of his mouth was a sharp, double-edged sword. His face was like the sun shining in all its brilliance.*
> —*Revelation 1:13-16*

Before we are introduced to what must happen, we may see the One who makes it happen—Jesus. He is with God, and he has the glory of God.

But he is our Jesus. He was born in our world; here he suffered and here he died. Once, when he was standing before one of the governors of our world—his head bowed, his face smeared with blood, and his strength failing—the governor said: "Here is the man!" (John 19:5). This governor thought that all the people would realize what a human and harmless spectacle this Jesus was. But on that day—Good Friday—hatred left no room for pity, and Jesus was crucified.

And now, here is the King! His face is an explosion of light, so that neither friend nor foe would dare set eyes on him. From his mouth comes the ultimate Word, a sword that cuts the world in two. And then his feet—don't forget his feet, because subjects kneel at the feet of a king. The kneeling bench for all the nations is at the feet of Jesus Christ. They are like bronze glowing in a furnace. Here he stands, in freedom and power—our brother and our God.

In their assembly, the servants of God, who are the followers of Jesus, are listening to the reader as he reads aloud the words of this book. When they hear these words, and when their hearts catch the vision of their exalted King, joy makes the voice of the reader tremble, and a thrill of exultation runs through the church. "Blessed is the reader; blessed are those who hear."

And when the assembly is dismissed, all of God's servants carry the message into the life of the world: Here is the King! World, gather around the book! Come and listen with us! Jesus is in heaven, and he is the King!

REFLECTIONS

Let this awesome picture of Christ wash over you. Then bow in silence before your King.

He Lives

REVELATION 1:17-20

> *"Do not be afraid. I am the First and the Last. I am the Living*
> *One; I was dead, and now look, I am alive for ever and ever! And*
> *I hold the keys of death and Hades."* —*Revelation 1:17-18*

God has given us the ability to remember the past. Our brains can store information in amazing quantities, and we can produce it at the flash of an impulse.

But the God who gave us the ability to retain the past has not allowed us to know the future. This decision of God is to the praise of his wisdom and for our own benefit.

Foolishly, we cannot stop trying to rend the curtain that God himself has spread before our eyes. To this very day, we try to read the path of the future in the entrails of chickens, the constellations of stars, the lines in the palm of a hand, or the shape of leaves in a teacup. There must be a mixture of anger and pity in the smile of God when, tonight, he sees fifty million people read their horoscopes.

God wants us to live by faith. And the book of Revelation is not going to change that rule. God did not give it to us so that we could have a schedule of future events, as some seem to think. God himself comes to us through this book.

After we have seen our Lord through the eyes of John, we may hear the Word of comfort that the Lord had John write down for us.

"Do not be afraid," Christ says. "You are going to an unknown future. You don't know a step ahead. As far as you know, your last step will lead you to death. But don't be afraid. I know you, and you may know me. I have conquered death. Trust me. When you have to take that last step, place all your trust in me. Death is not the end for you. I am."

When the church receives this Word in its assembly, it calls on the One who is the first and the last: We know where we come from; we know where we are going. We know where all things come from, and we know where all things are going. "For from him and through him and to him are all things. To him be the glory forever! Amen" (Rom. 11:36).

REFLECTIONS

How does knowing that Jesus has conquered death comfort you, in life and in death?

The Throne

REVELATION 4:1-5

I looked, and there before me was a door standing open in heaven. . . . and there before me was a throne in heaven with someone sitting on it.
—*Revelation 4:1-2*

One of the remarkable things about the book of Revelation is the way it speaks about God. Hardly ever is he called "God." Nearly always God is described as "he who sits on the throne."

This phrase is a message in itself. It is not a new message, of course. In the old songbook of the church, the book of Psalms, God is constantly described as the One who rules and is enthroned. Two psalms begin nearly the same way, yet with an important difference. Psalm 97 begins, "The LORD reigns; let the earth be glad." And the opening line of Psalm 99 is, "The LORD reigns; let the nations tremble." The reasons for joy and for trembling are spelled out in the book of Revelation. But it begins with the open door and the throne itself.

God is sitting on this throne in heaven, a throne above the universe. Above the threat of wars, plagues and famine, the fear of people, and the crying of children, we see a throne. Wars do not rage unchecked and crying does not go unheard because there is One who sits upon the throne.

Today, thanks to the Internet and television, we are in a better position than ever before to get a global picture of the world situation. Often, though, the news is mostly depressing or silly or infuriating. And television newscasts are interrupted constantly by messages about dog food and soap. After a half hour of this mixture, some of us turn away, mumbling that the world is crazy.

Indeed, much of human activity that makes the news makes little sense. That's why so many thinking people become cynical—and so many others don't think.

But now a door is opened. Look! A throne, and One who is seated on the throne! The quiet background of our restless history is the everlasting throne of God.

REFLECTIONS

How might this vision of God enrich your everyday life?

It Sings

REVELATION 4:6-11

And the four living creatures . . . day and night . . . never cease to
sing. —Revelation 4:8, RSV

John could not look God in the eye. He caught an impression of dazzling light that encircled the throne—a rainbow of colors.

Of course—the rainbow! Remember Noah? In one picture, the throne of God tells the whole story of the Ruler of the world. This Ruler executes judgment on sin as in the flood. Yet his wrath is held back by his own promise of mercy—the rainbow.

Around the throne are twenty-four thrones—two times twelve thrones. Twelve for the people of the old covenant, and twelve for the people of the new covenant. The church of all ages rules with her Lord in heaven.

The four living creatures represent creation, that is to say, the creation as God made it, unspoiled and unpolluted.

And creation sings.

We don't always hear that. To us, nature may seem mostly mute and indifferent. Human suffering does not seem to touch creation. Birds sing where people cry. Flowers grow where soldiers are buried. And nature can be cruel. Hailstorms can destroy crops; tidal waves smash lives and lands to bits.

But there is more to creation. It sings! It is the song of all creation to the Creator of us all.

Listen! It is not silent. It sings. Why don't you join in?

Open our eyes, God, and open the door so that we may see the throne and recognize you, the Creator and Redeemer of the world. Unplug our ears and open our hearts. Patiently teach us to join in the song of all creation to the God of all the creatures.

Wherever the throne is seen, the song is heard.

REFLECTIONS

Sing your own song of praise to the Creator, or use the words of the prayer near the end of this reading as your own prayer.

A Closed Book

REVELATION 5:1-5

I wept and wept because no one was found who was worthy to open the scroll or look inside. —Revelation 5:4

Nobody has yet found a theory that can explain the rise and fall of nations and the whole chain of happenings that we call history. Very loosely we talk about "progress" and "primitive societies" and the "future society," but we really don't know what we mean. The plan and purpose of events escape us. No one can read the script of history. The scroll is sealed.

We are like sailors on a fleet that has left the harbor with sealed orders for the expedition. Day in and day out we sail the rolling seas. But no one has been found worthy to open the scroll and execute the orders. Days turn to weeks, weeks to months. We keep guessing at the purpose of our mission. Yet we see nothing but the restless, endless sea.

"I wept and wept because no one was found who was worthy to open the scroll." There are moments when we admit our ignorance. Nobody seems to know where we are going.

Notice now that it is not an angel but an elder who says to John that he should stop crying. The elder represents the church. The servants of God do not only share the tears of all humanity, they also know the mystery of history—because they know Christ.

Of course we must not pretend to know more than we actually do. Some people and groups claim to interpret past history and the latest events in the light of the Bible. They even outline the course of future events and claim God's authority for their papers and books. They are an embarrassment to us and the church. They make the gospel itself seem unreliable to those who do not know the Lord.

Believers do not know all the answers. But they have a right to say to all people, "Stop crying. Jesus Christ will execute the plan of God."

REFLECTIONS

How does knowing and believing that "Jesus Christ will execute the plan of God" help you in your everyday living?

Worthy Is the Lamb

REVELATION 5:6-10

Then I saw a Lamb, looking as if it had been slain. . . .

—*Revelation 5:6*

John turns to look at the one who is worthy to open the book. The elder had said that this worthy one was the lion of the tribe of Judah. But when John looks, he sees not a lion but a Lamb.

And here is the whole surprise of the gospel: when all of Israel was looking for the lion who would break the yoke of its enemies, God sent a Lamb to take away the sins of the world. When people were eager to see the slaughter of the oppressors, the lion became a Lamb, and he himself was slaughtered.

The mystery of the gospel is also the offense of the gospel. For this reason Israel rejected its King, and it is the reason why even noble people of goodwill have refused the Redeemer. By his very looks, the slaughtered Lamb shows us that the wrath of God is so great that no one can hide. Sin is so bad that even the noblest must be saved by his blood.

When John sees the One who is worthy to open the scroll, he sees the revelation of God's compassion: he sees Jesus. The plan of God for the history of the world is executed by the Lion who appeared as the Lamb.

The Lamb is "standing" before the throne. That posture means that he possesses infinite power. But it is love-power. The Lion is a Lamb. And the whole world is at his mercy.

All the battles of God have been won—and shall be won—by the power and meekness of Jesus.

The great Word from the throne is that Jesus saves. Not only does he save the lost souls of wandering people, the Lamb directs the whole history of our planet to its eternal goal. He alone is worthy to take the scroll and open its seals.

So let all who have been ransomed by his blood now say, "Worthy is the Lamb!"

REFLECTIONS

What do people expect of Christ today? Would the "Lamb of God" imagery turn people off?

Worship

REVELATION 5:11-14

> *Then I heard every creature in heaven and on earth and under the earth and on the sea, and all that is in them, saying: "To him who sits on the throne and to the Lamb be praise and honor and glory and power, for ever and ever!"* —*Revelation 5:13*

The word *worship* comes from *worth-ship*. It's related to *worthy,* as in "worthy is the Lamb." To worship God means to give God what he is *worthy* to receive.

Worship will eventually unite the whole creation. The hearts of all people and the direction of all that lives will form a perfect harmony—not around a conference table but around the throne. The *end* of life is worship. The *goal* of living is praise.

When we offer proper worship, we are completely free.

For a picture of freedom by worship, put yourself in a stadium at a football game. But this time don't watch the game. Just watch the crowd—all those people different from each other in color, opinion, and character. On an ordinary day, in an ordinary room, you could not get six of them to say the same thing on any topic. But here they are unreservedly united in cheering on their team. For the moment, at least, they are entirely free from every private worry. Nobody's even thinking about the mortgage payments. The hope and happiness of every person there is wrapped up in their team's victory. Those fans in the stadium are a perfect parable of freedom by worship.

The goal of the cosmos is the praise of God. The universe will be free when all our streams of thought and all our aspirations converge on the throne of God.

Today we may already experience something of the freedom and unity of worship. In those rare moments when our prayers turn to praise, we are free. Health, house, money, misery, even sin and guilt are forgotten when we climb the stairway of praise.

In those moments when we have nothing to ask and everything to give, we make the great discovery that we were made for God. We realize that God and the Lamb are worthy of the worship of all that exists. And we find unity! Effortlessly we find each other in the praises of our God.

REFLECTIONS

If you are reading this with others present, read Revelation 5:12 as your song of praise to God. If you are alone, read it as you imagine saying it with the multitude described in verse 11.

Four Horses

REVELATION 6:1-8

They were given power over a fourth of the earth to kill by sword, famine and plague, and by the wild beasts of the earth.
—Revelation 6:8

The Lamb breaks the seals of God's book. This means Jesus carries out God's plan for the world.

When the first four seals are broken, horses are released. Those horses trample the world with fanatic fury. Some think that the first rider is a picture of Christ or of the gospel, because he is white and looks like the rider in Revelation 19:11. But you might also think of the four horsemen or chariots that Zechariah saw (Zech. 6). There, in the vision of Zechariah, they are God's patrols with power to execute his judgment. If the four horses in Revelation are related to the images in Zechariah, the white one is not a picture of the gospel but is merely a horse of a different color.

War, famine, and deadly plague go through this world like so many wild riders. Men and women tremble when they hear the stamping of their hoofs. All of us, even the most sheltered, have heard rumors of their noise, and millions of people have had firsthand encounters with the fury of these horses.

We have not been able to stop wars or to prevent them. Famines have oppressed parts of the world since the beginning, and experts predict that global warming means more and worse are coming. The open mouth of death has been receiving the victims of the four wild riders in dreadful quantities.

But here in Revelation we receive a new perspective: Christ is behind this chaos. That's not supposed to be an explanation. Far less is it a justification for permitting wars to go unchecked and famines to continue. Instead the vision is intended to strengthen the faith of God's servants. In the dark hour of fury, they should know not only that the Lamb is still there but that he is in command. It is the Lamb who breaks the seals of the book.

Our faith is stretched to believe in Jesus' might over the all-devouring powers of these torrents of evil.

REFLECTIONS

What dark events are occurring in the world as you read this? Does it stretch your faith to believe in Jesus' might over these events?

How Long?

REVELATION 6:9-11

> *They called out in a loud voice, "How long, Sovereign Lord, holy and true, until you judge the inhabitants of the earth and avenge our blood?"* —Revelation 6:10

The vision is focused on the foot of the altar. The dried-up blood on the stem of the altar represents the souls of those who were sacrificed for the cause of Christ.

These martyrs were slain "because of the word of God and the testimony they had maintained." Some of their names are in our church history books. God knows all their names—and all the blood, including the blood of the unnamed martyrs of our own time, people who thought it better to serve than to be popular. Other servants of God were killed in the jungle of American business. They would rather go broke than be disobedient.

The real suffering of the martyrs is not the pain in the body or in the pocketbook. Their deepest pain is expressed in their cry "How long, holy, faithful Master, how much longer will you wait? How long, Sovereign Lord, holy and true; how long?"

Every word is an appeal to God's own character and promises. Since God is the Sovereign Lord and since he can break human blades of grass by his breath, why does he allow this to go on and on? Since God is holy and true, intolerant of sin and unwavering in faithfulness, why do we live and die as if we have no defender?

When you have staked not only your style of living but life itself on the faith that Jesus is Lord, the most painful wound is the absence of the Lord. People deny this Lord everywhere. They kill the faithful and rob the righteous, and the Lord lets them get away with it. Sin and the devil are still ruling people. This goes on and on, so many years after Jesus has received the crown.

How long, Lord? How long will you hide your majesty, and how long will you allow your servants to bleed to death? Hear the cry of the martyrs. Open the gates of heaven. Come to our rescue. Let your weary children be refreshed by the glory of their Lord.

We must continue to wait, and we must remain faithful.

REFLECTIONS

What will you say to the Lord while you are waiting for him?

The Wrath of the Lamb

REVELATION 6:12-17

They called to the mountains and the rocks, "Fall on us and hide us from the face of him who sits on the throne and from the wrath of the Lamb!" —Revelation 6:16

This is a very disturbing picture of the day of wrath.

If you are reading this page before the day of wrath has come, you are still living in a world in which it is unclear that Jesus is Lord. Some people honor Christ and suffer for it; others deny him and prosper. As yet there is no real evidence that Jesus is Lord.

As long as the day of wrath has not yet come, the day of grace is still being extended. If the sun is still shining as you read this, if people are still laughing and church bells are still tolling, you are living in the day of grace. God's hands are still stretched out to all people, and God's voice still calls, tenderly but insistently, "Come home."

But even the patience of the Lamb has an end. The holy anger of the One who sits on the throne is reaching the point where it can no longer be contained. The earth will quake, and all temporary footholds will be gone. The blue sky will be ripped open, the stars will fall in a storm like fruit blown from a tree in an autumn gale. And the romantic moonlight will turn into a splash of blood.

Then people will run like frightened animals. Like ants they will hide in the crevices. This will be the day of wrath.

It sounds like a contradiction in terms—the *wrath* of the *Lamb*. Maybe that's why it's so hard to believe. Perhaps we are willing to believe that the Lion of Judah was revealed as a Lamb for the slaughter. But we must still be convinced that the Lamb is also the Lion. Even church members tend to lose sight of God's holiness—the perfect purity of his love and the depth of his wrath.

Right now God's grace allows us to know about it. If nothing else can bring us home, then let's be frightened into repentance and faith.

Pity the person who cannot even become afraid anymore.

REFLECTIONS

What place does the wrath of God have in your faith?

Sealed and Saved

REVELATION 7:1-8

"Do not harm the land or the sea or the trees until we put a seal on the foreheads of the servants of our God."   —Revelation 7:3

The command sounds: "Wait!"

Before the devastating winds are permitted to damage the world, the servants of God must be sealed.

A seal is a mark of ownership. Archeologists have dug up many ancient jars and vessels that still bear the seal of the owner, an impression in clay that shows to whom the pottery belonged. What we read about here is not the sealing of *things* but the sealing of *people*. God seals people by writing his name on them.

In our passage, twelve times twelve thousand people are sealed. Before the great disasters come, God says: "This one is mine; that one may not be harmed because he belongs to me; and she must go safely through the fire of the world because I love her." God's name is written on them. They are sealed in the name of the Father and of the Son and of the Holy Spirit. They have been set apart. They are in God's hand, and nothing— not even God's own judgment—can do them any harm.

These words of comfort are addressed to the same people for whom the whole book of Revelation is written. They are the church members who were hearing this scroll read in their assembly—the ones whom God calls blessed because they hear and keep his Word (Rev. 1:3). The angel who seals God's elect calls them "the servants of our God," which is the name for those who hear and keep the prophecy of this book (22:6-7). They are the ones who are being sealed here as the true Israel (3:9, 12), the faithful followers of the Lamb.

Twelve times twelve times one thousand stands for the complete number of all of God's people. The total number and every name is known to God. God knows his own. And God will not allow them to perish in the hour of trial.

We have no certainty of salvation in ourselves. We are not sure that we can stand up in the storm. But God has chosen us; God has called us. God has adopted us to be his children, and his everlasting arms will carry us through. Hallelujah!

REFLECTIONS

When have you had a strong sense of the "everlasting arms of God" carrying you through?

A Great Multitude

REVELATION 7:9-12

> *After this I looked, and there before me was a great multitude that no one could count, from every nation, tribe, people and language, standing before the throne and in front of the Lamb. They were wearing white robes and were holding palm branches in their hands.* —Revelation 7:9

In this vision, all of God's children are drawn to the throne of God and to the Lamb.

Something about that innumerable multitude makes us shiver with joy. Jesus had said, "When I am lifted up from the earth, I will draw all people to myself" (John 12:32). And here they are. Our Lord is faithful.

God's people have come from races that fought each other, from tribes that killed each other, from countries that oppressed each other, from tongues that misunderstood each other. But here they are, a crowd no one can count, a harmony we cannot imagine.

They have come *from* all these nations, tribes, peoples, and tongues. Their unity transcends everything that seemed to separate them in the world. Their loyalty was not to the nation, the tribe, the people, and the tongue. *Jesus* was their Lord, and to him they pledged fidelity. Theirs was the one holy, catholic, apostolic faith.

Our eyes see the vision and our hearts take courage, for the unity we seek is still so hard to express. Again and again we seem to be thrown back into the old units of the nation, the tribe, and the tongue. Our sins can still make us weep, but their robes are white. The victorious life still escapes us as we sink and sulk, but they are carrying palm branches to greet their King, who gives the victory.

The 144,000 and the great multitude are *not* two different groups. Both are what the angel lovingly calls "the servants of our God." In the first vision we may see, hear, and believe that God elects and protects and knows who are his own. In the second vision we may rejoice to know that the results of God's unconquerable grace will be a multitude no one can number. In spite of all obstacles and in spite of all divisions, no one will be able to count the multitude that will sing of God's unfailing grace.

REFLECTIONS

What lessons for your walk with God can you learn from this picture of the great multitude before the throne? Join with the multitude praising God, using the words of verse 12.

Intensified Living

REVELATION 7:13-17

> *"They are before the throne of God and serve him day and night in his temple; and he who sits on the throne will spread his tent over them."*
> —*Revelation 7:15*

The voice of the elder describes the life of the redeemed. He depicts them as people who have been journeying through the desert. Finally they have arrived in the promised land. What they lacked is now supplied. What they suffered is now forgotten. The feast has begun. Unending service in the presence of God fills all their days and nights.

Although the multitude of the redeemed comes from all nations, tribes, and tongues, their experience and their blessedness is expressed in terms of the Jewish Bible. All nations have been called to the light, but the light shone in Israel. Only by incorporation into Israel are the nations saved. The church is the *new* Israel, but it is, nevertheless, *Israel*.

Our future life is still *life*. The Eastern religions such as Hinduism and Buddhism that have been imported into North America—a bit restyled for our consumption—speak of *nirvana*. Their highest imaginable state is a blessed nothingness, when the flames are extinguished and life has ebbed into eternal oblivion.

The Christian Bible does not draw a blueprint of the future life. But we are told enough to know that the future is a sort of intensified living. The flame will burn brighter than ever. Instead of an ebbed-out existence, God's people will be riding the crest of the tide.

"They serve him day and night within his temple." The spiritual service that begins in this life is continued there endlessly and without interruption.

To young or immature Christians, this idea may arouse fears of boredom. The truth is that it will actually be a life of perpetual growing and flourishing. Boredom is the curse of the rich and the idle, for there is nothing more boring than living for self-gratification.

But the future is endless communion with an infinite number of people and angels in the ever-refreshing presence of our God.

REFLECTIONS

What aspects of our bright and active future make you want to praise God?

Prayer Power

REVELATION 8:1-5

. . . there was silence in heaven for about half an hour. . . . The smoke of the incense, together with the prayers of God's people, went up before God from the angel's hand. —Revelation 8:1, 4

When the seventh seal is opened, we expect to reach the summit. One by one the seven seals of the scroll are broken. Now comes the last one, the seventh, the number of fullness. But when the seventh seal is opened, nothing happens: "There was silence in heaven for about half an hour."

A great hush falls on the host of heaven. The choirs, which never tire of singing their hallelujahs, become quiet. No peals of thunder issue from the throne. And during this awe-inspiring stillness of heaven, the prayers of God's children rise to the throne of God.

Here we receive the assurance that God listens to our prayers. We need that certainty. Anyone who has ever prayed knows about the "psychological" help that we derive from this activity. If we unburden ourselves before God, we become calm. The first result of prayer is the emotional relief of "having said it all" to the Father. But that's not enough.

What assurance do we have that praying is more than our response to the very human need for a father-confessor? We need to know that there is someone who listens to our prayers.

This the Bible tells us in many places—but here in a very striking way. Our prayers reach the ears of God himself! Heaven becomes all ears because the saints are praying. "There was silence in heaven." Not only are we assured that God listens to the prayers of the saints—that's right, our prayers!—we are told that these prayers play a role in God's coming with judgment and salvation. God is moved to action by the prayers of his people.

When these prayers have gone from earth to heaven, an answer comes from heaven to earth (v. 5): "peals of thunder, rumblings, flashes of lightning and an earthquake"—all signs of the terror of God's coming. And if you think this answer does not fit your prayers, think again. What are you saying when you ask the Father to hallow his name and make his kingdom come? That's the kind of prayer to which heaven listens with breathless attention.

REFLECTIONS

How will this Scripture passage and reading affect your prayer life?

The Woman's Splendor

REVELATION 11:15-12:1

> . . . *a woman clothed with the sun, with the moon under her feet and a crown of twelve stars on her head.* —Revelation 12:1

A new vision is given to John. The vision covers all of history in a short series of pictures, and it explains that history to those who hear and believe the Word.

The woman represents the people of God from the beginning to the end of the world. Great is her glory. The sickle of the moon is her footstool. The sun is her brilliant robe, and stars crown her head.

Sun, moon, and stars used to be worshiped by the people of this earth. In fact, millions are still superstitious about these heavenly bodies. But God says by means of this vision that the sun, the moon, and the stars are but the decorations of his beloved one.

In the past people argued for a long time about whether the sun or the earth was the center of the universe. Does the earth turn around the sun or does the sun turn around the earth? Here God says, "My own people constitute the heart of the universe. Everything turns around them."

When astronauts landed on the moon for the first time, a few Christians thought the matter over and declared that humans were transgressing their limits. They thought that the moon was so much God's domain that humans should not be permitted to touch it. But God says: "My beloved is my holy possession, and my people form my holy domain. Woe to anyone who does violence to her! As for the moon, it's just her footstool."

This is how important the children of God are to their heavenly Father, who is also the Ruler of the universe. God declares that these lamblike children of his are the "salt" without which the earth would perish; they are the "light" without whom darkness would descend. God even declares that his people are the clue to the understanding of history.

The further explanation of the importance of the woman must be found in her Son, who is also her Lord.

REFLECTIONS

How do you know that you are important to God?

Delivery

REVELATION 12:1-2

She was pregnant and cried out in pain as she was about to give birth.   *—Revelation12:2*

One picture is worth a thousand words.

This picture also sums up two thousand years of history. God's people Israel gave birth to the Messiah. All the history before the birth of Christ can be summed up in one phrase: the people cried for the birth of the Son.

When we think of the origin of Jesus, we must first recognize that he came from the womb of Israel. Theirs—that is, the people of Israel's—was the adoption (sonship); theirs the divine glory, the covenants, the receiving of the law, the temple worship, and the promises. Theirs were the patriarchs, and from them we can trace the human ancestry of the Messiah (Rom. 9:4-5). We know that Jesus was not only man and Israelite "as to his earthly life"; we must also say who he is "through the Spirit of holiness" (Rom. 1:3-4). As such he is "the Messiah, who is God over all, forever praised!" (Rom. 9:5).

The fact remains that Israel brought forth the Messiah, who is the Son and the hope of the daughter of Zion. Therefore the whole of the Old Testament can be summed up in one symbol—the pregnancy of the people of God.

The vision does more than simply summarize history, it also interprets history. God explains to us why he formed and kept this nation of Israel: because this people had to give birth to Christ.

God had this purpose in mind when he called Abraham to be the blessing of all the families of the earth. For this reason God fenced the Israelites in with laws he gave through Moses. And God maintained his promises to David in spite of wicked kings and disobedient people because his steadfast mercy was aimed at the birth of the great Son of David.

You can't ever say a meaningful word about Israel if you forget that Jesus Christ explains the existence of Israel. And the whole history of the Old Testament is properly told in one picture—birth pangs, anguish to be delivered.

REFLECTIONS

When we read the Old Testament and the history of Israel, what should we be thinking of? Why?

Anti-Power

REVELATION 12:1-6

The dragon stood in front of the woman who was about to give birth, so that it might devour her child the moment he was born.
—Revelation 12:4

John sees the fiery red glow of the dragon, poised for the attack. He is the anti-Messiah. He is the other candidate for the throne of the world. Seven heads and ten horns tell of his gigantic intellectual and physical power.

The tail of the red dragon swept away a third of the stars. What do you think those stars represent? Angels? Princes? Or is this just an indication of the dragon's cosmic significance?

The dragon threatens the woman. He wants to make her Son his victim, because her Son is the opposing candidate for the throne of the world. Her Son is God's candidate.

This picture explains the history with which all the original readers were so familiar, and which all of us, the present readers, ought to know as well. Israel was loved and protected by God because of her Son. Israel was also attacked and threatened by the dragon because of her Son.

The attacks of the dragon were external: the Pharaoh in Egypt tried to kill the Savior of Israel by drowning the baby boys in the Nile. The Amalekites, the Philistines, and many other tribes also attempted to destroy God's people, but none succeeded.

Yet the Israelites were nearly destroyed by their own sins. We might call these sins the devil's internal attacks on Israel's existence. And here the dragon nearly succeeded. At times in the history of Israel God himself admitted that his people were no better than the nations he had destroyed because of their sins. Sometimes God's own people were no better than the people of Sodom and Gomorrah.

But God loved his sinful people. And the Lord remained faithful to his pledge that the daughter of Zion would give birth to the Son. For that reason, and for his own name's sake, he spared the woman from the fury of the dragon.

REFLECTIONS

What do the devil's "internal attacks" on you look like today? What comfort can you find from God's reactions to Israel's sins?

B.C. – A.D.

PSALM 2

> *She gave birth to a son, a male child, who "will rule all the nations with an iron scepter." And her child was snatched up to God and to his throne.*
> —*Revelation 12:5*

This is a remarkable description of the life and work of Jesus: He was born, and he was caught up to God and to his throne. He was born to serve, and he arose to reign. Here is our confession in one sentence.

The reason it can be stated so tersely is that the issue between this Son and the dragon is the throne. The Son's life was spared from the dragon's attack, and it was he, the Son of the woman, who went to the throne of God. The dragon was defeated. That's the short and glorious message.

We divide history into two parts. We indicate the years "before Christ" by writing B.C. behind the number. And we write A.D. in front of the number of the year in which we are now living.

If you ask a class of school kids what the letters "B.C." stand for, they are usually quick to answer correctly. But if you follow by asking what "A.D." stands for, they hesitate. They may guess that the "A" stands for "After," and then they think that the "D" should be a "C." They want to divide history into a time "Before Christ" and a time "After Christ."

But "A.D." actually stands for *Anno Domini,* which means "in the year of the Lord."

We have the sinful tendency to think that we are living "after Christ" instead of "under Christ." Countless people think of Jesus Christ as a past figure of history. But Jesus is not past; he is present. We are not living *after* he lived but *during* the reign of the Lord.

Since we are by nature shortsighted and unbelieving, we can go through our days without realizing that Jesus lives and that he is ruling over the world. Therefore we need to be reminded: "She gave birth to a son. . . . And her child was snatched up to God and to his throne."

The dragon's chances are past; his days are numbered. But we may forever number the days of the reign of our Lord.

REFLECTIONS

If you believe that "Jesus lives and he is ruling over the world," what impact does that have on your daily life?

The Devil on Earth

REVELATION 12:7-12

"For the accuser of our brothers and sisters . . . has been hurled down." —Revelation 12:10

When we say the word *heaven*, we are inclined to think of the place where God's children go when they die. Especially if one of our loved ones has recently left us "to be with the Lord," our thoughts turn to this person whenever we hear or read the word *heaven*. But when the Bible talks about heaven, it means the place from which this earth is ruled. Heaven is headquarters.

Since departed believers are "with the Lord," we must think of them as being in heaven. But whenever the Bible uses the word *heaven*, the accent is on the throne, the government of the world.

That's why the ascension is so significant. When Jesus had completed his work on earth, he went to the Father's throne in heaven. Since that time he has ruled, leaving the devil no ground to stand on. In the language of the book of Revelation, Michael and his angels hurled the devil out of heaven.

What Revelation describes as a war in heaven is the same event the gospel describes as Jesus' ascension to the throne. They are two sides of the same story. In the gospel the event is told from our point of view: Jesus was lifted up from the earth and he went to heaven. In Revelation we get the other side—the defeat of the demons by the faithful angels of God.

The devil is called "the accuser of our brothers and sisters." This does not mean that he slanders them—although he does that too. It means that he is their prosecutor. The devil used to make accusations against us that rang true in the courts of heaven. There was no sin of which we were not guilty, and there was no threat of God we could rightfully escape.

But now the Lamb has been slaughtered for our sins, and we have overcome "by the blood of the Lamb." And so the devil no longer has access to God's throne. Instead of an accuser, we now have an Advocate at the throne of God—Jesus, our Savior! Now the devil is "only" on earth. That sounds ominous, but it's really good news.

REFLECTIONS

Is the story of the ascension from heaven's point of view new to you? Why is it important to know?

The Persecuted Woman

REVELATION 12:13-17

When the dragon saw that he had been hurled to the earth, he pursued the woman who had given birth to the male child.

—*Revelation 12:13*

The Bible gives us no reason to expect quiet times for the church. The persecution of the woman continues after the ascension of the Son. After this event, God's people are still called "the woman" and the members of this body of people are called "the offspring of the woman" or, more fully, "those who keep God's commandments and hold fast to their testimony about Jesus" (v. 17). They are the people to whom the book of Revelation is addressed. They form the church of Jesus Christ, which must always be seen in her unity with Israel. The church in Revelation is not so much the *new* Israel as the *true* Israel.

Now the message is that the people of God, after the ascension of Jesus, will always be persecuted—more or less.

But this message comes to us as a Word of comfort and encouragement. We are told that the reason for our suffering is actually a happy one: the devil has only a short time.

People who are told they have only a year to live may try to pack all their remaining energy into some venture for the short time they have left. That picture fits the devil. He knows he has a limited territory and a short time left (v. 12). He has been thrown out of the driver's seat. Knowing that he has lost his bid for dominion and aware of impending doom, he strikes out in fury with all his remaining strength.

God is the woman's protector. He gives her "the two wings of a great eagle" so she can "fly to a place prepared for her in the wilderness." In the desert she may lack some culture and conveniences ("the fleshpots of Egypt"), but she is close to her God and safe from the dragon. And the good earth is also on the woman's side (v. 16).

The period of persecution is not going to outlast the endurance of the woman—a time, times, and half a time. Three-and-a-half years. God knows how long that is. For us it will be a whole year (how long it seems!), and two years (will it never end?), and then only half a year. And suddenly it will be over.

REFLECTIONS

Acquaint yourself—via the Internet—with places in our world where the Christian church is being actively persecuted. Pray that God will be their protector and that they may endure.

The Rule of the Beast

REVELATION 13:1-10

> *People worshiped the dragon because he had given authority to the beast, and they also worshiped the beast and asked, "Who is like the beast? Who can make war against it?"*
>
> *—Revelation 13:4*

Government under God is good. This we learn in Romans 13. Government that takes the place of God becomes a beast. This we learn in Revelation 13.

The government of a country can, and often does, surrender to the beast. That's probably why nearly all Christians are intuitively opposed to permitting a great deal of power to flow into the hands of only a few. We know the nature of the human race and the character of the beast who takes his orders from the dragon.

On the other hand, we also know that the government must have power to interfere, for the good of the citizens. Otherwise it is money that decides who the oppressor will be and who the oppressed. Mammon also takes orders from the dragon.

That's why we *must* interest ourselves in politics.

The Christians who read and heard this Scripture for the first time recognized the emperor of Rome as the beast who ruled the earth. These Christians knew from their own experience how people worshiped the beast. Maybe they themselves had asked, "Who is like the beast? Who can make war against it?" At that time it was unthinkable that the Roman Empire could fall.

Rome did fall. But the fall of Rome did not mean the end of the beast's rule. In the ninth century, Christians knew the beast. In the sixteenth century, Martin Luther had a name for the beast. And in the opening years of the twenty-first century, there is no shortage of those who persecute the Christian church.

Until the everlasting kingdom is revealed, the beasts rising from the political sea of nations will be permitted their blasphemies. It will last forty-two months or three-and-a-half years—a time, times, and half a time. That is, as long as the fury of the devil and the persecution of the woman continue.

REFLECTIONS

Who or what would you identify as a "beast" that is "rising from the political sea of nations" and attacking the Christian church today?

The False Prophet

REVELATION 13:11-18

Then I saw another beast, coming out of the earth. It had two horns like a lamb, but it spoke like a dragon. —*Revelation 13:11*

The second beast is not from the sea. That is to say, he does not come from the chaos of political powers. This beast rises from the earth, the ordered world that came from God's hands. And this beast is better-looking than the first beast. He even resembles the Lamb—though he speaks like the dragon.

This second beast represents the religious and cultural power that supports the first beast. No political power can stand merely by might. The beast needs might and meanness, but it needs more. It needs an ideology that justifies the worship of the beast. Every tyrant needs a prophet. Every dictator needs a manifesto.

The second beast makes up the enticing slogans everyone believes. The false prophet forms the ideas and composes the hymns of the beastly kingdom. He performs the miracles everyone admires. It is this false religion that makes so many people loyal to the order of the beast.

Did you notice that the kingdom of the beast is an exact caricature of the kingdom of God? It has a messiah, and it has signs and wonders. It aims at a new order that involves all of life. It even has a form of baptism, a sign to show that you belong. It is a mark not of God but of the beast.

The gospel is not an ideology. But the gospel of the kingdom does include a world-and-life view. We need Christian ideas spelled out in theories and programs that apply to politics and economics. We need Christian students who can pick apart the slogans of the false prophets with the scalpels of keen analysis. We need Christian schools and colleges. Christian businessmen have to speak up. Christian journalists must write sanely and soberly in a sea of madness.

If we are merely concerned with saving our souls, we are disloyal to the Lord and we surrender the country to the false prophets of our age.

Only the gospel of God's kingdom can give us the weapons we need to fight the beastly thoughts of the false prophet.

REFLECTIONS

Think of two or three false ideas and philosophies that threaten the church today. How can we fight against these false prophets?

They Don't Bow Before the Beast

REVELATION 14:1-5

These are those who did not defile themselves with women, for they remained virgins. They follow the Lamb wherever he goes. They were purchased from among the human race and offered as first-fruits to God and the Lamb. —Revelation 14:4

You would not think anyone could escape the rule of the beast and the cunning propaganda of the false prophet (Rev. 13). So it's comforting to view the vision of the redeemed on Mount Zion. The number 144,000 is mentioned again (see 7:4) so that we may realize anew that it is God who elects and protects and sanctifies.

At one time the prophet Elijah thought that no one had escaped the tyranny of Ahab and the false religion of Jezebel. "I am the only one left," he complained. But the God who elects and protects and sanctifies said to his prophet: "I reserve seven thousand in Israel—all whose knees have not bowed down to Baal" (1 Kings 19:18).

The church that escapes has been "redeemed from the earth"; that is, they have been bought by the blood of the Lamb. They are "virgins" or chaste; that is, single or married, they are single-mindedly faithful to their Husband, who is their Lord. They never consider God's commandments outdated by the theories of the false prophet.

They follow the Lamb wherever he goes. They have not created a Jesus after their own tastes—that innocent kind of false hero who never hurts anybody—but have obeyed the Christ of the Scriptures who gives his followers a cross to bear.

"No lie was found in their mouths; they are blameless." Of course they were sinners; otherwise they would not need the blood of the Lamb. But they were not hypocrites. They rejected outright the lie of their times, which was proclaimed as truth and honesty by the false prophet. They abided in the truth of Jesus.

It's almost unbelievable that such people can survive to the end. But it proves that neither the dragon nor the beast, neither today nor tomorrow—in fact, nothing at all—can separate us from God's love in Christ Jesus our Lord.

REFLECTIONS
Why do you follow the Lamb?

The Beginning of the End

REVELATION 14:6-12

Then I saw another angel flying in midair, and he had the eternal gospel to proclaim to those who live on the earth—to every nation, tribe, language and people. —Revelation 14:6

The preaching of the gospel is the beginning of the end. Now the flight of messengers (angels) has begun. Every nation, tribe, tongue, and people must hear that the end has begun because the eternal gospel is being proclaimed.

Now the message has come to all who dwell on earth. Through Christ, God, who formerly spoke to the sons of Abraham, Isaac, and Jacob, has now reached out to all people and to the whole world. God wants the whole earth back, and he wants all people in his kingdom. "Fear God and give him glory, for the hour of his judgment has come."

The church is the result of the gospel, and it marks the beginning of the end. Ever since Pentecost, we have been in the last days. No really new thing can be expected anymore. Of course the lines of history remain: we still experience good times, bad times, terrible times. Strictly speaking, however, it was all finished on Golgotha. Ever since the resurrection and the proclamation of the eternal gospel, the new world has begun.

The beginning of the end has come. Fear God and give him glory.

The people of God are in the world to proclaim loudly and clearly that the end is at hand, and that the kingdom has come and is coming. Whether it takes a few centuries more or less is of no importance when measured by the counsel of God. The decisions have been made.

The end is near. We don't say that in somber tones. That's the misinterpretation of cults and the misunderstanding of unbelief. When we say that the end is near, we are not announcing death. We are announcing the end of death.

We proclaim the good news that the end is near because we see the daybreak of a new age. Pain will have an end. Sin will have an end. All the certainties are given in the gospel. Thank God! The end is near!

REFLECTIONS

What does "The end is near" mean to you? How does it affect your daily living?

Dead Before the End

JOHN 11:17-27

Then I heard a voice from heaven say, "Write: Blessed are the dead who die in the Lord from now on."   —*Revelation 14:13*

Bad poetry and bad religion have tried to make death soft and innocent. They suggest that to be "enshrouded by the cloak of night" means we can sleep without the need to wake up for duty.

But human honesty and biblical realism hate death. No matter how many flowers and flowery phrases we use, we cannot hide its horror. Therefore when the voice says: "Write this: Blessed are the dead who die in the Lord from now on," we are receiving a revelation. We are learning something that we would not know without the special Word of New Testament prophecy.

The early Christians did not teach that humans have an immortal soul and a body made for the grave, as many people think today. They viewed themselves as one undivided being, and they regarded death as a judgment on our sinful existence. Yet they believed that in Christ they had escaped from the realm where sin and death rule. To them, dying was like bowing to your defeated enemy instead of sharing in the victory of your Lord.

If we don't share some of that feeling, we don't have an authentically Christian view of life and death. Submission to death is always like allowing a stranger to take what does not belong to him; it is like giving up what has already been claimed.

But now comes the Word we must accept in faith. The revelation says: "Blessed are the dead who die in the Lord."

"Blessed are the dead"?

That sounds ridiculous. But "blessed are the dead who die in the Lord" makes sense. "Dying in the Lord" is "from now on" a blessing. From now on, we bury those who die in the Lord in the good confidence that they will rise again. It only appears that they have been surrendered to the wrong master. They are the Lord's because they died in the Lord. They are not—and cannot—be beyond the power of Jesus.

Death is strong, but Jesus is stronger. Once we belong to Jesus, he does not let us go. Therefore there is sweetness in the death of God's children. But the sweetness is in Jesus—not in death.

REFLECTIONS

How is the view of death in today's Scripture and reading both realistic and comforting?

Harvest Time

REVELATION 14:14-20

I looked, and there before me was a white cloud, and seated on the
cloud was one like a son of man with a crown of gold on his head
and a sharp sickle in his hand. —*Revelation 14:14*

When they asked Jesus, in the night in which he was betrayed, if he was really the Christ, he answered: "You have said so. From now on you will see the Son of Man sitting at the right hand of the Mighty One and coming on the clouds of heaven" (Matt. 26:64).

His Jewish judges knew very well what Jesus was talking about. The Son of Man on the clouds of heaven was the one who received the everlasting kingdom out of the hands of God, according to Daniel 7:14.

But they did not believe that Jesus was the one through whom God would send the sickle into the human grain fields of this world. He did not look like the person of whom Daniel had spoken. He did not even look like the One of whom John the Baptist had said, "His winnowing fork is in his hand, and he will clear his threshing floor, gathering his wheat into the barn and burning up the chaff with unquenchable fire" (Matt. 3:12).

But that was exactly the mystery of the kingdom and the mystery of the King. Jesus said that first the Word of the kingdom had to be sown before the harvest of the world could be reaped. First a farmer went out to sow. First Jesus himself fell like a seed into the ground, in order to bring forth a harvest. By the grace and wisdom of God, Jesus' first coming inaugurated sowing time, but that did not mean that the harvest time wasn't coming. It ensured that there would be a harvest.

If the gospel is still being preached and the good news is still being broadcast while you are reading this, it is still sowing time. The weeds and the wheat are still growing together until it pleases God to harvest the wheat and burn the weeds.

We had better make sure that we are doing the right thing with the Word of the kingdom that is now being sown, for after sowing time comes harvest time.

You can stake your life on this: the One who now wears the golden crown is anxious to harvest what he has sown and to remove the weeds from the world.

REFLECTIONS

How does knowing about the inevitability of the coming judgment and "harvest" affect the way you live?

The End

REVELATION 21:1-4

"He will wipe every tear from their eyes."   —*Revelation 21:4*

If Jesus Christ is our Savior and Lord, we may already experience the beginning of the end. The everlasting gospel has brought us the only comfort available today. Right now nothing but the good news of Jesus Christ can still our sorrow. At this moment no one and no thing can give meaning to life but Christ alone. Yet this is only the beginning of the end.

The end means that we are fully comforted. In the end God will be fully revealed as our Comforter. He is certainly here today, but we cannot fully enjoy him yet. Somewhere we are still hurting. Every day we still sin. Our joy is still transitory and our happiness is not yet full.

But the end is coming. God will "wipe every tear" from our eyes. There are so many tears that only God can count them. There are hospitals full of people in physical pain. There are mental hospitals full of people who live with pain that can be even worse, pain that drives you out of your mind. And then there is spiritual sorrow that is beyond the reach of the most loving hand.

In the end, God will wipe away all tears.

The Christian religion does not picture a future of forgetfulness and nothingness, which pagans invented—and still accept—as the best ending of our tragedy. But the Bible does reveal that we will forget all the pain we suffered. There will be a legitimate forgetting. In one moment our tears will be wiped away. Our entrance into glory will so much outweigh all that we suffered and lacked that all traces of our sorrow will be forgotten in the joy to be revealed.

Once, Jesus pictured God as a father embracing his runaway son in an unforgettable welcome of salvation. But the gospel ends with a picture of God, like a mother, wiping away our tears. The journey was so long. We became so tired. We hurt all over.

And then, finally, we came home.

REFLECTIONS

Reflect on the wonderful homecoming that God will one day give you, and give thanks.

Last Warning

REVELATION 22:18-21

I warn everyone who hears the words of the prophecy of this scroll:
If any one of you adds anything to them . . . if any one of you
takes words away from this scroll of prophecy. . . .
—Revelation 22:18-19

A warning is not the same as a threat. A warning is intended to keep us from evil. A threat is the announcement of evil.

Parents are forever giving warnings to their children. "Be careful when you cross the street." "Don't accept rides from strangers." "Don't forget to drink your milk."

When the children grow up, they joke about it with their folks. But now they can see how those warnings showed how much their parents love them.

When sons or daughters leave the house, all grown up, they often get a kiss from their parents and a last word of warning.

And here on the last page of the Bible, when we are just about to close the book, we also receive a last word of warning. It is simply this: Don't tamper with the book.

We may not *add* anything to it. This Word is sufficient. Whatever we add is too much. So don't believe in teachings God has not revealed. And don't obey rules that God has not commanded.

We may not *subtract* anything from it either. This Word must be kept whole. Resist the tendency to reduce the Word to what is palatable, understandable, or workable.

We have received a Word from the Lord our God. This is *God*'s revelation. God has told us what he has done, what he is doing, and what he is going to do. God also arranged to have this all written down for us. We may have our differences about the interpretation of some of his words— no one understands it all, and we need each other and God's Spirit to understand. But for your life's sake, don't tamper with the book.

That's God's final warning. God loves us so much that he must warn us. Our very lives depend on what we do with the book.

REFLECTIONS

How does this warning apply to you personally? How might you be tempted to "add to" or "subtract from" God's Word?

Jesus Is Coming

Christmas is the first of Christ's two comings. We must now prepare ourselves for the second advent.

daylight

Jesus Is Coming

1 THESSALONIANS 1:1-10

". . . when the Son of Man comes, will he find faith on the earth?"
—Luke 18:8

The big event in December is, of course, Christmas, the date on which people traditionally remember that Jesus was born in Bethlehem, a small town five miles south of Jerusalem.

But there are really two comings of the Lord. The first one is remembered at Christmas. The second one is "near," the Bible assures us. If you are happy that Jesus came the first time, you should be overjoyed to know that he is coming again.

Christians cannot think of Christ's first coming, as a baby, without making ready for his coming as Lord.

You might say that the Bible has only one message: Jesus is coming! In Old Testament times people did not say that they were waiting for Jesus. They did not yet know his name. They were expecting a Savior they called "Son of David," or Messiah. Or they would simply say that they were waiting for the coming of the Lord. They looked forward to the day when God would set things straight in the world. They were always looking ahead, expecting what was to come.

The New Testament brings us Christ and all his benefits. Here we also learn that the complete revelation of God's kingdom involves two comings of Jesus: his coming in grace and his return in glory.

The message has not changed: *Jesus is coming!* And the people of the new covenant live just the way the people of the old covenant lived: always looking forward, always expecting what is coming.

Just as there is one Bible message—the coming of Jesus—there must be one response—readiness, faith!

In the midst of all the preparations for Christmas this month, we may not suppress the big question Jesus asked in Luke 18: When the Son of Man comes, will he find faith on the earth?

Let's live this month with gladness and soberness. We may enjoy what we receive—as long as we look forward to what is coming.

REFLECTIONS

How can we live this Christmas season—and always—in readiness and faith for the return of our Lord?

Misery and Hope

GENESIS 3:8-15

"And I will put enmity between you and the woman, and between your offspring and hers; he will crush your head, and you will strike his heel." —*Genesis 3:15*

When we read Genesis 3, we revisit the place where our misery started and where our hope began.

Our misery started when we broke our covenant with God.

Our hope began when God broke our alliance with the devil. God did not allow us to fall under the everlasting spell of the devil. Immediately God put *enmity* between him and us.

That was God's grace. He loved us. When we fell and sinned, God did not permit us to embrace evil but placed enmity between the children of Eve and the brood of the serpent. The unholy alliance between humans and the devil was broken the day it started. Instead of an alliance, God made it a battle: "I will put enmity between [the serpent] and the woman."

God pronounced a curse on the serpent. In the words of this curse, humanity's future was symbolized by the figure of a man fighting off a snake. In this fight the man is wounded and the snake is crushed. "He will crush your head, and you will strike his heel."

Further history and the rest of the Bible show us that people have not been doing so well in their fight against evil. The serpent's poison has deeply affected the behavior of us all. However, in Jesus, God came to our aid. That's the meaning of Christmas. Jesus delivered the decisive blow to our enemy—a blow from which the old serpent will never recover. And Christ has pulled us back to the service of God.

Now we are still fighting the serpent's offspring. Misery in all its ugly forms is still with us. "Deliver us from the evil one," we cry from our battlefield. But the time gets shorter and the hope gets brighter: "The God of peace will soon crush Satan under your feet" (Rom. 16:20).

God will crush the evil one. But he uses *our* feet.

REFLECTIONS

Do you sometimes feel you are losing the battle with the serpent and his poison? During those times, what "pulls you back to the service of God"?

The Silver Lining

GENESIS 9:8-15

I have set my rainbow in the clouds, and it will be the sign of the covenant between me and the earth. —Genesis 9:13

Human life is under a constant threat. We hate to talk about it. And we dislike people who bring it up. But no sober person can deny that we are living on the edge of a volcano. We are on the verge of a disaster every minute of our lives.

In this century, since September 11, 2001, we live under the cloud of another terrorist attack—perhaps many times more deadly than the one that brought down the twin towers. Rogue nations scramble to get the bomb and threaten to use it. Powerful nations already have enough nuclear weapons to destroy life on our planet. It will take only a few moments of panic or insanity.

Those who know the Bible fear the wrath of God. His earliest judgment was a flood that destroyed a world in revolt against him. God's wrath is really the cloud under which we live. God may use the reckless folly of sinister people to execute his wrath. In the past God has used the merciless Assyrians and the proud Babylonians. Let's pray that the Lord won't do it now.

God's wrath is very real. You and I get used to sin and rebellion against the sovereign God. But God will not tolerate it. The threat of his anger is bigger than people can imagine, and judgment is closer than most people think.

However, the clouds of God's wrath have a silver lining—the rainbow. God preserved the earth to make his own work of salvation possible. To this very day God has been faithful to the vow he made to the earth. For that reason the sun still shines on the evil and the good. God withholds the threat of destruction and tempers justice with mercy.

God wants all people to meet Jesus at Bethlehem before they meet him as the Judge of their lives. By his compassion, the present world continues to exist. Now is the time when people may flee the wrath that is coming.

If we know Jesus today as Savior and serve him as Lord, the last dark cloud of judgment will evaporate. We will live forever under the rainbow colors of his love.

REFLECTIONS

What hope and comfort does living under God's rainbow give you?

Hope of the Gentiles

GENESIS 12:1-3

> *Scripture foresaw that God would justify the Gentiles by faith, and announced the gospel in advance to Abraham: "All nations will be blessed through you."* —Galatians 3:8

For two thousand years God had a covenant with Abraham and his children—and with them only. You and I may not say that this arrangement was unfair to the Chinese and the Egyptians. We must study God's plan of salvation with diligence and adoration, but we may not try to make up a better one.

Praise the Lord: God did not forget those of us who had forgotten him and are not of Jewish birth. He was already thinking of us when he spoke to Abraham about "all the families of the earth." You can hear the gospel in Genesis 12:3, says Paul.

With the first coming of Jesus Christ, God turned to all people of all races. When Jesus was only forty days old, Simeon held the baby in his arms and said: "Here is a light for revelation to the Gentiles" (Luke 2:32)—that is, all those who are not Jews.

God did not change the covenant with Abraham. That covenant of grace is still in force. But now the Gentiles who believe in Jesus are also members of this covenant. And Paul, "the apostle to the Gentiles," was chosen by God to explain this plan for including the Gentiles and to begin its execution.

This teaching about the continuity of the covenant of grace from Abraham till today, and about the inclusion of the Gentiles by faith in Jesus Christ, has all sorts of implications. For one thing, our way into God's favor is always by way of Israel, by obtaining citizenship as children of Abraham. It does not matter if we are offspring of Native Americans or if we are sons and daughters of the Pilgrim fathers or of any other heroes of Gentile origin. Salvation is of the Jews, and God's blessing is in the covenant he made with Abraham.

However, since we, and even the Jews, may be included in the covenant of grace only by faith in Jesus, the question of our origins has become unimportant. It does not matter where you come from. It matters where you are!

REFLECTIONS

Give thanks that you are, by believing in Christ, a child of Abraham and a son or daughter of the covenant of grace.

God Is Here

EXODUS 40:33-38
> *. . . and the glory of the LORD filled the tabernacle.*
> —*Exodus 40:34*

> *Don't you know that you yourselves are God's temple and that*
> *God's Spirit dwells in your midst?* —*1 Corinthians 3:16*

When Moses finished building the tabernacle, God Almighty moved in. The glory of the Lord filled the tent. What an awesome moment!

You would think that with the presence of God so close and so visible, the people of Israel would have spent their days in reverence and obedience. But we know that during the years of wandering through the desert, the Israelites were often rebellious and disobedient.

The great miracle of the person of Jesus was that he came to us as God in the flesh: "The Word became flesh and made his dwelling (tabernacle) among us. We have seen his glory" (John 1:14).

You would think that since the presence of God has come so close that he meets us in the flesh, people would believe and live. But to this very day, unbelieving people say that Jesus could not have been God, that he was probably an ordinary man with an extraordinary faith.

Since the day of Pentecost, Christians together form the temple of God because the Spirit of God lives in them. Now God lives in his holy temple. God dwells in many lands and speaks in many tongues.

But many people still don't believe the gospel. Many think that if God is living anywhere on earth, it has to be in a multimillion-dollar temple with out-of-this-world furnishings.

Here is the simple truth: God lives today in men, women, and children who believe in Jesus. God's presence has become visible and tangible in lives that his grace has blessed and his Spirit has possessed.

And someday soon the glory of the Lord is going to cover the earth. Then nobody will say that it cannot be, that it isn't so. On that day we will experience what we have always believed. And others will see what their hearts refused to accept.

REFLECTIONS
You—along with other believers—are God's temple. God lives in you. As you think this through, what are some of the implications for your daily life? For your contact with non-Christians?

Holiness and Sinfulness

LEVITICUS 3:1-5

"You are to lay your hand on the head of your offering...."

—Leviticus 3:2

Whatever it may be that impresses us about God these days, it's likely not his holiness. A reading of the book of Leviticus may be just the medicine we need, because it is God's holiness that gives meaning to this book. Leviticus shows how the holy God may be approached by a sinful but chosen people under the rules of the old covenant. It took much more than changing a shirt before people could come into God's presence in a way approved by God.

Today many people seem to think not only that they can go to God at any time or place, in any manner, but also that God ought to be pleased if they give him any attention at all. This ignorance of God's very character may prove even more dangerous than handling high-voltage wiring if you are ignorant of electricity.

The God we worship is the same God who laid down all those "picky" regulations in the book of Leviticus. Israel was to seek God's presence, but the priests and the ordinary people had to observe strict rules and unbending requirements. The place was designated, the offering was prescribed, and the manner in which it was to be presented was outlined step by step. Any departure from the rules, even an unintentional error, was punished severely. At God's command, these rituals were maintained for hundreds of years.

Millions of animals died, first at the gate of the tabernacle and later in the court of the temple. Tens of thousands of Israelites stood there, pressing their palms on the heads of the animals presented for offering. With that gesture they transferred their intentions and feelings. When they saw the blood and the fire and the smoke, they bowed their heads, knowing that they stood in the grace of the holy God.

Here's something we must realize: we cannot approach God and live unless we come through Jesus Christ, who died for us. You and I must lay both our hands on Jesus. If we don't, we will regret it forever.

REFLECTIONS

How will this Scripture and reading affect the way you approach God?

Atonement Day

LEVITICUS 16:20-22

> *How much more, then, will the blood of Christ . . . cleanse our consciences from acts that lead to death, so that we may serve the living God!* —*Hebrews 9:14*

Jewish people who do not accept the Lord Jesus still observe *Yom Kippur,* the Day of Atonement. That was the only day of the year on which the high priest was allowed to enter the Holy of Holies to sprinkle blood on the mercy seat.

To get the whole picture of the atonement ritual, read Leviticus 16 a couple of times. And if you want to see how this ancient rite has been fulfilled by Christ, read Hebrews 9.

There were two goats used on Atonement Day. One was slaughtered and its blood was carried into the Holy of Holies by the high priest. That was the blood that covered the guilt of the people in the sight of God. It symbolized the blood of Christ, which covers our sins so that we are no longer guilty before God. Now our conscience is purified and we can serve the living God.

The other goat was held at the entrance of the tabernacle until the high priest came out and laid his hands on its head. Acting on behalf of all the people of Israel, the high priest confessed the sins of the people. He transferred them to this animal. Usually we call this second goat the "scapegoat"—a term we still use for someone who takes the blame. This goat not only received the blame but also carried the guilt away—far away into the wilderness. The people who chased the goat into the wilderness had to make sure it could never return.

Together those two goats constitute a blueprint of the redemptive work of Jesus. His blood has covered our sins in the sight of God, just as the blood of the first goat did. He became the scapegoat for all his people. Jesus our Savior was loaded with all our sins. And he carried them far, far away—as far as East is from West.

Jesus became our burden-bearer.

REFLECTIONS

What "burdens" of sin are you carrying that you need to put on Jesus today?

The Star of Jacob

NUMBERS 24:10-19

"A star will come out of Jacob; a scepter will rise out of Israel."
—*Numbers 24:17*

The Old Testament is full of pictures and prophecies that prefigure the future. All these promises and prophecies were given by God—usually through his servants. In this case, however, God used one of his enemies to speak of the hope of Israel.

The king of Moab saw the twelve tribes of Israel encamped on his doorstep. He became afraid and said, "This horde is going to lick up everything around us, as an ox licks up the grass of the field" (Num. 22:4).

That's why the king of Moab wanted to lay a curse on the people of Israel, an evil spell that would make them powerless. So he called in an expert whose name was Balaam. Balaam lived far away to the east, so it cost the king of Moab a lot of money to fetch him. But he figured it would be worth it: the curses Balaam knew would paralyze the children of Israel.

Ancient people knew—and feared—the realm of spirits, forces, and magic powers. And in modern times people have again become very curious about the occult, using it for scary entertainment and dangerous games. People like to play with fire.

But the God of Israel is sovereign also over the world of spirits, forces, and powers. This God had laid his blessing on the people of Israel. No power in the universe could turn God's blessing into a curse or his curse into a blessing.

That's how the tongue of Balaam was made a prisoner of God. Balaam opened his mouth to utter the curses for which he was paid, but instead he spoke the blessings God decreed. Three times he was supposed to curse; three times he blessed instead. And the fourth time topped it all: that time Balaam saw in the distance the mighty King who would come from Jacob, the star that would rise from Israel.

No power in the world can curse those who are blessed by this King.

REFLECTIONS

What evidence of people's belief in the occult have you heard about? Why is dabbling in the occult "playing with fire?""

Listen to Him!

DEUTERONOMY 18:15-22

> *For Moses said, "The Lord your God will raise up for you a prophet like me from among your own people; you must listen to everything he tells you."* —Acts 3:22

A prophet tells God's Word to people. Without prophets people don't know God or God's will. You cannot become a prophet by your own will—by growing a beard or by being stern or by shouting loudly. God appoints his own prophets.

God's greatest prophet in the Old Testament was Moses. God spoke directly through him. Through Moses Israel received its whole system of law and worship.

In his farewell address, Moses spoke of a prophet "like me" whom God would raise up. Moses warned that God would put his own words in that prophet's mouth. Therefore Israel had to obey that prophet unconditionally, for God himself would punish the disobedient.

Many years later two men quoted these words of Moses. They were speaking in the temple area to an audience that was eager to do what Moses had commanded. If you want to obey Moses, said Peter and John, you should listen to Jesus of Nazareth, for he is the prophet God promised through Moses.

These two men, Peter and John, were once on a mountain where they had the most wonderful experience. They saw Jesus transfigured by the radiance of heaven. God himself was on that mountain, and Peter and John were both lying on the ground, trying to hide in the dust. Then Moses and Elijah appeared, the two great spokesmen for God under the old covenant, and talked with Jesus.

Maybe Peter and John would have liked to hear something of the wisdom of Moses. Maybe they thought how great it would be to hear the voice of Elijah with their own ears. But then the voice of God said: "This is my Son, whom I love; with him I am well pleased. Listen to him!" (Matt. 17:5).

All people should stop paying attention to religious experts and false prophets. All people should do what God said on the mountain. "Listen to him!" We do not really know God unless we know him through the words and acts of Jesus.

REFLECTIONS

What does "listening to Jesus" look like in your life?

Immanuel

ISAIAH 7:10-17

All this took place to fulfill what the Lord had said through the prophet: "The virgin will conceive and give birth to a son, and they will call him Immanuel" (which means "God with us").
—Matthew 1:22-23

There was a king whose name was Ahaz. He was afraid because two other kings were going to attack his country. The prophet Isaiah said to king Ahaz, "Don't be afraid. God is with us." But the king did not want to listen to religious talk.

"You may ask a sign of the Lord your God," said the prophet. But the king said, "No, don't bother." And he added piously, "You may not test the Lord."

But Isaiah told Ahaz the unasked-for sign anyway: A virgin will give birth to a child, and his name will be called *Immanuel,* that is, *God-with-us.* Before the child grows up, Isaiah continued, the Lord will destroy your enemies, and your own country will be devastated as well.

We don't know anything about the circumstances of the birth of Immanuel, if, indeed, a boy with this symbolic name was born in the days of Ahaz and Isaiah. But the name-giving was a sign for a future event, the birth of Jesus. Many years after the prophet spoke, the virgin Mary gave birth to *Immanuel,* our blessed Savior. Then the sign of deliverance was fulfilled.

Notice that the sign of Immanuel was originally announced in the form of a threat: If God himself shows that he is with his people, woe to you if you still don't believe.

We have now received the ultimate sign of God's power and love. God is with us. Now we have no reason in the world to doubt God's intentions. He has decisively chosen to be on our side: *Immanuel!*

Now there may be no doubt in our mind and no fear in our way of living. God is not against us; God is for us. And if God is for us, who shall be against us?

Today the prophets of doom are getting too much of a hearing. They fail to see the sign—*Immanuel,* God-with-us. We must not get upset by their unbelieving talk. Immanuel is born. Therefore we will not be afraid.

REFLECTIONS

What "prophets of doom" do you hear these days? Does their message frighten you? Should it?

The Wonderful Name

ISAIAH 9:1-7

And he will be called Wonderful Counselor, Mighty God, Everlasting Father, Prince of Peace.   —*Isaiah 9:6*

This passage of Scripture describes the dawn of the kingdom of the Messiah. It's one of the most gripping prophecies of all, and it never fails to lift our spirits.

The prophecy of Isaiah 9 is introduced by statements about times that appear to be much like ours: truth is scarce (8:16-18), superstition abounds (8:19-20), and gloom is about to descend (8:21-9:1).

And then light bursts onto the anguished scene: "The people walking in darkness have seen a great light" (v. 2). There are strains of irresistible joy "as people rejoice at the harvest." Tyranny is ended and the "rod of their oppressor" is broken. Not only are the enemies overthrown, not only is the battle decided in the people's favor, the very weapons of war are destroyed in a blaze of fire (v. 5).

Then follows the cause of this blessed revolution: "For to us a child is born. . . ." The birth of a child is always a miracle. But now the child who is the Son of the living God has come. He becomes the ruler, and a new era begins: "The government will be on his shoulders . . . and of peace there will be no end."

The names declare who this Son of God is and what he does. *Wonderful Counselor* tells how he delivers people from stupidity. He liberates them from error and makes them wise to walk in the ways of God.

Mighty God announces that he is not bound by our dismal limitations. He will do his mighty and perfect work in the world of our failures.

Everlasting Father proclaims that he is wise and loving. On his arms all weary children will rest. He will comfort them in their hardship and pain.

Prince of Peace tells us that he brings the everlasting kingdom to this world. "Prince Shalom" is his name. Peace and justice will mark the country. And life will finally be what God intended it to be.

"The zeal of the LORD Almighty will accomplish this" (v. 7).

REFLECTIONS

How do these wonderful titles of Jesus speak to your needs today?

The Great Restoration

ISAIAH 11:1-9

A shoot will come up from the stump of Jesse; from his roots a Branch will bear fruit.   —*Isaiah 11:1*

So Joseph also went up ... to Bethlehem the town of David, because he belonged to the house and line of David.   —*Luke 2:4*

Jesse was the father of David. When the prophet Isaiah spoke of the "stump of Jesse," every Israelite knew what he was talking about. The kingdom of David had fallen like an oak that is cut down. Only the stump remained. The old glory was gone.

Now the prophet announces that the restoration of the house of David will be far more glorious than the reign of David or Solomon ever was. Just as a fallen oak often rises again through the shoots or suckers that grow out of its stump, so an offspring of David will arise, and he will rule as King of peace and glory.

First Isaiah gives a description of the qualities of this King (vv. 2-5). Then follows a picture of the land over which he will rule (vv. 6-9).

People have often said that this is what paradise must have looked like: the wolf and the lamb don't hurt each other; children laugh and play among harmless snails and serpents.

Maybe that's the way it was.

We do know that this is how it's going to be once Jesus has finished his work. The birth of Christ not only restored glory to the house of David, it also was the beginning of the restoration of creation. Jesus' work began in the hearts and lives of people. And when it is completed, peace and harmony will be restored in all that God has made.

The point of the picture is peace, *shalom*—a state of well-being without brokenness, hurts, or faults.

This is the picture that flashed before people's minds when they heard Jesus say that the kingdom of heaven was at hand. This kingdom is much closer now. Already the Son of David rules over our lives and families and churches. And his kingship is being extended by quiet but irresistible strength.

REFLECTIONS

Where in your life do you most feel the need for the *shalom* that has already begun but will one day be complete?

Wells of Salvation

ISAIAH 12

With joy you will draw water from the wells of salvation.
—Isaiah 12:3

"Let anyone who is thirsty come to me and drink."   *—John 7:37*

Almost every year there are severe droughts in some parts of the country. The sight of parched fields and ruined crops is very distressing. Nothing grows where there is no moisture. Life still depends on water.

In the Bible, water represents salvation. God himself is the well of salvation. Where God's goodness does not reach, life wilts. Life still depends on God.

Jesus is the Son of God. Just as a river carries water to a town from the springs in the mountains, so Jesus brings life itself from God to believers.

But it is not enough to have a mighty river running in front of your house. You might still die of thirst unless you yourself kneel down and put your lips to the water. Nobody can do that for you; you yourself have to drink. Only then can you sing with Isaiah, "Surely God is my salvation."

How do you drink the water Isaiah talks about?

Drawing from the wells of salvation is the same as coming to Jesus. Christ said, "Let anyone who is thirsty come to me and drink." And all these different words—*drawing, coming,* and *drinking*—may be replaced by one simple word: *believing.* Jesus himself said, "Whoever believes in me will never be thirsty" (John 6:35).

The experience of salvation is, among many other things, a matter of great joy. "With joy you will draw water from the wells of salvation." It has been rightly said that God's salvation aims at more than our happiness. But one of its first products is joy. It's a deep and lasting happiness, a visible contrast to those who do not know God's grace. Salvation gives joy!

Just as the well in ancient villages was the focal point of the good life—there was always the song of the girls, the meeting and greeting of people—so there is unending joy and daily singing among those who are drawing water from the wells of God.

REFLECTIONS

What does the "joy of salvation" look like in your life? How do you experience the deep happiness that comes from being saved?

The Comforter

ISAIAH 40:1-5

Comfort, comfort my people, says your God.   —*Isaiah 40:1*

It is the custom of the church in which I was ordained that the first official sermon is delivered in the presence of a number of elders and pastors. In my first sermon I had some incisive things to say (I thought) about certain weaknesses of the Christian church. I exposed them mercilessly. An elderly pastor tried to argue against my interpretation, but he lost the debate. By way of a parting admonition, he merely looked at me and said, "As long as you know that we must preach comfort."

Those words have never left me.

The Bible and the Christian confession give a richer than ordinary meaning to the word *comfort*. We certainly know the comfort of togetherness; we appreciate the silent handshake and the strong arm around the shoulders in times when grief is too deep for words. But people who are not Christians also experience this balm of human sympathy.

To us, comfort is an assurance we receive from God himself. It is a certainty God lays on our hearts, a certainty by which we are so strengthened that we have the power to endure the most wretched circumstances. We have acquired the habit of calling this our "only" comfort. It's not that we don't appreciate the other good things in life that offset suffering or lessen our pain. Yet there is only one certainty that pulls us through: "That I am not my own, but belong—body and soul, in life and in death—to my faithful Savior Jesus Christ" (Heidelberg Catechism, Answer 1).

Comfort is what everyone needs and what believers have. That doesn't mean everyone recognizes the need for this comfort. As long as we have a superficial knowledge of our needs, we have to do with the kind of comfort that human wisdom and sympathy can offer—the silver lining of the dark clouds and the silent handshake.

But the Bible and our confession speak of the *only* comfort, the comfort that meets our deepest need.

REFLECTIONS

Recall a time when you were in need of the kind of comfort and certainty only Jesus can provide. Did God provide you with his "comfort" and assurance? What form did that comfort take?

For Weaklings

ISAIAH 42:1-4

> *This was to fulfill what was spoken through the prophet Isaiah: . . .*
> *"A bruised reed he will not break, and a smoldering wick he will*
> *not snuff out. . . ."* —*Matthew 12:17, 20*

The Old Testament describes the coming Messiah as a mighty conqueror but also as a gentle pastor and a compassionate friend. "He gathers the lambs in his arms and carries them close to his heart; he gently leads those that have young" (Isa. 40:11). By strength Christ will redeem his people, but he will not despise what is weak: "A bruised reed he will not break, and a smoldering wick he will not snuff out."

A reed is certainly not a symbol of strength. A *bruised* reed is a sign of utter weakness. The light of a wick can be put out by a draft of wind. A *smoldering* wick is quenched by a mere puff of air. These figures of prophecy refer to people who have little vigor.

The good news is that when the glorious Messiah comes, he will be concerned with these weaklings. He will spare them and save their trembling lives.

The New Testament explains that this prophecy found fulfillment in the quiet ministry of Jesus to poor and sick people. He turned to those for whom we have no time. And he gave a great deal of attention to sick, small, weak, unimportant people.

What a surprise, and what good news for most of us! We, who are so impressed by power, must learn that Jesus turned to the helpless. We, who are inclined to pray that our children will get straight "A"s must remember that Jesus' tender mercy was poured out on those who would never rise to the top of the class.

The church must be very careful how it deals with those who are weak. If they are made to feel that they don't really belong because they cannot be heroes of faith and powerful in the Spirit, we are doing something wrong. Misfits and failures are welcome in the church, and they may require much of our time. Remember Christ's patience with them: A bruised reed he will not break, and a smoldering wick he will not snuff out.

REFLECTIONS

Pray specifically for someone you know who needs special care and attention from you and the church.

Never Alone

ISAIAH 43:1-4

"When you pass through the waters, I will be with you; and when you pass through the rivers, they will not sweep over you. When you walk through the fire, you will not be burned; the flames will not set you ablaze." —*Isaiah 43:2*

The Lord did not say to Israel and to us that we would never have to go through the fire and through the water. He did say, "When you pass through the waters, I will be with you" and "When you walk through the fire, you will not be burned."

We may not claim what God never promised. We may not think or teach that God will lead us only in "green pastures" and not in "dark valleys." But we must claim what God has promised—that he will go with us. God may demand of us that we cross a river or go through a fire, but we don't have to go it alone.

The people of Israel knew what that meant. They knew that their ancestors had once passed through the waters of the Red Sea and did not drown because the Lord was with them (Ex. 14). So they could also expect that in the darkest hour of their history, when they would be scattered throughout the nations, the Lord would lead them back through the water and the flames.

We should know this even better than the church of the old covenant, for we live after the birth at Bethlehem and the death on Golgotha. The Son of God has come to us, and he has become our trailblazer. He has walked through our deep waters, and he has passed through the flames. There is no danger he has not seen, no weakness he has not experienced, no temptation he has not faced.

In a sense we are reliving the pilgrimage of the people of Israel. The city is still beyond the horizon and the road is long. God has not promised to spare us the fright of passing through the waters. We may have to go through the flame. But God has promised that we will not drown. We will not perish.

Christ is with us and so we will reach the city, safe and sound.

REFLECTIONS

What "rivers" or "fires" threaten you now? What does it mean to you that Jesus will be at your side as you endure these things?

The Gospel Sound

ISAIAH 52:7-10

"How beautiful on the mountains are the feet of those who bring good news." —Isaiah 52:7; Romans 10:15

The tidings of the birth of Jesus is called the "good news" or "gospel." This expression comes from Isaiah's vision of the messenger of good news who approaches over the mountains to bring joy to Zion. Beginning with New Testament times, telling about Jesus is always "proclaiming good news."

The first good news was brought by a heavenly messenger who said: "I bring you good news of great joy" (Luke 2:10). That was the night Jesus was born.

Some of us have heard so often and so much about Jesus that we get accustomed to the gospel. That's dangerous. When the gospel becomes an old tale and the sermon a piece of information, we are in deadly danger, for the story about Jesus is, first and last, good news of great joy.

What is good news? Here's an example from The Netherlands, 1945. It was spring, following the most fearful winter Europe had ever known. Sons were murdered, fathers were powerless, daughters were insecure, and mothers could no longer give daily food to their children. People died of starvation. They cried to God under the heel of the Nazi oppressor. They met in churches. And in the long, dark nights—there was no electricity—they prayed fervently for freedom, for help, for a way out.

Then, on the evening of May 4, a rumor went throughout the country—an electrifying rumor that spread faster than a prairie fire: "It's over! The war is over! Peace!"

Not one healthy person sat still. Crowds poured into the dark streets. Someone started to sing a song of liberty. All were filled with joy.

This comes closest to what happened at Christmas. That night the heavens were opened and a voice said: "It's over! It's all over! Now the ends of the earth will see the salvation of our God."

REFLECTIONS

To what joyous event in your life would you compare the good news of what happened at Christmas?

The Suffering Messiah

ISAIAH 53:1-7

> *The eunuch asked Philip, "Tell me, please, who is the prophet talking about, himself or someone else?"* —*Acts 8:34*

Most Jewish people still reject Jesus because they cannot imagine a Messiah who would suffer. They think that the Messiah must be glorious. Yet Jesus himself said that if they would only read carefully, they would believe that he was the Messiah of whom the Old Testament spoke. Christ suffered "according to the Scriptures" And Isaiah 53 is the great chapter of his suffering.

But the Jews do not want to admit that Isaiah 53 speaks of their Messiah. Maybe this suffering servant of God is the prophet Isaiah, they say. Or maybe this passage speaks of the suffering of the Jewish nation.

We should talk about this passage with everyone but especially with Jewish people who still believe that it is a Word of God. We owe that to them, because it is through the Jews that we have received salvation in Jesus. We should ask them, "Who is this innocent one in Isaiah 53? It says here that he suffers under the wrath of God and that he does so in the place of others. Who is he?"

The Ethiopian who found Jesus as Savior was reading Isaiah 53 in the Jewish Scripture. He asked the right question: "Who is the prophet talking about, himself or someone else?"

Christians of many races may now explain Isaiah 53 to their neighbors (who may not have time for such things because there is one more week to go before Christmas). We must especially seek out the Jews who do not celebrate Christmas.

The Jews are the oldest sons and daughters among God's children. It's time for them to come home. Let's talk to them. We have the whole Old Testament in common. It's best to start with Isaiah 53. And then, beginning with "that very passage of Scripture," tell them the good news of Jesus (Acts 8:35).

REFLECTIONS

Would you be able to use the Bible to explain the good news to an inquirer? Why would Isaiah 53 be a good passage to use?

Who Can Endure?

MALACHI 2:13-3:4

But who can endure the day of his coming? Who can stand when
he appears? —*Malachi 3:2*

In the time of Malachi, people were praying for the day of the Lord:
"Come, O come, Immanuel."

The newly rebuilt temple was full of people. They were shedding tears
around the altar because they did not think the Lord really cared. They
doubted the truth of his promise. But still they cried for the Lord to come.

The word of the prophet gave them a rude awakening. "Yes," he thun-
dered, "the Lord is coming all right. Suddenly he will come to his temple.
But for many people, the advent of the Lord is not going to be a happy
event. In fact, who can endure the day of his coming? Who can stand
when he appears?"

Wouldn't it be a shock if Malachi were to take over the public address
system in one of our sprawling super shopping malls? Suddenly the
Christmassy music would stop and a dark voice would say: "Six more
days until Christmas. But who can endure the day of his coming? And
who can stand when he appears?"

Maybe it would not be such a shock. Someone might remark, "How
nice! They're giving Bible readings over the PA system." Someone else
might recall having heard these words before—in a really beautiful performance of the Messiah.

Words are so plentiful and truth is so scarce! The ancient temple was
also filled with words. "You have wearied the LORD with your words"
(2:17). But faith in God was lacking: "Where is the God of justice?" (2:18).
And faithfulness to the covenant of marriage was taken lightly (2:14-16).

The terror of God's appearance cannot be avoided by nice words, sweet
songs, or good sermons. It takes faith and faithful works, says the prophet.

We aren't just waiting for Christmas. We are expecting the appearance of the Lord. Therefore we must continue to have faith in him. If
we're married, we must remain faithful to our husbands and wives. And
we must love our neighbors as ourselves.

REFLECTIONS

How will this passage and reading affect your celebration of Christmas
this year?

Jesus Is Coming

MALACHI 4

"Surely the day is coming; it will burn like a furnace."

—*Malachi 4:1*

"Yes, I am coming soon."   —*Revelation 22:20*

"The day is *coming*. . . ." "The great and dreadful day of the Lord *comes*. . . ." "I am *coming*. . . ." These phrases set the tone for the last chapter of the Old Testament. And in the last chapter of the New Testament, the Spirit and the Bride say, "*Come*," and the Lord Jesus promises, "I am *coming* soon."

The Bible is framed by the word *coming*, both as a prayer and a promise.

That's why throughout history, God's people are taught not only to look back and remember and to look up and believe. We are encouraged especially to look *forward* and expect the coming of the Lord. This teaching is important for our understanding of God himself, as well as for learning an attitude God requires of us.

It is essential that we know God as "the One who is coming." For most people it is still easiest to think of God as an eternal deity, far above us. Even non-Christians have an inkling of God's existence. Unless we are totally insensitive to the deeper dimensions of life—the mystery of being, the riddle of dying, the aspirations of our spirits, the marvel of our bodies—we cannot avoid the conclusion that God exists.

But that's not enough. Bible-believing Christians believe in God as the *coming* One. He is not only above our world, he has walked here and will soon step into it once again.

That's why our confession of faith does not merely consist of statements about God. Faith involves an expectation of God's literal coming.

Say you are expecting guests this afternoon at 3 o'clock. As the time draws near, you'll find yourself saying, "Are they here yet? Do you see them coming? Yes, they're coming." The word *coming* describes your guests, and it says everything about your attitude during the time of expectation.

All the news about God in the Old Testament and the New Testament is summed up in three words: He is coming!

REFLECTIONS

How will you keep the *coming* of our Lord on your mind and heart this Christmas season?

Preparation

LUKE 1:13-17

"See, I will send the prophet Elijah to you before that great and dreadful day of the LORD comes." —*Malachi 4:5*

"And he will go on before the Lord, in the spirit and power of Elijah. . . ." —*Luke 1:17*

There are about four hundred years between the close of the book of Malachi and the beginning of the New Testament. One of the last Words God spoke to Malachi was that he would send Elijah the prophet. And the first thing the angel Gabriel said to the priest Zechariah was: "[Your son] will go on before the Lord, in the spirit and power of Elijah." The New Testament begins where the Old Testament left off. The Lord is coming, and Elijah will go before him.

God sent John the Baptist to prepare his people for the coming of the Lord. John the Baptist fulfilled his task "in the spirit and power of Elijah." Elijah was the man who told Israel to stop "wavering between two opinions." They had to break with their half-baked religion. Elijah called Israel to make a clear-cut decision: "If the LORD is God, follow him; but if Baal, follow him" (1 Kings 18:21).

If we want to be ready to meet the Lord, we must first be confronted by the message of John the Baptist: If the Lord is God, serve him, but if money is God, then serve it. Stop trying to go in two different directions at the same time.

We must meet John the Baptist if we are to meet Jesus. That means we must listen to the call of repentance and conversion. We can believe in Jesus only if we give up our other beliefs. If we say yes to Jesus, we must say no to all other lords.

It sounds a bit harsh in this season of goodwill. The sermons of John the Baptist don't make good Christmas cards. But there has always been a big gap between what God tells us and what we want to hear. You cannot get around John the Baptist if you want to meet the Lord.

REFLECTIONS

How you will make room for John the Baptist in this Christmas season?

It's God's Work

LUKE 1:26-38

> *"How will this be," Mary asked the angel, "since I am a virgin?"*
> *. . . "Even Elizabeth your relative is going to have a child in her*
> *old age, and she who was said to be unable to conceive is in her*
> *sixth month."* —Luke 1:34, 36

Why does God fulfill his promises in such strange, miraculous ways?

Remember Abraham and Sarah? All their lives they lived with the promise of a child. But they received the child only when it was abundantly clear that they could no longer have children. When it was humanly impossible, God gave them the child of the promise.

When we open the New Testament, the first thing we read about is a woman who is too old to have a baby. Then we're introduced to a woman who gets a baby before she has a husband. Through these two women God brought into the world children for whom the ages longed, and on whom our lot depends.

Doesn't God make it hard to believe? Don't you think most people would say that this is a wonderful story but that they don't believe it—at least not literally?

The message is that we cannot celebrate Christmas if we do not believe in God. Christmas is *God*'s work. The kingdom is *God*'s kingdom. John the Baptist was sent by *God*. Jesus was the Son of *God*. The whole event was the work of *God*.

These days we meditate on the star, the manger, and the virgin, but all the time we must listen to Isaiah's question: "Who has believed our message and to whom has the arm of the LORD been revealed?" (53:1).

It's good to sing carols, to catch the mood and enter into the spirit of the season. But it is not enough. "To whom has the arm of the LORD been revealed?"

In the child of Zechariah and Elizabeth, and even more in the Son of Mary, God has shown that salvation comes from him. Christmas is a time to praise the wonderful works of God! Only the believing acceptance of God's work gives us strength for today and hope for tomorrow.

REFLECTIONS

In the true spirit of the season, "praise the wonderful works of God."

Joseph

MATTHEW 1:18-25

> *Because Joseph her husband was a righteous man and did not want to expose her to public disgrace, he had in mind to divorce her quietly.* —*Matthew 1:19*

We must be stewards of whatever God entrusts to us. To some people God says, "Here is a million dollars." These people will have to account to God for what they did with all that money. Or God may say to some couple: "Here is a child for you to raise." These people must also give account to God. We are responsible for whatever God entrusts to us.

There was one man to whom God entrusted his own Son. That man was Joseph.

He was a "righteous man." That means that he was a God-fearing, law-abiding Israelite. He was a simple and honest man, the kind of person to whom God will entrust big things.

When he learned that his future wife was pregnant, he must have been heartbroken. He could have gone to the judge and had Mary punished for what he thought was her unfaithfulness (Deut. 22:23-24). But he loved his fiancée, so he decided to "divorce her quietly"—which does not mean that he wanted to sneak away. Instead he would leave her without making an official report, as he would normally be expected to do.

Then God spoke to him. God addressed him as "son of David," a title that was almost an embarrassment for the carpenter. God told the awe-struck Joseph that Mary was bearing a child who came from God. Joseph believed God. He responded in the direct and simple way by which believers are recognized: "He did as the angel of the Lord commanded him." He simply obeyed. In this case he obeyed by marrying Mary.

On two more occasions God spoke to Joseph in a dream (Matt. 2:19-20, 22). Both times Joseph immediately did as he was told. This man simply did what God said without *but*s or *if*s.

It appears that Joseph died before Jesus began his public ministry. When he had fulfilled his task, God called his steward home.

God laid his biggest gift in Joseph's calloused hands. And Joseph was faithful.

REFLECTIONS

What has God entrusted to you? What does "being faithful" with these responsibilities mean to you?

For Children Only

1 SAMUEL 2:1-10

He has brought down rulers from their thrones but has lifted up the
humble. —*Luke 1:52*

It makes little difference whether you listen to the song of Hannah, which she sang after she had received baby Samuel, or the song of Mary in Luke 1. Their songs may be personal, but they are not original. The material of their poems you can find everywhere in the Bible.

The content of their songs boils down to this: God is sovereign. God turns away from the proud and throws the arrogant from their thrones, but he helps those who are humble.

This is the right song to sing on the eve of Christmas. At Christmas, God turns away from all those who sit on their thrones and extends his hand to all who kneel.

Humility is the only gate through which we may reach Bethlehem.

Remember that at the beginning of our history, we wanted to be like God? Yes, and we have always wanted to build a tower that would reach the heavens. We are obsessed by the idea that we should be our own boss. We want to live by our own rules and elevate ourselves to the level of God.

But now comes Christmas. Instead of people becoming God, God becomes a person. And God says that if anyone on this planet wants to reach his or her destiny, that person must go to the manger of Bethlehem and kneel down.

There is no other entry into to the kingdom of heaven.

It's a simple tune, the song of Hannah and the song of Mary. Two women composing songs out of words that abound in the Scriptures: "He has brought down rulers from their thrones but has lifted up the humble." It's a song we all must learn—now or never.

Perhaps Christmas should be a feast that's only for children. Certainly the kingdom of God is only for those who become like children.

REFLECTIONS

Use the words of Mary's song (Luke 1:46-55) as your own song of praise to God.

Christmas

LUKE 2:1-7

For God so loved the world that he gave his one and only Son, that whoever believes in him shall not perish but have eternal life.
—*John 3:16*

Together with millions of people all over the world, we remember today that God has shown us his love. Now we join the host of thankful people and say, "Thank you, heavenly Father, for the gift of Jesus Christ. Thank you for showing us how much you love us."

The love of God is directed to the world. "God so loved *the world.*" The world means all people. We may not limit this gift of God's love to ourselves, our family, our group, our nation. God so loved *the world!*

God loved. Therefore God gave. It may be possible to give without love, but it is impossible to love without giving.

God gave his Son, his one and only Son. That's how much he loved us. In the giving of his Son, God's love has been revealed. We must read the story carefully and believe it with our hearts. A child was born in Bethlehem. By that child, God shows how much he loves us, for that child was God's Son.

Nothing else will convince us that God loves us. You may be enjoying kindness this Christmas, and other good things, but there is always enough unhappiness that we sometimes wonder if God really loves the world. We know God's love not by looking at the gifts on our table but by looking at his gift in the stable. There, as the proof that he loves us, God has given all he has to give. It's all in this child, wrapped in swaddling cloths and lying in a manger.

God's only Son was "given" to us. Now we may receive him. We must go on our knees and accept this gift. Please do not refuse what God's love has prepared.

A thousand tongues cannot describe the riches of this gift. "Whoever believes in him shall not perish but have eternal life." In this gift we receive the Giver. In Bethlehem we meet our God. In Jesus we have life.

REFLECTIONS
Thank God for giving us all he has to give!

Choir Directors

LUKE 2:8-14

"Glory to God in the highest. . . ."   —*Luke 2:14*

We really should "harken" a little better when the "herald angels" sing. The angels never sang "glory to the newborn king." That's because the newborn king had taken off his royal robes. He had set his glory aside, coming not to be served but to serve. Nor did the angels mention the "goodwill to men" so many Christmas card poets celebrate.

But the angels did sing "Glory to God." God must have told them to teach the people of the world how to sing. Then the angels started with the line that came most naturally to them: "Glory to God in the highest."

We have a hard time learning this first line.

God's first commandment is this: "You shall have no other gods before me." In other words, "Glory to God in the highest." And the first thing we are taught to pray is "Hallowed be your name." In other words, "Glory to God in the highest."

Today people often greet each other by asking, "Did you have a nice Christmas?" We could turn that into a question about spiritual life and ask, "Does it come a little easier, now, to say, 'Glory to God in the highest?'"

God has brought salvation to the world. And the angels have become the choir directors of creation. The whole created world must learn to sing "Glory to God in the highest."

The result of Jesus' coming into the hearts of believers is a reordering of their lives. From now on, God is first. The whole of our lives are reorganized to bring glory to him. This transformation is the new song we are slowly learning to sing.

Even the angels must be disappointed by the world's singing. But they too must wait until Christ has finished his work. And when that day comes, when God is "all in all" or "everything to everybody," the whole cosmos will sing one song. All people, all creation, and all angels will sing "Glory to God in the highest."

REFLECTIONS

After your Christmas celebration is it easier to sing "Glory to God in the highest"?

The Changing of the Guard

LUKE 2:25-38

"Sovereign Lord, as you have promised, you may now dismiss your servant in peace. For my eyes have seen your salvation. . . ."

—Luke 2:29-30

God had promised Simeon that he would not die before he had seen the Messiah. On this day, the Holy Spirit guided Simeon into the temple, where he met Mary and Joseph with their baby. Then Simeon took Jesus in his arms and sang his song: "Now may your servant, Lord, according to your word depart in exaltation. My peace shall be serene, for now my eyes have seen your wonderful salvation."

Simeon was not asking for death. He was speaking as a watchman whose watch had ended. He is the representative of the true Israel. An old woman, Anna, of the tribe of Asher, also came to greet the Redeemer.

Simeon is described as someone who was looking "for the consolation of Israel." And Anna was one of many who were "looking forward to the redemption of Jerusalem."

The Bible brings these people onto the scene as "the Israel within Israel," the true people of God whose hearts burned with Messianic hopes and whose lips said daily prayers for the redemption of Jerusalem.

Now their eyes are blessed because they see the baby in the temple. Here their watch has ended. Simeon sings the swan song of the old covenant: "Now dismiss your servant in peace, for my eyes have seen your salvation." And Anna, who is from the tribe of Asher, one of the least among the sons of Jacob, sees the remnant of that tribe coming to greet the light of day after a long and dreary night. And now the Old Testament exits.

It is the end of one watch and the beginning of another. The guard has changed. Now the people of the Messiah, the true Israel of the new covenant, are the saints who watch and wait and pray. And soon "the night of weeping shall be the morn of song."

REFLECTIONS

What can you learn for your spiritual journey from the examples of Simeon and Anna?

The Boy Jesus

LUKE 2:41-52

"Didn't you know I had to be in my Father's house?" . . . But his mother treasured all these things in her heart. —Luke 2:49, 51

The annual trip to Jerusalem must have been one of the highlights for the Jews who lived in Galilee. They travelled on foot, of course. And they made the trip in a big group. They must have sung along the way—the book of Psalms includes a special section of songs for pilgrims on their way to Jerusalem: Psalms 120-134.

Mary and Joseph observed the Passover in Jerusalem and returned to Nazareth. But three days after the group left, Jesus was still sitting at the feet of the rabbis in the temple court. He was the center of attention: "Everyone who heard him was amazed at his understanding and his answers."

When his anxious parents found him, Mary asked, with gentle reproof, why he had caused them so much concern. Then Jesus gave that revealing answer: "Didn't you know I had to be in my Father's house?"

At twelve years old our Savior knew he had special obligations to God, his Father. But it is impossible to say how much he knew of his real relationship to God and of the Father's will for his life.

Mary took careful note of Jesus' words. She must have lived between fear and joy as she observed the life of her Son and Savior. Twelve years earlier she had sung a hymn that sounded much like Hannah's. Maybe now she was thinking that since Hannah had given up her Samuel for the Lord's service, she could not withhold her Jesus.

Jesus was perfectly human. His parents knew the secret of his birth, but no one else would have guessed at the time that he was also the Son of God.

We should not be perturbed to discover that Jesus was at one time an eager, gifted, but ordinary Jewish boy. After all, he came not to make us superhuman but perfectly human.

It is a fruit of Jesus' work that today there are many ordinary human beings who are happy in the service of their heavenly Father. And some of these people are only twelve years old.

REFLECTIONS

Why do you suppose Luke included in his gospel this one look into Jesus' childhood?

Down to Earth

MARK 6:1-6

Then he went down to Nazareth with them and was obedient to them. —*Luke 2:51*

Most of Jesus' life on earth was very ordinary, just as our lives are ordinary. He lived the routine of day and night, meals and work. And he was related to his parents and brothers and sisters, just as we are related to ours.

Joseph probably died young. He was still alive when Jesus was twelve years old, but after Jesus began his official ministry when he was thirty, Joseph's name is not mentioned. We do hear of Jesus' mother, brothers, and sisters (Mark 3:31; 6:3). The idea that Jesus was the only child of Mary was invented when people began to worship Mary's virginity.

As the oldest boy in the family, Jesus must have had to work hard—especially if Joseph passed away while Jesus was still young. By God's wise decision, we know nothing about Jesus' life from when he was a baby until the time he was twelve years old. Then we are told about his trip to the temple. And then follow eighteen years of which we know nothing.

People have made up many stories about Jesus' childhood miracles. But they are the work of pious imagination. You can be sure that Jesus simply worked for a living. He did not turn stones into bread or use the kind of magic you see on television. In Nazareth, the town where he grew up, people called Jesus "the carpenter" (Mark 6:3). That tells the story. In small towns, people know each other. Jesus was simply known as the carpenter.

Ordinary work is a beautiful thing. Otherwise Jesus could not have spent most of his life doing a carpenter's job. So if I were a carpenter today, I'd say, "It's time to get back to the daily routine. Back to work."

Jesus is coming. And when the Lord comes back and finds us at our ordinary work—whether it's in the factory, on the farm, at the office, at school, or in the kitchen—it's perfectly all right. After all, that's what he did himself for most of his years on earth.

REFLECTIONS

What does Jesus' "ordinary life" as a child and then later as a carpenter say to you about your "ordinary" daily routine?

To Seek and to Save

LUKE 5:27-32

"For the Son of Man came to seek and to save what was lost."
—*Luke 19:10*

"I have not come to call the righteous, but sinners to repentance."
—*Luke 5:32*

Ask the crowds that have just celebrated Christmas why Jesus came into the world. Or stop a worship service and have every person there write one short sentence about why Jesus came into the world.

What answers would we get? Some, I'm sure, would be way off the mark.

It's also possible that some answers would be correct but different from each other. The New Testament has different ways of stating the mission of Jesus. It describes that mission as announcing the kingdom, as destroying the works of the devil, as doing the Father's will, and as glorifying God.

But there is one basic answer we should all know: Christ came to seek and save people who are lost. He came to save sinners.

Why is it so important for us to know this purpose of Jesus' mission?

First, for our own comfort. Because all of us are lost, all of us need to be saved. Jesus said, "I have not come to call the righteous, but sinners to repentance." When he told the scribes and Pharisees, "It is not the healthy who need a doctor, but the sick," he wasn't giving them a clean bill of health. He was telling them that they needed to realize their need for him. There is not a person who does not need Jesus.

We must also know this purpose of Jesus' mission as members of his church. If our Master came to seek and to save those who are lost, we are compelled to follow his example. We have to go out of our way to find those who are "lost" in order to "seek and to save" them.

Only the lost can be found. Only sinners can be saved. Candidates for salvation are always those who are least likely. Those who are "not good enough" can be saved. But those who are self-satisfied do not know they need Jesus.

REFLECTIONS

What would "going out of your way" to share the good news look like in your life? Are you willing and able to do that, if given the opportunity?

Year End

PSALM 130

> *If you, LORD, kept a record of sins, Lord, who could stand? But with you there is forgiveness, so that we can, with reverence, serve you.* —*Psalm 130:3-4*

Every nation and many regions have their own customs for observing the change from one year to another. In North America we try to make New Year's Eve the noisiest night of the year. It differs from place to place, of course, but in most places people whoop it up to a lunatic pitch.

What sort of national nervous disorder is this? Fear, maybe?

Christians do not have to walk around today as if we were the last of the Pharisees. But we should at least be sober-minded, for we have a few things to discuss with our God.

This year is past. "If you, LORD, kept a record of sins, Lord, who could stand?"

Can we take ten minutes today to think about our sins of the past year? Do we have the time, the spiritual sensitivity, and the moral seriousness to think for ten minutes of all of our failures in the past year? And could we then put them into words and confess them before God?

"But with you, there is forgiveness."

Picture God writing on every page of the calendar of the past year: Forgiven, forgiven, and again forgiven! Through tears of gratitude, see God writing "Forgiven" with the blood of Jesus.

Only when the past does not plague us anymore can we be serene in the present and prepare for a look at the future.

We cannot look into the future, and we won't pretend we can. The newspapers and magazines will try to make their forecasts today and tomorrow. Once again the charlatans and stargazers will make a pretty penny on the superstitious children of our technological age. But we will place our trust in God.

We know only one thing about the future: Jesus is coming!

REFLECTIONS

Consider taking that ten minutes to think about and confess your biggest failures of the past year—and give thanks for the joy of knowing that God has completely forgiven them all.

Index